Intelligent Manufacturing Systems

This book offers an in-depth exploration of the evolution, implementation, and impact of modern technologies in manufacturing. This book provides a comprehensive analysis of cyber-physical systems, the Internet of Things (IoT), cloud computing, artificial intelligence (AI), and big data analytics, demonstrating their role in optimizing design, production, and management processes. With detailed case studies, structured literature reviews, and real-world applications, this guide is an essential resource for scholars, researchers, and professionals aiming to understand and leverage the advancements in Intelligent Manufacturing Systems.

Key Features:

- Provides an overview of digital twin technology, enabling virtual replication of physical assets for simulation, analysis, and optimization.
- Examines the role of IoT in connecting devices and sensors to enhance data collection, monitoring, and decision-making processes.
- Discusses the applications of AI and ML in predictive maintenance, quality control, and production optimization.
- Explores about intelligent robotics that can sense, learn, adapt, and make autonomous decisions during manufacturing.
- Examines the interaction between human workers and intelligent systems, focusing on enhancing productivity and safety.

Intelligent Manufacturing Systems

Digitalization of Industrial Production

Edited by
P. Suresh, Pravin Kumar Singh, T. Poongodi,
R. Gopal, and P. Senthil

CRC Press
Taylor & Francis Group
Boca Raton London New York

CRC Press is an imprint of the
Taylor & Francis Group, an **informa** business
A CHAPMAN & HALL BOOK

First edition published 2027
by CRC Press
2385 NW Executive Center Drive, Suite 320, Boca Raton FL 33431

and by CRC Press
4 Park Square, Milton Park, Abingdon, Oxon, OX14 4RN

CRC Press is an imprint of Taylor & Francis Group, LLC

ISBN: 9781032949352 (hbk)
ISBN: 9781032949383 (pbk)
ISBN: 9781003582465 (ebk)

DOI: 10.1201/9781003582465

Typeset in Times
by codeMantra

Contents

About the Editors

P. Suresh is a professor in the Department of Mechanical Engineering and also serves as Controller of Examinations at J.J. College of Engineering and Technology, Tamil Nadu, India. He has also served as the University-level Academic Coordinator at Galgotias University, Delhi NCR.

He received his Ph.D. in the Faculty of Mechanical Engineering from Anna University, Tamil Nadu, in 2014. He completed his Master of Engineering in Engineering Design from Bharathiyar University, Coimbatore, in 2001 and his Bachelor of Engineering from University of Madras, Chennai, in 2000.

With over 25 years of experience in academia and research, his areas of expertise include optimizations, machinability of materials, composite materials, and metal matrix composite materials. He has authored more than 55 research publications in reputed international journals, conferences, and book chapters published by Elsevier, Springer, IET, and other leading publishers.

Pravin Kumar Singh is an accomplished academician and researcher in the field of Mechanical Engineering, currently serving as an associate professor at Galgotias University, Greater Noida, India. With over 8 years of teaching and research experience, he holds a Ph.D. in Manufacturing Engineering from NIT Jamshedpur, specializing in vibratory welding techniques and materials processing.

His core areas of expertise include advanced welding technology, robotics welding, smart manufacturing, 3D printing, and sensors and transducers. He has contributed extensively to academia through peer-reviewed publications in SCI/Scopus-indexed journals, through book chapters with Springer and Elsevier, and as an editor of reputed international conference proceedings. He is also a reviewer for several renowned journals under Elsevier and IOP.

A strong advocate of industry–academia collaboration, he has coordinated numerous internships and skill development programs in partnership with top-tier companies such as BOSCH, TSPDI, and Prinston Engineering Ltd. He has also played key roles in institutional development, including NAAC accreditation processes, curriculum innovation, and student mentorship initiatives.

T. Poongodi is presently working as a professor in the Department of Computer Science and Engineering, School of Engineering at the Dayananda Sagar University, Bangalore, India. She received her Ph.D. in Information Technology (Information and Communication Engineering) from Anna University, Tamil Nadu, India. She is the author of over 50+ (Scopus-indexed) book chapters, including some reputed publishers such as Springer, Elsevier, IET, Wiley, De Gruyter, and CRC Press, and 30+ (SCI/Scopus) international journal articles and conference papers. She has published 15+ authored/edited books in the areas of Internet of Things (IoT), data analytics, blockchain technology, artificial intelligence (AI), machine learning, and healthcare informatics, published by renowned publishers. With over 20 years of extensive experience in teaching and multidisciplinary research, she has been recognized with several prestigious awards, including the Research and Innovation Award and Excellence in the Area of Research & Innovation/Academic Excellence from Galgotias University, Delhi-NCR. She is a senior member of The Institute of Electrical and Electronics Engineers.

R. Gopal received his Master's degree from the Department of Computer Science and Engineering, Anna University, India, in 2010 and his Ph.D. degree from the Department of Information and Communication Engineering, Anna University, India, in 2018. He is currently working as an assistant professor at the College of Engineering, University of Buraimi, Oman. His research interests span wireless sensor networks, malicious node detection, cooperative network, and IoT. He received a grant of 40,000 OMR from the Ministry of Higher Education and Research and Innovation and a grant of 10,000 OMR in an internal funded project. He has served on many technical program committees and as a reviewer in reputed journals like Wireless Personal Communication (Springer). He has a list of publications in reputed journals, has been an editor for three Scopus-indexed books, and has published nine book chapters.

P. Senthil received his Master's degree in Mechanical Engineering from Bharathiyar University, India, in 2002 and his Ph.D. in Mechanical Engineering from Anna University, India, in 2012. He is currently serving as a senior lecturer at the College of Engineering and Technology, University of Technology and Applied Sciences, Muscat, Sultanate of Oman.

His research interests include squeeze casting, pressure die casting, non-ferrous composites, rapid prototyping, and process optimization. He has published extensively in reputed international journals and conference proceedings. He has also contributed to the academic community by serving on various technical program committees and acting as a reviewer for several esteemed international journals.

Contributors

Mona Ahmad Alharazi
Awon Tech Company
Makkah, Saudi Arabia

Mohd. Amjad
Department of Computer Engineering
Jamia Millia Islamia
New Delhi, India

Sundaravadivazhagan Balasubaramanian
Department of Information and Technology
University of Technology and Applied Sciences-Al Mussana
Al Mussana, Oman

Vanitha C. N.
Department of Information Technology
Karpagam College of Engineering
Coimbatore, Tamil Nadu, India

Chanakyan Chandrasekaran
Department of Mechanical Engineering
Global Academy of Technology
Bengaluru, Karnataka, India

Amar Y. Jaffar
Department of Computer and Network Engineering
College of Computing Umm Al-Qura University Makkah
Makkah, Saudi Arabia, UAE

Kanya Devi Jayabalan
Department of Computer Science and Engineering
Dayananda Sagar University
Bengaluru, Karnataka, India

Bilal Ahmed Naushad Kalburgi
eLIMS from Drug Discovery
Eurofins
Bengaluru, Karnataka, India

Jaggannagari Kavitha
Department of Computer Science and Engineering
Koneru Lakshmaiah Education Foundation
Hyderabad, Telangana, India

Pankaj Kumar
Department of Computer Science & Engineering
G. L. Bajaj Institute of Technology and Management
Greater Noida, Uttar Pradesh, India

Gurunathan Manikandan
Department of Mechanical Engineering
Velammal College of Engineering and Technology
Madurai, Tamil Nadu, India

Maniraj Mariraj
Department of Mechanical Engineering
Sree Sakthi Engineering College
Coimbatore, Tamil Nadu, India

Gousia Thahniyath Mulla
Department of Computer Science and Engineering
Dayananda Sagar University
Bengaluru, Karnataka, India

Kavitha Nagarajan
Science & Humanities Department
Sri Eshwar Engineering College
Coimbatore, Tamil Nadu, India

Keerthivasan Navaneethakrishnan
Department of Mechanical Engineering
J.J. College of Engineering and Technology
Tiruchirappalli, Tamil Nadu, India

Anusuya P.
Department of Information Technology
Karpagam College of Engineering
Coimbatore, Tamil Nadu, India

Ashoka Varthanan Perumal
Department of Mechanical Engineering
Sri Krishna College of Engineering and Technology
Coimbatore, Tamil Nadu, India

Mathiyalagan Ponnusamy
Department of Mechanical Engineering
J.J. College of Engineering and Technology
Tiruchirappalli, Tamil Nadu, India

Pragya
Department of Computer Science and Engineering
G. L. Bajaj Institute of Technology and Management
Greater Noida, Uttar Pradesh, India

Banu Priya R.
Department of CSE, School of Engineering
Dayananda Sagar University
Bengaluru, Karnataka, India

Adarsh Priyadarshi
D&T Pro, Eligere Technologies
Gurugram, Haryana, India

Ashok Raj Rajendran
Department of Mechanical Engineering
J.J. College of Engineering and Technology
Tiruchirappalli, Tamil Nadu, India

Rifa Nizam Khan
Jamia Millia Islamia
New Delhi, India

Aradhna Saini
Department of Computer Science and Engineering
G. L. Bajaj Institute of Technology and Management
Greater Noida, Uttar Pradesh, India

Kanakaprabha Selvakumari
Department of Artificial Intelligence and Machine Learning
Malla Reddy College of Engineering
Hyderabad, Telangana, India

Vijayan Selvarangam
Department of Mechanical Engineering
J.J. College of Engineering and Technology
Tiruchirappalli, Tamil Nadu, India

Mouleeswaran Singanallur Kumaresan
Department of Computer Science and Engineering
Dayananda Sagar University
Bengaluru, Karnataka, India

Shashi Kant Singh
Deapartment of Computer Science & Engineering
Sanskaram University
Jhajjar, Haryana, India

Sivaramakrishnan Sivakumar Sivasankari
Department of Artificial Intelligence and Machine Learning
New Horizon College of Engineering
Bengaluru, Karnataka, India

Rajiv Subramanian
Department of Mechanical Engineering
E.G.S. Pillay Engineering College
Nagapattinam, Tamil Nadu, India

Poongodi Thangamuthu
Department of CSE
Dayananda Sagar University
Bengaluru, Karnataka, India

Swapna Thouti
Department of ECE
CVR College of Engineering
Hyderabad, Telangana, India

Rajendran Chinnasamy
Department of Mechanical Engineering,
Sri Krishna College of Engineering and Technology,
Coimbatore, Tamil Nadu

Rengaraj Gurumoorthy Vidhya
ULM University
Ulm, Germany

Ramadas Vinu
Department of Electronics and Communication
Dayananda Sagar University
Bengaluru, Karnataka, India

Natarajan Venkateswaran
Department of CSE
Dayananda Sagar University
Bengaluru, Karnataka, India

1 Transformer-Based Computer Vision Technique for Improving Manufacturing Quality

Bilal Ahmed Naushad Kalburgi, Adarsh Priyadarshi, Natarajan Venkateswaran, and Poongodi Thangamuthu

1.1 EVOLUTION OF COMPUTER VISION APPLICATIONS IN MANUFACTURING

Manufacturing processes have long been the drivers of industrial growth and the resultant economic growth. It has contributed to rising standards of income and living in many nations. While there are several drivers for manufacturing growth, such as market opportunities, favorable government policies, availability of raw materials, and other resources, a key driver for manufacturing growth is indeed technology and innovation. Hence, it is no coincidence that the roles of technological and innovation changes through various industrial revolutions we have seen so far have had a lasting improvement and impact on the manufacturing sector and thereby on economic and societal growth.

The First Industrial Revolution that began in the 1700s with the introduction of steam engines marked the advent of technological changes that impacted production in a big way. Prior to the First Industrial Revolution, most of the production operations were hand-based. The introduction of steam engines and the increased use of machine tools gave rise to the factory system for manufacturing. Since then, we have seen every industrial revolution leave its profound impact on manufacturing growth. With the Second Industrial Revolution, the impact of technology on manufacturing heralded an era of "mass manufacturing" characterized by stable, efficient, and large-scale manufacturing processes from the late 19th century. Many areas of the world underwent a period of rapid industrialization during this time. The Third Industrial Revolution launched the information age and characterized the shift of the economy from traditional industries to one based on information technology. The digital revolution so enabled made possible the use of technology in digital format, and from a manufacturing perspective, this also led to the application of digital technologies to manufacturing. The invention of the transistor, the integrated circuit chip, and the microprocessors that contained hundreds of these transistors led to the

DOI: 10.1201/9781003582465-1

development of the home computer and the internet. Computing and computational devices became more widely available and used. The invention of the World Wide Web in 1989 led to the spread of the digital revolution to millions of users. By 2000, cell phones began to be used and became as ubiquitous as the digital computers. The Fourth Industrial Revolution in the early 21st century has really transformed the technological landscape with a plethora of technologies such as artificial intelligence (AI), 3D printing, genome editing, robotics, augmented reality, and their applications. All these technologies, especially AI, have had a profound impact on manufacturing. The application of AI-based technologies in manufacturing has led to more responsive, flexible, and efficient manufacturing processes, also referred to as "Smart Manufacturing".

1.1.1 Computer Vision in Manufacturing

Computer vision, a field of Artificial Intelligence, can be thought of as an interdisciplinary area that can extract useful information from images. Computer vision works similarly to how humans operate in understanding the visual world. Computer vision aims to develop systems that can "see" and interpret the world around them, enabling automated visual understanding through the application of computer vision models and theories. As noted above, the various industrial revolutions have helped in the development and application of technologies in various spheres, including manufacturing. Not surprisingly, the development of computer vision has some parallels with the earlier industrial revolutions. Although the first camera was invented by Kodak in 1884, major developments in computer vision happened in the period up to the early 21st century with the advent of deep learning neural networks as vision happens to be one of the data and computationally intensive areas to pursue. The growth of computing power in terms of faster computers and better techniques to handle vast image data that was available during this period led to major developments in computer-based vision. Common computer vision techniques include feature extraction, object detection and tracking, image classification, image segmentation, facial recognition, etc.

Computer vision in manufacturing is of more recent origin commensurate with the development of capabilities in this area. Computer vision is applied in a wide range of industries, including automotive, aerospace, transportation, pharmaceutical, robotics, etc. In 2021, data from IBM shows that 51% of computer vision applications are in manufacturing, and it was ranked as one of the ten key technologies for manufacturing. Key technologies related to computer vision include attempts to derive 3D representations from 2D images in 1963, the development of multilayer neural networks in 1966, and the development of the neocognitron in 1979 by Fukushima, which helped the model detect patterns and local features using an architecture that mimicked the human visual system structure. The neocognitron led to the development of convolutional neural networks (CNNs), which are one of the most widely and successfully used computer vision technologies today. More recently, the unprecedented success of transformers in the domain of Natural Language Processing (NLP), as highlighted by successful applications such as ChatGPT, led to efforts to develop transformer architecture-based computer vision applications. In this context, the recent entrant in this area is "vision transformers" (ViTs), whose application in manufacturing is the subject of this chapter and therefore is reviewed in more detail.

Major applications of computer vision in manufacturing today are several, including automated quality control, predictive maintenance, inventory management, industrial safety and reducing workplace hazards, assembly line optimization, defect detection and improved product reliability, labeling and packaging, robotic guidance, custom manufacturing, and the optimized use of resources. Given the rapid strides of computer vision applications in manufacturing so far, the future looks very bright and promising indeed. In conjunction with other AI technologies, computer vision would facilitate greater automation and attainment of higher-quality benchmarks in manufacturing. Autonomous manufacturing that can operate round the clock with a skeletal workforce could become a reality across many industries. Recent developments in Generative AI promise to open a new world of possibilities with powerful Large Language Models that are being developed for videos and images. Generative AI models can be applied in manufacturing for product design, production planning, automated quality inspection, etc. Recent Augmented Reality (AR)/Virtual Reality (VR) vision-based technologies integrated with AI can be used for various manufacturing applications, such as industrial safety design and robotics applications.

1.2 INTRODUCTION

1.2.1 Vision Transformers

Prior to the development of transformers, computer vision was dominated by CNN-based models. Even today, CNNs represent some of the most successful models of choice for computer vision applications. Several classical image processing and computer vision-based tasks were handled by a variety of CNN models [1–4]. A comprehensive summary of CNN models and their analysis, applications, and prospects is given by Li et al. [5]. Although quite successful and widely used for computer vision, CNN models have a few limitations. Notably, these models have a fixed receptive field and may not effectively capture spatial hierarchies and relationships in the data, which can limit their performance on tasks requiring an understanding of more intricate relationships between objects or components of an image. Frequently, in image processing, they capture the local features well but struggle with global contexts.

ViTs do address these limitations of CNNs and are based on the transformer architecture [6] that has had tremendous success in many NLP-based applications, including sentiment analysis, text summarization, machine translation, and predicting words. Transformers' notable feature is the attention mechanism, which helps in modeling long-range dependencies with models that learn global contexts.

While transformer models enjoyed huge success in NLP areas, the success of transformers in NLP motivated many to adopt the transformer approach for tasks involving computer vision, which led to the development of ViTs [7]. It was shown that transformers can be applied to a sequence of image patches to model computer vision tasks such as image classification, leading to the introduction of ViTs [8]. The performance of the ViT does not offer significant benefits when trained on smaller datasets, but it does well for larger datasets.

1.2.2 Role of ViTs in Manufacturing

Manufacturing processes involve a wide range of equipment and machinery that work as per applicable procedures and operations to convert raw materials to finished products. As discussed, the Second Industrial Revolution began with the advent of mass manufacturing operations and processes. The Third Industrial Revolution featured the application of information and digital technologies into manufacturing. For example, we saw the application of automation technologies in manufacturing during this phase. The Fourth Industrial Revolution saw the introduction of Internet of Things (IoT) and robotics-based technologies in the manufacturing domain. The automation application, IoT, robotics, smart sensors, connectivity and network-based cognitive sensing, data analytics, and AI models have given rise to "Smart Manufacturing" now. These digital and information technologies are transforming traditional manufacturing processes into intelligent, efficient, and autonomous processes.

Computer vision-based technologies have long been used in manufacturing, and more recently, ViTs play an important role in the application of computer vision to manufacturing. There are several applications [9] of ViTs in manufacturing in diverse areas, such as quality control, predictive maintenance, supply chain management, process optimization, and inventory optimization, besides human–robot collaboration. Most of the literature discusses ViTs and CNN models for manufacturing-related computer vision applications.

Quality control is a principal area where ViTs have been used in manufacturing in various industries. A detailed review regarding the recent use of ViTs for quality control is given below under the literature review [9–13]. It can be seen that ViTs have been used successfully for a variety of manufacturing applications, and in many cases, they perform as well as or outperform the CNN models in the image processing tasks. And there are variants of ViTs developed to do away with some of the problems and challenges with vanilla ViTs [14–16]. Where the conventional ViTs have not been adequate, improved and innovative variants of these models have also been developed and applied [17].

This is not to say that ViTs are without any limitations. The challenges and applications associated with ViTs are discussed next.

1.2.3 Challenges and Applications in ViTs

Although ViTs have proven their ability in a wide range of tasks involving computer vision, there are several challenges in the implementation part. The significant challenges are in using the self-attention mechanism, which consumes a lot of processing capacity and memory. It is highly challenging to implement on mobile phones and embedded systems where the available resources are limited. Moreover, a huge volume of data is required to train the ViT model, and it would be very hard to preprocess the data since it is heterogeneous. For instance, the labeled data in medical imaging will be very limited. Furthermore, the quality of the training dataset has a huge impact on the ViT; if the dataset's size is too small or biased, the model may not generalize as well. Interpretability is another issue since it is difficult to understand how the model makes decisions because of the complexity in the attention process. Eventually, there is a requirement for a detailed study in optimizing the ViT architectures for various domains like 3D object recognition and video analysis, since the unique challenges are not addressed in the presently available frameworks. Generally, although ViT models are delivering outstanding performance on a wide range of computer vision applications, there are still significant challenges to be handled before they can be widely used for several more real-world problems.

ViTs in manufacturing improve production efficiency and quality control by detecting defects in real time. It assists in predicting machinery failures and optimizing processes, improving safety and coordination in human–robot collaboration; it tracks shelf availability and automates stock counting in inventory management. The challenge is to integrate seamlessly with the existing systems, which ensures real-time processing. Some more challenges are maintaining data security to ensure the confidentiality of sensitive information and ensuring higher precision in process monitoring, inventory management, and defect detection. Furthermore, it is expensive to manage the initial setup, which includes maintenance expenses as well. ViTs are a cutting-edge technology bridging the interpretation gap between machines and humans.

- While implementing ViTs, the fundamental challenge lies in the inherent complexity. Moreover, they require a huge dataset and substantial computational power. With scalability in perspective, the requirements of computational power and model size impose a barrier in wide-range adoption, specifically in small-scale industries.
- Due to the complex architecture, ViT models are often viewed as black boxes. In applications such as healthcare and autonomous vehicles, it is vital to understand the decision-making process in the ViT. It is a significant challenge to ensure interpretability in safety-related applications.
- The training phase of ViTs requires a huge dataset, raising concerns about data security and privacy. The ethical and legal considerations are significant while collecting and storing sensitive information. The model should comply with regulations when it delivers the result accurately.
- The settings in an industrial sector are ever changing and highly dynamic. ViTs should be adaptable to unpredicted events and different weather conditions. There should be a generalized model to face the challenges in diversified conditions.
- To ensure seamless human–machine coordination, more advancements are required in UI design, gesture recognition, and NLP.
- Finding standard pre-trained weights that are appropriate for different inputs, such as image, audio, and text remains challenging. Hence, deep insight is required to reveal the underlying principles of ViTs.
- At present, there are possibilities to extract the features directly from the convolutional layers without using positional embeddings. It may lead to information loss in case the input size differs from the training size.
- Lightweight models are appropriate for mobile devices, and deep learning models are extensively used in them as they have gained much popularity in recent years. However, the computing resources available on mobile devices

are insufficient to run Vision Transformers (ViTs) due to constraints in cost, size, and computational capacity. Decreasing the model size to operate ViT models in mobile devices is a significant challenge.

- The performance of a model is highly influenced by choosing the relevant features. When training a deep ViT model, it is unable to generate different representations. Hence, learnable parameters and introducing additional modules are required, whereas it results in an overhead issue. To solve this problem, advanced techniques are essential to introduce modified architectures and various data augmentations.

The applications of ViTs span diversified problems, which include image classification, image segmentation, image compression, image denoising, object detection, and anomaly detection. ViT models compete with CNNs for classifying images with large-scale image datasets. ViTs in object detection improve accuracy by finding out the relationship among objects in a global context. In image segmentation, it plays a role in segmenting pixels into regions, and it increases efficiency in autonomous driving and medical imaging. ViT models can also detect anomalies in images such as unusual patterns or defects in the surface.

1.3 LITERATURE REVIEW

Although there are several applications of ViTs in manufacturing [9], many of them are in the domain of quality control. One such problem is detecting and classifying missing bolts from train components [10]. They used different ViT and CNN models and their variants for this problem. To enhance robustness, feature-wise normalization, shearing, rotation, and brightness adjustment techniques were brought into application. The CNN models had many false negatives, detecting missing bolts as cases where the bolts were present. They found that the pre-trained ViT models performed much better than all other models, showing the efficacy of leveraging transfer learning for these applications. Despite an accuracy as high as 93%, various constraints, such as finite memory, limited dataset size, and environmental dependencies such as lighting and camera angle, could hinder real-world deployment. The present research gaps include lightweight models, handling environmental constraints, model compression, and ease of deployment.

The authors looked at modeling the recognition of fines in coal particles in a conveyor line and the characterization of particle sizes in the underflow of a hydrocyclone. The study uses ViT-B32 and ViT-B16 models with varying patch sizes and attention maps to visualize the parts of an image on which the model focuses, enhancing explainability [11]. GoogLeNet and MobileNetV2 were used as benchmarks to compare the performance between traditional methods and ViTs in case of detection of fine particulates in coal fields. This included preprocessing steps like resizing, normalization, and data augmentation to improve robustness and prevent overfitting.

The authors have looked into the case of applying ViTs and other CNN-based models for Industrial Visual Inspection while considering three use cases explicitly [12]. These are damage detection in sheet metal flooring, wooden load spaces, and recognition and character localization as a foundation for wagon matching with an internal database. Based on their study, they recommended the application of ViTs for Industrial Visual Inspection noting that ViTs perform better than typical CNN models being used, no significant difference is shown in convergence speed compared to CNNs, and they can handle datasets of smaller size commonly utilized in Industrial Visual Inspection well.

An interesting application of ViTs for the detection of defects in leather is reported in the proposed study [13]. One of the challenges in defect detection and classification is the availability of sufficient images with high resolution to show the defects and not miss them. Any subtle defects may be missed if processed as a low-resolution image. In addition, the manufacturing environment may include variations in viewing angle, lighting, and other factors, which may change the appearance of the leather without constituting a defect. They have discussed two variants of ViTs suitably developed for anomaly detection. The results show the ViTs outperform the CNN models in terms of defect classification accuracy and in highlighting the defective regions of interest. A comparative analysis between CNN-based models, like ResNet-50, Inception-V3, and EfficientNet-B0, and ViTs for detecting specific defects such as folding marks, loose grain, and pinholes was conducted by the authors using a dataset of 3,600 low-resolution images across six defect categories. The ViT was able to achieve a superior classification accuracy, up to 93.89%, and lower validation loss (0.1846). For the visualization, heat maps were used, pinpointing defect regions more accurately than CNN models. While ViTs proved effective in detecting subtle defects, future work may address the optimization of these models further, for even smaller datasets, in industrial applications.

The authors have discussed the development and application of a dynamic vision transformer that focuses on capturing both local and global features of the defect [14]. They developed a hybrid transformer architecture with a focus on reducing computational complexity while improving local detection accuracy similar to CNN models. Their results suggest that such hybrid transformers can be developed that can outperform all other models for these kinds of tasks. Its key techniques include hybrid window attention for combining window and pooling attention to reduce computational complexity; dynamic token normalization to allow the model to capture both global context and local details; and deep learning for the convolutional operations and the attention mechanism for efficient defect detection using specific datasets—NEU and DAGM. Its primary limitation happens to be that it does not include real-world defects. Future study can extend its application in other areas such as medical imaging.

A hybrid model named ViV-Ano is proposed for detecting and localizing anomalies in manufacturing by applying a combination of ViTs and variational autoencoders [15]. By leveraging deep learning, ViV-Ano captured both global and local features from image data, thereby improving both anomaly detection accuracy and localization precision. Image patches were processed through a ViT, which captured relationships across image regions, and a variational autoencoder compressed these features for reconstruction, allowing for anomaly detection by comparing reconstructed and original images. To estimate normal data distributions, the model incorporates a Gaussian mixture model, which helps in anomaly detection by understanding data patterns. ViV-Ano performed better than or similar to existing models on datasets like MNIST, CIFAR-10, and MV-TECH, particularly when it comes to industrial defect detection scenarios.

The authors have proposed an idea to develop a variant of the ViT model for anomaly detection [16]. This study presented an approach that leverages ViTs for detecting anomalies in industrial images without the requirement of labeled anomalous data. This involved the integration of a ViT-based autoencoder, a memory module, and a coordinate attention mechanism to capture global image features and localize anomalies precisely. It was thereafter tested on MVTec AD and BeanTech AD datasets for anomaly detection cases that correspond to simulated industrial world scenarios. In anomaly detection, the model achieved image-level AUROC values averaging 91.2% and 93.0% for pixel-level accuracy. Despite all its strong promising performance, the high computational cost of the model due to memory storage requirements suggests future work in optimizing the memory module for better efficiency and enhanced scalability.

Another application of ViTs for detecting defects in fasteners utilizing a model that combines both CNN type model and a transformer-based model is described [17]. It showed that the integrated model which utilized a knowledge distillation framework performed better when compared to the baseline models. A combination of the Swin transformer and EfficientNet is used as a teacher model to capture both local and global features. ResNet-18, a knowledge distillation technique, is used for faster and real-time processing on edge devices. Quantization is then applied to reduce the size and speed up inference time, and data is enhanced using augmentation techniques and Generative Adversarial Networks (GANs). Deployment on resource-constrained devices is always a challenge to maintain good accuracy while performing heavy computation and compression.

ViTs have been used for surface defect classification in aluminum surfaces [18]. A custom ViT model includes a 16 * 16 patch divisor and a transformer encoder that applies multihead self-attention and layer normalization, followed by a multilayer perceptron layer added as the final classifier for the output. Against CNN models such as VGG19, DenseNet, and ResNet, it obtained a superior accuracy and F1 score for aluminum surface defect detection. The comparatively smaller dataset size in real-world situations is a challenge for this type of work. Collaboration with manufacturing industry is essential as it will provide the large datasets that are required for the study in an industrial application.

A review of ViTs in biomedical applications has been reported in the proposed work [19]. While exploring ViTs for biomedical applications, they have mentioned various models, including the application of the standard ViT model, the MoViT, designed for mobile and edge devices (a lightweight version), and hybrid models combining ViT and other architectures such as CNNs for improved image segmentation and depth estimation. To use ViTs in biomedical applications, limitations such as computational power with an increase in the number of patches, extensive dataset for training, and interpretability come in the way. While MoViTs show promise, their biomedical application is currently limited. There is room for exploration, particularly in real-time diagnostics and monitoring on mobile devices while also enhancing the interpretability for building trust in automated medical diagnosis.

While most applications of ViTs in manufacturing seem to have been for quality assurance, the application of these technologies in pharmaceutical manufacturing lines, for preventive maintenance, has been mentioned [20]. This study introduces ManuTrans, a predictive maintenance model, which is based on deep learning transformers. It uses the encoder module of the transformer architecture to process raw sensor data from pharmaceutical manufacturing lines. Their model based on transformers was able to predict the instant in time of the next malfunction occurrence (in production cycles), evaluate the manufacturing line's health condition, and also predict the severity of such malfunction. The study has optimized the number of attention heads and encoder layers as part of the hyperparameter analysis. Future development could include efforts to pinpoint the exact faulty location in addition to predicting when the next fault would appear.

There are also innovative applications of ViTs to image data pertaining to maintenance [21]. They have applied ViTs to analyze vibration signal data related to motor bearing faults. Data from Case Western Reserve University Bearing Failure Library includes vibration signals for various bearing conditions, like in inner races, outer races, and balls. Through conversion of one-dimensional vibration data into two-dimensional time-frequency images through Short-Term Fourier Transforms, an accuracy of 98.8% with ViTs, outperforming CNNs (93.3%) and Deep Neural Networks (89.2%), was achieved.

A novel hybrid model integrating CNNs was proposed by the authors with the attention mechanism of transformers for detecting the faults in the rolling elements of industrial machines [22]. A combination of CNNs, for their local feature extraction, and transformers, for the global spatial analysis, was used. It was trained on the Case Western Reserve University dataset. A high fault classification accuracy of 99.62% and an average fault detection time of 38.4 ms were achieved through this model. Despite all its effectiveness, the model has certain limitations, such as potential sensitivity to varying data distributions and the need for further real-world testing in diverse industrial environments.

The authors explore the development of a model that integrates digital twin technology with a ViT framework to enhance quality in mechanical production and its assembly [23]. Here, the authors implemented geometric deviation, material properties, and assembly conditions for predicting assembly performance, specifically applied to composite bolted joints in aircrafts. The applied model achieved promising accuracy with a Root Mean Square Error of 0.105 kN, matching finite element analysis results, thus validating the Digital Twin-based Assembly Vision Transformer (DTA-VIT)'s predictive power. This approach, however, demands extensive data for training, and further research is required to improve computational efficiency or to extend the applicability of the model to broader contexts in assembly quality management.

Another recent article by the authors presents a model based on improvement of quality assurance in manufacturing by integration of Machine Learning, transfer learning, and ViTs into an architecture called ETLViT [24]. This system employs a three-layered approach with a cyber-physical system, which captures product images, then transmits data to a cloud server, and finally, processes images to detect faults using ETLViT. This model outperformed other methods by a remarkable 99% accuracy in defect prediction on casting and metal surface datasets. However, the model's reliance on high computational resources is a limitation. Future exploration should focus on further optimization of the ensemble model and its adaptation to real-world industrial settings.

A very comprehensive review of Automated Visual Inspection for Quality and Maintenance has been reported in the proposed work [25]. They looked at several cases for VI from both manufacturing and maintenance use cases. They have divided the entire set of use cases of four types such as binary classification, multi-class classification, localization, and multi-class localization. All these use cases are answered by mainly three types of models for object detection, image classification, and segmentation. They also looked into comparing a wide range of models applied for these problems. From the context of ViTs, the ViT models have performed quite well in comparison to other models with very good median accuracies and F1 scores. They recommend the acceleration and application of ViTs in the Automated Visual Inspection domain.

Multiple research gaps exist in the application of ViTs across the manufacturing and its related domains. A significant challenge is posed by memory and computational constraints, in particular, for real-world deployment on resource-constrained edge devices. Model generalization is affected by small datasets; this emphasizes the need for industrial collaboration to acquire large-scale datasets. Models are also sensitive to environmental dependencies such as lighting conditions and certain camera angles; this impacts the accuracy in defect detection. Approaches existing currently also struggle to incorporate real-world industrial defects and are thereby dependent on benchmark datasets. Exploring advanced model compression techniques, such as quantization, and developing lightweight ViTs remain crucial for improving inference speeds and deployment feasibility. Further, for balancing the trade-off between computational efficiency and accuracy, optimization is required. At the same time, methods for fault localization are needed for pinpointing the defect locations exactly. ViT-based models often suffer from issues and challenges with regard to memory and scalability. Hence, optimization for diverse datasets and applications is required. The lack of labeled data necessitates unsupervised approaches for enhancing the utility with regard to anomaly detection. Furthermore, for critical applications such as medical diagnostics, interoperability of ViT models must be improved, fostering trust in automated systems. For tasks requiring consistent accuracy, it is essential to optimize models for real-time deployment and adapt them to dynamic industrial environments. ViTs show sensitivity to data distribution variation. This impacts the generalization in hybrid models. In the context of real-time diagnostics and monitoring in biomedical applications, this remains unexplored. In settings with low resolution, subtle defects are often missed, necessitating improvements in the performance of models with respect to smaller-size datasets. Techniques such as hybrid window attention, introducing computational complexity, are though effective, but require simplification. In conclusion, energy efficiency enhancement and improvement of ViT models for deployment on a cyber-physical system is vital for practical and large-scale adoption across industries.

1.4 PROPOSED METHODOLOGY

An essential manufacturing process in which, onto a mold with a hollow cavity, molten metal is poured is called casting, which further forms a desired shape after letting it settle and solidify. It is a technique used widely across industries to make complex parts with intricate geometries. However, the whole process is prone to defects, which might compromise the performance and quality of the product. These defects are irregularities, which are unwanted and might emerge due to temperature fluctuations, procedural issues, or material inconsistencies. Common defect types include burrs, pinholes, blowholes, shrinkage cavity, material defects, mold, pouring metal defects, and metallurgical flaws. Each of these defects is a unique anomaly, which might destroy the working of the product, thereby making their detection and removal essential in casting industries. Traditionally, quality control for casting relies on manual inspection. Although skilled, human inspectors are inherently always limited to subjective judgment and fatigue, which could introduce the risk of defect identification inconsistencies. Furthermore, manual inspections are time-consuming and each part must be inspected properly. This can result in various bottlenecks, driving up costs, and leading to operational losses. Thus, the casting industries are seeking automated solutions that enhance both the efficiency of defect detection and the accuracy.

Now, for the above-mentioned reason, the dataset from Pilot Technocast is used for defect detection. In this, the dataset consisted of top-view images of a submersible pump impeller, which is a rotating iron or steel disc with vanes that transfer energy from the motor to the fluid in the centrifugal pump. The images were captured under consistent lighting conditions using a Canon EOS-1300D TSLR camera. Each image was 300 × 300 pixels and converted to grayscale to focus on texture and visibility. The dataset consists of 7,348 images divided into two categories: defective and non-defective.

Before training, this dataset needed to be pre-processed like resizing, normalization, and augmentation to simulate different conditions in the industry, allowing the model to learn from a broader range of defect appearances and improve the ability to generalize them.

In recent years, computer vision models have always been leading in automating defect detection by analyzing images. For that, convolutional neural networks have been the primary architecture for such tasks. They are capable of recognizing spatial hierarchies and also visualizing patterns like edges, shapes, and textures by using various convolutional filters. However, when it comes to capturing long-range dependencies, for instance, if defects are subtle or spread across various regions of the image, they have limitations. For this, ViTs have recently emerged as a promising alternative. It provides tasks where capturing global relationships within an image is crucial. ViTs, unlike CNNs, which apply convolutions, divide an image into patches and process them as a sequence. This approach of following a patch-based method allows ViTs to capture the broad range and long dependencies, making them very efficient. Based on the self-attention mechanism, each patch can attend to any other patch in the image. In this study, the pre-trained ViT model is fine-tuned for defect detection. This way, though the core transformer layer retains the knowledge gained from large datasets, only the classifier head requires training. With the advanced capabilities of ViTs, the defect detection process has become faster, less reliant on manual inspection, and more accurate. It offers a modern solution, which leads to a more reliable quality control process and reduces inconsistency and inefficiency.

1.4.1 Data Preprocessing

The dataset used initially consisted of images sized 300 × 300 pixels, which were again resized to 227 × 227 pixels to fit onto the model architecture, individually; this was done through various data manipulation techniques. These techniques included ideas like flips, rotations, cropping, adjusting brightness, altering exposure levels, and varying light conditions for simulating the diverse industrial environment specifications. Additionally, with rotations, flips, and varying light conditions, this was augmented. From the dataset, we selected 2,500 images for training and 500 images for testing. This ensured a balanced distribution for both non-defective and defective classes. The preprocessing and augmentation aimed to enhance model generalizability across various defect patterns and types.

Normalization: To standardize the data and make it easier to process the requirement, it is used to scale the input values (X) to a specific range (0 and 1).

$$X' = \frac{(X - X_{\min})}{(X_{\max} - X_{\min})} \tag{1.1}$$

Adjusting Brightness: I is the original image intensity, and β is the brightness offset. Adding β to each pixel value leads to a brighter or darker image.

$$I' = I + \beta \tag{1.2}$$

Rotation: The function $I(x,y)$ represents the intensity at coordinates (x,y) in the original image. Here, θ is the angle of rotation in radians. The coordinates (x,y) are transformed using a rotation matrix to new coordinates, calculated as:

$$x' = x\cos(\theta) - y\sin(\theta) \tag{1.3}$$

$$y' = \sin(\theta)\cdot x + \cos(\theta)\cdot y \tag{1.4}$$

$$I'(x, y) = I\big(x\cos\theta + y\sin\theta - x\sin\theta + y\cos\theta\big) \tag{1.5}$$

1.4.2 Model Architecture

To explain ViT's superiority in certain aspects, we draw a comparison between CNN and ViT architecture for defect detection using the casting defect dataset. The comparison of CNN and ViT models is described in Table 1.1. We use these two streamlined models below; each model is designed to classify images of casting products into defective and non-defective categories.

1.4.3 Convolutional Neural Networks

A CNN model follows a step-by-step structure with a straightforward layer arrangement in order to capture all the features in the images effectively [5]. The architecture

TABLE 1.1
Comparison of CNN and ViT Models

Features	CNN	ViT
Feature extraction	Employs convolutional filters for extracting local features with no global context	Employs self-attention for capturing global relationships in patches
Model complexity	Less computationally expensive than ViTs	Higher computational cost
Data requirements	Performs well on both small and large datasets	Large dataset is required to perform well
Inductive biases	Strong inductive bias for local features like edges and curves	Minimal inductive bias as it learns the features directly
Performance on small datasets	Performs better on smaller datasets due to built-in bias	Tends to overfit on small datasets
Interpretability	Easy understanding with learned filters	Complex understanding due to attention mechanisms

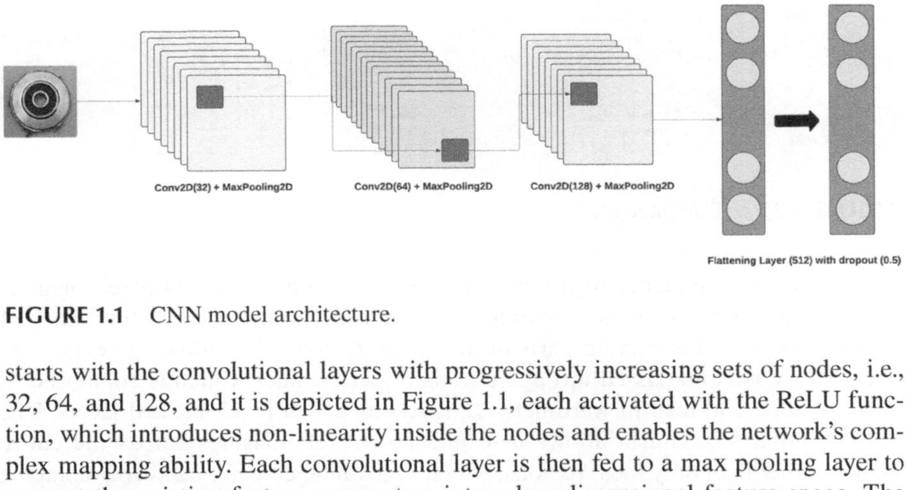

FIGURE 1.1 CNN model architecture.

starts with the convolutional layers with progressively increasing sets of nodes, i.e., 32, 64, and 128, and it is depicted in Figure 1.1, each activated with the ReLU function, which introduces non-linearity inside the nodes and enables the network's complex mapping ability. Each convolutional layer is then fed to a max pooling layer to convert the existing feature parameters into a low-dimensional feature space. The convolutional layers are followed by a flattening layer, which transforms the 2D feature map to a 1D vector. This 1D vector is then sent to the dense layer, where a fully connected layer with 512 units and ReLU activation functions acts as the primary learning function. A dropout layer with a dropout of 0.5 is included, which reduces overfitting. Finally, an output layer with a single neuron and sigmoid activation helps with binary classification, with them either being defective or non-defective. The equations used in the CNN model are provided in Table 1.2.

1.4.4 Vision Transformers

The ViT architecture model employs ViT-B/16 architecture, and it is shown in Figure 1.2. It was initially pre-trained to fit a larger dataset, which is optimized to capture both local and global relationships within the image. The ViT first embeds

TABLE 1.2
Equations Implemented in the CNN Model

Process	Equation
The convolutional output O with input feature map I and filter K with dimensions w and h	$O(i,j)=\sum_{m=0}^{h-1}\sum_{n=0}^{w-1} I(i+m,j+n)\cdot K(m,n)$
ReLU activation function	$f(x)=\max(0,x)$
Flattening layer	$\text{Flatten}(O)=\left[O_{1,1},O_{1,2},\ldots,O_{m,n}\right]$
Output layer with **sigmoid** activation	$\sigma(x)=\frac{1}{1+e^{-x}}$

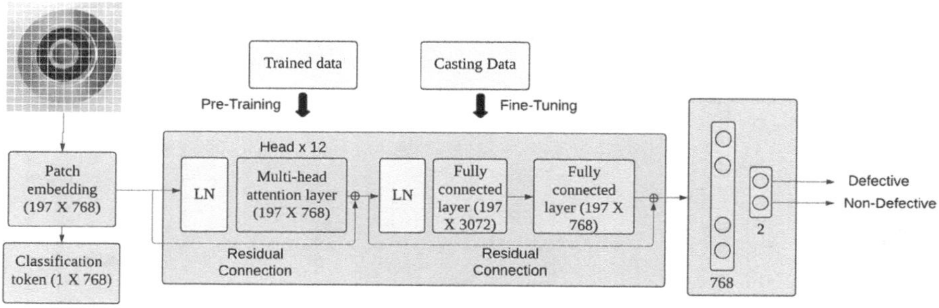

FIGURE 1.2 ViT architecture.

the images as a sequence of patches. Specifically, each 224 × 224 pixel image is bundled into 16 × 16 patches creating a sequence of 196 flattened vectors. Each of which represents the smaller parts of the image region. The following vectors are then embedded and passed through a transformer encoder, which is composed of self-attention and feed forward network layers arranged in 12 stacked layers. The self-attention mechanism allows it to understand relationships across the entire image rather than only local regions, which is advantageous for capturing complex different patterns on casting surfaces. Finally, toward the end, a classifier head, i.e., a linear head, outputs a binary classification score. This enables ViTs to capture intricate different characteristics often ruled out by CNN models, which only rely on local spatial hierarchies. The equations used in ViT models are provided in Table 1.3.

Due to the above comparison, we chose the ViT model for casting defect detection due to its ability to capture a wider range of dependencies within an image. This feature allows it to understand and detect subtle distributed defects across the casting surface. Unlike CNNs, which excel at local feature extraction, ViTs' self-attention mechanism makes them take into account the relevance of different image patterns, making them highly effective in scenarios where patterns are not localized, as can be seen in this case. Figure 1.3 describes the dimensionality reduction representation, which is compared with CNNs.

TABLE 1.3
Equations Implemented in the ViT Model

Processes	Equations
Image to Patch Embedding: with the input the size of the image is 224 × 224 split into 16 × 16 patches; each patch is flattened to a vector	$\text{Patch}_i = \text{Flatten}\left(X_{p\times p}\right)$
Linear Embedding: each patch is linearly projected into a vector of special embedding dimension D using learned weights matrix W	$E_i = \text{Patch}_i \cdot W$
Positional Embedding: to retain positional information	$Z_0 = \left[E_1 + P_1, E_2 + P_2, \ldots, E_{196} + P_{196}\right]$
Self-Attention Mechanism	$\text{Attention}(Q,K,V) = \text{softmax}\left(\frac{QK^T}{\sqrt{d_k}}\right)V$
Multihead Attention	$\text{MultiHead}(Q,K,V) = \text{Concat}\left(\text{head}_1, \text{head}_2, \ldots, \text{head}_h\right) \cdot W_O$
Feed Forward Network	$FFN(x) = W_2 \cdot \text{ReLU}\left(W_1 \cdot x + b_1\right) + b_2$
Classifier Head (Linear)	$f(x) = Wx + b$ $x, W \in R^{768}$ $b.y \in R^2$

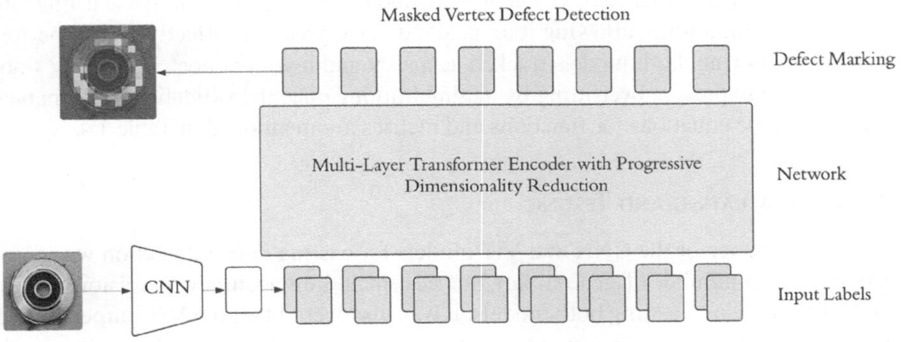

FIGURE 1.3 ViT dimensionality reduction representation.

1.4.5 Loss Function and Position Monitoring

For both CNN and ViT models, since they are employed for binary classification, we have used binary cross-entropy as the loss function, which measures the divergence between predicted possibilities and true labels, and this function is calculated as shown below:

Toward the end, the Adam Optimizer, as depicted in the table above, is used for both models, which is a widely adopted optimization method due to its adaptive learning rate feature, which allows for better and faster convergence. It combines the benefits

TABLE 1.4
Functions and Metrics

Functions and Metrics	Equations
Binary Cross-Entropy Loss Function	$L = -\frac{1}{N}\sum_{i=1}^{N}\left(y_i \log(p_i) + (1-y_i)\log(1-p_i)\right)$
Adam Optimizer	
• m_t = first moment estimate	$m_t = \beta_1 m_{t-1} + (1-\beta_1) g_t$
• v_t = second moment estimate	$v_t = \beta_2 v_{t-1} + (1-\beta_2) g_t^2$
• Bias-corrected moment estimate	$m_t = \frac{m_t}{1-\beta_1^t}, v_t = \frac{v_t}{1-\beta_2^t}$
• Parameter update	$\theta_t = \theta_{t-1} - \alpha \frac{m_t}{\sqrt{v_t} + \epsilon}$
Precision	$\text{Precision} = \frac{\text{True Positives}}{\text{True Positives} + \text{False Positives}}$
Recall	$\text{Recall} = \frac{\text{True Positives}}{\text{True Positives} + \text{False Negatives}}$
F1 Score	$F1 = 2 \cdot \frac{\text{Precision} \cdot \text{Recall}}{\text{Precision} + \text{Recall}}$

of both AdaGrid, an adaptive grid optimization technique designed to improve the efficiency and performance of vision models, and RMS-prop, an adaptive learning rate optimization algorithm, allowing it to handle diverse gradients effectively. For performance monitoring, both models tracked accuracy and loss per epoch with early stopping applied to prevent overfitting by halting training once the validation performance plateaued. The equations for functions and metrics are mentioned in Table 1.4.

1.4.6 Evaluating and Testing

The performance of the CNN and ViT models for casting defect detection was compared using a number of general key metrics, including accuracy, precision, recall, and F1 score. Upon testing both models, it was discovered that the ViT outperformed the CNN in terms of performance. Higher recall and improved F1 scores were attained by the ViT model, indicating that it is more adept at capturing these scattered flaws throughout casting sequences. The CNN's lack of global pattern perception can have certain drawbacks, even though it still performed exceptionally well at local feature extraction within its range. On the other hand, local and global dependencies are successfully captured by the ViT's self-attention mechanism, which is crucial for detecting flaws that can differ in shape and location. Consequently, the ViT outperformed the CNN in general defect recognition, exhibiting a better capacity to identify and capture faulty structures throughout the area. The experimental setup details are provided in Table 1.5.

A variety of testing techniques were used to cross-check the generalizability of each model. To assess each model on untested data, the dataset was first divided into training and testing sections. Cross-validation was then employed to confirm the

TABLE 1.5
Experimental Setup

Simulation	
Notebook server	24.5.0
Python	3.12.4
IPython	8.25.0
Frameworks	
Torch	2.4.0
Pillow	10.3.0
TensorFlow	2.18.0
Supporting Tools	
pandas	2.2.2
Matplotlib	3.8.4
NumPy	1.26.4
Training Configuration	
AdamOptimizer	
• Learning rate	5×10^{-5}
• Weight decay	1×10^{-4}
Loss Function	Cross-Entropy Loss
Epochs	15
Model	
ViT-B-16 Pre-trained ViT	ViT model pre-trained on ImageNet-21k (14 million images, 21,843 classes) at resolution 224 × 224, and fine-tuned on ImageNet 2012

robustness of each model. By splitting the data into multiple subsets, cross-validation rotates until every subset has been tested, training on one subset and validating on others. By correcting possible overfitting, this method can provide us with a more thorough understanding of the model across various data sets. Furthermore, stratified sampling provides consistency and dependability in performance evaluation by guaranteeing that each batch during training and testing preserves the original dataset's defect distribution. In defect detection, where intricate visual cues and variations are crucial for precise classification, this comparison highlights the significance of transformer-based models like ViTs.

1.5 USE CASE DESCRIPTION

Casting is a crucial manufacturing process as melted metal is poured into a mold with a hollow cavity to form a desired shape after being allowed to settle and solidify. Many industries use this method to create complex parts with intricate geometries. However, the entire process is vulnerable to flaws that could lower the product's performance and quality. These defects are undesired irregularities that could result from variations in temperature, inconsistent materials, or problems with procedures. Blowholes, pinholes, burrs, shrinkage cavities, mold, material defects, pouring metal defects, and metallurgical flaws are examples of common defect types. Since each of these flaws is a distinct anomaly that could prevent the product from functioning, it is crucial for the casting industry to identify and eliminate them. Traditionally, quality control for casting relies on manual inspection. Although skilled, human inspectors are inherently limited to subject judgment and fatigue, which could introduce the risk of defect identification inconsistencies. Furthermore, manual inspections are time-consuming, and each part must be inspected properly. This can result in various bottlenecks, driving up costs and leading to operational losses. Thus, the casting industries are seeking automated solutions that enhance both the accuracy and efficiency of defect detection. Now, for the above-mentioned reason, the dataset from Pilot Technocast, consisting of 7,348 grayscale images of 300 × 300 pixels, was used for defect detection in submersible pump impellers. In this, the dataset consisted of top-view images of a submersible pump impeller, which is a rotating iron or steel disc with vanes that transfer energy from the motor to the fluid in the centrifugal pump.

1.6 COMPARATIVE ANALYSIS OF CNNs AND ViTs FOR CASTING DEFECT DETECTION

CNNs operate by the application of convolutional filters for extracting local features such as edges, shapes, and textures. Primarily, the limitation arises from their fixed receptive fields, which focus on localized information and fail to grasp long-range dependencies across the images. All the layers in CNNs process the images sequentially, with pooling layers reducing computational and dimensionality complexity. This structure is efficient but often sacrifices global information critical for complex defect detection. In tasks where defect features are localized and prominent, such as small cracks, or single blowholes, CNNs excel. However, they struggle when complex defects distributed across the surface, such as shrinkage or subtle irregularities come into question. However, the ViTs divide the image into fixed-size patches, treating these as sequential inputs of data. Each of the patch is embedded into a vector and passed through a self-attention mechanism, which enables the model to capture global inter-patch relationships. Contrary to CNNs, ViTs lack inductive biases, relying entirely on the data for learning. This approach is data-intensive, but it allows models to excel for recognizing dispersed patterns across the images. This

TABLE 1.6
Comparison of the CNN and ViT for Casting Defect Detection

Metric	CNN	ViT
Training accuracy	98.84%	99.78%
Validation accuracy	93.50%	94.86%
Recall	0.89	0.92
F1 score	0.91	0.94
Training time/epoch	~3 minutes	~6 minutes
Memory usage	~2.3 GB	~3.9 GB

architecture is inherently parallelizable and can process multiple patches simultaneously. However, this comes at the cost of increased computational and memory requirements. The comparison of CNNs and ViTs based on the above-mentioned evaluation metrics is given in Table 1.6.

1.7 RESULTS AND DISCUSSION

Plots here depict the increasing training/validation accuracy and decreasing loss over the epochs. Early stopping is applied to prevent overfitting when validation performance plateaus. The bar charts show balanced "Defective" and "Non-defective" image counts in training/testing datasets. The histogram with decision threshold at 0.5 highlights classification confidence, predicting probabilities distribution.

1.7.1 Training and Validation Loss

The *X*-axis and *Y*-axis describe the Epochs and Loss (number of training iterations vs. measure of error during training and testing). Initially, both training loss and test loss are high, which indicates that the model is learning. Thereafter, the training loss gradually decreases to near zero and shows that the model fits the training data. The test loss shows variability and initially increases, which indicates overfitting at the beginning but later stabilizes after a few epochs. After the fifth epoch, the gap between the training and test losses increases, indicating signs of overfitting, as the model performs better on the training data than on the test data, as shown in Figure 1.4a and b.

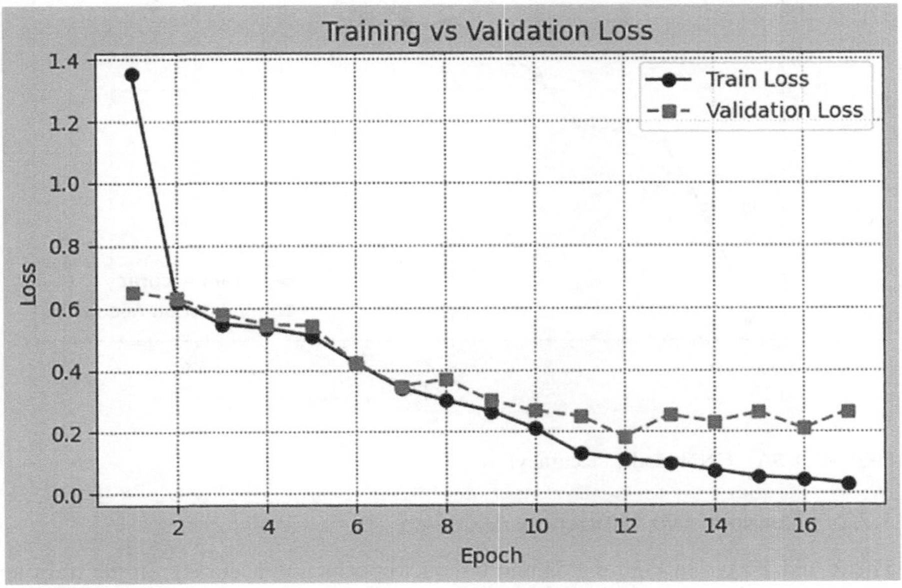

FIGURE 1.4A CNN model (loss).

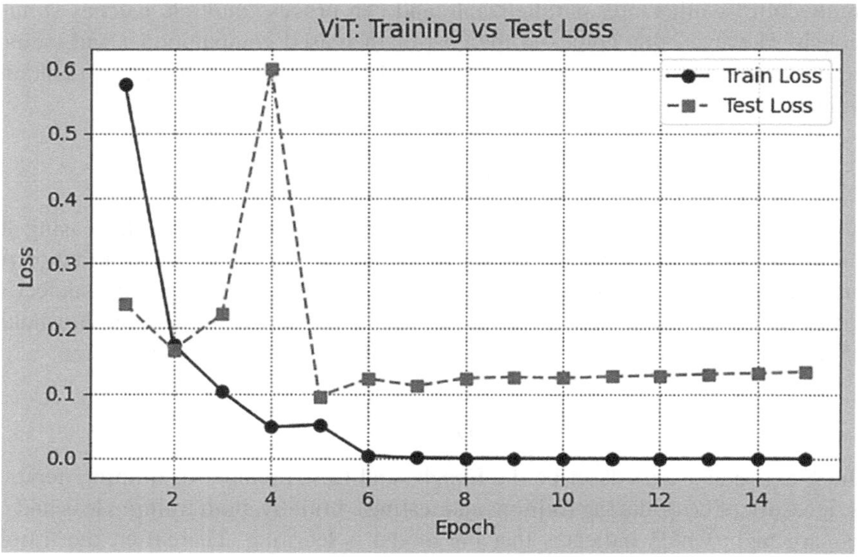

FIGURE 1.4B ViT model (loss).

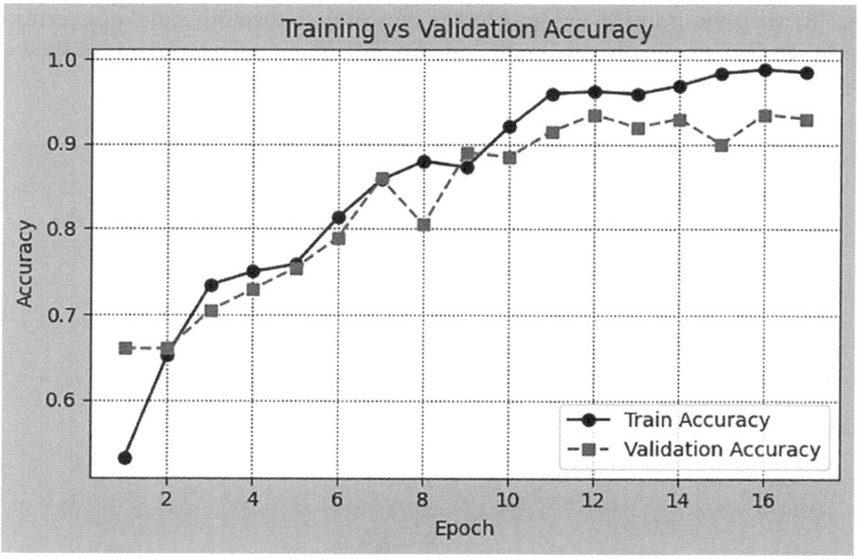

FIGURE 1.5A CNN model (accuracy).

1.7.2 Training and Validation Accuracy

The *X* and *Y*-axes in Figure 1.5a and b depict epochs and accuracy; in the training accuracy, it can be seen that there is a rapid increase, which nearly reaches 100% by the sixth epoch, thereby indicating that the model fits the training data perfectly.

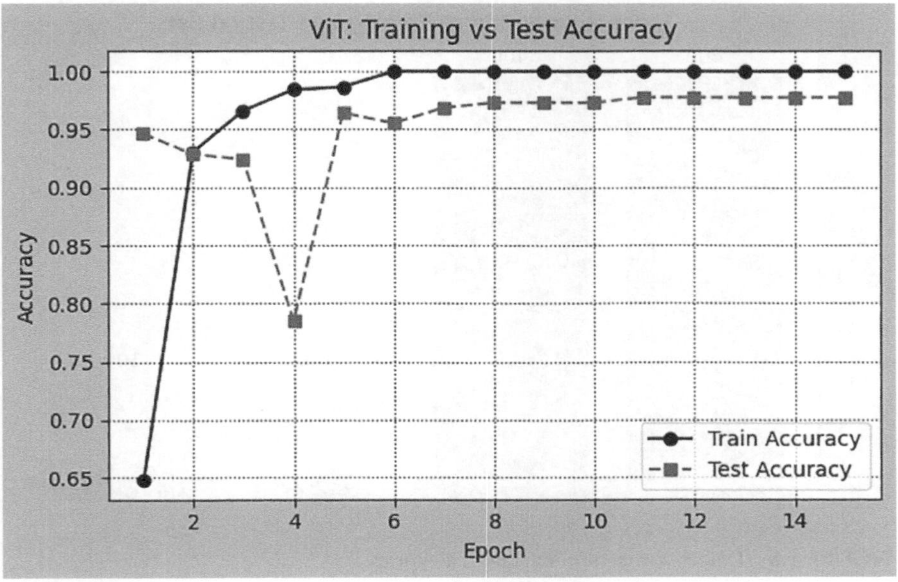

FIGURE 1.5B ViT model (accuracy).

For the test accuracy, the initial increase shows a dip around the third epoch. After more epochs, the test accuracy approaches ~95%, thereby showing high generalization performance. Overall, the loss graph suggests that the model overfits as the training loss is near zero, while the test stabilizes at a higher value.

The accuracy graph indicates good training performance but highlights a risk of overfitting as the test accuracy does not match the scale of training accuracy.

1.7.3 Class Distribution

The class distribution bar chart in Figure 1.6 is a visual representation of the balanced nature of the training and testing datasets. The *X*-axis denotes four categories: train-non-defective, train-defective, test-non-defective, and test-defective, while the *Y*-axis indicates the sample count. The dataset consists of 400 "non-defective" images and 400 "defective" images, which is used for training, ensuring equal representation of classes for training, and for testing, an additional set of 100 non-defective images and a set of 100 defective images are being used even the balance throughout.

1.7.4 Predicted Probabilities Distribution

The histogram of probabilities provides insights into the confidence levels of the ViT and the CNN model when classifying images as defective or as non-defective. The ViT model demonstrates a tighter clustering of probabilities around the true class labels, which results in a narrower spread when compared to the CNN model. This suggests that the ViT produces predictions with higher confidence as compared to

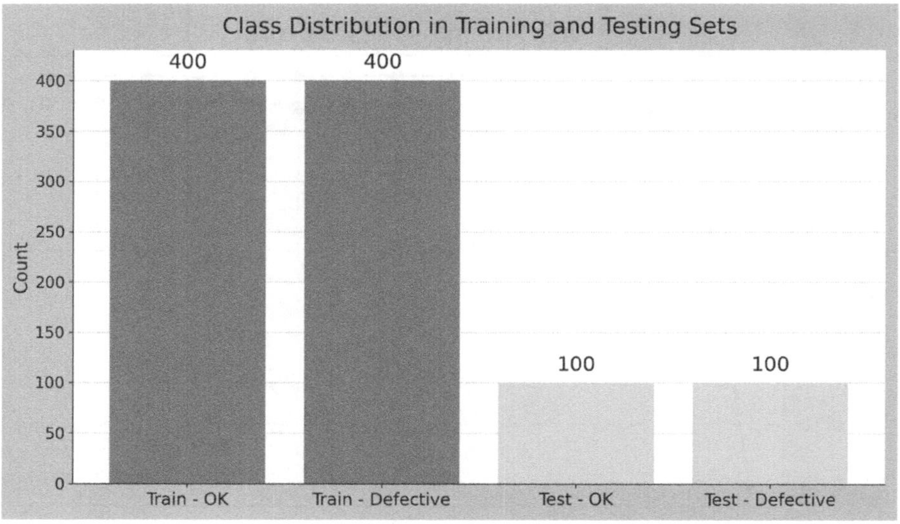

FIGURE 1.6 Defective and non-defective categories.

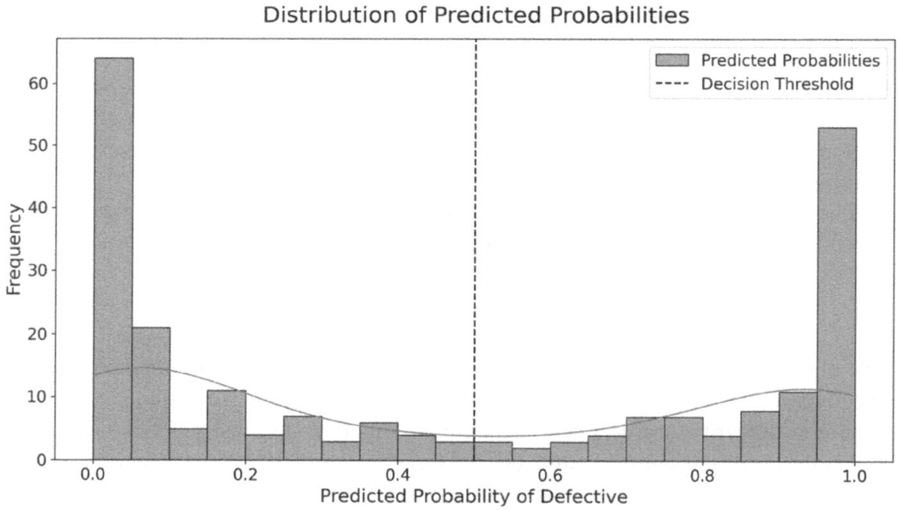

FIGURE 1.7 Predicted probability distribution of defective and non-defective.

the CNN, which reflects its superior feature extraction and classification capability. The CNN model, on the other hand, displays a slightly wider spread, which suggests sporadic ambiguity and incorrect classifications, especially for borderline cases. Because the ViT can more effectively distinguish subtle defect patterns, we can conclude that it achieves higher prediction and recall values, as illustrated in Figure 1.7. The robustness in real-world defect detection tasks is highlighted by the ViT's lower misclassification rate when compared to the CNN.

1.8 CONCLUSION

This study analyzed 2,000 images of submersible pump impellers—1,600 defective and 400 non-defective—using two deep learning approaches: a CNN and a ViT. Image preprocessing was performed through resizing, augmentation, and normalization to enhance the model's generalizability. The CNN, which comprises convolutional and pooling layers along with dropout, achieved a validation accuracy of 93.5% and a peak training accuracy of 98.84%, although minor overfitting was observed. While effective for detecting localized defects, CNNs struggled with subtle or dispersed patterns due to their focus on local features. In contrast, the ViT-B/16 model, using self-attention on 16 × 16 image patches and fine-tuned with frozen base layers, demonstrated superior performance. It reached a test accuracy of 94.86% and an overall weighted accuracy of 99.6%, excelling in identifying complex and scattered defects. This highlights ViTs' robustness and generalization capability over CNNs, though at a higher computational cost.

Looking ahead, research should explore hybrid architectures that merge CNN efficiency with ViTs' global context understanding, enabling deployment in resource-limited industrial environments. Further directions include optimizing ViT models for real-time applications, leveraging transfer learning across manufacturing domains, and developing lightweight ViT variants for edge devices. Integrating ViTs with IoT and Smart Manufacturing systems could also support predictive maintenance and adaptive quality control. As ViT technology matures, emphasis should shift toward creating interpretable, scalable, and real-time solutions, unlocking new possibilities for intelligent automation in industrial defect detection.

REFERENCES

1. Krizhevsky, A., Sutskever, I., and Hinton, G. E. "ImageNet Classification with Deep Convolutional Neural Networks." In *Advances in Neural Information Processing Systems*, vol. 25, edited by F. Pereira, C. J. C. Burges, L. Bottou, and K. Q. Weinberger, pp. 1097–1105. Curran Associates, Inc., 2012.
2. Wu, Zifeng, Chunhua Shen, and Anton van den Hengel. "Wider or Deeper: Revisiting the ResNet Model for Visual Recognition." *Pattern Recognition* 90 (June 2019): 119–133.
3. Wang, Chao, Dong Chen, Lian Hao, Xiaoyan Liu, Yijie Zeng, Jun Chen, and Guangyu Zhang. "Pulmonary Image Classification Based on Inception-v3 Transfer Learning Model." *IEEE Access* 7 (October 2019): 146533–146541.
4. Zhang, Kai, Yu Guo, Xiaocheng Wang, Jie Yuan, and Qiang Ding. "Multiple Feature Reweight DenseNet for Image Classification." *IEEE Access* 7 (January 2019): 9872–9880.
5. Li, Zewen, Fan Liu, Wenjie Yang, Shouheng Peng, and Jun Zhou. "A Survey of Convolutional Neural Networks: Analysis, Applications, and Prospects." *IEEE Transactions on Neural Networks and Learning Systems* 33, no. 12 (December 2022): 6999–7019.
6. Vaswani, Ashish, Noam Shazeer, Niki Parmar, Jakob Uszkoreit, Llion Jones, Aidan N. Gomez, Łukasz Kaiser, and Illia Polosukhin. "Attention Is All You Need." In Advances in Neural Information Processing Systems 30, edited by Isabelle Guyon, Ulrike von Luxburg, Samy Bengio, Hanna M. Wallach, Rob Fergus, S. V. N. Vishwanathan, and Roman Garnett, pp. 5998–6008. Curran Associates, Inc., 2017.

7. Ruan, Bo-Kai, Hong-Han Shuai, and Wen-Huang Cheng. *"Vision Transformers: State of the Art and Research Challenges." arXiv preprint*, arXiv:2207.03041v1 (July 7, 2022).
8. Dosovitskiy, Alexey, Lucas Beyer, Alexander Kolesnikov, Dirk Weissenborn, Xiaohua Zhai, et al. "An Image Is Worth 16×16 Words: Transformers for Image Recognition at Scale." In *International Conference on Learning Representations (ICLR), Virtual Conference*, May 3–7, 2021.
9. Rane, Nitin. "Transformers in Industry 4.0, Industry 5.0, and Society 5.0: Roles and Challenges." *SSRN* (2023). https://dx.doi.org/10.2139/ssrn.4609915.
10. Alif, Mujadded Al Rabbani, Mahbub Hussain, Graham Tucker, and Simon Iwnicki. "BoltVision: A Comparative Analysis of CNN, CCT, and ViT in Achieving High Accuracy for Missing Bolt Classification in Train Components." *Machines* 12, no. 2 (2024): 93. https://doi.org/10.3390/machines12020093.
11. Liu, Xiu, and Chris Aldrich. "Multivariate Image Processing in Minerals Engineering with Vision Transformers." *Mineral Engineering* 208 (2024).
12. Hütten, Nils, Richard Meyes, and Tobias Meisen. "Vision Transformer in Industrial Visual Inspection." *Applied Sciences* 12, no. 11 (2022): 11981. https://doi.org/10.3390/app122311981.
13. Smith, Antony Douglas, Shuang Du, and Kurien. "Vision Transformers for Anomaly Detection and Localisation in Leather Surface Defect Classification Based on Low-Resolution Images and a Small Dataset." *Applied Sciences* 13, no. 15 (2023): 8716. https://doi.org/10.3390/app13158716.
14. Ding, Chao, Donglin Tang, Xianghua Zheng, Qiang Wang, Yuanyuan He, and Long Zhang. "DHT: Dynamic Vision Transformer Using Hybrid Window Attention for Industrial Defect Images Classification." *IEEE Instrumentation & Measurement Magazine* 26, no. 2 (April 2023): 19–28.
15. Choi, Bonghee, and Jungsoo Jeong. "ViV-Ano: Anomaly Detection and Localization Combining Vision Transformer and Variational Autoencoder in the Manufacturing Process." *Electronics* 11, no. 15 (2022): 2306. https://doi.org/10.3390/electronics11152306.
16. Yang, Qifan, and Ruicheng Guo. "An Unsupervised Method for Industrial Image Anomaly Detection with Vision Transformer-Based Autoencoder." *Sensors* 24, no. 8 (2024): 2440. https://doi.org/10.3390/s24082440.
17. Sampath, Vignesh, Iñaki Maurtua, Juan José Aguilar Martín, Ander Iriondo, Iker Lluvia, and Andoni Rivera. "Vision Transformer-Based Knowledge Distillation for Fasteners Defect Detection." In *Proceedings of the International Conference on Electrical, Computer and Energy Technologies (ICECET 2022)*, July 20–22, 2022, Prague, Czech Republic.
18. Zhao, Jihai. "Surface Defect Classification with Vision Transformer." In *2022 3rd International Conference on Intelligent Design (ICID)*, Nanjing, China, 2022.
19. Teh, Shem, Saaveethya Sivakumar, and Foad Motalebi. "Vision Transformers for Biomedical Applications." In *2024 International Conference on Green Energy, Computing and Sustainable Technology (GECOST 2024)*, Miri, Sarawak, Malaysia, 2024.
20. Kavasidis, Isaak, Efthimios Lallas, Vassilis C. Gerogiannis, Theodosia Charitou, and Anthony Karageorgos. "Predictive Maintenance in Pharmaceutical Manufacturing Lines Using Deep Transformers." *Procedia Computer Science* 220 (2023): 576–583.
21. Zim, Abid Hasan, Aeyan Ashraf, Aquib Iqbal, Asad Malik, and Minoru Kuribayashi. "A Vision Transformer-Based Approach to Bearing Fault Classification via Vibration Signals." In *Proceedings of the 2022 APSIPA Annual Summit and Conference*, November 7–10, 2022, Chiang Mai, Thailand.

22. Saeed, Ali, M. Usman Akram, Muazzam Khattak, and M. Belal Khan. "An Interpretable Hybrid Framework Combining Convolution Latent Vectors with Transformer Based Attention Mechanism for Rolling Element Fault Detection and Classification." *Heliyon* 10, no. 21 (2024): e38993.
23. Liu, Yuming, and Qingyuan Lin. "A Digital Twin-Based Assembly Model for Multi-Source Variation Fusion on Vision Transformer." *Journal of Manufacturing Systems* 76 (October 2024): 478–501.
24. Arora, Aashish and Rajeev Gupta, Intelligent and Automated Product Quality Assurance System using Machine Learning, *Journal of Electrical Systems* 20–6s (2024): 2452–2463
25. Hütten, Nils, Marcos Alves Gomes, Felix Hölken, Ksenija Andricevic, Richard Meyes, and Tobias Meisen. "Deep Learning for Automated Visual Inspection in Manufacturing and Maintenance: A Survey of Open-Access Papers." *Applied System Innovations* 7, no. 1 (2024): 11. https://doi.org/10.3390/asi7010011.

2 Production and Operations Management for Intelligent Manufacturing

Maniraj Mariraj, Gurunathan Manikandan, and Ashoka Varthanan Perumal

2.1 AN OVERVIEW OF PRODUCTION AND OPERATION MANAGEMENT FOR INTELLIGENT MANUFACTURING

Intelligent manufacturing integrates the emerging Internet of Things (IoT), bigdata, digital twins (DTs), cloud computing, and fifth-generation mobile networks with automation to effectively face the unprecedented challenges arising in the manufacturing sector [1]. In addition, wireless sensor networks, RFID technology, and mobile computing provides edge in intelligent approaches in the manufacturing sector [2]. The customized product requirements based on dynamic demands lead to effective implementation of open manufacturing resources and capabilities through cloud manufacturing [3]. The design by feature and automated feature recognition approaches used in Computer Aided Process Planning increases the functionality in optimizing the machine tools, cost, time, jigs, and fixtures, as well as the sequence of processes [4]. Process capability in the manufacturing sector is analyzed in three layers, namely, universal level, shop floor level, and machine level, for accurately planning the processes. Further, rule-based intelligent process planning is adopted for the confirmation of compatibility in automated process planning of products in consideration with features as well as process requirements [5].

Strategic deployment of machines and workforce to meet customer demand through an optimal production schedule not only reduces the production cost but also maximizes the profit of the manufacturing plant. Scrap rates, changeover duration, labor cost, and consumption of energy are some of the constraints considered in optimizing the schedule of production lines [6]. Scheduling in a mass customized product environment needs a specific approach to minimize the work-in-process inventories as well as maximize product output based on the application domain [7]. In real time, there is a challenge in scheduling for a mass customized product environment since the processing of data is huge at the operation level, product level, and system level. For any group of products, the generic bill of materials of the parent item is a more suitable option for process planning.

DOI: 10.1201/9781003582465-2

2.2 IMS TECHNIQUES IN TOTAL QUALITY MANAGEMENT (TQM)

The core concepts of TQM – customer focus, top management commitment, continuous improvement in the process, employee engagement, supplier partnership, and performance measures – are still relevant and also augmented with IMS techniques in the Industry 4.0 scenario. In general, several researchers point out the emergence of TQM 4.0 as an enhanced approach that integrates conventional TQM methodologies with many IMS techniques [8–11]. The relevance of TQM in the era Industry 4.0 was discussed by many researchers, and they pointed out that the data-driven ability of the IMS techniques helps any conventional TQM methodologies reap benefits never realized before, like an increase in productivity (up to 86% in some studies), noticeable cost reductions (reported in 83.3% of relevant studies), and marked improvements in product quality (observed in 87.9% of studies). These improvements arise from the strategic application of technologies such as the Industrial IoT, artificial intelligence (AI), big data analytics, and digital twins, which enable real-time monitoring, predictive analytics, and automated decision-making [12–17].

2.2.1 Impact of AI/Machine Learning (ML) on TQM Function

The major benefit of TQM over earlier quality assurance techniques is that TQM focuses on the prevention of defects through proactive detection in any product/service. Especially, the use of AI/ML techniques like machine vision realizes this major advantage [18]. Table 2.1 summarizes the application of various AI/ML techniques in the TQM techniques.

TABLE 2.1
Integration of TQM and IMS Techniques

TQM Techniques	Purpose	Enhancement Through AI/ML
Seven basic QC tools, root cause analysis, FMEA, lean six sigma	Proactive identification of quality issues in the manufacturing processes	Predictive Quality Software early defect detection, automated root cause analysis
KANBAN, visual inspection, management by wandering around	Visual inspection of various processes to identify defects and assembly issues	Machine Vision enhances the defect identification and provides greater accuracy and speed than management by wandering around
Quality function deployment, Hoshin Kanri, seven new management tools, benchmarking	Data/information analysis and work flow analysis for better overall quality management	Modern Quality Management Software incorporates cloud computing and AI to automate the data/information analysis
Design for six sigma, design FMEA, lean manufacturing	Focused customer requirements analysis for better design and development of product/service	Extended Reality Systems for providing immersive, interactive guidance for quality dimensions and process adherence, effectively augmenting the human intelligence

2.2.2 IoT and TQM

IoT is considered to be the major enabler of Industry 4.0 [19] in the industrial production of complex products for enhanced customer satisfaction. It helps in the real-time monitoring of product/service quality at various stages of production and helps in early detection. IoT enables seamless communication and data exchange among a vast network of devices, machines, and human elements. This capability is crucial for Quality 4.0, as it facilitates real-time data collection and analysis from smart systems that are essential for advanced quality control and informed decision-making. Today, IoT connects not only the devices but also people, allowing the data/information to be collected and used for better coordination and control of decisions. IoT also allows computers and automated systems to collect the data/information without human errors [20]. Figure 2.1 illustrates the benefits of IoT in TQM.

2.2.3 Robotics and Automation in TQM

Many of the productivity and ergonomics challenges were addressed by novel robotics and automation solutions, facilitating improved product/service quality. Robots are designed to substitute human hardships in carrying out challenging manufacturing tasks. These robots perform a wide variety of tasks like assembling, material handling, packaging, painting, and welding. They excel at repetitive and precise tasks, resulting in improved production rates and reduced cycle time. These advantages transform the robotics and automation into muscles of Industry 4.0, resulting in agility and efficiency

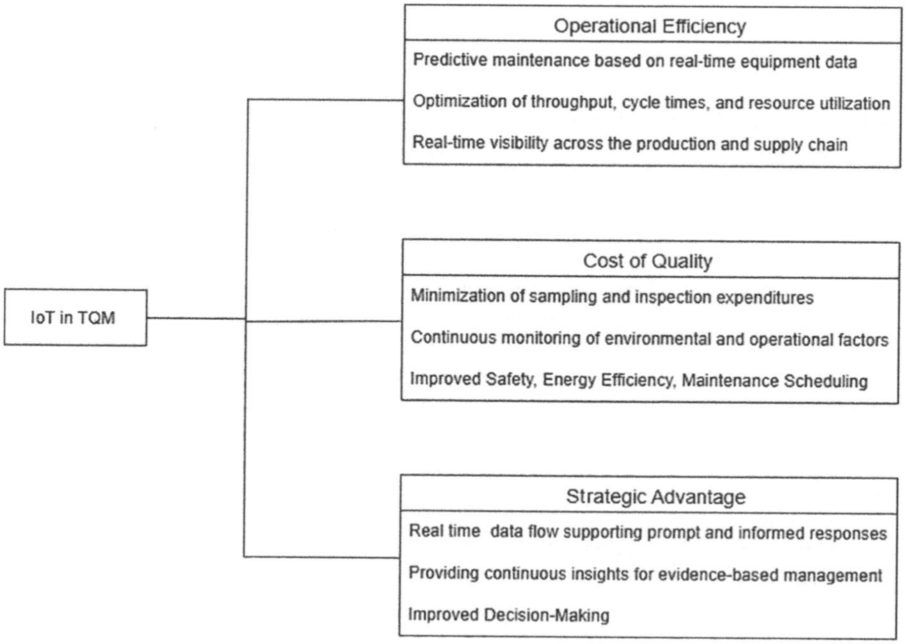

FIGURE 2.1 IoT in TQM.

enablers [18]. In the current scenario, customer demands are growing, and in order to meet them, TQM techniques should be applied to achieve smart manufacturing systems, and robotics and automation is a significant enabler for it.

The major benefits of robotics and automation can be summarized as follows.

- Smart manufacturing process with agility, reconfigurability, and high responsiveness to change with respect to the customer requirements
- Data-driven optimization of physical systems through the automation of physical production systems
- Zero defects manufacturing and predictive maintenance
- Holistic quality management approach to achieve the sustainability of organization

  This sophisticated robotics and automation enables an organization to address challenges in the three vital phases of quality management:
  - **Design Quality**: design as per the customer requirements, i.e., increased customer involvement in the product/service realization
  - **Conformance Quality**: increased variety at affordable cost, i.e., increased level of mass customization
  - **Performance Quality**: more dynamic process adjustments and self-corrected control systems for zero defect manufacturing targets.

2.2.4 Big Data Analytics (BDA) in TQM

The primary objective of the BDA in the TQM is to effectively use the raw data/information collected for ascertaining the customer requirements in the entire product/service life cycle. It serves as a direct link between raw data/information provided by the customer into actionable points required for a smart manufacturing system [21]. BDA in TQM is much very important to identify meaning, interpreting the patterns of change and enabling the prediction of performance capabilities (Table 2.2).

2.2.5 Digital Twins and Simulation in TQM

The main objective of digital twins and simulation in the TQM is to simulate product and process design for quality testing and prevent subsequent defects in the product life cycle. Digital twin technologies create industrial equipment,

TABLE 2.2
Big Data in TQM

TQM		BDA		Benefits
Quality control Quality assurance Quality optimization	→	Prediction Correlation Correlation analysis	→	Performance prediction Data integration and processing System performance prediction Optimized decision-making

TABLE 2.3
TQM and DT&S

Core Components of a Digital Twin and Applications	
Physical entity ® Virtual model	Data and algorithm
Product twin, asset twin, factory twin, end-to-end twin; quality defect problem-solving, predictive maintenance	Discrete event simulation for factory production lines, hybrid simulation for complex systems, prototyping

production line, and supply chain processes. These models allow TQM personnel to simulate real-world conditions, helping to identify bottlenecks if any and predict failures without affecting actual production [18]. A new development in the digital twin is the development of lightweight digital twin systems for industrial robots with the aim of perfect synchronization between physical equipment and virtual models to improve accuracy and reduce associated implementation costs [22]. This development drives even some smaller organizations to go for the Industry 4.0 technologies (Table 2.3).

A critical core aspect of this DT&S is in-process quality improvement, in-process sensing data for continuous process monitoring, diagnosis, and control. Traditional quality control techniques emphasize the detection of change or adjustments after detection of poor quality, but DT&S-assisted TQM techniques focus on the root causes for the defect occurrence, online correction, and most importantly prevention instead of detection of defects [18]. Thus, the significant impact of IMS techniques in the TQM is a transformation of quality from a separate, reactive inspection function to an inherent, continuous, and predictive function attached throughout the entire manufacturing lifecycle. This leads to significantly higher first-time quality, reduced rework, scrap, and warranty costs, and a stronger brand reputation built on consistent product reliability. It also changes the role of quality professionals from inspectors to data analysts, system optimizers, and proactive problem-solvers.

2.3 INTEGRATION OF IMS WITH SUPPLY CHAIN MANAGEMENT (SCM) – REVITALIZING THE OBJECTIVES AND GOALS OF SCM

Conventional SCM focuses on the broader objectives of efficiency, optimizing inventories, and synchronizing the production schedule with the suppliers. However, the contemporary global economic space, identified by increasing complexity and demands for mass customization, requires a significant shift in the way supply chains and manufacturing operations are managed [23]. Industry 4.0 has provided ample scope for the traditional supply chain integrated with the sophisticated IMS techniques for a new 'Smart Supply Chain' or 'Digital Supply Chain' or 'Intelligent Supply Chain' to achieve autonomy, dynamism, flexibility, and precision in manufacturing operations. Table 2.4 summarizes the key functions of SCM enhanced by the IMS techniques.

TABLE 2.4
SCM Functions Integrated with IMS

SCM with IMS	AI/ML	IoT	Advanced Robotics and Automation	BDA	Digital Twins/ Simulation
SCM	Forecasts demand, optimizes logistics, and enables adaptive supply chains.	Enhances real-time tracking of goods and inventory across the supply chain. Fosters collaboration.	Automates material transport (Automated Guided Vehicles-AGVs/–Autonomous Mobile Robots-AMRs) and optimizes warehouse operations.	Drives efficiency with predictive analytics for demand planning and cost savings.	Creates virtual models of supply chain processes to identify bottlenecks and optimize flow.

2.3.1 SCM and AI/ML

AI/ML are central to data analysis, decision support, and enterprise resource planning systems. These technologies empower systems to learn from huge volumes of datasets, adapt to dynamic changes, and optimize various workflows across the manufacturing operations. Generative AI, for instance, assists production managers in tasks such as authoring data entries, scheduling operational tasks, and creating consistent cost templates. Research reveals that the overall efficiency of the supply chain is significantly increased with the use of AI/ML algorithms in the demand forecast, optimal order fulfillment, and transportation route planning [24]. With tools like generative AI in the supply chain planning, vast improvement is seen in the strategic sourcing and supplier relationship management. The accurate predictive capability of AI tools in the business offers better demand forecasting and inventory management, eliminating both the excess inventory and the risk of emptying stocks. This is the most crucial element of control for organizations adopting Just In Time as a competitive strategy in their entire operations. Also, significant cost savings and delivery time reduction were reported in the literature in the application of ML-powered algorithms in dynamic routing, changing delivery paths in real time due to the abrupt changes in traffic and weather [25]. Also, AI/ML techniques in enterprise resource planning systems can effectively handle large volumes of real-time data to obtain smarter routes using logistics data and accurate forecast demand [26].

However, AI/Ml-enabled SCM is still in the nascent stage due to the following constraints [27]:

- Availability of vast datasets
- Comprehensive supply chain data from diverse sources
- Lack of data standards

Organizations employing AI/ML in their SCM should focus on data standardization, technological implementation difficulties, upskilling the workforce for adaptation, critical ethical, and cybersecurity considerations.

2.3.2 IoT and SCM

The effectiveness of the SCM is greatly affected by the limited integration and collaboration among suppliers, manufacturers, and customers. However, with the use of IoT technologies, the efficient handling of the continuous stream of data generated from these stack holders is possible and will result in accurate demand forecasting, optimal inventory, and significant cost savings in the entire supply chain [26]. IoT technologies in the SCM optimize warehouse management and logistics operations with their capability in real-time goods tracking and automated inventory management, significantly increase operational efficiency, and reduce costs. These IoT-assisted SCM systems can automatically modify their functions by predicting operational risks and potential production delays before they occur. This is mainly due to the capability of IoT technologies in real-time tracking of goods and inventories, accurate predictive analytics, and comprehensive digital supply chain integration (Table 2.5). It also provides a better degree of trust, transparency, and the establishment of robust data-sharing protocols among all supply chain partners, leading to more collaborative and integrated business models. Often, IoT devices, like sensors and RFID tags for the products, help real time on line tracking of goods, proper monitoring of product/service conditions (e.g., temperature for perishable items), and improving inventory management. For example, IoT supports cold chain logistics in the food sector by ensuring quality during transport.

2.3.3 SCM and BDA

BDA is critical to various SCM processes, including demand forecasting, inventory management, logistics, and risk management. Organizations use ML algorithms, such as neural networks and support vector machines in demand forecasting and planning. Here, BDA enhances demand forecasting accuracy by analyzing the huge volume of historical and real-time data. Many researchers highlighted BDA's role in optimizing inventory levels and distribution routes, reducing costs, and improving efficiency in logistics operations [25,28–30].

BDA provides real-time visibility and predictive analytics to remove disruptions. Therefore, supply chain complexities were resolved through enhancing resilience, data-driven risk assessment, and response strategies. Another modern-day expectation from the society especially from the legislators is that organizations should

TABLE 2.5
SCM Transform into Digital Supply Chain

SCM Key Functions	Primary Activity	Digital Supply Chain	Features of Digital Supply Chain
Procurement Logistics Inventory	Sourcing Transportation Stock with respect to demand	IoT-enabled SCM integrates all these activities	Self-organize and self-optimize, predicting operational risks and potential production delays before they occur

comply sustainability and circular economy requirements. BDA facilitates sustainable SCM by optimizing resource use and reducing emissions. In particular, BDA, combined with Industry 4.0 technologies, supports sustainable procurement and waste reduction in manufacturing.

Logistics and transportation functions of SCM are improved through BDA's capability in real-time data analysis for route optimization and fleet management. BDA is accurately matching supply and demand, resulting in enhancement of operational efficiency in transportation. BDA is very much capable of providing accurate risk management due to its power of analyzing vast data on external disruptions (political instability, pandemic, etc.) and internal risks (supplier reliability). However, the BDA in SCM is effective only if the organization proactively acts on the following challenges:

- Poor data quality and fragmented data silos
- Complexity in Closed-Loop Supply Chains
- Cybersecurity risks
- Lack of top-level management support, financial assistance, expertise, and processes

2.3.4 SCM and Advanced Robotics and Automation (ARA)

One of the major difficulties in the implementation of efficient SCM is that most of its activities are repetitive and monotonous in nature, resulting in human fatigue and a huge amount of errors. However, ARA technologies, such as collaborative robots (cobots), autonomous guided vehicles (AGVs), and robotic process automation, are changing the SCM into error free function. ARA technologies enhance operational efficiency, flexibility, and resilience in response to increasing demands for faster, more sustainable supply chains.

Many researchers highlighted the effectiveness of ARA applied in various SCM processes, including warehousing, logistics, manufacturing, and customer point delivery [31–34]. Warehousing and Inventory Management: Cobots and AGVs improve warehouse operations by automating material handling, picking, and inventory checks. AGVs employed in the warehouse systems optimize the multi-robot collaboration through advanced path planning, reducing bottlenecks, and improving the efficiency. Modern-day logistics uses many automation technologies like vision-guided vehicles and drones in its logistics and transportation operations.

Manufacturing and Assembly: Cobots assist in vehicle assembly and other manufacturing tasks, reducing ergonomic strain and enhancing productivity. Cobots allow human workers to focus on complex tasks, fostering human–robot collaboration. Customer Point Delivery: ARA, including drones and autonomous delivery vehicles, optimize customer point delivery, enhancing speed and safety. Procurement and Supply Management: ARA streamlines procurement processes by automating repetitive tasks like contract management and supplier coordination, resulting in reducing errors and improving efficiency in purchasing. Table 2.6 summarizes the benefits of ARA in SCM.

TABLE 2.6
Benefits of ARA-Integrated SCM

SCM Processes	ARA	Benefits
Warehousing	Cobots, AGVs, robotic process automation	Operational efficiency
Logistics		Flexibility and scalability
Manufacturing		Workplace safety and ergonomics
Customer point delivery		Sustainability
Procurement and Supply Management		Resilience

In order the reap the benefits of ARA-integrated SCM, organizations should focus on the following challenges:

- High Implementation Costs
- Skills Gaps and Workforce Training
- Integration with Legacy Systems
- Safety and Ethical Concerns
- Data Security Risks

2.3.5 Digital Twins/Simulation in SCM

Effective and efficient management of SCM is crucial for organizations in the contemporary competitive business operations. Poor collaboration between supply chain partners, complex logistics networks, and high inventory costs are the major drawbacks of the conventional SCM. However, with the emergence of Industry 4.0, many digital tools provide significant improvements in the SCM. Among them, the most proven technique is digital twin. Digital Twin is defined as the virtual representation that faithfully represents any physical system, process, or object. By creating the virtual counterpart of the physical process, organization can gain intelligence to increase the responsiveness of the SCM [35]. Even though DT evolved as a digital tool for manufacturing operations, due to the visual representation capability, it is now widely used in logistics and supply chain. DT-based SCM provides more resiliency, offering more monitoring and decision support [36]. In inventory management, DTs help accurate inventory control by continuously monitoring critical factors such as demand signals, supplier lead times, and production variability. This capability supports the implementation of just-in-time inventory strategies, which effectively reduce working capital requirements without compromising service quality. In addition, with its accurate predictive capability, DTs can offer an optimal level of safety stock required under various risk scenarios, ensuring minimum or zero capital in the inventory.

DTs in the field of logistics and transportation optimize transportation networks, analyze traffic patterns, improve overall logistics operations, and increase the efficiency of operations. This is due to their capability in the competitive and strategical planning of distribution center locations, transport routing, and the better optimization of truck routes, resulting in smoother and cost-effective movement of goods.

Especially, during the risk assessment, there is a conflict between efficiency and resilience. But the capabilities of DTs facilitate organizations to maintain lean operations, also improve their ability to detect, respond to, and recover from disruptions with optimal physical buffer stocks.

However, DTs in SCM face several challenges:

- **Higher Capital Cost:** Developing and maintaining DTs requires substantial infrastructure and expertise, resulting in greater implementation costs.
- **Cybersecurity Threats:** Due to the large volume of real-time data, integration across its function increases vulnerability to cyber threats.
- **Interoperability Challenges:** Isolated departments and poor standardization in the data formats affect the seamless collaboration across supply chain stakeholders.
- **Predictive Capability limitations:** DTs' reliance on historical data affects the accurate prediction of rare or unprecedented events.

Researchers highlighted that modern-day business operations need to be more visible, employ optimal operations, and be more resilient in the uncertain global economic environment. Also, the economic performance of business should be aligned with environmental responsibility, which demands the organizations to transition from reactive problem-solving to proactive in all the SCM operations. This transition is made possible by the contemporary DT technologies in the logistics and SCM.

2.4 MAINTENANCE MANAGEMENT (MM) AND IMS TECHNIQUES

Traditional manufacturing operations are affected by sudden machine break downs, resulting in reduced productivity and costly unplanned downtime. To avoid this, Production and Operations Management (POM) personnel should move from scheduled or reactive maintenance to condition-based, predictive asset management. This could be a strategic advantage for organizations targeting global competition. Conventional POM uses a preventive maintenance strategy, which could result in high prevention costs due to the unnecessary maintenance activities based on time duration or machine process iterations. Therefore, Industry 4.0 prescribes organizations to go for predictive maintenance, an appropriate trade-off between the costlier reactive maintenance and too much preventive maintenance [37]. The capability of IMS techniques is critical to the success of this predictive asset management. IMS techniques, in particular, cater to the following activities of MM (Table 2.7).

2.4.1 MM AND AI/ML

The effectiveness of predictive maintenance is improved by the application of AI/ML algorithms. Techniques such as neural networks and support vector machines are central to processing vast amounts of sensor data, enabling accurate fault diagnosis and the prediction of remaining useful life for critical components. These AI/ML applications lead to substantial gains in efficiency and reductions in maintenance costs. Recently, due to the advancement in the semi-conductor technology,

TABLE 2.7
IMS Techniques in MM

MM with IMS	AI/ML	IoT	Advanced Robotics and Automation	BDA	Digital Twins/ Simulation
MM	Predicts equipment failures by analyzing historical and real-time data. Enables proactive maintenance scheduling.	Monitors critical machine parameters (vibration, temperature) to detect potential failures.	Reduces manual effort in maintenance tasks, handles hazardous repairs.	Transforms raw data into actionable insights for predictive maintenance.	Simulates machine performance to predict failures and optimize maintenance schedules.

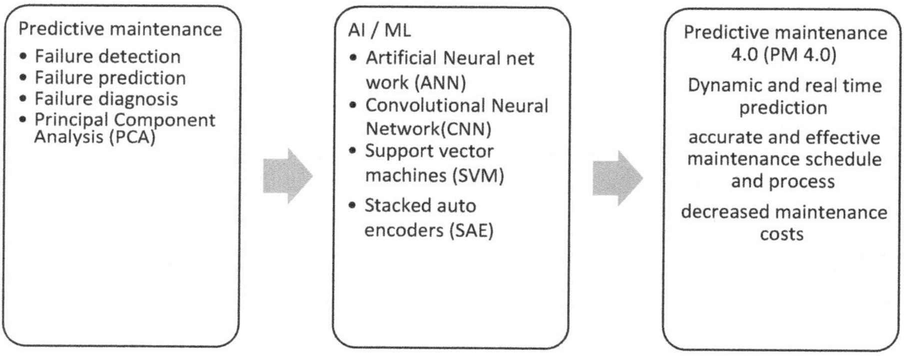

FIGURE 2.2 Predictive maintenance transformation PM 4.0.

the AI/ML algorithms are improved and matured in terms of classification and regression. This capability results in more accuracy in the fault diagnosis and prediction of remaining useful life. Researchers [38–40] pointed out the significance of AI/ML algorithms in the predictive maintenance modules, namely, (i) failure detection, (ii) failure prediction, and (iii) failure diagnosis, resulting in better performance and accuracy than the reactive maintenance/preventive maintenance (Figure 2.2).

2.4.2 Challenges in PM 4.0

However, organizations needs to address the following challenges:

- Huge volume of generated data for engineers and data scientists in finding the proper ways to understand, analyze, use, and store them
- Sustainability, including social, economic, and environmental factors, which are strongly affected by maintenance
- Lack of failure-related data
- Cybersecurity

2.4.3 MM and IoT

IoT is important for real-time data monitoring and collection in manufacturing operations. Embedded sensors continuously track data and parameters, providing crucial insights into machine performance, product quality, and energy consumption. This real-time data is critical for predictive maintenance, as IoT sensors closely track a machine's parameters – such as run-time hours, energy consumption, temperature, vibration, and wear and tear – to detect and repair defects before they cause breakdowns, thereby streamlining operations and reducing costly downtime [41].

i. **IoT in Condition Monitoring**

   Equipment health is very important from the profitable business perspective, and real-time monitoring of operational parameters, like temperature, vibration, and utilization rate, is crucial for detecting malfunctions in the operation. IoT solutions offer better equipment health through condition monitoring, equipment status data, and process information. This allows better MM, shifting the focus from intermittent periodic checks to greater asset health through condition monitoring.

ii. **Failure Detection**

   Researchers pointed out that advanced models in the MM involving IoT with AI/ML algorithms are capable of analyzing the IoT telemetry data to classify equipment faults and predict potential failures before they occur, frequently estimating the remaining useful life of components. This approach leads to both detection and prediction of future failures, facilitating proactive maintenance activities.

iii. **Failure Prediction**

   Contemporary research [42] on MM focuses on the hybrid approaches that combine statistical AI (e.g., ML, data mining) with symbolic AI (e.g., ontologies, logic rules), which are proposed to automate decision-making processes. This hybrid approach eliminates the difficulty involved in the processing of heterogeneous industrial data. Due to the proper and effective integration of statistical and symbolic AI, degradation models perform with valid reasoning for failure and event prediction.

IoT-assisted MM focuses on the intelligent, self-optimizing, and transparent and autonomous maintenance systems. These autonomous maintenance systems significantly reduce human error and optimize resource allocation in the maintenance activities and improve human trust and quicker adoption, especially in safety-critical industrial environments.

2.4.4 ARA and MM

Contemporary research [43] suggests that use of ARA in MM has evolved due to the emphasis on predicting maintenance issues instead of fixing equipment after breakdowns. Especially, in contemporary manufacturing and mining operations, cobots, AI, and digital twins are important technologies employed to improve maintenance systems. In Industry 4.0, conventional MM transforms into Maintenance 4.0 with its capability in analyzing real-time data for fault prediction and process optimization, enhancing efficiency, sustainability, and safety. Robotics is increasingly used in harsh environments like mining, where automated systems handle dangerous tasks. Cobots work alongside humans, improving safety and flexibility in maintenance tasks. The integration of robotics and automation in maintenance is likely to grow, with innovations like autonomous robots and enhanced AI systems making maintenance even more efficient. Through ARA, most of the maintenance activities can be made safer or even replaced entirely. Inspections that are very dangerous and time-consuming, as preparations are needed for safety, can be easily done by an automated inspection process. In addition, by automating preventive maintenance tasks with a cloud-based maintenance solution, the effectiveness of the maintenance can be ensured. Improved maintenance compliance results in improved running of equipment and decreased breakdowns.

By using customized MM software, organizations can automate the time-based tasks of the maintenance activities. In addition, this software stores all the relevant information on the maintenance activity, which enables the maintenance personnel to make decisions based on the facts. With IoT devices and ARA, condition monitoring becomes simpler and leads to a more accurate maintenance schedule. Because of this, costs associated with unnecessary maintenance can be reduced.

2.4.5 BDA in MM

Predictive maintenance, using ML algorithms and IoT sensor data analysis, plays an important role in reducing downtime and maintenance costs. This BDA enables organizations to analyze a large amount of data from IoT devices, sensors, and operation systems to extract valuable insights and helps in informed decision-making for maintenance managers. Predictive maintenance models can make use of the capability of BDA in analyzing the hidden patterns, trends, and correlations in the maintenance data. This approach not only helps in accurately predicting component failures immediately, but also contributes to the reliability and safety of industrial systems by reducing the risk of unwanted breakdowns [39].

BDA integrates with MM to create smart maintenance systems:

- IoT and Sensors enable real-time data collection from industrial equipment, forming the backbone of predictive maintenance.
- Cloud Computing platforms like Hadoop and Spark process large datasets, improving scalability and accessibility.
- AI and Deep Learning applications in manufacturing and energy sectors improve fault detection and decision-making.

BDA applications in the maintenance of various industrial sectors reported by the researchers [44–46] include the following:

i. **Manufacturing:** Predictive maintenance improves production efficiency, with studies reporting a 5%–15% reduction in downtime.

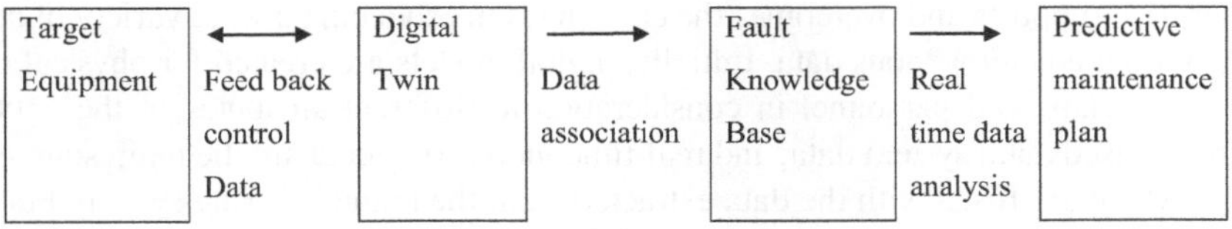

FIGURE 2.3 DTS and MM.

ii. **Energy:** Predictive analytics optimizes asset management in power plants and oil refineries, enhancing reliability.
iii. **Transportation:** Big data ensures fleet reliability, with telematics reducing maintenance costs in 80% of Class 8 trucks in North America.
iv. **Healthcare:** While less common, BDA supports equipment maintenance in medical facilities.

2.4.6 Digital Twin and Simulation in MM

The digital twin is a digital model of a real world physical product, system or process that serves as a digital counterpart of it for the purposes such as simulation, testing, monitoring and maintenance. The main objective of DTS Digital Twin and Simulation (DTS) in MM is to simulate machine performance to predict failures and optimize maintenance schedules. Digital twins, which are virtual replicas used for simulation and optimization, enhance maintenance by providing real-time data analysis. Predictive maintenance consists of analyzing the data from condition monitoring, fault diagnosis, and failure prediction. When these activities were carried out manually, huge errors are likely to occur. However, DTS can provide organizations with accurate design optimization, fault prediction, and fault diagnosis, which are essential to perform the data processing required for predictive maintenance (Figure 2.3).

With respect to the visualization maintenance, manual operators cannot obtain complete fault information. But the comprehensive visualization capabilities of DTS intuitively display virtual visualization models of the equipment, facilitate interaction with the physical entities of the equipment, and display the real-time status and fault information of the equipment to the maintenance personnel. DTS simulates the equipment in running condition, collects the equipment data that changes dynamically with time, and can provide a more intelligent service application than conventional predictive maintenance, which can realize the long-term dynamic maintenance of the equipment.

2.5 DIGITAL TWIN TECHNOLOGY IN SCHEDULING AND INVENTORY MANAGEMENT OF INTELLIGENT MANUFACTURING SYSTEMS

Scheduling of intelligent manufacturing based on digital twin technology creates virtual models with real-time physical entities to optimize the production cost and efficiency of the production. The dynamic approach in scheduling the intelligent manufacturing enterprise supports and overcomes the challenges in producing a wide variety of products with the heterogenous data. Initially, digital models are created for physical entities, materials, and personnel in consideration to different attributes of the entities. Sensor-based data, system data, and real-time monitoring data are the main sources of data, which are fused with the data extracted from the manufacturing system. Further algorithms are used in scheduling the workshop to minimize the maximum completion time using fitness function. The average completion time, maximum completion time, utilization rate of equipment, production cost, and energy consumption cost are the indicators of parameter measures of the production efficiency of intelligent manufacturing [47]. In general, to overcome the correlation of features, processes, and machine tools in scheduling of any operation, a three-layer processing super-network model was effectively used based on identification of similarity of attributes available in the features. The data for the digital twin workshop was integrated by performing data extraction, data loading, and data transformation [48]. Unpredictable market demands necessitate demand-driven production planning and scheduling in intelligent manufacturing, thereby requiring dynamic planning in inventory management. There is proper oversight of the executable schedule apart from the customer demand in scheduling of manufacturing and inventories. Simulation-based planning considers the initial production orders as input, further integrating with the enterprise resource planning to replan and reschedule the manufacturing environment [49].

2.6 CONCLUSION

Traditional POM functions rely on the skill/knowledge level of the personnel involved and are often reactive, which result in the below par organizational excellence. But due to the rising demands of the customer in the product/service quality, increased variety, and statutory requirements of sustainability in resource utilization, organizations should strategically apply proactive, data-driven POM functions to stay relevant in the competitive market.

IMS techniques like AI/ML, IoT, ARA, BDA, and digital twins and simulation offer excellent avenues for the POM functions and strengthening the organization through interconnected cyber-physical systems for IMS. These wholesome and inclusive transformations bring forth significant benefits: more customized and high-quality product/service to customers at low cost with shorter duration of time. In addition to these benefits, organizations can also meet the continuously growing sustainability and environmental challenges easily.

However, organizations willing to adopt the integration of IMS and POM should address the following challenges:

- Increased cost of technology implementation
- Robust cybersecurity measures for the effective and safe interconnected systems
- Workforce skill gap in adopting the digital transformation
- Complexities in managing a huge volume of data from different sources

In order to mitigate these challenges, organizations should strategically invest in the IMS techniques, follow continuous learning, and radically shift to an organizational and cultural shift to the digital transformation.

REFERENCES

1. Zhou L, Jiang Z, Geng N, Niu Y, Cui F, Liu K, Qi N. Production and operations management for intelligent manufacturing: a systematic literature review. *Int J Prod Res* 60:2, 808–46 (2022).
2. Yang H, Kumara S, Bukkapatnam STS, Tsung F. The internet of things for smart manufacturing: a review. *IISE Trans* 51:11, 1190–216 (2019). https://doi.org/10.1080/24725854.2018.1555383
3. Yang C, Lan S, Shen W, et al. Towards product customization and personalization in IoT-enabled cloud manufacturing. *Cluster Comput* 20, 1717–30 (2017).
4. Besharati-Foumani H, Lohtander M, Varis J. Intelligent process planning for smart manufacturing systems: a state-of-the-art review. *Proc Manuf* 38, 156–62 (2019).
5. Al-wswasi M, Ivanov A, Makatsoris H. A survey on smart automated computer-aided process planning (ACAPP) techniques. *Int J Adv Manuf Technol* 97, 809–32 (2018).
6. Angizeh F, Montero H, Vedpathak A, Parvania M. Optimal production scheduling for smart manufacturers with application to food production planning 2020/06. *Comput Electr Eng* 84, 106609 (2020).
7. Aydin AO, Tunali S. A conceptual framework for scheduling purposes in mass customisation systems: an agent-based approach. *Int J Mass Customis* 3:2, 208 (2009).
8. Yang CC, Jou YT, Lin MC, Silitonga RM, Sukwadi R. The development of the new process of design for six sigma (DFSS) and its application. *Sustainability.* 14:15, 9294 (2022).
9. Crowe B, Gaulton JS, Minor N, Asch DA, Eyet J, Rainosek E, et al. To improve quality, leverage design. *BMJ Qual Saf* 31:1, 70–4 (2022).
10. Santos G, Sá JC, Félix MJ, Barreto L, Carvalho F, Doiro M, et al. New needed quality management skills for quality managers 4.0. *Sustainability* 13:11, 6149 (2021).
11. Dobni CB, Wilson GA, Klassen M. Business practices of highly innovative Japanese firms. *Asia Pac Manag Rev* 27:3, 155–62 (2022).
12. Sader S, Husti I, Daróczi M. Quality management practices in the era of industry 4.0. *Zesz Nauk Politech Częstochowskiej Zarządzanie* 35, 117–26 (2019).
13. Sahrane A, Elouadi A. Essential models and key concepts of quality 4.0. *J Oper Manag* 2:1, 1–7 (2022).
14. Ali K, Johl S. Soft and hard TQM practices: future research agenda for industry 4.0. *Total Qual Manag Bus Excell* 14:19, 11917 (2022).
15. Din A, Asif M, Awan M, Thomas G. What makes excellence models excellent: a comparison of the American, European and Japanese models. *TQM J* 2020. https://doi.org/10.1108/TQM-06-2020-0124
16. Yaqub MZ, Alsabban A. Industry-4.0-enabled digital transformation: prospects, instruments, challenges, and implications for business strategies. *Sustainability* 15:11, 8553 (2023).
17. Maganga DP, Taifa IW. The readiness of manufacturing industries to transit to quality 4.0. *Int J Qual Reliab Manag* 40:7, 1729–52 (2023).
18. Drystek A. What is quality 4.0 in manufacturing? [Internet]. Acerta. 2024 [cited 2025 July 27]. Available from: https://acerta.ai/blog/what-is-quality-4-0-in-manufacturing/
19. Radanliev P, De Roure D, Page K, Nurse JRC, Mantilla Montalvo R, Santos O, et al. Cyber risk at the edge: current and future trends on cyber risk analytics and artificial intelligence in the industrial internet of things and industry 4.0 supply chains. *Cybersecurity* 3:1, 13 (2020).
20. Bibby L, Dehe B. Defining and assessing industry 4.0 maturity levels – case of the defence sector. *Prod Plan Control* 29:12 (2025). https://doi.org/10.1080/09537287.2018.1503355
21. Wang J, Xu C, Zhang J, Zhong R. Big data analytics for intelligent manufacturing systems: a review. *J Manuf Syst* 62, 738–52 (2022).

22. Hu B, Cheng D, Fu Y, Song X, Bi Y, Zhao Q, et al. An equipment-level digital twin method for industrial robots for machining. *Int J Prod Res* 1–19 (2024). https://doi.org/10.1080/00207543.2024.2446953
23. Chaudhary A, Sharma V, Alkhayyat A. *Intelligent Manufacturing and Industry 4.0: Impact, Trends, and Opportunities*. Routledge & CRC Press. Available from: https://www.routledge.com/Intelligent-Manufacturing-and-Industry-40-Impact-Trends-and-Opportunities/Chaudhary-Sharma-Alkhayyat/p/book/9781032627618
24. Choi TM, Kumar S, Yue X, Chan HL. Disruptive technologies and operations management in the industry 4.0 era and beyond. *Prod Oper Manag* 31:1, 9–31 (2022).
25. KPMG [Internet]. [cited 2025 July 28]. KPMG 2024 CEO Outlook. Available from: https://kpmg.com/xx/en/our-insights/value-creation/kpmg-global-ceo-outlook-survey-2024.html
26. Recent Development and Technology Trends in Supply Chain Management [Internet]. 2024 [cited 2025 July 28]. Available from: https://www.panorama-consulting.com/trends-in-supply-chain-management/
27. Rana J, Daultani Y. Mapping the role and impact of artificial intelligence and machine learning applications in supply chain digital transformation: a bibliometric analysis. *Oper Manag Res* 16, 1641–66 (2022).
28. Runtuk JK, Sidjabat F, Jsslynn, Jordan F. Big data in supply chain management: a systematic literature review. *Green Intell Syst Appl* 2:2, 108–17 (2022).
29. Hallikas J, Immonen M, Brax S. Digitalizing procurement: the impact of data analytics on supply chain performance. *Supply Chain Manag Int J* 26:5, 629–46 (2021).
30. Zhang G, Yang Y, Yang G. Smart supply chain management in Industry 4.0: the review, research agenda and strategies in North America. *Ann Oper Res* 322:2, 1075–117 (2023).
31. Chauhan A, Brouwer B, Westra E. Robotics for a quality-driven post-harvest supply chain. *Curr Robot Rep* 3:2, 39–48 (2022).
32. Han H, Li J. Leveraging industry 4.0 technologies for sustainable supply chain management: a systematic review. *Clean Logist Supply Chain* 16, 100246 (2025).
33. Rainer Jr. RK, Richey Jr. RG, Chowdhury S. How robotics is shaping digital logistics and supply chain management: an ongoing call for research. *J Bus Logist* 46:1, e70005 (2025).
34. Flechsig C, Anslinger F, Lasch R. Robotic process automation in purchasing and supply management: a multiple case study on potentials, barriers, and implementation. *J Purch Supply Manag* 28:1, 100718 (2022).
35. Guo D, Mantravadi S. The role of digital twins in lean supply chain management: review and research directions. *Int J Prod Res* 63:5, 1851–72 (2025).
36. Zaidi SAH, Khan SA, Chaabane A. Unlocking the potential of digital twins in supply chains: a systematic review. *Supply Chain Anal* 7, 100075 (2024).
37. Zhu T, Ran Y, Zhou X, Wen Y. A survey of predictive maintenance: systems, purposes and approaches. *IEEE Commun Surv Tutor* 28, 633–71 (2025).
38. Shaheen BW, Németh I. Integration of maintenance management system functions with industry 4.0 technologies and features—a review. *Processes* 10:11, 2173 (2022).
39. Kiangala KS, Wang Z. An effective predictive maintenance framework for conveyor motors using dual time-series imaging and convolutional neural network in an industry 4.0 environment. *IEEE Access* 8, 121033–49 (2020).
40. Fernandes J, Reis J, Melão N, Teixeira L, Amorim M. The role of industry 4.0 and BPMN in the arise of condition-based and predictive maintenance: a case study in the automotive industry. *Appl Sci* 11:8, 3438 (2021).
41. Sharma M, Tomar A, Hazra A. Edge computing for industry 5.0: fundamental, applications, and research challenges. *IEEE Internet Things J* 11:11, 19070–93 (2024).
42. Dey S, Chatterjee S, Mondal R, Ghosh R. Revolutionizing smart devices: integrating federated learning with IoT for advanced digital innovation. *Int J Smart Sustain Intell Comput* 1, 57–67 (2024).

43. Werbińska-Wojciechowska S, Winiarska K. Maintenance performance in the age of industry 4.0: a bibliometric performance analysis and a systematic literature review. *Sensors* 23:3, 1409 (2023).
44. Judijanto L, Uhai S, Suri I. The influence of business analytics and big data on predictive maintenance and asset management. *Eastasouth J Inf Syst Comput Sci* 1, 123–35 (2024).
45. Achouch M, Dimitrova M, Ziane K, Sattarpanah Karganroudi S, Dhouib R, Ibrahim H, et al. On predictive maintenance in industry 4.0: overview, models, and challenges. *Appl Sci* 12:16, 8081 (2022).
46. Batko K, Ślęzak A. The use of Big Data Analytics in healthcare. *J Big Data* 9:1, 3 (2022).
47. Hu J, Yao Y, Liu F. Optimization and scheduling of intelligent manufacturing workshop based on digital twin technology. *Proc Computer Sci* 262, 1194–201 (2025).
48. Liu Z, Chen W, Zhang C, Yang C, Cheng Q. Intelligent scheduling of a feature-process-machine tool supernetwork based on digital twin workshop. *J Manuf Syst* 58:Part B, 157–67 (2021).
49. Ma G, da Silva ER, Møller C. Digital twin-based demand-driven production planning and scheduling system: a new conceptual framework. *Proc CIRP* 130, 705–10 (2024).

3 Generation and Optimization of Mid-Term Production–Distribution Plan Using Metaheuristic Techniques

Ashoka Varthanan Perumal, Kavitha Nagarajan, Rajendran Chinnasamy, and Maniraj Mariraj

3.1 INTRODUCTION

The importance of an integrated Mid-Term Production–Distribution Plan (APDP) has been highlighted in this chapter. This chapter focuses on developing such a plan for a leading bearing manufacturing company that produces a similar product family across three geographically distinct plants. The objective is to optimize production and distribution decisions over a multi-period planning horizon. To achieve this, the APDP is generated using four widely recognized metaheuristic techniques: Simulated Annealing (SA), Genetic Algorithm (GA), a hybrid GA–SA approach referred to as the Memetic Algorithm (MA), and Discrete Particle Swarm Optimization Algorithm (DPSOA). Through the integration of several cost components, including normal production, extended production, contract production, product holding, backorders of goods, labor hiring/layoffs, and trip-based transportation expenses, the present research focuses on generating an efficient mid-term production–distribution plan. It also determines the quantities to be transported from each manufacturing factory to various demand centers during each time period. Demand allocation is integrated with schedule generation, ensuring a coordinated and efficient planning process. The performance of the metaheuristic techniques is benchmarked against a solution derived using LINGO, popular operations research software that employs the conventional branch-and-bound method [1]. Among the tested approaches, the DPSOA provides a more efficient plan with lower total cost while maintaining solution feasibility and balance in workforce allocation.

The development of these advanced planning models is non-linear programming in nature. Unlike linear programming, which guarantees a unique global optimum under convexity, non-linear programming deals with complex, curved relationships and often encounters multiple local optima. This complexity makes the solution process more challenging and requires specialized mathematical techniques

DOI: 10.1201/9781003582465-3

such as gradient-based algorithms, Lagrange multipliers, and Karush-Kuhn-Tucker conditions. Non-linear programming is widely applied in areas such as structural design, engineering process optimization, economic modeling, financial portfolio optimization, and machine learning. Building on this foundation, an Integer Non-Linear Programming-based production–distribution model is implemented using the discrete swarm optimization [2]. This model is incorporated to a real-world dataset from the bearing manufacturing sector to alleviate multi-period manufacturing distribution planning problems. The PSO-based approach is compared against GA, SA, and MA for performance benchmarking. The PSO-generated plan effectively determines the optimal allocation of production activities, inventory levels, and workforce across all plants to meet customer demand over a 12-month planning horizon. It also specifies the quantities shipped to each demand center in every time [3]. Furthermore, the DPSO framework incorporates an innovative constraint-handling mechanism that avoids discarding infeasible solutions and eliminates the need for complex penalty parameter. This leads to improved computational efficiency and enhanced overall solution quality.

3.2 DISCRETE NON-LINEAR OPTIMIZATION USING INTEGER VARIABLES

Most real-world problems inherently possess non-linear characteristics [4]. Although linearizing variable relationships can simplify the modeling process, it often compromises optimality. On the other hand, introducing excessive non-linearity can make the problem computationally intractable. Therefore, in this study, non-linear relationships are included only when essential and justified by the problem requirements (Equation 3.1).

The ultimate aim of the work is to minimize the overall cost (Z), expressed as:

Normal production, contracted production, extended production, recruiting, unfulfilled demand, stock holding, and transport costs computed on a per-trip basis are some of the cost components that make up the objective function (Total Cost, Z).

The primary objective function along with the associated constraints is:

$$\text{Min } Z = \sum_k \sum_i [(NP_{ki}CN_i) + (S_{ki}CS_i) + (OT_{ki}CO_i) + (I_{ki}CI_i) + (H_{ki}CH_i) + (F_{ki}CF_i)] + \sum_k (B_k CB_k) + \sum_k \sum_i \sum_j (TR_{kij}CT_{ij}) \tag{3.1}$$

Equations (3.2–3.4) define the quantities manufactured under regular time, extended production, and outsourcing, respectively. Among them, the extended production relation indicted in Equation (3.3) is non-linear because extended production hours are typically distributed across the available workforce; the interaction between total workforce size and extended hours cannot be captured accurately with a simple linear form. This non-linear formulation therefore more realistically models how additional labor capacity is generated through overtime. In addition, outsourced production is assumed to occur in fixed batch quantities, as reflected in the outsourcing equation. Equation (3.4) is employed for finding the externally sourced units.

$$NP_{ki} = P_{ki} * W_{ki} * D_{ki} \forall k \text{ and } i \tag{3.2}$$

$$OT_{ki} = O_{ki}\left(\frac{P_{ki}}{T_i}\right)W_{ki} \forall k \text{ and } i \tag{3.3}$$

$$S_{ki} = SB_i SN_{ki} \forall k \text{ and } i \tag{3.4}$$

The following is a definition of the worker-related constraints: While Equations (3.6–3.8) outline the recruiting and layoff criteria, Equation (3.5) determines the total number of employees across the three factories for each of the eight periods. These constraints ensure that layoffs are allowed only when there is no recruiting, extended production, or outsourcing activity. Incorporating these conditions adds to the model's non-linearity; however, they are necessary to reflect practical considerations. In countries like India, layoffs are generally considered a last resort, making it essential to enforce these constraints when solving the model using GA, SA, MA, and DPSOA techniques.

$$W_{ki} = W_{k-1i} + H_{ki} - F_{ki} \forall k \text{ and } i \tag{3.5}$$

$$H_{ki} F_{ki} = 0 \forall k \text{ and } i \tag{3.6}$$

$$O_{ki} F_{ki} = 0 \forall k \text{ and } i \tag{3.7}$$

$$S_{ki} F_{ki} = 0 \forall k \text{ and } i \tag{3.8}$$

- **End Inventory** (Equation 3.9): Inventory at the close of a period equals the total units available at that factory (opening inventory + current-period production + receipts, if any) minus the total units transported from that factory to dealer point during the period.
- **Unmet Demand Units** (Equation 3.10): Unfulfilled/unmet demand units in a period are the total expected requirement across all dealer point minus the total quantity transported to those centers from all factories in that period.

These relationships ensure proper tracking of stock balances and any shortfall that must be carried as backorders or lost sales, depending on model assumptions.

$$I_{ki} = (N * P_{ki} + O * T_{ki} + I_{k-1i} + S_{ki}) - \left(\sum_j P * R_{kij}\right) \forall k \text{ and } i \tag{3.9}$$

$$B_k = \left(\sum_j F * D_{kj}\right) - \left(\sum_i \sum_j P * R_{kij}\right) \forall k \tag{3.10}$$

According to the trip limitations, Equation (3.11) is used to determine the frequency of trips required to convey goods from an individual factory to consumers over all time durations, and the results are limited to a whole number. An "equal to or more than" condition is added to the equation to prevent rounding down when solving.

$$TR_{kij} \geq \left(\frac{PR_{kij}}{CP_i} \right) \forall k, i \text{ and } j \tag{3.11}$$

Equations (3.12–3.18) serve as binding constraints, which limit the assigned values to the decision variables within permissible ranges.

$$0 \leq S_{ki} \leq S \text{ and } _{kimax} \tag{3.12}$$

$$0 \leq O_{ki} \leq O \text{ and } _{kimax} \tag{3.13}$$

$$0 \leq H_{ki} \leq H \text{ and } _{kimax} \tag{3.14}$$

$$0 \leq F_{ki} \leq F \text{ and } _{kimax} \tag{3.15}$$

$$Wki \text{ and } _{kimax\,kimin} \tag{3.16}$$

$$0 \leq I_{ki} \leq I \text{ and } _{imax} \tag{3.17}$$

$$B_k \geq 0 \forall k \tag{3.18}$$

$O_{ki}, S_{ki}, H_{ki}, F_{ki}$ and TR_{kij} are restricted to integers.

Equations (3.16–3.18) do not require explicit integer restrictions since their associated decision variables (W_{ki}, I_{ki}, and B_k) are intrinsically integer-valued.

3.2.1 Notations

P_{ki}: Factory i's mean productivity per employee per shift over time k

W_{kimax} is the peak number of employees that can be employed in factory i during period k throughout all three shifts.

W_{kimin}: The bare minimum of employees needed in factory i for a day (three shifts/day) during period k

D_{ki} is the cumulative number of working days for factory i during period k.

O_{kimax}: Factory i's maximum allowable extended production hours for period k

T_i is the total number of hours worked in a factory shift.

H_{kimax} is the maximum number of employees that factory $_i$ may hire during period k.

F_{kimax} is the maximum number of employees that factory I may lay off throughout period k.

SBi: The batch quantity of goods that can be contracted out from the facility

S_{kimax}: The production ceiling of the factory i during period k through outsourcing or subcontracting

I_{imax}: Maximum units holding capacity in factory i

FD_{kj}: Predicted requirement at the center j in period k

CP_i: Vehicle capability to transport goods from factory i per travel

CN_i: Planned production expense per product in factory i

CS_i: Third-party/outsourced production expense per unit in factory i

CO_i: Extended time production expense per unit in factory i

CB_k: Penalty incurred per unit of unfulfilled demand in a given period k

CI_i: Expense for holding inventory per unit in factory i

CH_i: Recruiting cost/worker in factory i

CF_i: Downsizing/firing expense/worker in factory i

CT_{ij}: Trip expense from factory i to request center j

3.2.2 Factors Affecting Decision

The major decision variables that govern the production–distribution plan are as follows:

NP_{ki} products manufactured from a regular output during the specified time frame k in factory i

SN_{ki} batches of products that may be subcontracted in the period j from factory i

S_{ki} products manufactured through a third party/outsourcing during period k in factory i

O_{ki} overall extended hours throughout the period k in factory i

OT_{ki} products manufactured through extended hours during period k in factory i

W_{ki} number of labors working in a day for three shifts during period k in factory i

H_{ki} number of workers recruited during period k in factory i

F_{ki} number of labors terminated during period k in factory i

I_{ki} inventory units at the end of time horizon k in factory i

B_k total unmet demand in time frame k

PR_{kij} products shipped from plant i to demand center j during period k

TR_{kij} total trips made from factory i to demand center j in period k

3.3 PRESUMPTIONS

The following presumptions and policy choices served as the foundation for the development of the quantitative model:

- All factories generate goods of the same quality.
- Each factory is subject to maximum inventory limits, but there is no minimum inventory requirement.
- Ordering in advance is prohibited; any unfulfilled demand during one period cannot be carried over to the following.

3.4 SOLUTION METHODOLOGY

Production planning problems are typically classified as NP-hard [5]. When integer variables and non-linear relationships are involved, solving a production–distribution problem optimally within polynomial time becomes especially difficult. As both the number of variables and the level of non-linearity increase, the problem's complexity escalates exponentially, categorizing it as NP-complete [6]. To effectively tackle this complexity, the production–distribution problem in this study is addressed using LINGO along with four metaheuristic methods: GA, SA, MA, and DPSOA. All metaheuristic approaches were coded using C language and compiled in the Cygwin editor.

3.4.1 A Conventional Method

To establish a feasible initial solution, **LINGO** commercial software was used. The model was first run with LINGO's default non-linear solver, and then with its optional global solver, which is designed to handle nonconvex non-linear programming and can provide globally optimal solutions for certain Integer Non-Linear Programming formulations. Nevertheless, with an increasing number of integer variables, performance deteriorates significantly. The same problems were solved using non-traditional optimization techniques like GA, SA, MA, and DPSOA.

3.4.2 Genetic Algorithm

GA is frequently employed to address a variety of problems with optimization [4]. GAs, which have their roots in natural selection and heredity, evolve a population of potential solutions instead of enhancing a single one [5]. The approach usually produces optimal or nearly optimal solutions by repeatedly applying genetic operators across many generations [6–10]. Each individual (chromosome) in the population is assigned a fitness value derived from the problem's objective function, and a survival-of-the-fittest selection mechanism favors higher-fitness individuals for reproduction [11]. The step-by-step procedure for implementing GA is given below.

1. **Initialize**: Create a starting population of random strings that represent the variables used to make decisions.
2. **Evaluate**: Compute the fitness of each string.
3. **Genetic Operators**: To create a new population, use division (selection), crossover, and mutation.
4. **Iterate**: Test the termination condition and assess the new population. Repeat the operator-evaluation cycle if the requirements are not met [12].

3.4.3 Solution

The chromosome (solution string) structure used in this study is shown in Figure 3.1. The symbols represent:

- O: Integer-coded extended time hour.
- SN: Batch size of subcontracted (outsourced) units, encoded as an integer.
- H/F: Integer-coded number of workers recruited or laid off.

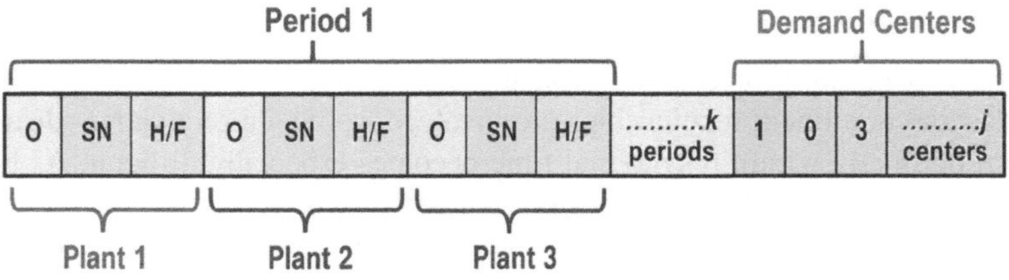

FIGURE 3.1 The solution string.

This is a revolutionary demand allocation technique where each demand center gene in the chromosome encodes the sequence in which the production plants/factories satisfy that particular center's predicted demand. For example, if the first demand-center gene holds the value **1**, Plant/factory 2 is given first priority. Any unmet remainder is next assigned to Plant/factory 1, and any residual after that to Plant/factory 3 (in a three-plant system).

3.4.3.1 Demand-Allocation Codes

- **0** → Plant / Factory 1 → Plant / Factory 2 → Plant / Factory 3
- **1** → Plant / Factory 2 → Plant / Factory 1 → Plant / Factory 3
- **2** → Plant / Factory 2 → Plant / Factory 3 → Plant / Factory 1
- **3** → Plant / Factory 3 → Plant / Factory 1 → Plant / Factory 2
- **4** → Plant / Factory 3 → Plant / Factory 2 → Plant / Factory 1
- **5** → Plant / Factory 1 → Plant / Factory 3 → Plant / Factory 2

3.4.4 GA Process

Step 1: **Initial Population**: A randomly chosen initial population of chromosomes is produced. Although it may also result in longer computation times, a greater population size typically increases the chances of discovering an optimal or nearly optimal solution [13]

Step 2: **Fitness Evaluation**: By entering the parameters into the objective function, each chromosome that meets the problem constraints is assessed. The resulting fitness score indicates how good the outcome is overall.

Step 3: **Selection**: For reproduction, chromosomes with greater fitness are selected. In this study, tournament selection is used as one of several selection strategies. This approach increases the likelihood that stronger chromosomes will be chosen for reproduction more than once by having each chromosome participate in two tournaments against other chromosomes in the pool.

Step 4: **Crossover**: Crossover promotes gene exchange between selected parent chromosomes, creating offspring that combine features from both parents. This genetic mixing accelerates convergence toward optimal solutions. A multipoint crossover technique is used here due to the relatively long chromosome length, with a high crossover probability to ensure diversity and progress toward optimality.

Step 5: **Mutation**: Mutation preserves population diversity by introducing small random alterations in a chromosome. In contrast to crossover, mutation happens very infrequently inside a single chromosome in order to prevent upsetting promising solutions. Swap mutation is implemented in this work with a minimal probability of occurrence.

Step 6: **Sorting and Replacement**: All parent and offspring chromosomes are evaluated after undergoing selection, crossover, and mutation, and the best-performing chromosomes proceed to the next generation. Chromosomes violating any constraints are discarded.

Step 7: **Termination**: Once the predetermined number of generations is reached, the process of evolution is repeated.

3.5 SA ALGORITHM

A stochastic, neighborhood-based search algorithm called SA was created to address combinatorial optimization issues. Inspired by the annealing process in metallurgy, when atoms settle into a stable, low-energy crystalline structure through progressive preservation, the SA approach was first introduced by Kirkpatrick et al. [14]. SA increases the reasons for reaching the global ideal optimization value by periodically accepting subpar solutions to prevent becoming entangled in local optima [15]. Effective parameter tuning is critical for the performance of SA. Key parameters include:

- Rate of cooling (alpha α)
- Beginning temperature (t_i)
- Final temperature (t_f)

The resulting convergence behavior and search trajectory are controlled by this parameter. The beginning temperature should be high enough to provide extensive investigation for "annealing," and it should be progressively lowered to the final temperature to refine the solution. Equations (3.19–3.21) illustrate the equations for the rate of cooling, beginning temperature, and final temperature, as per Bennage and Dhingra [16,17].

$$\alpha = \left(\frac{\ln p_i}{\ln p_f} \right)^{\frac{1}{n-1}} \tag{3.19}$$

$$t_i = \frac{(f_{\min} - f_{\max})}{\ln p_i} \tag{3.20}$$

$$t_f = \frac{(f_{\min} - f_{\max})}{\ln p_f} \tag{3.21}$$

where,

p_i = acceptance rate at the initial point (0.95)
p_f = final likelihood of acceptance (1.3 E^{-15})
n = quantity of iterations
f_{max} = highest solution value
f_{min} = bare minimum expected solution

3.5.1 Solution Methodology

The initial solution is a randomly coded string as shown in Figure 3.1. By entering the decoded values of this initial solution into the objective function, it is assessed. This initial solution is then used to generate a series of neighboring solutions. ΔE, or the variation in objective function values between the best neighbor and the current solution, is calculated. The new current solution for the following iteration is accepted if $\Delta E > 0$, which indicates that the neighbor is superior. The cooling rate (alpha α) is then multiplied to the beginning temperature to update it, thus lowering it progressively over iterations. Acceptance is decided computationally even if the neighboring solution is worse (i.e., $\Delta E \leq 0$). Equation 3.22 generates a stochastic value in the interval [0,1] and evaluates it using the Metropolis acceptance criterion.

$$\text{Stochastic value } (r) \leq e^{\frac{-\Delta E}{T}} \tag{3.22}$$

As per the acceptance rule (based on the Metropolis criterion), the inferior neighbor is accepted, and the temperature is then reduced. If not, additional neighbors are created and evaluated at a similar temperature. This neighbor-generation step is repeated up to a number of times equal to the string length. If no improving neighbor is found after these attempts, the algorithm retains the present solution and the temperature is then lowered. At the end of each temperature stage, termination conditions, viz, reach of final temperature and/or iteration limit, are checked.

3.6 MEMETIC ALGORITHM

GA is highly flexible and can be combined with other methods or problem-specific heuristics [13,18,19]. In many applications, hybridizing algorithms yields better performance than using stand-alone metaheuristics such as GA or SA [20]. MAs belong to this class of hybrid GAs: They retain the population-based search framework of GA while embedding powerful local improvement strategies to tackle hard optimization problems [21]. By integrating domain-specific heuristics with evolutionary search, MAs exploit both intensification and diversification [22,23]. In the present study, GA provides global exploration over the population, and SA is employed as a local search algorithm around each chromosome, prior to the initiation of the next generation. All GA and SA parameter settings described earlier are used jointly to generate the mid-term production–distribution plan under the MA framework.

Step 1: Initialize parameters P_m, P_c, t_i α, t_f, and n
Step 2: Set the initial sample size m

Step 3: Select the size of the population/strings
Step 4: Initiate the process of reproduction, crossover, and mutation (GA)
Step 5: Sort the best m solutions
Step 6: Begin local search by considering each and every solution using SA
Step 7: Obtain the best population of size m after local search
Step 8: Reduce the temperature t_i for all solutions
Step 9: Check for termination criteria. Else continue till the set number of iterations

3.7 DISCRETE PARTICLE SWARM OPTIMIZATION ALGORITHM

A recently developed and well-known metaheuristic method, the DPSOA, is used to solve the NP-hard Integer Non-Linear Programming production–distribution problem. The outcomes of GA, SA, and MA solutions are then benchmarked with the outcomes of DPSOA. In DPSOA, potential solutions are shown as particles with the corresponding velocities traveling through the search space. Each particle keeps track of its personal or local best, which is the finest position it has attained thus far. A particle modifies its trajectory in order to move closer to an ideal solution by considering two important factors: the personal or the individual best solution and the universal or global best solution [24]. The search for the optimum is an iterative process driven by information shared between local and global bests. This mechanism mirrors human decision-making, where individuals consider both their past successes and the successful strategies of others [25–27]. In DPSOA, a binary coded string of solution is created with each particle represented as $Xn = (xn1, xn2\ldots, x_{nd})$, where $n = 1,2\ldots,N$ d is the total number of binary-encoded decision components (determined by the problem variables and the number of bits assigned to each). Each particle also maintains a vector's velocity $Vn = (V_{n1}\ldots V_{nd})$, whose components are real-valued parameters that guide probability-based bit updates. These velocities are revised at every iteration (t) according to the DPSO velocity update rule (Equation 3.23).

$$v_{nd}^{t+1} = \omega v_{nd}^{t} + r_1\theta_1\left(b_{nd}^{t} - x_{nd}^{t}\right) + r_2\theta_2\left(g_d^{t} - x_{nd}^{t}\right) \tag{3.23}$$

Particle's personal (local) best position (b_{nd}) and the swarm's global best position (g_d) are denoted in the PSO velocity update, respectively. The amount of the prior velocity that is carried forward or the "momentum" is determined by the inertia weight $\omega \in [0,1]$. Both the particle's individual best position (local) and the swarm's universal best position (global best) are weighted by the learning coefficients θ_1 and θ_2. These terms of learning are stochastically scaled by independent uniform random values $r_1, r_2 \sim U(0,1)$.

The new positions of the particles are determined using Equations (3.24) and (3.25).

$$x_{nd}^{t+1} = \begin{cases} 1, \text{if } r < S\left(v_{nd}^{t+1}\right) \\ 0, \text{otherwise}; \end{cases} \tag{3.24}$$

$$S\left(v_{nd}^{t+1}\right) = \frac{1}{1 + \exp\left(-v_{nd}^{t+1}\right)} \tag{3.25}$$

3.7.1 DPSOA Procedure

The production–distribution problem is solved by the suggested DPSOA, which combines an effective constraint-handling mechanism with a population-based search approach. This approach enables the algorithm to effectively guide solutions out of infeasible regions, ensuring faster convergence toward feasible and high-quality solutions.

Step 1: Initial swarm

A swarm of initial binary population is created randomly as shown in Figure 3.1. The initial random solutions should abide by the constraints discussed earlier.

Step 2: Swarm fitness

After decoding each of the N solution strings, the decoded values are entered into the objective function (Equation 3.1) to determine the overall cost. This process determines the fitness of each string.

Step 3: The greatest in the world and locally

Next, the global best and the local best are initialized. Each particle's local best position (b_{nd}) and present position (x_{nd}) are the same at the beginning. The global best position (g_d) for each dimension is determined by the positions of the particles in the best-performing solution string in the entire swarm.

Step 4: New velocity

Initially, all velocities are set to zero. The updated particle's velocity for each is then measured using Equation (3.26), which is a modified form of Equation (3.23). In this approach, the uniform random numbers r_1 and r_2, used in the standard velocity update rule (Equation 3.24), are omitted. The revised velocity computation for V_{nd} is presented in Equation (3.26).

$$v_{nd}^{t+1} = \omega v_{nd}^{t} + \theta_1 \left(b_{nd}^{t} - x_{nd}^{t} \right) + \theta_2 \left(g_d^{t} - x_{nd}^{t} \right) \tag{3.26}$$

Step 5: A new position generating technique that handles constraints better

At iteration $t + 1$th, each position bit x_{nd} is updated using Equations (3.24) and (3.25), yielding either 0 or 1. If the resulting solution violates any constraint, the bit-generation step is repeated until a feasible configuration is obtained. Because x_{nd} is probabilistically reassigned based on r, the swarm can escape infeasible regions quickly and reliably.

3.8 APPLICATION OF THE METAHEURISTIC ALGORITHMS AND VALIDATION

The mathematical model is applied to a major bearing manufacturer in India operating three plants/factories in the southern region. Finished goods are shipped directly to six customers nationwide and to two northern warehouses that serve additional regional demand; customer locations 4 and 5 correspond to these North India warehouse demands. Large automakers and retail stores make up the remaining clients. Tables 3.1 and 3.2 show demand information for each of the eight demand centers and the number of working days across the eight monthly periods, respectively. Tables 3.3 and 3.4 provide a summary of cost parameters, stock areas, and other inputs. Factory 2 is the largest production facility, but factories 1 and 3 are more highly automated, so productivity rates differ across plants/factories. Storage capacities also vary by site. Transportation is modeled on a per-trip basis rather than the per-unit shipping cost used in many earlier studies. All three factories use trucks of similar capacity, so vehicle capacity is assumed equal across plants.

TABLE 3.1
Trends in Demand

	Demand, in Lakhs of Units							
	Demand Center, *j*							
Duration, *k*	**1**	**2**	**3**	**4**	**5**	**6**	**7**	**8**
1	3.20	4.20	4.80	22.20	20.30	3.25	2.85	3.10
2	3.25	4.25	3.85	21.60	20.05	4.15	2.30	3.15
3	3.75	4.05	2.65	22.22	20.10	4.15	2.55	3.15
4	3.25	3.65	3.15	22.50	21.10	4.15	2.15	3.20
5	3.55	4.15	3.15	22.20	20.11	4.10	2.85	3.15
6	3.45	4.15	3.80	20.10	20.10	3.75	3.10	2.59
7	3.86	4.55	3.65	21.25	20.45	3.15	3.65	3.20
8	3.65	4.75	4.60	22.15	20.80	4.40	3.20	3.40

TABLE 3.2
Total Days Scheduled for Manufacturing

Planning Month, K	1	2	3	4	5	6	7	8
Days	21	24	25	22	25	25	25	25

TABLE 3.3
Transportation Expenses

	Cost of Transportation (*Rs*)							
	Request Center, *j*							
Plant, *i*	**1**	**2**	**3**	**4**	**5**	**6**	**7**	**8**
1	10,400	12,300	9,850	22,500	19,900	7,500	8,600	7,900
2	1,500	2,500	4,500	23,600	22,000	6,400	7,200	8,000
3	4,800	5,500	9,100	22,800	24,500	2,500	3,000	5,200

TABLE 3.4
Other Expenses and Related Information

Parameters and Expenses	Plant 1	Plant 2	Plant 3
Average manufacturing cost per unit, (₹)	42	40	43
Average cost of production per unit for extended time CO, (₹)	45	42	46
Average third party/outsourcing cost per unit, (₹)	46	44	47
Recruiting and training each employee CH, (₹)	1,300	1,200	1,500
Cost of firing each employee CF, (₹)	3,500	2,800	4,300
Unit carrying cost of inventory CI, (₹)	0.22	0.2	0.23
Beginning inventory in units Io	100,000	120,000	80,000
The maximum quantity of inventory that can be kept on hand at any given time *I*max	800,000	1,050,000	625,000
Average productivity per worker per shift in the number of units *P*	832	752	816
Total number of current workers (*W*)	72	136	82
W_{max} is the maximum number of workers on rolls at any given time	79	144	88
The bare minimum of employees needed at any particular time (W_{min})	72	136	82
Total number of shifts	3	3	3
Hours of work for each shift	8	8	8
The average penalty cost per unit of unmet demand comprising both goodwill and profit loss CB, (₹)	75	75	75
Transportation capacity in units per trip CP	125,000	125,000	125,000

Each factory was dedicated to specific customers: Factory 2 served Customers 1, 3, 5, and 7; Factory 3 handled Customers 2, 6, and 8; while demand from Customer/Warehouse 4 was split between factories 1 and 3, with the majority managed by factory 1. This allocation strategy was historically based on distribution costs and local product availability. As a result, demand allocation across plants/factories was never optimized. Production planning was done in isolation for the forecasted demand of each assigned customer. This fragmented approach led to excessive reliance on extended time and outsourcing in certain factories, even when unused normal production capacity existed in other. Consequently, the company incurred higher overall costs, faced increased backorder, and experienced customer dissatisfaction. The lack of coordination effectively made the plants operate as independent entities. The proposed model addresses these inefficiencies by reducing overall planning costs and enabling optimal demand allocation across all plants based on minimum manufacturing cost. In addition, it generates a comprehensive mid-term production–distribution plan to ensure effective utilization of resources across the network.

3.9 COMPUTATIONAL RESULTS AND DISCUSSION

The production–distribution problem was solved using LINGO software. To test whether the global optimum would naturally yield integer decision variables, the integer non-linear coding problem was relaxed to a non-linear programming issue. This relaxed model converged to a global optimum of ₹ 2,126,638,000 in 17 seconds, but key variables F_{ki}, I_{ki}, W_{ki}, and TR_{kij} converged to fractional values. Simple rounding produced infeasibilities and required full precomputation. Equations (3.6)–(3.8) were also relaxed in the LINGO run, and this reduced the model's non-linearity. Integrality constraints were then reinstated, and the default non-linear solver (not the global solver) was used with a 2-hour time limit. The model failed to reach optimality; the best feasible solution obtained was ₹ 2,131,164,000. LINGO reported an objective bound value of ₹2,126,680,000 during the run. It was fixed as the lower bound value or the benchmark value.

3.9.1 GA Solution

The process was tested over run lengths ranging from 50.00 to 15,000.00 iterations to accommodate problem size and complexity. Multiple GA parameter settings were explored, including crossover probability, mutation probability, and population size. Beyond a certain population threshold, computation slowed with little improvement in solution quality. The best-performing GA settings identified through these experiments are listed below.

Initial chromosome pool size (m) = 100
Genetic crossover rate (P_c) = 0.9
Mutation rate (P_m) = 0.1
Generation count (n) = 13,000

As iterations increased, solution quality improved. The best cost ₹ 2,120,170,367 was reached at the 13,000th iteration in 14 minutes. As shown in Figure 3.2, the cost dropped from ₹ 2,134,971,075 at iteration 50 to the best value at iteration 13,000. For plotting, discrete checkpoints were recorded: Cumulative best values after 1–50, 1–100, 1–1,000, ... up to 15,000 iterations were plotted as shown in Figure 3.2.

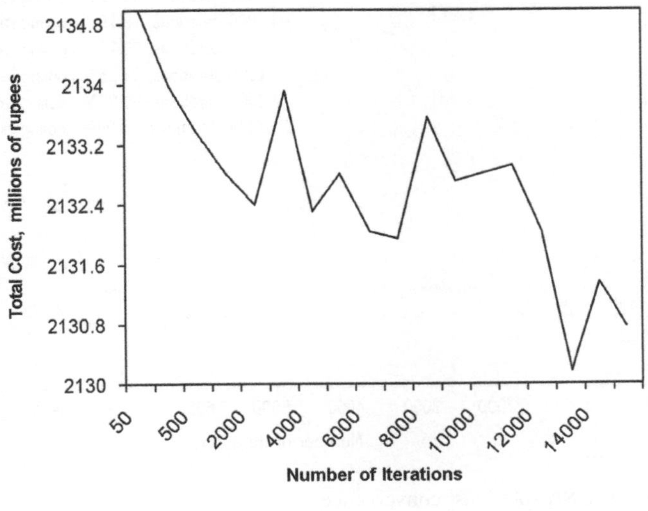

FIGURE 3.2 Convergence of the GA solutions.

3.9.2 SA Solution

Similar to GA, the SA algorithm was executed for multiple iterations to evaluate performance. Figure 3.3 illustrates representative runs demonstrating the algorithm's convergence toward improved solutions. The results indicate that SA achieves a reasonably good solution within 900 iterations; however, additional iterations were performed to mitigate the risk of poor decision-making. The ideal answer was obtained in about 50 seconds when the algorithm was run 1,000 times at a cooling rate of 99.35%. This was the best performance reported. Around the 100th iteration, the algorithm improved from an initial feasible solution of ₹ 2,144,847,475 to the best answer of ₹ 2,133,603,498.

3.9.3 MA Solution

The MA was executed for multiple iterations, similar to GA and SA, using the same parameter settings. Figure 3.4 illustrates the convergence trend of MA toward the best solution. The results are recorded and plotted at discrete intervals, such as after 100, 1,000, and up to 15,000 iterations. The convergence pattern demonstrates consistency, with the algorithm steadily improving as the iteration count increases. The finest solution of ₹2,129,392,467 was achieved in the 41st minute, after 13,000 iterations.

3.9.4 DPSOA Solution

Swarm size, learning factors θ_1 and θ_2, and inertia weight (ω), in addition to the number of iterations, are the four main criteria that affect the performance of the DPSOA. The same "eight-period" problem is chosen, and several experiments are carried out utilizing the bearing production dataset in order to ascertain the ideal parameter choices. Nonetheless, even with comparatively small swarm sizes, DPSOA is known

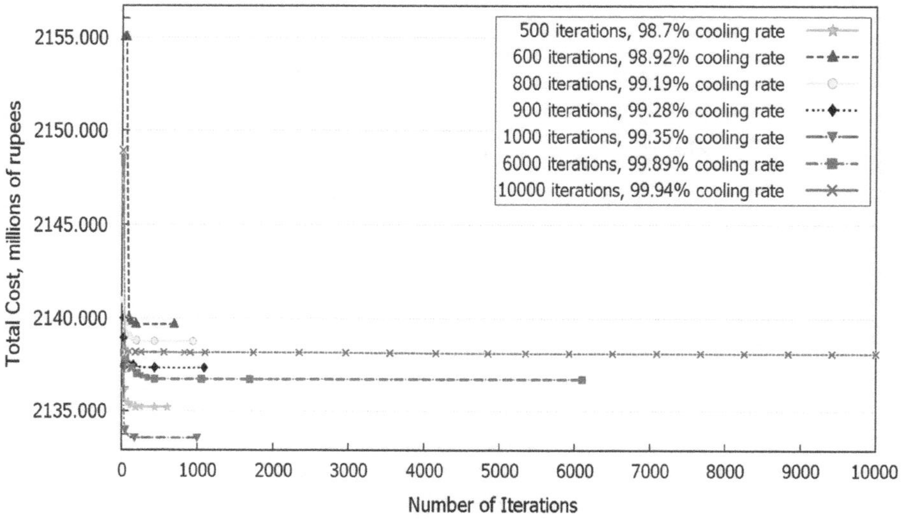

FIGURE 3.3 The SA solutions' convergence.

FIGURE 3.4 Convergence of solutions for MAs.

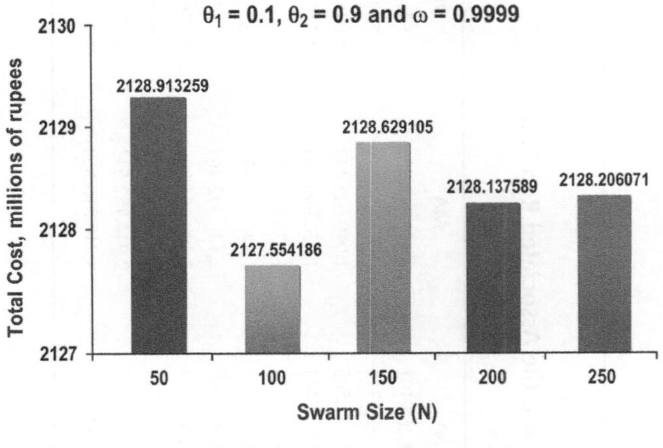

FIGURE 3.5 Solutions are compared according to swarm size.

to converge to high-quality solutions [28]. A good solution was obtained with a moderate swarm size of 100, as illustrated in Figure 3.5, although greater swarm sizes only provided slight increases in consistency. The best solution was obtained for the following combination of the governing parameters: $\theta_1 = 0.1$ and $\theta_2 = 0.9$ and $\omega = 0.9999$. All experiments were conducted using the velocity Equation (3.26), excluding the use of uniform random numbers

Initial experiments on the *eight-period demand* instance showed that the DPSOA converged to a best solution value of ₹ 2,127,554,186 in 481 seconds outperforming GA, SA, and MA, and coming very close to the LINGO objective bound. Motivated by this performance, additional multi-period cases (2 through 12 periods of demand) were solved using DPSOA and compared against GA, SA, and MA results. The best outcome from the three runs is shown in Table 3.5, accompanied by the average

TABLE 3.5
For Metaheuristic Methods, Solutions, and the Associated Run Time

Periods, *k*	Solution, ₹				Time, seconds			
	GA	SA	MA	DPSO	GA	SA	MA	DPSO
II	521,404,479	524,262,191	522,168,839	521,581,238	121	36	897	105
III	785,270,395	791,315,714	784,884,869	783,980,398	211	38	1,264	174
IV	1,051,062,247	1,057,577,505	1,049,627,147	1,048,006,063	336	41	1,505	238
V	1,319,349,515	1,325,867,444	1,316,995,851	1,315,509,848	461	43	1,740	296
VI	1,579,214,617	1,584,877,328	1,578,952,558	1,575,069,678	588	45	1,988	358
VII	1,848,683,304	1,855,309,485	1,848,497,370	1,844,790,976	702	47	2,287	411
VIII	2,130,180,357	2,133,603,498	2,129,392,467	2,127,554,186	840	50	2,460	481
IX	2,405,704,432	2,416,261,507	2,399,761,006	2,396,658,709	913	51	2,771	562
X	2,679,392,253	2,685,276,144	2,670,671,386	2,665,896,045	1012	53	3,056	643
XI	2,948,855,540	2,949,331,523	2,944,782,572	2,935,969,040	1,137	56	3,311	725
12th periods	3,223,397,807	3,233,025,622	3,213,210,552	3,207,537,318	1,249	57	3,544	804

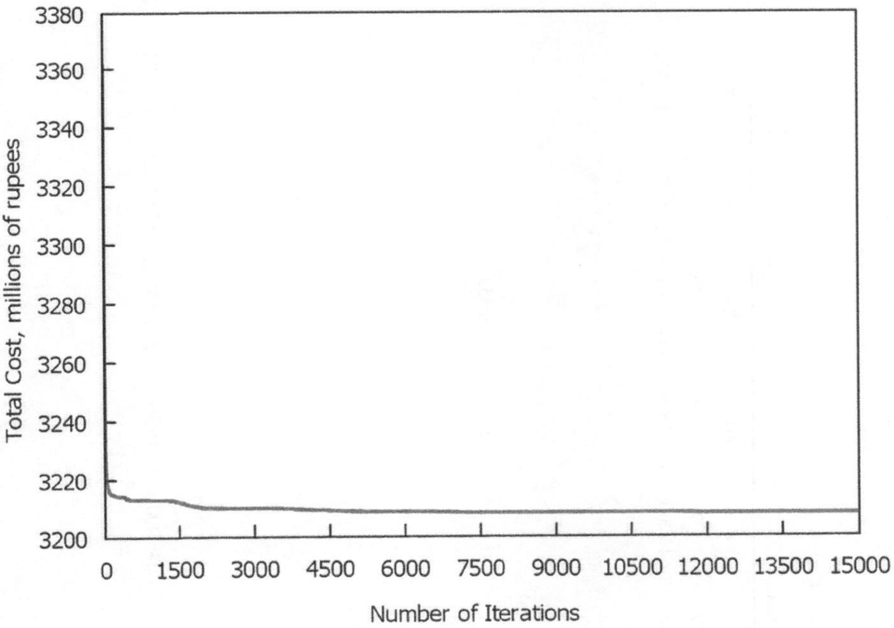

FIGURE 3.6 DPSOA solution convergence for the 12-period problem.

solution times (seconds). DPSO outperformed other methods in 10 of the 11 test cases. Convergence behavior for the *12-period* problem is illustrated in Figure 3.6, which shows that high-quality feasible solutions emerge within the first few hundred iterations.

For factories 1, 2, and 3, the comprehensive mid-term production–distribution plans produced by the DPSO algorithm for the 12 demand periods are shown in Tables 3.6–3.9, respectively. Based on the data, it can be concluded that factories 1 and 2 are making the most of their labor force. Furthermore, compared to the other factories, Plant 2 uses extended time and outsourcing more frequently. Only at factory 3, inventory holding is advised. A summary of the overall unmet demand for each of the 12 periods is provided in Table 3.9.

3.10 CONCLUSION

In 10 of the 11 multi-period production–distribution problems, the DPSOA had better performance than GA, SA, and MA. To benchmark DPSOA's effectiveness, it is benchmarked against the results obtained using LINGO, commercial optimization software that employs the traditional branch-and-bound algorithm. A comprehensive plan was developed using DPSOA for three geographically distributed manufacturing factories/plants. This multi-factory multi-product multi-customer production–distribution plan includes the details of the number of products manufactured in each factory in all period. It also indicates the number of labors required in each period,

TABLE 3.6

Plant 1's Mid-Term Production–Distribution Plan Using the DPSO Solution

APDP	Period, *k*											
Parameters	**I**	**II**	**III**	**IV**	**V**	**VI**	**VII**	**VIII**	**IX**	**X**	**XI**	**XII**
No of worker	79	79	79	79	79	79	79	79	79	79	79	79
Usual production, units	1,422,016	1,644,200	1,708,828	1,512,744	1,711,928	1,701,128	1,644,200	1,708,828	1,643,201	1,555,472	1,555,472	1,623,200
Contact production, units	50,000	-	-	-	-	-	-	-	-	-	-	-
Extra time production, units	121,355	-	-	-	-	-	-	15,432	16,452	-	-	-
Inventory, units	-	-	-	-	-	-	-	-	-	-	-	-
Demand Center	Number of Units Sent[a]											
1	-	-	-	-	-	-	-	-	-	-	-	-
2	-	-	-		-	-	-	-	-	-	-	-
3	-	-	-	-	-	-	-	-	-	-	-	-
4	-	-	-	-	-	-	-	-	-	-	-	-
5	171,7472	1,643,200	1,708,928	1,511,744	1,708,928	1,708,928	1,643,200	1,725,360	1,659,632	1,577,472	1,577,472	1,643,200
6	-	-	-	-	-	-	-	-	-	-	-	-
7	-	-	-	-	-	-	-	-	-	-	-	-
8	-	-	-	-	-	-	-	-	-	-	-	-

[a] denotes the number of units sent to the demand centers

TABLE 3.7
Plant 2's Mid-Term Production–Distribution Plan Using DPSO Solution

APDP Parameters	Period, *k* I	II	III	IV	V	VI	VII	VIII	IX	X	XI	XII
No of workers	142	134	134	134	134	134	134	134	134	134	134	134
Usual production, units	2,334,592	2,123,200	2,845,688	2,478,924	2,456,488	2,456,488	2,807,200	2,978,488	2,123,200	2,587,512	2,512,312	2,712,200
Contact production, units	50,000	-	40,000	70,000	-	-	-	-	-	-	16,000	14,000
Extra time production, units	3,345,76	267,876	163,232	378,008	280,720	218,756	378,788	378,748	345,108	378,748	347,108	355,508
Inventory, units	-	-	-	-	-	-	-	-	-	-	-	-
Demand Center	Number of Units Sent[a]											
1	350,000	355,000	385,000	325,000	375,000	355,000	396,000	375,000	358,000	384,000	340,000	310,000
2	420,000	425,000	415,000	375,000	425,000	425,000	475,000	485,000	445,000	425,000	430,000	422,000
3	450,000	395,000	275,000	325,000	325,000	390,000	375,000	470,000	405,000	376,000	390,000	412,000
4	1,702,168	1,748,776	1,932,920	1,904,632	1,961,208	1,862,064	1,840,208	1,864,496	1,878,208	1,792,920	1,832,920	1,957,208
5	-	-	-	-	-	-	-	-	-	-	-	-
6	-	-	-	-	-	-	-	-	-	-	-	-
7	-	-	-	-	-	-	-	-	-	-	-	-
8	-	-	-	-	-	-	-	-	-	-	-	-

[a] denotes the number of units sent to the demand centers

TABLE 3.8

Plant 3's Mid-Term Production–Distribution Plan Using the DPSO Solution

APDP	Period, *k*											
Parameters	**I**	**II**	**III**	**IV**	**V**	**VI**	**VII**	**VIII**	**IX**	**X**	**XI**	**XII**
No of workers	87	87	87	87	88	88	88	88	88	88	88	88
Usual production, units	151,2276	1,456,200	1,564,008	1,243,584	1,576,576	1,876,776	1,787,700	1,889,876	1,754,500	1,698,724	1,679,824	1,789,800
Contact production, units	20,000	0	0	0	0	0	0	0	0	0	0	0
Extra time production, units	142,616	0	0	0	0	0	0	0	0	0	0	0
Inventory, units	3,032	5,208	277,064	25,024	208,736	520,304	518,112	447,544	482,784	254,400	24,016	-
Demand Center	Number of Units Sent[a]											
1	-	-	-	-	-	-	-	-	-	-	-	-
2	-	-	-	-	-	-	-	-	-	-	-	-
3	-	-	-	-	-	-	-	-	-	-	-	-
4	547,832	441,224	279,080	355,368	238,792	137,936	294,792	360,504	326,792	393,080	362,080	272,792
5	332,528	371,800	291,072	588,256	382,072	411,072	411,800	364,640	372,368	527,528	467,528	471,800
6	335,000	405,000	425,000	425,000	400,000	385,000	325,000	460,000	440,000	390,000	410,000	397,000
7	295,000	250,000	275,000	225,000	295,000	300,000	375,000	330,000	290,000	288,000	310,000	292,000
8	300,000	325,000	325,000	310,000	325,000	279,000	350,000	380,000	290,000	314,000	365,000	344,824

[a] denotes number of units sent

TABLE 3.9
Total Unfulfilled Demand from DPSO Solution

Periods, k	I	II	III	IV	V	VI	VII	VIII	IX	X	XI	XII
Total Unmet Demand, Units	0	0	0	0	0	0	0	0	0	0	0	176

inventory, and backlog levels of all the products and detailed distribution plan. It also provides detailed workforce levels across all planning periods for each plant. A key strength of the DPSOA approach lies in its efficient constraint-handling mechanism, which avoids the use of complex penalty parameters while ensuring feasible and robust solutions. Additionally, an innovative demand allocation strategy was applied, enabling effective distribution of customer requirements across different manufacturing plants/factories and demand centers.

REFERENCES

1. Hillier, F. S. and Lieberman, G. J. *Operations Research Concepts and Cases*, New Delhi: Tata McGraw-Hill, 2005.
2. Vieira, G. E. and Ribas, P. C. “A new multi-objective optimization method for master production scheduling problems using simulated annealing”, *Int. J. Prod. Res.*, Vol. 42, No. 21, pp. 4609–4622, 2004, https://doi.org/10.1080/00207540410001733869.
3. Jayaraman, V. and Ross, A. “A simulated annealing methodology to distribution network design and management”, *Eur. J. Oper. Res.*, Vol. 144, No. 3, pp. 629–645, 2003, https://doi.org/10.1016/S0377-2217(02)00153-4.
4. Chan, F. T. S. and Chung, S. H. “Multi-criteria genetic optimization for distribution network problems”, *Int. J. Adv. Manuf. Technol.*, Vol. 24, No. 7, pp. 517–532, 2004, https://doi.org/10.1016/j.apm.2009.10.005.
5. Knosala, R. and Wal, T. “A production scheduling problem using genetic algorithm”, *J. Mater. Process. Technol.*, Vol. 109, No. 1–2, pp. 90–95, 2001, https://www.jstor.org/stable/30133023.
6. Aytug, H., Khouja, M. and Vergara, F. E. “Use of genetic algorithms to solve production and operations management problems: a review”, *Int. J. Prod. Res.*, Vol. 41, No. 17, pp. 3955–4009, 2003, https://doi.org/10.1080/00207540310001626319
7. Deb, K. *Optimization for Engineering Design–Algorithms and Examples*, New Delhi: Prentice-Hall, 2003.
8. Raja, K., Arumugam, C. and Selladurai, V. “Non-identical parallel-machine scheduling using genetic algorithm and fuzzy logic approach”, *Int. J. Services Oper. Manag.*, Vol. 4, No. 1, pp. 72–101, 2008, https://doi.org/10.1504/IJSOM.2013.052837
9. Sivakumar, G. D. and Shahabudeen, P. “Design of single-stage adaptive Kanban system using genetic algorithm”, *Int. J. Services Oper. Manag.*, Vol. 4, No. 1, pp. 125–144, 2008, https://doi.org/10.1016/j.cie.2007.10.017.
10. Gokilakrishnan, G., Varthanan, P.A., Sreeharan, B.N., Nithiyapathi, C., Kavitha, N., and Rajendran, C. “Simulation based swarm intelligence optimization to develop manufacturing distribution plan”, *Int. J. Interact. Des. Manuf.*, Vol. 19, pp. 3855–3865, 2025, https://doi.org/10.1007/s12008-024-01980-2.
11. Park, B. J., Choi, H. R. and Kim, H. S. “A hybrid genetic algorithm for the job shop scheduling problems”, *Comput. Ind. Eng.*, Vol. 45, No. 4, pp. 597–613, 2003.

12. Diaby, M. "Successive linear approximation procedure for generalized fixed-charge transportation problems", *J. Oper. Res. Soc.*, Vol. 42, No. 11, pp. 991–1001, 1991, https://doi.org/10.1504/IJOR.2009.026936.
13. Chan, F. T. S., Chung, S. H. and Wadhwa, S. "A hybrid genetic algorithm for production and distribution", *Omega J. Manag. Sci.*, Vol. 33, No. 4, pp. 345–355, 2005, https://doi.org/10.1007/BF03396524.
14. Kirkpatrick, S., Gelatt, C. D. and Vecchi, M. P. "Optimisation by simulated annealing", *Science.*, Vol. 220, No. 4598, pp. 671–680, 1983, https://doi.org/10.1016/0262-8856(95)98863-O.
15. Varthanan, P. A., Murugan, N., Kumar, G. M., and Parameswaran, S. "Development of simulation-based AHP-DPSO algorithm for generating multi-criteria production–distribution plan", *Int. J. Adv. Manuf. Technol.* Vol. 60, No. 1, pp. 373–396, 2012, https://doi.org/10.1007/s00170-011-3606-x.
16. Boudia, M. "Coordination of production planning and distribution", *4OR*, Vol. 6, No. 1, pp. 93–96, 2008, https://doi.org/10.22060/miscj.2016.832.
17. Varthanan, P. A., Murugan, N., and Kumar, G. M. "A simulated annealing algorithm for the generation of multi-factory aggregate production plan." *J. Manuf. Sci. Prod.* Vol. 9, No. 3–4, pp. 171–182, 2008, https://doi.org/10.1504/IJVCM.2010.033613.
18. Chan, F. T. S. and Chung, S. H. "Multicriteria genetic optimization for due date assigned distribution network problems", *Decis. Support. Syst.*, Vol. 39, No. 4, pp. 661–675, 2005, https://doi.org/10.1016/j.dss.2004.03.004.
19. Lawrynowicz, A. "Production planning and control with outsourcing using artificial intelligence", *Int. J. Services Oper. Manag.*, Vol. 3, No. 2, pp. 193–209, 2007, https://doi.org/10.1504/IJENM.2014.066813.
20. Varthanan, P. A., Murugan, N., and Kumar, G. M. "A simulation based heuristic discrete particle swarm algorithm for generating integrated production–distribution plan", *Appl. Soft Comput.* Vol. 12, No. 9, pp. 3034–3050, 2012, https://doi.org/10.1016/j.asoc.2012.05.001.
21. He, T., Wang, H., and Yoon, S. W. "Comparison of four population-based meta-heuristic algorithms on pick-and-place optimization", *Proc. Manuf.* Vol. 17, pp. 944–951, 2018, https://doi.org/10.1007/s00170-023-12346-5.
22. Mistry, M., Gupta, R., Jain, S., Verma, J. V., and Won, D. "Parameter optimization for surface mounter using a self-alignment prediction model." *Solder. Surf. Mount Technol.* Vol. 35, No. 2, pp. 78–85, 2022, https://doi.org/10.1108/SSMT-01-2022-0008.
23. Mahmud, S., Chakrabortty, R. K., Abbasi, A., and Ryan, M. J. "Switching strategy-based hybrid evolutionary algorithms for job shop scheduling problems." *J. Intel. Manuf.* Vol. 33, No. 7, pp. 1939–1966, 2022, https://doi.org/10.1007/s10845-022-01940-1.
24. Gokilakrishnan, G., Ganeshkumar, S., Anandakumar, H., and Vigneshkumar, M. "A critical review of production distribution planning models." In *2021 7th International Conference on Advanced Computing and Communication Systems (ICACCS)*, Vol. 1, pp. 2047–2051. Coimbatore: IEEE, 2021, https://doi.org/10.5281/zenodo.7938110.
25. Varthanan, P. A., Murugan, N., and Kumar, G. M. "An AHP based heuristic DPSO algorithm for generating multi criteria production–distribution plan." *J. Manuf. Syst.* Vol. 32, No. 4, pp. 632–647, 2013, https://doi.org/10.1016/j.jmsy.2013.05.014.
26. Ruben, R. B. and Varthanan, P. A. "Application of total interpretive structural modeling (TISM) approach for analysis of barriers in deploying circular supply chains." *Indian J. Sci. Technol.* Vol. 12, No. 24, p. 24, 2019, https://doi.org/10.1016/j.heliyon.2023.e22506.
27. Tseng, C. T. and Liao, C. J. "A discrete particle swarm optimization for lot-streaming flow shop scheduling problem", *Eur. J. Oper. Res.*, Vol. 191, No. 2, pp. 360–373, 2008. https://doi.org/10.1007/978-3-642-25944-9_9.
28. Gokilakrishnan, G. and Varthanan, P. A. "Development of manufacturing-distribution plan considering quality cost." *Int. J. Enterprise Netw. Manag.* Vol. 10, No. 3–4, pp. 280–304, 2019, https://doi.org/10.1504/IJENM.2019.103157.

4 Big Data in Intelligent Manufacturing

Amar Y. Jaffar, Mona Ahmad Alharazi, Jaggannagari Kavitha, Swapna Thouti, and Kanakaprabha Selvakumari

4.1 INTRODUCTION

Modern technologies such as automation, data analytics, Artificial Intelligence (AI), Machine Learning (ML), the Internet of Things (IoT), and Cyber-Physical Systems (CPS) signify a substantial shift from conventional processes. It can be the idea of a smart factory, where people and machines collaborate to create manufacturing environments that are incredibly sensitive, efficient, and flexible. The next generation can be manufactured to increase production efficiency, lower operating costs, and improve production quality. The combination of data analytics, machines, and algorithms that study data and gradually enhance their routine is the essence of a smart industrial system. Decision-making and changes to the manufacturing processes are based on real-time feedbacks. Businesses can improve workplace safety, reduce energy consumption, and better manage other resources through proactive data-driven efforts.

The big data term refers to the massive amount, variety, and speed of data generated every day from a variety of sources in manufacturing. These sources can be supply chains, sensors placed into the machines, and consumer contacts. The data can be used to generate useful insights by collecting it directly. Data analytics can be defined in intelligent manufacturing as the process of analyzing massive amounts of structured and unstructured information using advanced algorithms. Knowledge about operational performance, spotting inefficiencies, and outputs are all possible through this data. Big data enables manufacturers to monitor their operations in almost real time and make informed choices, which was not possible with traditional data processing methods. Big data serves the basis of intelligent decision-making, which is the crucial development of smart manufacturing systems. The connection of the factory system is the major driver to this change. IoT devices in factories are turning into data-rich settings, where all machinery, goods, and processes are continuously observed with data being be collected in the platforms.

Traditional manufacturing has evolved into a data-driven ecosystem by the combination of big data and intelligent manufacturing systems. This enables real-time intensive care, prognostic preservation, and decision-making. Modern skills such as IoT, AI, and cloud computing are efficient and increase the product quality. The unstructured data generated by sensors, supply chains, and machines is properly

DOI: 10.1201/9781003582465-4

analyzed and can be helpful. This chapter analyzes the use of big data analytics in intelligent manufacturing systems, focusing on how facts collected from many sources such as production lines, company systems, and IoT devices improve modern manufacturing's efficiency, sustainability, and adaptability. Using predictive analytics and real-time 24-h care enables proactive decision-making, reduces failures, and improves resource use. Along with real-world case studies demonstrating how big data is impacting manufacturing industries such electronics and cars, this chapter additionally addresses problems with data processing, storage, and security.

4.1.1 Overview of Intelligent Manufacturing

Modern technologies like automation such as AI, IoT, and intelligent manufacturing are the next stage in the industrial production. A more intelligent and responsive production system can better adjust to shifting conditions. And, for more conventional manufacturing techniques, a cyber physical system can establish a smooth link between the digital and physical worlds through computer-based algorithms and physical processes. The capacity to gather and examine massive sums of data is produced in the production process to this paradigm. The production of system is interconnected from the supply chain logistics to the machine performance to the producers of the decision-making to the streamline processes to the output.

Manufacturing not only improves operational efficiency but also enhances creativity and innovation. The intelligent manufacturing system, presented in Figure 4.1, has become increasingly important in the global market as a result of Industry 4.0. It is intended for the development of highly automated and autonomous production environments, thereby increasing productivity, reducing cutting costs, and improving quality. The market needs to cut waste and meet higher environmental requirements through the implementation of technologies, opening the door to more efficient, flexible manufacturing systems.

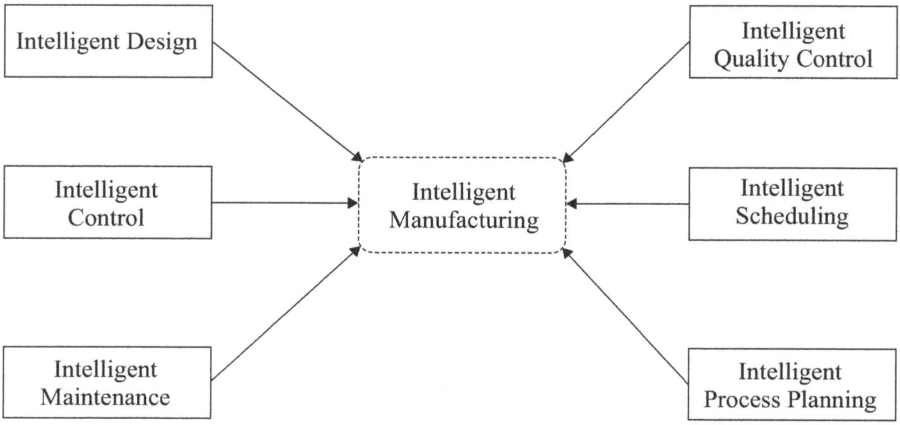

FIGURE 4.1 Intelligent manufacturing system.

4.1.2 Big Data in Manufacturing

The term big data describes the huge collections of facts produced in the manufacturing process by supply networks, manufacturing system, sensors, and machines. Big data in industry includes not only massive amounts of data but also a variety of data kinds and high-speed data streams. It relies on advanced technologies for processing and analyzing data in real time, unlike traditional data management, which works with limited, setup datasets. Big data can be collected from a variety of sources like robots, control systems, automated machinery, environmental sensors, and IoT. Data variables such as temperature, weight, machine performance, and production speed are measured by these instruments. Production lines generate both structured and unstructured data. Big data technologies enable the storage, processing, and analysis of these large and diverse datasets, providing valuable insights through advanced analytics and predictive modeling. These capabilities help to improve operational efficiency, optimize production processes, support predictive maintenance, and enhance decision-making in manufacturing sector. Manufacturers identify patterns and trends in massive databases using advanced algorithms. They improve quality control and optimize operations, which can be data-driven decisions. Big data analytics can forecast when machines are likely to fail, enabling predictive maintenance, reducing unplanned downtime, and saving money. Logistics, inventory control, and demand forecasting can optimize supply chains, ensuring that right quantities are available when needed. The big volume of the data can be handled and stored by using bigdata technologies like Hadoop, Apache spark, and platforms.

Figure 4.2 shows that big data manufacturers can extend to the data infrastructure and conduct analysis. The volume and complexity of the data generated by these technologies have increased significantly, creating challenges in data storage, processing, analysis, and decision-making. The efficient production systems obtain even deeper insights to the operations in the modern technologies like big data. The transforming data can promote innovation, efficiency, and other improvement in manufacturing processes; the big data plays the important part in modern manufacturing. The data can be essential for enterprises looking for a competitive edge in the global market.

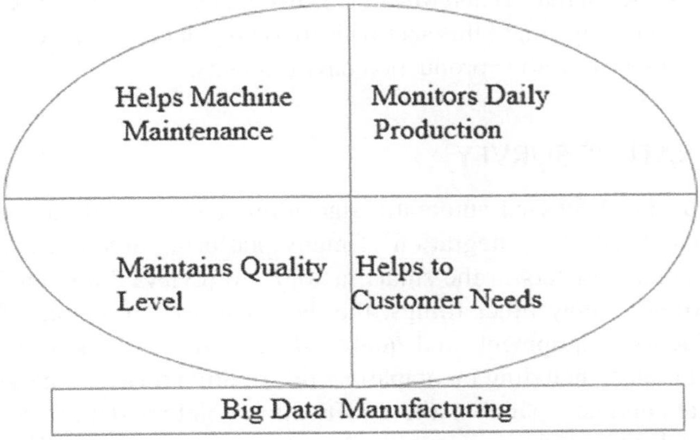

FIGURE 4.2 Big data manufacturing.

4.1.3 Need for Big Data

The consumer demand, operational expenses, other standards of the quality, and the complexity of the production are becoming increasingly prevalent challenges in the manufacturing sector. The speed, depth, and precision to the education sector are not mentioned in the traditional sector of data collection and processing, which is sufficient to these challenges. The big data has more capacity to handle and massive volumes of the varied and information identified throughout the production lifecycle. Big data can help manufacturers to identify inefficiencies, minimize downtime, and boost overall effectiveness thorough predictive analytics for the service and supply chain management in real-time machine monitoring. These data can be modern knowhows such as IoT and AI, which also move from the reactive to the proactive methods, to address serious issues. In addition, big data can be more encouraging inventiveness to the customization in the manufacturing sector. The individual goods quickly adjust to shifting consumer demands of the preferences in the market trends. These insights can further enhance environmentally sound manufacturing methods, decrease waste, and support other optimizations. Big data is an essential tool for businesses to keep their competitive era of the market by the digital transformation Industry 4.0. Intelligent manufacturing enables better decision-making, improves the efficiency of operations, and provides higher product quality in the world that is more variable.

4.1.4 Scope of This Chapter

This section analyzes the challenges of big data in the manufacturing sector, with a specific stress on its use in enabling intelligent manufacturing processes. The fundamental ideas of big data are more integrate and how the process can be affects industrial processes like quality control, real-time production, and other predictive maintenance. This chapter examine the challenges of big data in manufacturing and possible solutions, and dives into actual case studies to demonstrate its successful implementations. The new developments and the new highlights of big data and modern technologies, like AI and Machine learning, and their influence on the future are discussed. The key aim of this section is to use big data to enhance efficiency and creativity in other innovative production environments.

4.2 LITERATURE SURVEY

L. Shen et al. [1] discussed automatic algorithm research and data mining problems associated with the integration of many platforms in smart factories. First, several data platform sets in the smart factory are reviewed and analyzed in this research. Among many other things, the data platform in a smart factory comprises production, equipment, and quality data platforms. These data platforms have several issues, including incompatible information formats, massive data sets, and rapid data updates, which make it difficult to combine data from several platforms. Second, this study proposes the big data analysis-based difficulty mining technique for multi-set data platform integration. The method uses intelligent data processing and analysis to achieve automatic fusion between data platforms. Good results are achieved through the implementation of the recommended strategy and algorithm in an actual smart factory.

C. Zhou *et al.* [2] reported a new business and brainy industrial zone score technique that integrates rule-based modeling, Analytic Hierarchy Process, and AI models, proposed in this piece using industrial and intelligent industrial areas as an example. Using big data technologies, gather both organized and unstructured data from various foundations, such as past records, market trends, real-time operational data, and expert opinions. The performance is regularly monitored by this system, which offers thorough and accurate ratings to aid in business and governmental decision-making.

According to C. Zhou *et al.* [2], the production efficiency and green innovation efficiency are the two major ways that big data application improves the environmental performance of manufacturing companies. The effect of big data applications on enhancing ecological performance has been more apparent as corporate digital innovation orientation has improved. This offers helpful suggestions for heavily polluting companies looking to use big data to execute digital transformation strategies to enhance environmental performance; the results mentioned above offer a theoretical foundation for the relationship between big information utilization and enterprise environmental sustainability.

The study by N. Bhosale et al. [3], as an overview, provided an innovative method for refining excellence controller in the age of Industry 4.0 using real-time mechanization and widespread data analysis. In addition to ensuring that all examinations are carried out consistently and correctly, this also eliminates human mistake. In addition, the data from these automatic procedures may be analyzed in real time for recurrence and identification of anomalies in real time, which aids in upholding proper quality control measures. A higher-quality product and improved efficiency and affordability for those who are producing the goods are the advantages.

R. Rajnoha and J. Hadač [4] reported the findings of a thorough analysis of recent professional literature with the express goal of providing an expanded and systematic perspective on the condition of this topic today and its potential developments in the future. Both quantitative and qualitative research methodology methods are used to address this extremely complex research challenge. The article's primary source is an in-depth review of the literature that includes 187 important and 36 more recent research papers from 2012 to the present that are available in the Web of Science and Scopus databases. According to our findings, there are seven essential strategic variables that determine whether big data analytics can be a significant and effective driver of commercial value generation in IoT smart industries.

G. Salierno *et al.* [5] developed a digital twin model in the railway industry, which is presented in this chapter. We particularly stress how crucial big data is to helping railroad corporations make decisions and how crucial it is to building digital representations of real-world things in railway systems. The results we obtained demonstrate that the performance of actual railway changes in terms of data opinions is accurately captured by the digital twin model of railway switch opinions, and is based on artificial data.

X. Zhu ***et al.*** [6] showed that, by creating virtual models, simulating production processes, monitoring equipment operation, and carefully allocating resources, digital twin technology bridges the gap between the real and virtual worlds. Real entity layers, transmission of data layers, data layers, tools and visualization levels, and application layers are all part of the system's design. Simulation, data processing and evaluation, continuous evaluation and forecasting, simulation and optimization, system integration, and testing are each component of its implementation.

According to **M. Poltavtseva and E. Aleksandrova** [7], advanced manufacturing solutions are currently being constructed on top of big data. Large businesses are starting to use distributed heterogeneous (multi-modal) industrial big data platforms. But there are also more and more attacks on these systems every day. Because multi-modal big data systems are heterogeneous, they are particularly susceptible. The system for access control is the most vulnerable. It is challenging to control access and create a single security policy when heterogeneous components have different information structuring and security methods. The new method uses multivariate optimization to identify the best unified security strategy. The access control subsystem's final architecture includes elements of distributed auditing, analysis, and the creation and application of security policies.

According to **C. Ge** ***et al.*** [8], microstrip series-fed line arrays and a substrate integrated waveguide-based power division make up the proposed antenna. By frequently loading inverted rectangular branches on either side of the microstrip line, series-fed line arrays are able to attain broadband characteristics. This antenna array uses the substrate integrated waveguide the internet, which is noted for having fewer losses than the standard microstrip feed network, for its feed network design.

A. Wan et al. [9] presented an intelligent control system based on big data, AI, and industrial net technologies to digitize the entire liquor supply lifecycle. It optimizes the customer experience and operational effectiveness through applications for purchase delivery, product distribution, and flavor recommendation. The product distribution app improves supply chain efficiency by coordinating production and stock levels, while the flavor recommendation app suggests acceptable alcoholic beverage flavors using data fusion and fuzzy neural networks.

V. Beliakova ***et al.*** [10] used digital twin expertise to predict how long a nonstop casting machine's mold would last. The design of the digital twin of a continuous casting machine is explained, and scientific and technical literature is analyzed. The digital twin's database structure is based on the electronic passport. As a result, a mix of architecture is used. We provide machine learning methods for figuring out the mold's copper walls' hydraulic and thermal properties. These models served as the foundation for the continuous casting machine's digital replicate of the cast.

According to **Z. Jingwen** ***et al.*** [11], in the intelligent manufacturing sector, an enhanced PRO-PSO algorithm is suggested to attain effective performance in anomaly location and product quality control. Simulations confirmed the strong impact of data characteristics on the model's routine, as well as the effect of the number of neurons on the detection accuracy and danger of misjudgment. The model reaches an accuracy of 88.02% in anomaly detection, 1.13% in false detection, and 99.4% in place after optimization.

As discussed by **J. Zhu and X. Chen** [12], AI and mechanism assessment play a crucial part in consumption structure; yet, the issue of erroneous outcome evaluation exists. The evaluation of the mechanism of consumption structure under AI is an incomprehensible challenge that cannot be resolved by using the traditional consumption model. In order to assess and examine the mechanism of invention and optimization, this investigation suggests a data mining technique. The consumer market is assessed using the relative income consumption theory, and the indicators are categorized based on the mechanism evaluation requirements to minimize the elements that interfere with the mechanism assessment.

G. Xie *et al.* [13] noted that the data analysis application needs of metering device status detection, effective operation and upkeep of the collection system, and equipment quality evaluation can no longer be met by the current abnormality monitoring and diagnostic model as the application of power consumption information collection systems continues to deepen, company scope continues to expand, and the functional applications continue to grow. Due to the large number of pieces of equipment and a complex working environment, the current operation maintenance model can only identify issues when the equipment fails because it lacks fault ability diagnosis and screen assistance from technology.

A. Jaffar *et al.* [14] provided a multi-modal strategy that used expert analysis, a 44-item Big Five Inventory survey, and non-verbal clues (facial expressions, head stances, and body poses) to predict all five-character traits of the Big Five model. Using the Face Emotion Recognition Plus dataset, the facial expression module trains a Convolution Neural Network model with an accuracy of 95.14%. We evaluated questionnaire responses, data from human–robot connections, and expert opinions to identify the Big Five characteristics of 16 individuals who were vocally interacting with the humanoid robot NAO.

Table 4.1 presents the various big data applications of intelligent manufacturing advances in the digital twin technology and big data analytics to the industrial sectors to the comparative study. Recent advances include the use of big data to improve

TABLE 4.1
Comparative Analysis of Big Data Applications in Intelligent Manufacturing

References	Research Focus	Key Contribution	Novelty & Impact
L. Shen *et al.* [1]	Smart factory data integration	Suggests an automatic fusion method for integrating multiple data sets.	Improves smooth data transfer by employing clever data processing to overcome data incompatibility problems.
C. Zhou *et al.* [2]	Industrial zone rating	A hybrid approach for performance evaluation that combines AI, Analytic Hierarchy Process, and rule-based modeling.	Unique system that combines several data sources to provide accurate industrial evaluations.

(*Continued*)

TABLE 4.1 (*Continued*)
Comparative Analysis of Big Data Applications in Intelligent Manufacturing

References	Research Focus	Key Contribution	Novelty & Impact
C. Zhou *et al.* [2]	Environmental performance in manufacturing	Creates a system for automated, real-time quality checking.	Improves real-time production problem diagnosis while removing human error.
N. Bhosale et al. [3]	Industry 4.0 quality control	Creates a system for automated, real-time quality checking.	Improves real-time production problem diagnosis while removing human error.
R. Rajnoha and J. Hadač [4]	Big data analytics in IoT smart manufacturing	The contribution of big data to the creation of corporate value.	Identifies seven strategic variables that influence effective big data utilization in manufacturing.
G. Salierno *et al.* [5]	Digital twin in railway systems	Creates digital twins for railway decision-making using big data.	Demonstrates how well digital twin models capture the behavior of railway switches in real time.
X. Zhu *et al.* [6]	Digital twin framework	Introduces an intelligent manufacturing system using a structured digital twin.	Uses a multi-layered system architecture to create a link between the real and virtual worlds.
M. Poltavtseva and E. Aleksandrova [7]	Security in multi-modal industrial big data	A technique for optimizing security on diverse big data systems.	Presents a multivariate method for coordinating security tactics across many data platforms.
C. Ge *et al.* [8]	Microstrip series-fed line arrays and substrate integrated waveguide	Branch loading inverted rectangle for broadband properties.	Lower losses in contrast to conventional microstrip feed networks.
A. Wan *et al.* [9]	Intelligent liquor supply chain	Optimizes the distribution of liquor and the client experience by using a control system driven by AI.	To combine big data with fuzzy neural networks to provide personalized beverage recommendations.
V. Beliakova *et al.* [10]	Digital twin for casting machine	Uses machine learning to predict how long a mold will last in casting machines.	Uses a digital twin structure based on an electronic passport for predictive maintenance.
Z. Jingwen *et al.* [11]	PRO-PSO algorithm in manufacturing	Uses an enhanced algorithm to improve anomaly detection and product quality.	Reduces false positives while achieving a high anomaly detection accuracy of 88.02%.

(*Continued*)

TABLE 4.1 (*Continued*)
Comparative Analysis of Big Data Applications in Intelligent Manufacturing

References	Research Focus	Key Contribution	Novelty & Impact
J. Zhu and X. Chen [12]	AI in consumption structure assessment	Uses data mining powered by AI to assess economic consumption.	Limits of standard models in evaluating the dynamics of market consumption.
G. Xie *et al.* [13]	Metering device fault detection	Presents a fault diagnostic system for power consumption monitoring driven by AI.	The gap in preventive maintenance, lowering power grid breakdowns.
A. Jaffar *et al.* [14]	Personality prediction via multi-modal analysis	Uses physical and face analysis in conjunction with the Big Five Inventory to identify personality traits.	Predicts personality traits with 95.14% accuracy using Convolution Neural Network for facial recognition.

environmental sustainability, AI-powered systems, and the algorithms of the automated fusion in various smart factories. Digital twins are used in manufacturing and railway systems to improve efficiency and decision-making. These advances include AI-based anomaly detection, prediction, and solutions to security issues in multi-modal big data platforms. This information shows that AI and big data are integrated into the current business settings.

Algorithm: Big Data-Driven Intelligent Manufacturing System

Input: Real-time information from enterprise systems, equipment, sensors, and IoT devices

Output: Improved quality control, predictive maintenance, and production efficiency

STEP-BY-STEP ALGORITHM

1. **Start**
2. **Data Collection**
   Capture both organized and unstructured data from production systems, machines, and IoT sensors.
3. **Data Preprocessing**
   Filter and clean up data that is redundant or noisy.
   To provide uniformity, standardize various data formats.
4. **Data Storage**
   Use a scalable big data platform (like Hadoop, Spark, or Cloud Storage) to store processed data.
5. **Real-Time Monitoring**
   Use real-time data streams to continuously monitor production and machine performance.

6. **Feature Extraction**
   Determine the cycle time, error rates, and energy usage, among other key performance indicators.
7. **Predictive Maintenance**
   Use AI/machine learning models to plan maintenance and identify possible issues.
8. **Anomaly Detection**
   To spot differences from typical operational behavior, apply deep learning models.
9. **Process Optimization**
   Examine real-time data to make dynamic adjustments to production parameters.
10. **Quality Control**
    Use AI models and image processing to automate defect identification.
11. **Supply Chain Integration**
    Link supply chain systems with production data to forecast demand.
12. **Digital Twin Simulation**
    For testing and optimization, create a virtual model of manufacturing operations.
13. **Energy Efficiency Analysis**
    Monitor and maximize energy use for environmentally friendly production.
14. **Decision Support System**
    Using dashboards, give managers and operators valuable insights.
15. **Security and Access Control**
    Put strong cybersecurity safeguards in place to safeguard large data in industry.
16. **Data Visualization**
    Display analytics findings with interactive reports and dashboards.
17. **Continuous Learning**
    Use self-learning AI models and feedback loops to enhance system performance.
18. **Deploy Optimized Model**
    Use improved models in production to increase productivity.
19. End

4.3 APPLICATIONS OF BIG DATA IN INTELLIGENT MANUFACTURING

The concept of smart industry refers to the process of improving industrial operations by participating systems, connecting physical and cyber abilities, and utilizing information, including the emergence of big data. There is a growing need to examine additional industries to identify the key factors and implementation pathways for smart manufacturing adoption. Although sectors such as biochemistry and biology have shown increasing interest in advanced technologies, smart manufacturing adoption has been uneven across different industries. The development of big data presents a chance to handle much more data and use analytics to act on it for better prognostics and diagnoses. Analytics will be further made easier in the upcoming by a healthier big data setting which includes smart industrial concepts like numerical twins; yet, it is probable that subject matter information in solution production will still be required [15].

The goal is to find and group academic publications about applied strategies that are relevant to production maintenance and applications of Figure 4.3. Our study's foundation is a thorough, methodical literature analysis that includes a two-step hunt strategy along with extra cleaning and organization. We estimate and demonstrate the possible effect of data analysis on the topic of upkeep based on our search results [16]. A proactive strategy for investigating and creating clever models and techniques for effective data analysis and use is required. Developing novel approaches that can handle the complexities of big datasets and guarantee both the timely extraction of relevant information and the accuracy of studies is essential. These kinds of research projects are now essential for meeting the growing requirement for strong data processing abilities across a range of sectors [17]. Table 4.2 shows the applications for the big information in the intelligent Industry.

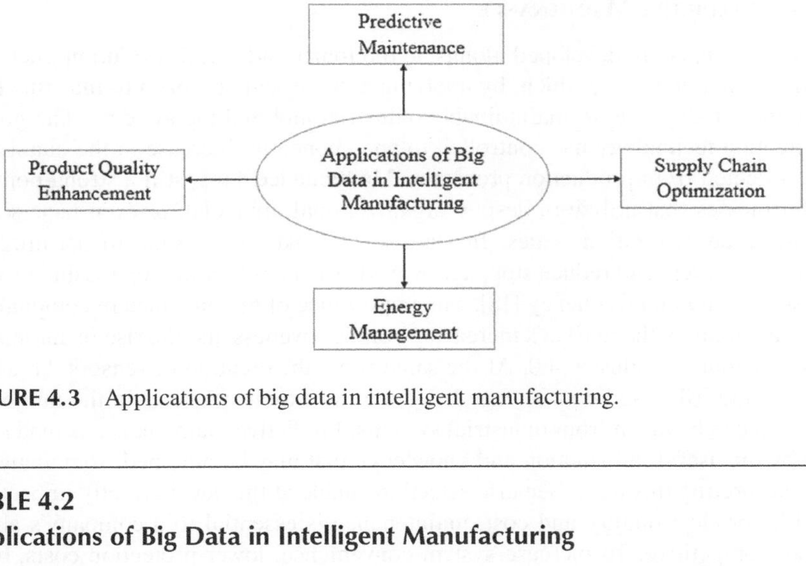

FIGURE 4.3 Applications of big data in intelligent manufacturing.

TABLE 4.2
Applications of Big Data in Intelligent Manufacturing

Application Area	Description	Benefits
Predictive maintenance	Analyzes sensor data using machine learning to predict breakdowns of equipment before they occur.	Prolongs the life of equipment, decreases maintenance expenses, and minimizes downtime.
Quality control and defect detection	Real-time product flaw detection with AI-powered image processing and big data analytics.	Lowers waste, improves product quality, and cuts down on recalls.
Supply chain optimization	Optimizes supply chain operations through the analysis of demand, inventory, and logistical data.	Minimizes delays, saves operating costs, and enhances inventory management.

(Continued)

TABLE 4.2 (*Continued*)
Applications of Big Data in Intelligent Manufacturing

Application Area	Description	Benefits
Smart factory automation	Uses real-time data and IoT sensors to make automated production decisions.	Boosts production, decreases human error, and improves efficiency.
Energy efficiency management	Improves energy use in manufacturing facilities and keeps an eye on trends in energy consumption.	Lowers energy expenses, encourages sustainability, and enhances resource use.
Process optimization	Reduces inefficiencies and improves operations by analyzing production data.	Enhances manufacturing efficiency overall, reduces waste, and boosts throughput.
Product lifecycle management	Makes use of data analytics to analyze product performance and improve next developments.	Decreases time-to-market, boosts innovation, and increases product reliability.

4.3.1 Predictive Maintenance

Several concepts are developed alongside the fourth industrial revolution, including predictive maintenance, which, by applying a numerical approach to machine preservation, is today vital to maintainable industrial and making systems. The growth of detection technology has controlled to an exponential increase in the quantity of data collected from production processes. Maintenance 4.0 is still a strong point for the businesses that utilize it, despite organizational, financial, or even facts source and machine restoration issues. In statistic, it makes it possible to optimize the engine's life cycle and reduce stoppage as well as expenses, while increasing production superiority and frequency [18]. The importance of maintenance in companies is made apparent by the market's increasing competitiveness and the rise in automation brought about by Industry 4.0. At the same time, the creation of sensors, broadcast devices, and IoT-based data storage has led to an exponential rise in the number of facts that can be taken from industrial systems. Predictive maintenance is made possible by the useful information and knowledge that may be obtained from analyzing and interpreting this data. Because selections made at this level directly impact factors like product quality and cost, maintenance is essential to a company's ability to stay competitive. To increase system convenience, lower protection costs, boost effective presentation, and aid in managerial, AI tools, particularly machine learning, show great potential in the study of massive volumes of data that are right now eagerly available [19]. In recent years, there have been many growths in structure operation and maintenance. To better manage building maintenance, a variety of data and communication technology (ICT) solutions have been positioned. Building protection processes, however, remain to be inefficient and result in significant energy waste. The purpose of this framework is to offer suggestions for how to make use of preventive upkeep for construction projects. Data collection, data processing, creation of models, defect statement, and model enhancement are the five phases that make up the framework. In this article, a sports facility was chosen as a case study to illustrate the agenda. Using building mechanization systems and IoT devices, facts were gathered from several HVAC installations. Then, failures were projected using a deep learning model [20]. Predictive maintenance for basic machinery systems under IoT surveillance is the major topic of this article. Traditional predictive maintenance methods encounter challenges because of the dearth of extensive historical data, and these schemes might be difficult to model because of their difficulty, variety of typologies, and short working lifespans. We provide a unique clustering-based method that detects possible machinery issues to solve this problem. The suggested method consists of giving decision-makers the authority to create predictive maintenance plans according to the recommended fault classification's dependability. We highlight the practicality and efficacy of our approach in anticipating problems and improving maintenance procedures by a case study utilizing actual device data from a transport vehicle's doors, especially a bus [21].

4.3.2 Supply Chain Optimization

By accounting for unidentified variables that support efficiency and robustness, the model recognizes uncertainty. The primary objectives are cost reduction, on-time delivery, and optimization of important decision factors including production setups, quantities, levels of inventory, and backorders. When compared with conventional models, extensive imitations and numerical results validate the mockup's ability to provide accurate responses to supply chain issues that are always evolving. Large-scale real-world applications may encounter difficulties due to the substantial computing complexity introduced by the integrated model [22]. Supply chain optimization is the process of optimizing resource utilization to enhance the production and distribution supply chain's performance and efficiency. Experts in supply chain optimization have long found scheduling to be a challenging task, particularly as a dispersed industrial system. In order to address the supply chain development issue in a Decision-Making System (DMS), the current study considers two essential sustainability factors: the economic and environmental. Optimizing the whole order delivery time, transportation expenditures, and manufacture costs, while limiting environmental contamination and product excellence, all pay to the economic side. It has been formalized as a mixed-integer linear programming perfect to address the issue [23]. Many companies believe that supply chain management is at the front of their product delivery. The supply chain management uses a variety of optimization methods to increase process efficiency. To advance the efficacy of the supply chain management analysis, the predictable stochastic gradient approach was recommended in this study. Finding the most suitable movement patterns for the best items is the main goal of a successful supply chain since it helps choose which suppliers to offer to various clients. Therefore, the goal of this study is to create a real multi-echelon supply chain through using variables like risk, time, and cost [24]. Potential problems have left the global supply chain highly vulnerable, and any link failure might compromise the system's security. From the manufacturer's perspective, this article examines a disruption scenario when a distribution center failure and a supply delay happen at the same time. With the goal of achieving the highest possible profit, a healthy supply chain optimization perfect is created based on a mix of active and sensitive protection methods, such as the manufacturer's mitigation inventory of raw materials, favorite for temporary circulation sites, and vagaries to invention design. Latin hypercube sampling, example average approximation, and scenario reduction approaches are used to approximate the recommended stochastic development model with demand indecision as a varied integer linear software design model [25]. Using an outlet store and a distributor as supply chain entities, the current study investigates how carbon emissions affect supply chain coordination. Also, two system types centralized and decentralized are included in the study. Using the standard optimization method, a centralized scheme analyzes the revenue of the whole amount chain, counting the profit of a distributor and a retailer. A decentralized system, on the other hand, applies the Stackelberg sequence for profit optimization and independently evaluates the turnover of a distributor and a retailer [26].

4.3.3 Energy Management

To meet the growing demand for energy, slow down weather change, and promote supportable progress, renewable energy sources have become a viable alternative. Microgrid schemes are used to participate these systems in a dispersed fashion. This offers a set of technology answers that enable information sharing between the dispersed cohort centers and consumers, suggesting that they require suitable management. An information and control scheme that offers the necessary features to ensure that the producing and delivery systems supply energy at the lowest likely operating costs is known as vigor administration in microgrids [27]. Energy management systems are thought to be vital components of smart grids. A viable solution to the quest for sustainability, efficiency, stability, and durability is a combined energy management system driven by machine learning. With an emphasis on important topics like renewable energy sources, energy management platforms, energy storing systems, interchange in energy danger management systems, demand-side control systems, grid mechanization, and self-healing systems, an in-depth examination of recent research and trends has been carried out [27]. The technology, which is based on a genetic algorithm, gives the user suggestions on how to better control the home's energy requirements. These recommendations consider not only the changing cost of power but also user comfort and optimization for solar energy consumption. In order to incorporate the user's desire into the algorithm, past data about the times at which the applications have been used is utilized statistically [28]. An energy organization approach for combined energy systems with electricity, heat, and hydrogen multi-energy storing is planned in order to overcome the difficulties in multi-energy connection decision-making brought on by the intricate relationships and substantial fights of interest among several units in integrated energy systems. First, the construction of the combined energy system is intended and the precise model of the system's primary mechanisms is established based on the connection relationship of the multi-energy flows of heat, electricity, and hydrogen. Second, dimensional assessment indices such as energy storing device life, load fulfillment rate, and new energy application rate are targeted to completely describe the system's stability, economy, and ecological protection when it is in operation [29]. The smart microgrids are now feasible because of the recent advances in the field of sensors, which have greatly improved the monitoring and control of many different energy factors. To optimize the managing of electric vehicles, electrical storage systems, and other deferrable loads like heat hearts, this work provides an original concept of an energy management system for grid-connected poly age group microgrids. This model's main novelty is that it includes climate comfort variable star, considers the decrease of energy storage volume in the control strategy, and penalizes surplus dumping. A smart, maintainable building has been used as a case study for the idea [30]. To meet the need for thorough energy planning and smooth transitions between these phases, the study investigates experimental, scientific, and cross approaches for microgrid sizing and optimization-based energy management strategies. Important conclusions highlight how crucial ideal sizing is to lowering expenses and carbon dioxide emissions while maintaining system dependability. The integrated approaches that concurrently address energy management and size, as well as the potential of new services like smart grids and electric cars to improve sustainability and energy effectiveness, are highlighted in this review from an educational perspective [31].

4.3.4 Product Quality Enhancement

The most important aspect of business competitiveness is product quality. The main step in creating quality is product processing. The improvement of data processing and gathering capabilities in smart factories serves as the foundation for data-based quality control. We separated the slow change of superiority features into three conditions depending on the variation of the slow value of superiority features, treated the production process as a data processing unit, and regarded the development of changes in the invention excellence state as a procedure of processing quality appearances data in order to decrease the amount of invention value complications. After that, we established a classification model of process apparatus parameters [32]. Actions aimed at raising a product's quality level and, as a result, lowering waste levels ensure improvements in present items. We must take exact meticulously considered development steps because of the rapidly shifting manufacturing environment and abrupt shifts in client expectations. In order to be ready for future changes in the market, it is also critical to predict favorable product developments. This issue remained unsolved. The goal of this training was to offer a system for forecasting the excellence of possible product prototypes that would arise from the suggested alterations to the product's landscapes. Current client expectations are considered by this process [33]. The goal was to create a universal model that aids in enhancing product quality by consistently recognizing the reasons behind product incompatibilities and the steps taken to resolve them. The model may be implemented in any product quality control system. To verify the perfect for the mismatch of the mechanical seal in alloy 410, the fluorescence projection method was used to identify the porosity cluster. The SMART(-ER) approach was used to create the analysis's goal [34].

4.4 BIG DATA TOOLS AND PLATFORMS FOR MANUFACTURING

For modern manufacturing groups to make knowledgeable and data-driven decisions, data analytics is essential. To develop better goods, industrial processes, and customer services, traditional approaches to data analytics must be enhanced toward advanced data analytics in light of the increasing global competition.

This uses all the data's potential to make decisions and obtain insights fast. Real-time analytics, augmented analytics, and predictive analytics are instances of application industries [35]. More than ever before, companies must dynamically change how they execute business processes to fit current business scenarios to meet the ever-increasing demands of the global marketplace. Companies will have a significant advantage over rivals if they can assess the health of their processes, estimate how best they will develop, and take proactive control of them based on accurate forecasts. To achieve event-based forecasts and allow active control of commercial processes, the study at hand takes advantage of the potentials in big data predictive analytics [36]. We built a service-oriented trade big data admission platform architecture, described the platform's main machineries, and described the platform's function based on the needs analysis of complicated products. In particular, the platform offers dispersed computing engines, algorithmic pieces, graphic pieces, and visual study tools for multifaceted produce manufacture. It additionally includes big data admission, preprocessing, packing, and investigation [37]. One of the most essential elements of intelligent systems is data analytics, which increases automation to new levels of efficiency, safety, and dependability while also reducing the apparent complexity for the user. These include root cause analysis, plant imitation and optimization, analyzing trade-offs between produce quality demands, process monitoring and anomaly detection using virtual sensors, and knowledge extraction from data [38].

Figure 4.4 provides the big data tools for major trend connecting manufacturing companies with information technology. However, unlike ICT-related businesses, some minor and medium-sized industrial companies might not accept and apply big data knowledge. The factors (technological, organizational, and environmental) moving the adoption of big data analytics systems in manufacturing SMEs are explored in this paper using the Technology–Organization–Environment (TOE) Framework typical [39]. Table 4.3 provides the big data tools for manufacturing.

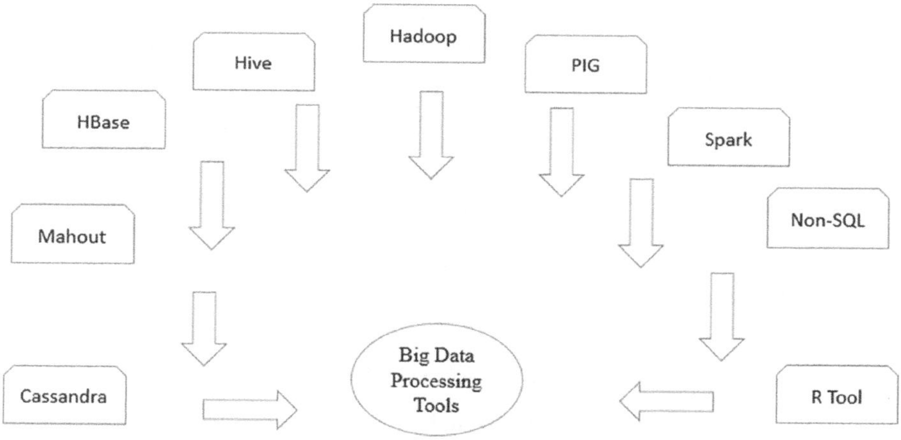

FIGURE 4.4 Big data processing tools.

TABLE 4.3
Big Data Tools and Platforms for Manufacturing

Category	Tool/Platform	Key Features	Uses in Manufacturing
Data storage	Apache Hadoop	Scalability, fault tolerance, and distributed storage	Handles and keeps vast amounts of sensor data
Data processing	Apache Spark	Analysis in real time and in-memory processing	Quick processing of data produced by machines
Industrial IoT (IIoT)	Siemens MindSphere	IIoT platform based in the cloud, real-time monitoring	Process optimization and predictive maintenance
Data analytics	KNIME	Machine learning, visualization, and data integration	Quality control, defect detection
Cloud computing	AWS IoT Analytics	Analytics and data processing on the cloud	Data analysis on the plant floor for optimization
Predictive analytics	IBM Watson IoT	AI-driven analytics, anomaly detection	Optimization of the supply chain and predictive maintenance
Manufacturing execution systems	GE Predix	Asset tracking and industrial analytics	Smart manufacturing, equipment performance tracking
Edge computing	Microsoft Azure IoT Edge	Edge-based AI and analytics, low-latency processing	Automation and real-time monitoring on manufacturing floors

4.5 RESULT AND ANALYSIS

The impact of large amounts of data in intelligent manufacturing systems: cost reduction trends, efficiency in production, maintenance prediction accuracy, and defect detection rate.

4.5.1 Production Efficiency Improvement

Real-time monitoring, automation, and predictive insights are all rendered possible by big data analytics, which improves production efficiency. The proportion of the obtained production efficiency over a 5-year period following the start of big data solutions is shown in the graph below.

Figure 4.5 shows how the use of big data in intelligent industrial has improved production efficiency over the years. Automation, predictive insights, and real-time monitoring are all made available by big data analytics, which improves production efficiency. The percentage develop in production efficiency over a period of 5 years with the introduction of big data solutions can be seen in the graph below. The trend shows a steady rise in production efficiency, demonstrating the effectiveness of data-driven decision-making and procedure optimization.

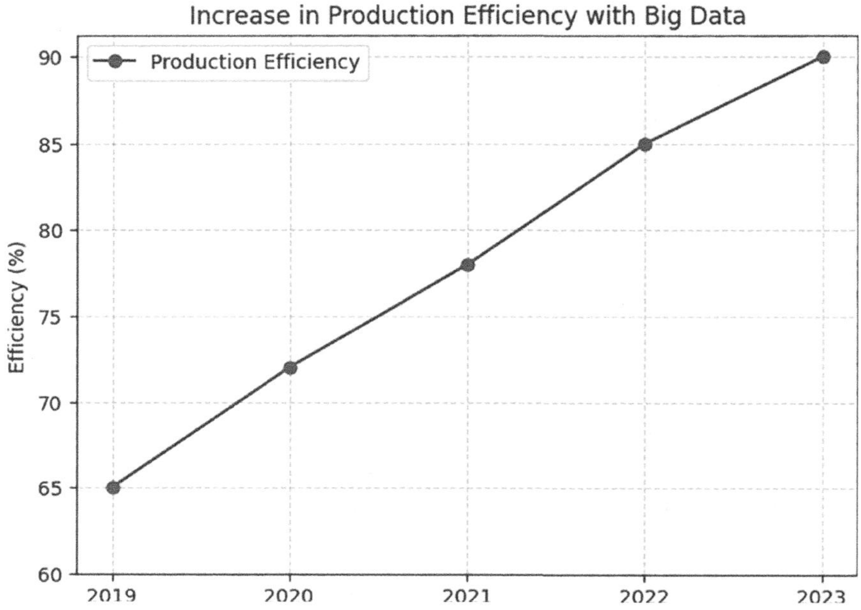

FIGURE 4.5 Production efficiency improvement.

4.5.2 Predictive vs. Reactive Maintenance Accuracy

Figure 4.6 provides the predictive maintenance reductions in unplanned downtime. The efficacy of reactive and predictive maintenance over time is compared in the graph above. Predictive maintenance extends asset life and decreases failures by achieving a greater accuracy rate (92%) than reactive maintenance (65%).

4.5.3 Defect Detection Rate Using Big Data

The application of AI-driven big data analytics improves manufacturing quality control. The following graph displays the percentage of errors identified before the shipment across multiple production cycles in Figure 4.7.

4.5.4 Cost Reduction Trends with Big Data Implementation

Big Data reduces inefficiency and improves resource allocation, which reduces costs. Cost reduction patterns over a 5-year period are shown in Figure 4.8.

Big Data reduces waste and maximizes resource allocation, which lowers costs. Cost reduction patterns over a 5-year period are depicted in the graph in Figure 4.8. The big data analytics significantly enhances intelligent manufacturing's cost-effectiveness, identification of errors, predictive maintenance accuracy, and production efficiency. These results show how manufacturing businesses may use big data to establish a more effective, cost-effective, and high-quality production environment.

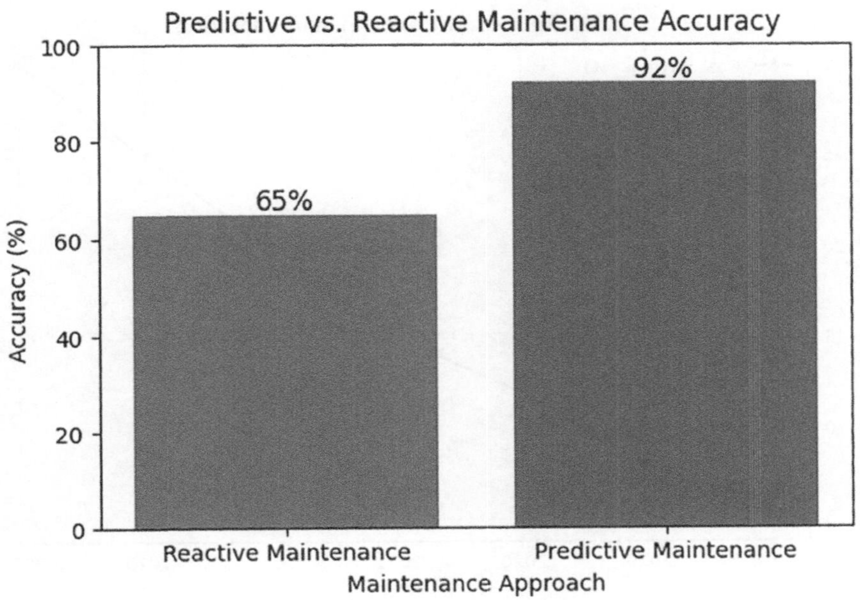

FIGURE 4.6 Predictive maintenance accuracy.

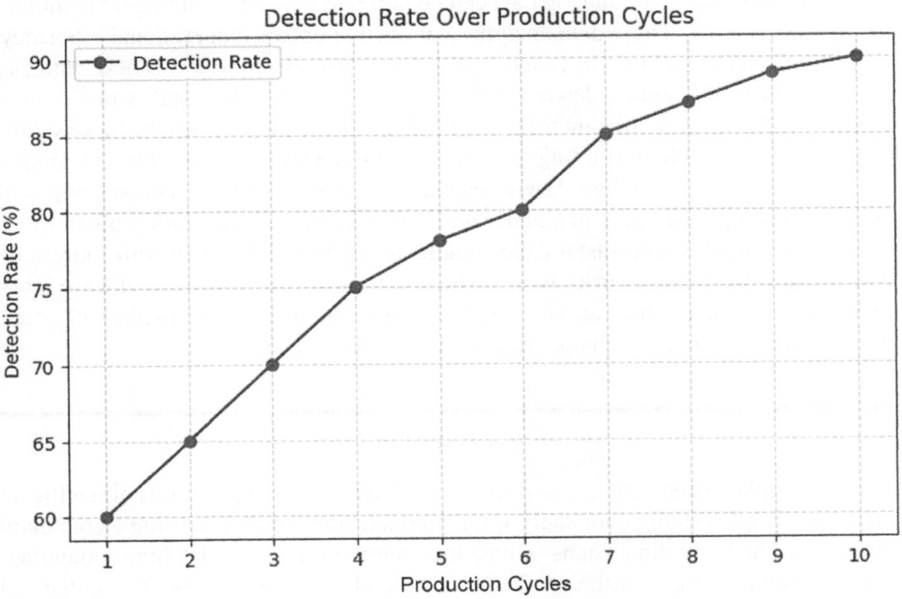

FIGURE 4.7 Detection rate over the production cycles.

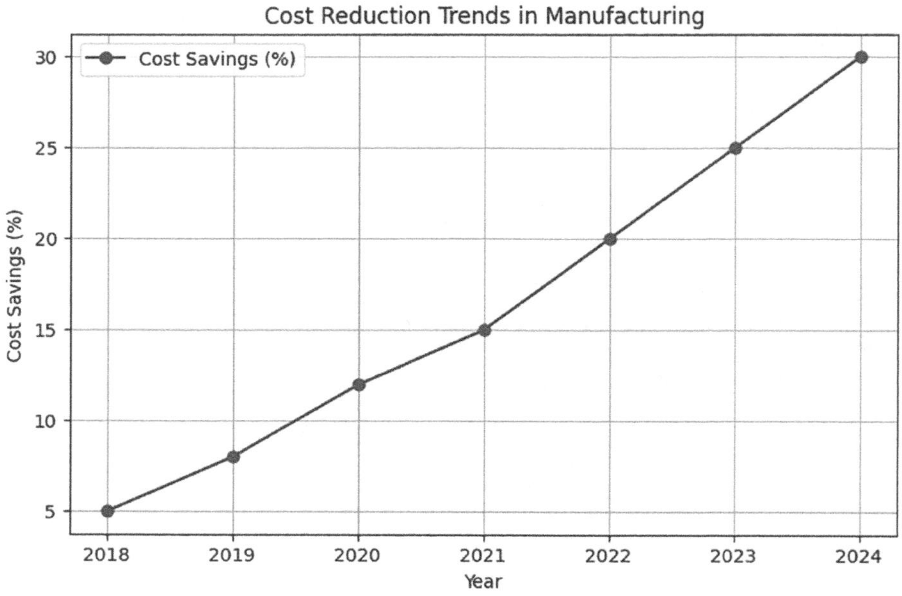

FIGURE 4.8 Cost reduction and trends in manufacturing.

4.6 FUTURE TRENDS AND RESEARCH DIRECTIONS

The edge computing, AI, and big data can be more influenced in intelligent manufacturing in the future. These data analytics can further enhance operational efficiency, decrease decision-making time, and enable more predictive models. These data can be analyzed in the source; latency reduction allows real-time insights in dynamic contexts and plays a significant role. The block chain technology is to be more significant in the supply chain running and other manufacturing systems. The integration of big data analytics and digital twins enables the creation of virtual copies of physical systems for predictive maintenance and optimization process. Future possibilities involve big data-powered sustainable manufacturing methods, along with addressing data privacy and other security issues. The real-time data processing and wave intelligent manufacturing innovation is to identified in the trends and research projects; the production systems can be more flexible and ecological.

Case Studies

Predictive upkeep and actual time decision-making are key applications of intelligent manufacturing, with big data analytics, manufacturing, and IoT serving as the main examples. The large dimensions of data are identified from the machine's manufacturing system to improve the product quality and other operations. The enhanced predictive maintenance in the machine learning algorithms and the other identification lowers costs and the production efficiency. The cloud-based Siemens platform uses big data to support smart manufacturing systems. Siemens combines production data across the global to identify and prevent malfunctions. Businesses can increase the optimize manufacturing lines to this strategy. For instance, MindSphere is recognizing the bottlenecks and data-driven solutions. These studies in the automotive industry identify opportunities for more intelligent and effective use of big data.

FOXCONN'S AI-DRIVEN QUALITY CONTROL

The electronics industry uses AI and big data to improve quality control in the manufacturing of smart phones. High-speed cameras and IoT collect datasets that are used by AI models to find flaws. They greatly decreased in the 30% of the machine learning which is identified by product quality and reduced work expenses. The data-driven approach improves the precision and efficiency of large-scale production by enabling accurate analysis, real-time monitoring, and informed decision-making.

4.7 CONCLUSION

The new era of industrial manufacturing approaches emphasizes big data as the key component of intelligent production, enabling better production, efficiency, and innovation. Big data plays a major role in facilitating real-time decision-making processes and the sustainable behavior. These issues include resource limitations, market volatility, and operational efficiencies, which can be addressed through predictive models, networked systems, and data analytics. The data continues to grow in technologies like IoT, AI, and other industrial usage. Human-centric and automated systems can be increasingly important to the 5.0 sector. Data exchange, sustainable practices, and the creation of next-generation technologies, along with real-time processing and data analytics, are future trends and research directions. These developments of the industry provide alternatives for productivity, imagination, and decision-making. Big data's role is a game-changing factor in intelligent manufacturing in the future.

REFERENCES

1. Shen, L., F. Wang, Z. Zhou, and R. Xu. "Research on the Difficulty Mining Algorithm for the Integration of Multiple Sets of Data Platforms Based on Big Data Analysis in Smart Factories." In *Proceedings of the 2024 IEEE 3rd International Conference on Electrical Engineering, Big Data and Algorithms (EEBDA)*, Changchun, China, 2024, 1444–1448. https://doi.org/10.1109/EEBDA60612.2024.10485802
2. Zhou, C., W. Wang, M. Tian, J. Liang, D. Zhang, and H. Li. "The Application of Big Data and AI Analytics in Rating Industrial and Smart Manufacturing Districts: Challenges and Opportunities." In *Proceedings of the 2024 3rd International Conference on Big Data, Information and Computer Network (BDICN)*, Sanya, China, 2024, 70–78. https://doi.org/10.1109/BDICN62775.2024.00020.
3. Bhosale, N., S. B. Sollapur, M. R. Borade, V. J. Vijayalakshmi, D. Aulakh, and P. Kodmalwar. "Enhancing Quality Control in the Age of Industry 4.0 through Real-Time Automation and Big Data Analysis." In *Proceedings of the 2024 15th International Conference on Computing Communication and Networking Technologies (ICCCNT)*, Kamand, India, 2024, 1–6. https://doi.org/10.1109/ICCCNT61001.2024.10724744.

4. Rajnoha, R., and J. Hadač. "Strategic Key Elements in Big Data Analytics as Driving Forces of IoT Manufacturing Value Creation: A Challenge for Research Framework." *IEEE Transactions on Engineering Management* 71 (2024): 90–105. https://doi.org/10.1109/TEM.2021.3113502.
5. Salierno, G., L. Leonardi, and G. Cabri. "A Big Data Architecture for Digital Twin Creation of Railway Signals Based on Synthetic Data." *IEEE Open Journal of Intelligent Transportation Systems* 5 (2024): 342–359. https://doi.org/10.1109/OJITS.2024.3412820.
6. Zhu, X., C. Li, J. Mai, J. Yang, and Z. Kuang. "An Empirical Study on the Digital Twin System of Intelligent Production Line." In *Proceedings of the 2024 4th International Conference on Computer Science and Blockchain (CCSB)*, Shenzhen, China, 2024, 280–286. https://doi.org/10.1109/CCSB63463.2024.10735491.
7. Poltavtseva, M., and E. Aleksandrova. "Improving Access Control in Heterogeneous Industrial Big Data Systems." In *Proceedings of the 2024 International Russian Automation Conference (RusAutoCon)*, Sochi, Russian Federation, 2024, 260–265. https://doi.org/10.1109/RusAutoCon61949.2024.10694121.
8. Ge, C., M. Gao, H. Niu, H. Yuan, C. Wang, and X. Zhang. "A Broadband SIW-Feed Microstrip Array Antenna for Millimeter-Wave Applications." In *Proceedings of the 2024 International Conference on Microwave and Millimeter Wave Technology (ICMMT)*, Beijing, China, 2024, 1–3. https://doi.org/10.1109/ICMMT61774.2024.10671789.
9. Wan, A., K. Luo, L. Yang, B. Liu, X. Fan, and Q. Zhang. "Digital Transformation in Liquor Supply – Full Lifecycle Intelligent Control System." In *Proceedings of the 2024 IEEE 2nd International Conference on Image Processing and Computer Applications (ICIPCA)*, Shenyang, China, 2024, 478–483. https://doi.org/10.1109/ICIPCA61593.2024.10709230.
10. Beliakova, V., A. Beliakov, and D. Topolsky. "Predictive Analysis of the Remaining Useful Life of the Continuous Casting Machine Mold through the Introduction of Digital Twin Technology." In *Proceedings of the 2024 International Ural Conference on Electrical Power Engineering (UralCon)*, Magnitogorsk, Russian Federation, 2024, 368–372. https://doi.org/10.1109/UralCon62137.2024.10718987.
11. Jingwen, Z., M. Zhu, and Y. Zhang. "Research on Product Quality Control Algorithm System of Intelligent Manufacturing Based on Big Data." In *Proceedings of the 2024 International Conference on Computers, Information Processing and Advanced Education (CIPAE)*, Ottawa, ON, Canada, 2024, 527–533. https://doi.org/10.1109/CIPAE64326.2024.00102.
12. Zhu, J., and X. Chen. "Research on the Impact and Mechanism of Artificial Intelligence on Consumption Upgrading." In *Proceedings of the 2024 IEEE International Conference on Information Technology, Electronics and Intelligent Communication Systems (ICITEICS)*, Bangalore, India, 2024, 1–5. https://doi.org/10.1109/ICITEICS61368.2024.10625343.
13. Xie, G., Liu, Y., Zhang, H., Wang, J., and Li, Q. "Research on Fault Diagnosis of Electric Power Collection Equipment Based on Big Data Analysis." In *Proceedings of the 2024 IEEE 7th Information Technology, Networking, Electronic and Automation Control Conference (ITNEC)*, Chongqing, China, 2024, 1748–1756. https://doi.org/10.1109/ITNEC60942.2024.10733325.
14. Jaffar, A., Ali, S., Iqbal, K. F., Ayaz, Y., Ansari, A. R., Fayyaz, M. A. B., and Nawaz, R.. "A Comprehensive Multimodal Humanoid System for Personality Assessment Based on the Big Five Model." ***IEEE Access*** 12 (2024): 84261–84272. https://doi.org/10.1109/ACCESS.2024.3412931.
15. Moyne, J., and J. Iskandar. "Big Data Analytics for Smart Manufacturing: Case Studies in Semiconductor Manufacturing." *Processes* 5, no. 3 (2017): 39. https://doi.org/10.3390/pr5030039.

16. Baum, J., C. Laroque, B. Oeser, A. Skoogh, and M. Subramaniyan. "Applications of Big Data Analytics and Related Technologies in Maintenance—Literature-Based Research." *Machines* 6, no. 4 (2018): 54. https://doi.org/10.3390/machines6040054.
17. Zhang, C., W. Li, H. Zhang, and T. Zhan. "Recent Advances in Intelligent Data Analysis and Its Applications." *Electronics* 13, no. 1 (2024): 226. https://doi.org/10.3390/electronics13010226.
18. Achouch, M., M. Dimitrova, K. Ziane, S. Sattarpanah Karganroudi, R. Dhouib, H. Ibrahim, and M. Adda. "On Predictive Maintenance in Industry 4.0: Overview, Models, and Challenges." *Applied Sciences* 12, no. 16 (2022): 8081. https://doi.org/10.3390/app12168081.
19. Cardoso, D., and L. Ferreira. "Application of Predictive Maintenance Concepts Using Artificial Intelligence Tools." *Applied Sciences* 11, no. 1 (2021): 18. https://doi.org/10.3390/app11010018.
20. Bouabdallaoui, Y., Z. Lafhaj, P. Yim, L. Ducoulombier, and B. Bennadji. "Predictive Maintenance in Building Facilities: A Machine Learning-Based Approach." *Sensors* 21, no. 4 (2021): 1044. https://doi.org/10.3390/s21041044.
21. Zero, E., M. Sallak, and R. Sacile. "Predictive Maintenance in IoT-Monitored Systems for Fault Prevention." *Journal of Sensor and Actuator Networks* 13, no. 5 (2024): 57. https://doi.org/10.3390/jsan13050057.
22. Douaioui, K., O. Benmoussa, and M. Ahlaqqach. "Optimizing Supply Chain Efficiency Using Innovative Goal Programming and Advanced Metaheuristic Techniques." *Applied Sciences* 14, no. 16 (2024): 7151. https://doi.org/10.3390/app14167151.
23. Beheshtinia, M. A., P. Feizollahy, and M. Fathi. "Supply Chain Optimization Considering Sustainability Aspects." *Sustainability* 13, no. 21 (2021): 11873. https://doi.org/10.3390/su132111873.
24. Alkahtani, M. "Supply Chain Management Optimization and Prediction Model Based on Projected Stochastic Gradient." *Sustainability* 14, no. 6 (2022): 3486. https://doi.org/10.3390/su14063486.
25. Wang, N., J. Chen, and H. Wang. "Resilient Supply Chain Optimization Considering Alternative Supplier Selection and Temporary Distribution Center Location." *Mathematics* 11, no. 18 (2023): 3955. https://doi.org/10.3390/math11183955.
26. Kumari, N., Y. K. Rajoria, A. Chauhan, S. J. Singh, A. P. Singh, and V. K. Sharma. "A Supply Chain Coordination Optimization Model with Revenue Sharing and Carbon Awareness." *Sustainability* 16, no. 9 (2024): 3697. https://doi.org/10.3390/su16093697.
27. García Vera, Y. E., R. Dufo-López, and J. L. Bernal-Agustín. "Energy Management in Microgrids with Renewable Energy Sources: A Literature Review." *Applied Sciences* 9, no. 18 (2019): 3854. https://doi.org/10.3390/app9183854.
28. El Makroum, R., A. Khallaayoun, R. Lghoul, K. Mehta, and W. Zörner. "Home Energy Management System Based on Genetic Algorithm for Load Scheduling: A Case Study Based on Real Life Consumption Data." *Energies* 16, no. 6 (2023): 2698. https://doi.org/10.3390/en16062698.
29. Peng, B., Y. Li, H. Liu, P. Kang, Y. Bai, J. Zhao, and H. Nian. "Design of Energy Management Strategy for Integrated Energy System Including Multi-Component Electric–Thermal–Hydrogen Energy Storage." *Energies* 17, no. 23 (2024): 6184. https://doi.org/10.3390/en17236184.
30. Ennassiri, Y., M. de-Simón-Martín, S. Bracco, and M. Robba. "Energy Management System for Polygeneration Microgrids, Including Battery Degradation and Curtailment Costs." *Sensors* 24, no. 22 (2024): 7122. https://doi.org/10.3390/s24227122.
31. Agha Kassab, F., R. Rodriguez, B. Celik, F. Locment, and M. Sechilariu. "A Comprehensive Review of Sizing and Energy Management Strategies for Optimal Planning of Microgrids with PV and Other Renewable Integration." *Applied Sciences* 14, no. 22 (2024): 10479. https://doi.org/10.3390/app142210479.

32. Yan, X., and G. Duan. "The Real-Time Prediction of Product Quality Based on the Equipment Parameters in a Smart Factory." *Processes* 10, no. 5 (2022): 967. https://doi.org/10.3390/pr10050967.
33. Pacana, A., and D. Siwiec. "Predicting Quality of Modified Product Attributes to Achieve Customer Satisfaction." *Designs* 8, no. 2 (2024): 36. https://doi.org/10.3390/designs8020036.
34. Pacana, A., and D. Siwiec. "Universal Model to Support the Quality Improvement of Industrial Products." Materials 14, no. 24 (2021): 7872. https://doi.org/10.3390/ma14247872.
35. Voigt, T., Migenda, N., Schöne, M., Pelkmann, D., Fricke, M., Schenck, W., & Kohlhase, M. "Advanced Data Analytics Platform for Manufacturing Companies." In *2021 26th IEEE International Conference on Emerging Technologies and Factory Automation (ETFA)*, Västerås, Sweden, 01–08. IEEE, 2021. https://doi.org/10.1109/ETFA45728.2021.9613499.
36. Krumeich, J., S. Jacobi, D. Werth, and P. Loos. "Big Data Analytics for Predictive Manufacturing Control—A Case Study from Process Industry." In *2014 IEEE International Congress on Big Data*, Anchorage, AK, USA, 530–537. IEEE, 2014. https://doi.org/10.1109/BigData.Congress.2014.83.
37. Wei, L., Y. Huang, Q. Zhao, and H. Shu. "Big Data Analysis Service Platform Building for Complex Product Manufacturing." In *2019 IEEE 4th International Conference on Cloud Computing and Big Data Analysis (ICCCBDA)*, Chengdu, China, 44–49. IEEE, 2019. https://doi.org/10.1109/ICCCBDA.2019.8725665.
38. Vodenčarević, A., and T. Fett. "Data Analytics for Manufacturing Systems." In *2015 IEEE 20th Conference on Emerging Technologies & Factory Automation (ETFA)*, Luxembourg, Luxembourg, 1–4. IEEE, 2015. https://doi.org/10.1109/ETFA.2015.7301541.
39. Tang, W., and S. Chaveesuk. "Big Data Analytics System Adoption in SMEs of Manufacturing." In *2021 IEEE 6th International Conference on Computer and Communication Systems (ICCCS)*, Chengdu, China, 28–32. IEEE, 2021. https://doi.org/10.1109/ICCCS52626.2021.9449100.

5 Deep Learning for Intelligent Manufacturing

Sivaramakrishnan Sivakumar Sivasankari,
Ramadas Vinu, and
Rengaraj Gurumoorthy Vidhya

5.1 INTRODUCTION

Through improved automation, process optimization, and the development of predictive capabilities, deep learning is transforming intelligent manufacturing. Real-time defect identification, visual inspections for quality control, and sensor data-driven predictive maintenance are some of the key uses. Even the in situ process control of additive manufacturing is being improved. As the nature of tracking dependencies over time is well managed with recurrent networks, analyzing a spatial data type is amazingly facilitated with such techniques as convolutional neural networks (CNNs). In fact, the quality of in situ process control used in additive manufacturing is being further improved too. While the performance of recurrent networks can be leveraged for effectively dealing with time dependency issues, for analyzing spatial dependency issues, techniques like CNN can be used effectively. It improves flexibility, productivity, and quality while minimizing costs. The ideas that are in line with the Industry 4.0 Intelligent manufacturing has the potential to substitute some characteristics of human mental labor in the production process. This results in more intelligent, efficient, and customized manufacturing. The future direction of the manufacturing sector is determined by this. Scheduling production in workshops is a fundamental element of an intelligent manufacturing system. In theory, the management of production can be addressed through order scheduling. The real-world production environment is complex and often subject to change. It has numerous unpredictable factors at play. As a result, various dynamic real-time events frequently take place, such as equipment malfunctions, emergency order placements, and order cancellations. It is evident that actual production systems are inherently dynamic and uncertain. Deep learning focuses on the methodologies and importance of the learning process in the setting of massive data. Deep learning is on the edge of becoming a widely accepted and applied learning and service technology. Deep learning models are dominating tasks that involve process optimization, quality assurance, and predictive maintenance. By understanding trends in sensor data, pictures, and operational metrics, they are able to provide flawless flaw detection, prediction of equipment failure, and dynamic adjustment of parameters for best performance. The result of such a competitive advantage in contemporary manufacturing is less downtime, more productivity, and quality products. Deep learning systems' versatility

DOI: 10.1201/9781003582465-5

also enables manufacturers to switch from strict, rule-based automation to more intelligent, flexible solutions. The transition from the traditional system to autonomous provides a better performing system. These autonomous systems are mostly data-driven systems which learn from the past. Therefore, deep learning-based intelligent manufacturing is about building smarter factories that can foresee problems. Depending upon the problem they adjust to changes to improve the performance. Then solution is incorporated across industries.

Deep learning is a branch of machine learning that models intricate patterns in data using artificial neural networks. Structures consisting of layers of neurons similar to human brain can process input data. Each neuron receives inputs, apply the weights, and then pass the output through an activation function (like ReLU or Sigmoid). The hidden layer extract features through nonlinear transformations. The output layer provides the prediction or classifications. In Backpropagation, weights are adjusted during training to minimize the errors. Activation Functions (like ReLU or Sigmoid) determine neuron outputs. Overfitting & Regularization is the method used to prevent models from memorizing data with techniques like dropout. Using methods like gradient descent to minimize loss functions is known as optimization. Transfer Learning is the method of reusing pre-trained models for new tasks.

5.2 LITERATURE REVIEW

By the usage of deep learning, the quality assurance and defect identification have greatly benefited. In the intelligence manufacturing, visual inspections are frequently performed using CNNs [1]. CNNs are more accurate than conventional image processing techniques for detecting surface flaws on industrial products [2]. CNNs along with attention procedures work together to identify minute flaws. Thus, improving the accuracy of quality evaluations. The techniques like anticipating malfunctions and streamlining maintenance plans lower expenses and downtime. The manual inspection is replaced with automated problem identification in products [3]. In smart manufacturing, all manufacturing equipment is accessed via wireless network. This equipment is observed by sensors and managed by a sophisticated computer in order to reduce costs and increase system productivity [4]. Current advancements in the internet of things (IoT) and cloud computing deliver essential technologies to improve contemporary production [5]. These are used in numerous manufacturing control procedures, such as schedule preparation, diagnosis and assessment, predictive maintenance, and quality [6]. On the other hand, intelligent manufacturing systems can outperform traditional manufacturing systems because they can analyze, self-learn, and comprehend complexity. They can also accumulate and analyze enormous amounts of data to progress product quality, decrease production costs, and shorten time-to-market [7]. The end-to-end prototype aimed at multiple phases of machine calculation of speed, which is encouraged by current deep learning research in smart manufacturing. A deep convolutional Long Short-Term Memory (LSTM) deep convolutional encoder and decoder architecture makes up the model. When compared to the most advanced predictive models, extensive empirical assessments utilizing real-life information from a UK metallic wrapping plant demonstrate the benefit of the suggested approach [8]. The reviews of deep learning's role in intelligent manufacturing highlight methods, opportunities, and challenges. They discuss various models like CNNs and RNNs, emphasizing automated feature engineering, big data handling, and hybrid replicas while addressing data-driven challenges in smart manufacturing [9]. The framework of an attribute attentional LSTM takes a system of electrical archives as input to abstract features. Later, various qualities are merged into the characteristic attention network, which can alter the status of each attribute inevitably. Subsequent, the reweighted features are nourished into the well-being forecast section to establish time-based requirement for the manufacturing structure [10]. Semiconductor crackers are extensively castoff in combined circuit-oriented chips. The composite process of production is easy to reason numerous imperfections. Consequently, the flaw detection of semiconductor wafers is an important means to ensure their yield and productivity [11], a data-driven optimization model of industrial service in intelligent manufacturing procedure using deep learning algorithm and resource agent, and a data-driven resource representative that represents available manufacturing resources. The asset representative is an intelligent element of object making part, which consumes controlling purposes of data processing and service in management [12]. Sensor data is analyzed using deep learning models, such as LSTM networks and Recurrent Neural Networks (RNNs), to monitor the state of machinery [13]. Adaptive process control in manufacturing systems is made possible by deep reinforcement learning. By automatically optimizing machining parameters, these algorithms raise output and enhance product quality. Cyber-physical systems use real-time analytics to make smart decisions about resource allocation and process redesign by combining deep learning with IoT and big data.

5.3 ARCHITECTURES OF DEEP LEARNING FOR INTELLIGENT MANUFACTURING

Intelligent manufacturing on the other hand is practice of deep learning to boost efficiency, precision, and automation in production processes. There are numerous ways, each addressing specific challenges within the domain of manufacturing. The following sections outline key techniques that use deep learning toward intelligent manufacturing.

5.3.1 Architecture of Siamese RPN

The Siamese Region Proposal Network (Siamese RPN) is an architecture that properly allows precise real-time object tracking according to the combination of a Siamese network and an RPN. It employs two similar neurons for extracting feature maps by comparing the template image (reference) and the search image (current frame) as shown in Figure 5.1. Cross-correlation is used to extract a response map indicative of similar regions. These regions are arranged by the RPN by proposing bounding boxes and refining along the way [14]. Officially, it is known as an architecture that is hybrid and does object detection and tracking very effectively, owing to its ability to adapt to scale, perspective, and appearance diversity, especially in dynamic and crowded environments.

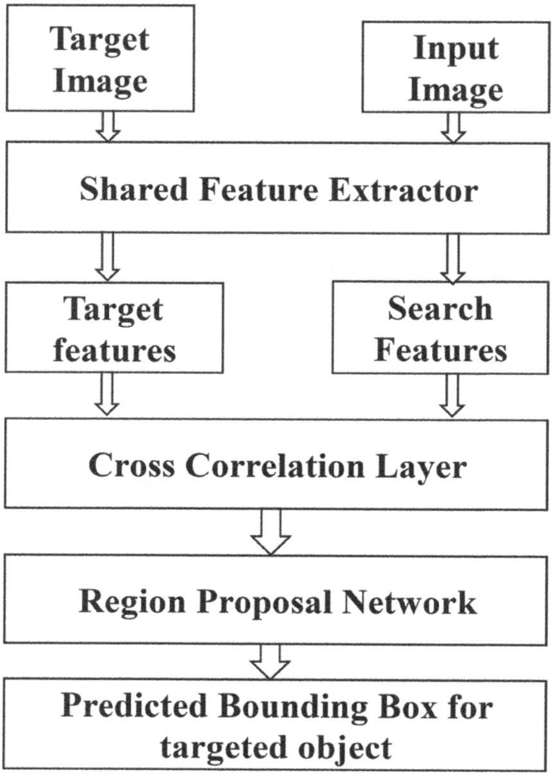

FIGURE 5.1 Siamese RPN (Siamese RPN).

The source of Figure 5.1 is the adapted modified version of deep feature-based Siamese network for Visual Object Tracking – Su lang kim – 2022.

The Siamese RPN is considered to be an architecture of deep learning, combining the concepts of the Siamese network and RPNs. The foremost impression behind it is to track objects through a sequence of images or frames using a Siamese network. Region proposals for object detection are to be made by the Siamese RPN as it tracks the objects [15]. The Siamese RPN has been used in the domain of intelligent manufacturing for object tracking and monitoring in dynamic situations.

Siamese RPN Object Tracking in Assembly Lines. The capacity to track the flow of parts, components, or products from one station to another is necessary for complex assembly lines. Siamese RPN can be used to supervise specific components during the assembly process to guarantee that they are positioned accurately and within predefined boundaries. This is particularly helpful in the production of electronics and cars, where exact tracking is required to ensure quality.

Siamese RPN for Quality Control in High-Speed Production. Siamese RPN can be applied in scenarios where there is a movement of products at a fast pace, for example during the processes of labeling or packing. This approach may monitor the correct alignment positioning and quality of moving items on conveyors at high speed, and spotting any anomalies instantaneously. So this does enable the real time, quality assurance which means the post production checks are minimal.

Automation and Robotics Control Siamese. RPN is excellent in the accurate localization of the target object within the factory or in a robotic pickup and or placement activity. It ensures that robotic arms are accurately pointed during action in dynamic situation where the object shifts or changes attitude. When high precision or attention is required in performing a task, this technique improves the accuracy and flexibility of the robotic operations.

5.3.2 Architecture of Multi-Objective Optimization (MOO)

In intelligent manufacturing, MOO is handled with the integration of deep learning approaches which are referred to as DL-MOO. Enhancing product quality, reducing energy use, increasing the throughput, and decreasing costs of production are the focus of the intelligent manufacturing activities.

Figure 5.2 shows the architecture called DL-MOO based on MOO of deep learning, which provides effective solutions to complex manufacturing problems where several objectives, namely, cost, quality, energy efficiency, and throughput, are targeted by means of deep learning models combined with MOO techniques. After pinpointing the decision factors and optimization objectives, the architecture performs some analysis and gathers necessary data. Estimates of various configurations are typically done using a neural network as the deep learning model. The solution domain is then scanned, and trade-offs among objectives are accomplished via MOO approaches such as evolutionary strategies or Pareto front optimization. The best options are assessed, and the model is improved based on input. The results ultimately inform automated process modifications or decision-making in real-time production settings.

5.3.3 Architecture of LSTM

LSTMs are a specific type of RNN that specializes in identifying long-term addictions in time-series information. Based on past sensor data and operating conditions, they are utilized for more precise predictive maintenance, predicting when a machine is likely to break.

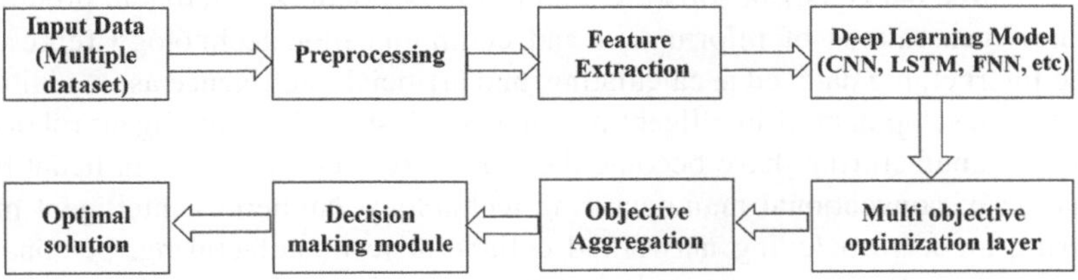

FIGURE 5.2 DL-MOO architecture.

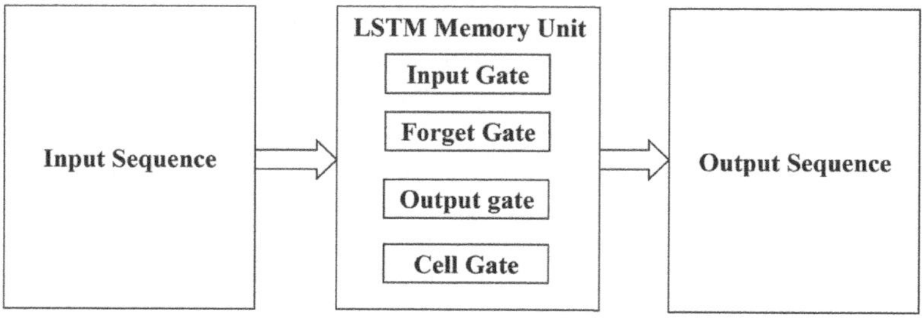

FIGURE 5.3 LSTM system.

Figure 5.3 is referred and modified from the research gate. Figure 5.3 shows the LSTM system. The LSTM unit receives an input *x*(*t*) at each time step, and outputs a corresponding hidden state *h*(*t*). The amount of input that ought be extra to the cell state is determined by the input gate. How ample of the prior memory (cell state) should be retained is resolute by the forget gate. The input and prior memory is castoff to apprise the cell state. The production gate uses both the updated memory and the current input to determine what the next output should be. For predictive analytics in tool monitoring, a variety of models such as CNNs and RNNs are used, allowing automated feature abstraction and efficient big data management. Intelligent manufacturing systems can make dynamic adjustments based on production demands and resource availability, thanks to deep learning's assistance with modeling and scheduling. Through precise forecasting, Convolutional LSTM Autoencoders optimize manufacturing processes and energy usage by predicting machine speed in real time. Although these techniques demonstrate the potential of deep learning in intelligent manufacturing, issues including model selection, data quality, and interaction with current systems continue to be major obstacles that must be overcome for wider adoption.

5.3.4 Architecture of Intelligent Manufacturing Systems

The basic concept behind intelligent manufacturing is to effectively encompass communication technology with intelligent equipment that will automate the manufacture process, gather various types of data during the making process using various perception technologies, upload the data to an industrial server via industrial Ethernet and other communication channels, process and analyze the data under the supervision of Manufacturing Execution System software, connect to enterprise resource management software, and ultimately achieve intelligent production. The new generations of information and communication technology represented by the Internet, big data, edge calculating, and artificial intelligence as in addition to the quick development of intelligent machinery, illustrated by intelligent robots and additive manufacturing, have become the main forces behind the significant transformation of conventional manufacturing technology. Numerous intelligent manufacturing models, including networked collaborative manufacturing, personalized customized production, service-oriented manufacturing, value-added operation and maintenance services, and public research and design, are emerging as a result of the

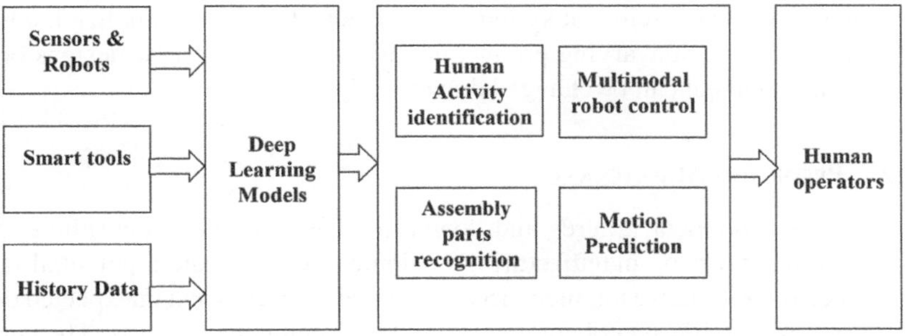

FIGURE 5.4 Intelligent manufacturing system.

integration of manufacturing and the Internet. An efficient method of continuously promoting new development momentum in the manufacturing sector is to provide solutions for the new mode of intelligent manufacturing by enhancing the fundamental technology and security support capabilities of manufacturing and Internet convergence development.

The source of Figure 5.4 is from by referring intelligent manufacturing systems in pandemic and beyond a framework and impact assessment [16]. Figure 5.4 shows the block diagram for intelligent manufacturing systems. This illustrates the integrated framework that connects various components. The data is collected using sensors and smart tools. The acquired data uses deep learning models to identify the pattern, make decisions, and learn automatically from the data. The applications like assembly parts recognition, motion prediction, and multimodal robot control use deep learning techniques. The human operator monitors the process and intervenes the process if needed.

5.4 APPLICATIONS

5.4.1 Quality Control and Inspection

Quality control in manufacturing has been predominantly achieved through manual inspection or through rules-based systems. CNNs have made it possible to automate defect detection processes onsite with a notable increase in accuracy. The technology inspects products at times using high-definition photographs and detects any minute imperfections available on the product and classes them accordingly for extent of damage. Automated visual inspection thus reduces human error and creates the possibility for improved consistency across operations. In intelligent manufacturing, quality regulator and examination practice cutting-edge technologies such as artificial intelligence, machine vision, and the IoT to guarantee that properties meet challenging quality standards in real time. Automated systems perform quantity acceptances, notice defects, and verify necessities more correctly than manual approaches because they practice high-resolution cameras and sensors. Such systems can notice microscopic irregularities in multifaceted goods or identify patterns even in high-speed manufacturing environments, thanks to deep learning models, including CNNs. The intelligent systems reduce defect rates, minimalize the waste, and guarantee for the unvarying product quality. According to new designs or customer requirements, it can be changed dynamically.

5.4.2 Predictive Maintenance

It diminishes equipment failures and downtime. Deep learning algorithms examine data from sensors on manufacturing equipment to anticipate a potential failure before it occurs. Predictive maintenance is designed to circumvent unexpected downtime, maximize the lifespan of equipment, and save maintenance costs. The purpose of predictive maintenance is to determine when a portion of machinery might fail so that service disruption can be diminished and the scheduling of part replacement can be optimized [17]. In order to address failure prediction difficulties, deep learning techniques, in particular, RNNs and associated LSTM parameters, can handle sensor data and perform analysis over time. These models enable the fast action and warnings in reaction to situations by translating complicated sequences, trends, and patterns across systems.

Finding anomalies: Anomaly finding is the procedure of identifying rare patterns in the behavior of equipment that may indicate an approaching malfunction. Autoencoders and LSTM networks are examples of anomaly detection models that monitor sensor information (such as temperature and shuddering) to identify withdrawals from typical behavior [18]. It can be used to keep an eye on devices like motors, pumps, and compressors and alert operators to any strange activity. This makes it possible to identify problems early.

Fault Classification: It classifies the various types of machine failures. Deep learning classification models such as CNNs and RNNs use labeled datasets to classify different types of faults from image or sensor data. Applications: helpful in identifying the kind of gearbox or motor failure, for instance, when various fault types call for various repair techniques. It makes it easier to identify the exact issue so that maintenance staff can quickly create appropriate fixes.

Remaining useful life prediction: It indicates how long a machine or component will last before breaking down mechanically. The remaining useful life is estimated using deep learning models, particularly LSTM and RNN models. It is based on research into the equipment's deterioration patterns over time. In dynamic machinery, such as engines, turbines, and heavy industrial equipment, the remaining useful life is frequently monitored [19]. This helps in providing information for maintenance scheduling. This makes it possible to schedule maintenance as efficiently as possible, which effectively lowers downtime and extends the equipment's lifespan.

5.4.3 Process Optimization

Deep learning can enhance factory operations by analyzing production line data, locating bottlenecks, and suggesting fixes. In this field, the Reinforcement Learning (RL) subset of deep learning works very well. In RL, the agent acquires decision-making skills by interrelating with the backgrounds and getting response in the system of motivations or consequences [20]. Our style is ideal for complex multi-stage production processes where ordinary optimization methods are ineffectual. Process optimization, carried out by advanced skills such as AI, machine learning, IoT, and real-time analytics, aims to enhance production processes in intelligent manufacturing. Optimization systems analyze data from production lines to anticipate problems and suggest solutions. This reduces waste and downtime. Through the implementation of deep learning algorithms, the process parameters are changed because of the shifts in demand or variations in raw materials. With the help of optimization, the smart manufacturing system increases the quality of final products.

5.4.4 Autonomous Systems and Robotics

With deep learning, robots are able to perform complicated tasks with great precision. The robots with the help of computer vision can navigate around, recognize objects, and perform assembly tasks with incredible precision. In order to achieve greater efficiency and safety, collaborative robots are being created to align their abilities with the humans.

5.4.5 In situ Process Control in Additive Manufacturing

In situ process control refers to the real-time monitoring and modification of the printing process. It aims to ensure consistent quality and minimize defects. Machine learning algorithms examine the data collected by sensors on various characteristics, such as temperature and layer deposition to find anomalies [21]. Feedback systems make dynamic adjustments to variables like laser power and material feed rates to sustain ideal conditions. This control process, performed layer by layer, enhances accuracy, reduces waste, and bolsters the reliability and structural integrity of parts produced through additive manufacturing.

5.5 CASE STUDY

A manufacturing firm implemented robots fitted with deep learning-based vision systems to perform sensitive assembly tasks. The robots adapted their movements in real time, resulting in a 20% enhancement in assembly precision.

5.5.1 LSTM in Automotive Plants

The LSTM models are implemented in a large automotive factory keeping track of the robotic arm. The models were successful in identifying the vulnerability with a 90% accuracy. This has helped in bringing down the unwanted breakdowns by a further 30%. In a car factory, the manufacture of goods in a large scale through robotic arms is the most crucial factor [22]. Proper maintenance of the mechanical arms has to be done to conduct the functioning in a long period. The mechanical arms are slow movers. If any breakdown takes place, it will lead to idle margin times. So, the car factory has been able to effectively tackle the problem by bringing in a premonitory support procedure with the help of long transient memory.

5.5.1.1 How LSTM Functions in Prescient Support

Models based on the LSTM are seen to be largely skilled in controlling information without any disruptions and changes in the learning environment, thus making them useful in the prediction and maintenance of machine conditions through proper maintenance [23]. The information is derived from various sensors attached to the machine's automatic arms, incorporating information based on its activities, including vibrations, temperature, force, and other measures that determine the robustness especially on machine parts.

This data is handled by the LSTM model, which is ready to identify common functional examples, as well as anomalies that could suggest a risk of malfunction. By learning from past breakdowns and maintenance logs, the model develops knowledge of what precedes a glitch. Once trained, the LSTM model is applied to continuous checking. The sensor information is granularly decomposed to identify any deviations from the normal course of behavior, thus predicting weaknesses in the mechanical arms. Benefits achieved are as follows. The LSTM model executed at the plant achieved 90% accuracy in predicting possible weaknesses in the mechanical arms [23]. This means that nine out of ten predicted failures were accurate, thus enabling support teams to focus on the most relevant issues and not get distracted by undesired ones. Moreover, with the help of exact forecasts, they were in a position to minimize negative breakdowns by 30%. Furthermore, with proactive maintenance, they were in a position to schedule their time of repair in what was considered a scheduled time. Sudden happenings frequently result in massive costs solely attributed to fixing and repairing damaged parts with manufactured time lost. The plant benefited from massive reserves saved through predictions alone. The reduction in unexpected setbacks proved that not only was there smoothness in the process but gains were recorded in terms of functional capacity. The predictive maintenance strategy ensured that the plant maintained high productivity with minimal disturbances. Due to specific anticipations, traditional maintenance prevents minor issues from becoming critical delays. Besides prolonging the life cycle of the robotic arms and other equipment, this reduces repair costs and enhances the profit from speculation. The LSTM models' successful deployment in predictive maintenance for the car plant is a sign of the general tendency to introduce AI and artificial intelligence to Industry 4.0. AI-driven predictive analytics allows companies to make a shift from reactive to proactive maintenance [24]. This not only reduces costs but also fosters gradual improvement and progress at assembly.

5.5.2 Manufacturing with CNN-based Defect Detection

Essentially, silicon wafers are the main combined substrates applied in the production of semiconductors. The functionality of a chip can be jeopardized by a fault, notwithstanding if it is micro, leading to serious economic complications as well as adverse effects on one's reputation. In response to the need to resolve this plight, the company utilized a framework of deep learning that was design based on a CNN that focused on inspecting minute faults within wafers. This case study will closely evaluate the ways through which the inspection accuracy improved significantly, as well as the extensive reduction seen in inspection durations.

Key challenges are low rates of defect recognition. Conventional techniques normally ignore small flaws, subsequent in expensive reworks or rejected products. The production line had blocks, and throughput was limited due to the slowness of manual inspection. Even skilled inspectors had trouble seeing little faults, predominantly when they were tired. The Implementation for CNN-Based Defect Detection is as follows. A system built on CNNs, a type of deep learning algorithm that is perfect for image analysis, was implemented by a semiconductor manufacturer. Along the inspection range, high-resolution cameras were positioned to take close-up pictures of every wafer. These pictures were important in creating a dataset that contained wafers that are normal and flawless. Wafers that have known micro-defects, like fractures, scratches, external objects, or uneven textures [25]. Experts exactly marked the dataset, classifying flaws according to location, type, and severity. The CNN model remained accomplished using this data as the basis. The CNN model remained qualified by means of the annotated dataset. The CNN expanded the ability to recognize characteristics that are important for defect detection, such as minute variations at the pixel level that point to a flaw. The CNN model identified patterns linked to supervised learning. The CNN model identified patterns linked to different kinds of faults through supervised learning. It was able to distinguish between real flaws and allowable modifications as a result. Iterative training was used to progress the model's accuracy, lower false positives, and make sure it could identify a variety of flaws. For real-time inspection, the trained CNN was incorporated into the production line. In a matter of seconds, the CNN examined the pictures taken as each wafer moved through the imaging station, pointing out any flaws for examination. Wafers that the system recognized were either thrown away or forwarded to human specialists for additional examination.

After CNN-based flaw detection was incorporated, the manufacturer's quality control procedure saw significant enhancements. The following key benefits as followed. Only wafers free of flaws advanced to the following stage of production. The CNN exhibited superior accuracy in flaw finding when compared to manual examination. The CNN system's real-time processing allowed for quicker decision-making and a quicker reaction to possible quality problems. By retraining on fresh datasets, the CNN model might be readily modified to examine other wafer or material kinds, providing adaptability for upcoming production requirements. A comparatively recent semiconductor manufacturer employed a system based on a CNN to check the wafers for micro-defects. Improved detection rates and reduction of inspection periods by about 50% were reported due to the application of the model of deep learning in the inspection process.

A chemical manufacturing plant used RL to optimize reaction times and temperatures, leading to a 15% increase in production yield while reducing energy consumption by 10%.

5.5.3 Optimizing Chemical Manufacturing with RL

Efficiency and production are key success factors in the severely competitive chemical production sector. An RL system was used in a chemical production facility to optimize temperature and reaction durations, two crucial parameters in chemical reactions. The goal was to increase production and reduce energy used in order to save a significant amount of money. As a result, the factory could able to reduce its energy usage by 10% and increase its output yield by 15%. This case study examines the advantages of the transition from RL to manufacturing process optimization.

Among the key problems the plant faced were unused chances for a higher production yield resulted from fixed working conditions that limited the ability to maximize output. The high energy requirements of chemical processes resulted in significant operational costs and negatively impacted the environment. In traditional optimization techniques, it is difficult to determine the relationship between reaction time and yield. To solve these problems, the chemical manufacturing company implemented an RL system to make decisions by interacting with an environment. The objective of the RL agent is to determine the ideal temperature and reaction time parameters in order to optimize yield and reduce the amount of energy [26]. Gathering historical data from the plant's production operations was the first step, and it included various conditions for the reaction (e.g., timeframes, temperatures, pressures), yields corresponding to each set of criteria, and measures of energy consumption. The following elements were used in the design of the RL agent. State Space is described the reaction's current state, including variables like temperature, reaction duration, and energy usage. Action Space is the range of possible actions the agent can take, like changing the temperature or reaction time. Reward Function specified the objectives of the agent. A number of elements were combined to determine the reward, including maximizing output yield, reducing energy use, and penalizing circumstances that resulted in subpar products.

5.6 CHALLENGES AND CONSIDERATIONS

Deep learning presents significant opportunities for intelligent manufacturing, but several challenges must be overcome. Deep learning offers massive potential for intelligent manufacturing; there are challenges that need to be addressed are as discussed below.

5.6.1 Data Quality and Availability

Large amounts of high-quality data are necessary for deep learning models to be trained effectively. In the manufacturing sector, data can often be noisy, incomplete, or inconsistent. To ensure the success of deep learning applications, it is vital to focus on precise collection of data and preprocessing. In intelligent manufacturing, information availability and quality are critical because they have a direct behavior on how well analytics, AI-driven systems, and decision-making procedures work. Accurate, comprehensive, consistent, and timely data guarantees that machine learning models and algorithms can produce trustworthy predictions and insights. The term "data availability" explains the persistent and easy admittance to real-time data from many sources, such as commercial systems, sensors, and IoT devices. When collective, they make predictive maintenance, effective resource allocation, and streamlined production processes possible. Vigorous data management techniques are critical for the achievement of smart manufacturing programs since deprived data quality or limited access can result in poor judgments, operational incompetence, and missed opportunities.

5.6.2 Model Interpretability

In particular, deep neural networks tend to be realized as unfamiliar due to their complex internal structures. Defining in what way models make decisions is vital in production, where safety and dependability are crucial. Research on interpretable AI models that essence on decision-making developments is increasing.

The internal structures of deep neural networks and other deep learning are always complicated. In manufacturing, the decision-making is crucial because of the safety and reliability consideration. The decision-making procedure is an important area of study in intelligent manufacturing. The "model interpretability" refers to the capacity to understand decision-making of models, which are sometimes unpredictable. In manufacturing industry, decisions can impact safety and efficiency. So it is important to ensure that AI models not only serve a function but also provide transparency and accountability. Interpretability is essential for troubleshooting and system confidence. This enables engineers to track the path taken by a model to come for a certain recommendation or forecast. In order to help users, comprehend model behavior, make educated adjustments, and adhere to safety or regulatory requirements, approaches, such as feature reputation, Shapley Additive Explanations, and local surrogate models, are employed to explain difficult decisions.

5.6.3 Computational Resources

The computational power and memory requirement is very high for large architectures of training deep learning models like CNNs or RNNs. For manufacturers who do not have the access to high-performance computing resources, training of deep learning models is challenging. For the extensive use cases of industries, developing deep learning models requires huge computational power. High-performance equipment, cloud services, and specialized hardware accelerators (such as GPUs and TPUs) are often important to achieve the requirement. High training and implication times can postpone model deployment, limit scalability, and increase costs. The sophisticated hardware, software, and data processing skills needed to enable IoT, AI, and machine learning technologies, which are referred to as computational resources in intelligent manufacturing. These resources, which manage enormous volumes of real-time data produced by sensors, robotics, and production systems, include strong processors, edge computing devices, cloud platforms, and fast networks. In manufacturing operations, predictive analytics, process optimization, and adaptive decision-making are made possible by efficient computational resources. They ease activities like supply chain management, digital twin simulations, and quality inspection, guaranteeing smooth direction and integration across all the parts of a smart factory. Scalable and effective computational resources are crucial for meeting Industry 4.0's demands for speed, precision, and flexibility as production becomes more data-driven.

5.6.4 Scalability and Maintenance of AI Models

It has been noted that moving from successful implementation of any particular deep learning solution in experimental ways to manufacturing can be challenging, largely based on the idea that regular maintenance, along with the potential need to continuously train new approaches based on new data, new pieces of equipment, or new manufacturing goals, has higher maintenance costs. There is an increase in the demand for computation in the manufacturing process. Deep learning solution development at measure requires huge infrastructure investments across different production lines or manufacturing sites. In addition, every new setup can call for separate training, adaptation, and computational resources [27]. The flexibility of smart systems, in regard to intelligent manufacturing, is achieved by the continuous update of AI models. By so doing, it achieves cumulative complexity without any loss in performance. To offer distributed data processing and model deployment over a large number of systems or factories, AI models should support large volumes of data. In turn, this demands powerful infrastructure, such as edge-cloud computing. Maintaining includes activities like repeatedly updating models with new data, specifying idea meanings, and optimizing processes in order to meet changing settings and specifications. Such activities and processes are simplified through automated systems designed for combined learning integration and retraining processes, and model performance. AI models are maintained with respect to changing demands and specifications in intelligent manufacturing systems through scalability.

5.6.5 Handling High-Dimensional and Noisy Data

High-dimensional data is produced in large measures during manufacturing (e.g., sensor data photos videos and telemetry) that may contain redundant data or be noisy. Complex data can cause deep learning models to overfit or lose important indications. Noisy data can result in reduced model accuracy, unproductive models, longer exercises periods, and higher computing expenses. Large volumes of complex data including telemetry information images, videos, and sensor data are produced in manufacturing settings. Important indications may be obscured by the noise or unnecessary details that are generally present in this data. The inability of deep learning models to differentiate noise from data leads to overfitting. This may reduce accuracy and increase processing costs. Handling noisy data in intelligent manufacturing includes addressing challenges like complex datasets. It difficult to extract meaningful data from the sensor data and logs. To achieve this, advanced methods like dimensionality reduction (e.g., Principal Component Analysis (PCA), t-distributed Stochastic Neighbor Embedding (t-SNE)) and noise filtering (e.g., Kalman filters, smoothing algorithms) are used [28]. Additionally, deep learning models such as autoencoders help to identify patterns in noisy data. Robust data preprocessing, feature selection, and model regularization are also employed to improve model accuracy. AI systems can make predictions or decisions in spite of the noisy data.

5.6.6 High Costs of Implementation

Incorporating deep learning in manufacturing industries requires the major investment in relations of hardware, software, setup, and expert personnel. This makes a huge barrier for small- and medium-sized businesses or industries who have less budget. Such industries face the challenges in implementing the deep learning-based intelligent manufacturing because of high cost. The large data can make the deep learning models to be easily overfitted that are patterns which are not transferable to other datasets. The manufacturing system is often prone to work under the difficult environment in which the deep learning models are dependable on circumstance. The overfitting high-dimensional data can be effortlessly overfitted by deep learning models, which can discover patterns that are not transferable to other datasets. This is particularly problematic in manufacturing, where models must be dependable and consistently perform under a variety of circumstances. In adding to decreasing the model's dependability, overfitting has an adverse effect on safety which is essential in industrial settings. The considerable investment needed for cutting-edge technologies, infrastructure, and staff training is the main cause of the high implementation charges in intelligent manufacturing. Acquiring IoT-enabled apparatus, robotics, edge computing systems, AI-driven software, and high-speed communication networks is essential to set up smart factories, but these might be unaffordable, particularly for small- and medium-sized businesses. The expenditures are further increased by keeping cybersecurity and integration inheritance systems with contemporary technologies. Costs are increased further by the fact that these systems need to be designed, implemented, and managed by qualified experts. However, the initial costs can be compensated over time by improved product quality and quantity.

5.6.7 Dynamic Manufacturing Environments

The manufacturing environment is dynamic because of variations in product categories, materials, machine configurations, and workflows. Such variability can affect the efficiency of a model in deep learning trained on static datasets. In dynamic situations, models may not regulate well in the case of deviations, which might result in incorrect predictions or decisions. The rapidly changing demands, measures, and outside influences characterize dynamic manufacturing surroundings, which demand real-time adaptation of the system. Quite often, dynamic settings are also marked by diverse consumer requirements, complex supply chains, and multiple production inputs. The ability to make decisions based on real-time data and forecasts is enabled through quick decision-making techniques and real-time analytics, while intelligent manufacturing achieves this through leveraging artificial intelligence, as well as IoT, in controlling changing dynamics [29]. It involves deep learning algorithms that optimize processes related to schedules in construction, for example, machines through efficiency, affordability, and ability to regulate based on changing market dynamics and processes. The dynamic environment of changing productivity involves extremely flexible systems that were specifically put in place and engineered to respond well to change, variations in design, and unscheduled interruptions. These involve sophisticated technologies, robots, artificial intelligence, and changes enabled through IoT. Production lines can change over between different tasks, fine-tune the usage of resources allocated toward different tasks in the line, and even extend the processes as the need arises due to the dynamic nature of the environment [30]. It values flexibility over other traits that a static system lives by. Deep learning takes these kinds of environments further with the inclusion of tools like predictive analytics and development optimization. As a result, the need for downtime or waste is lessened with the efficient usage of resources like energy or materials. The need for Industry 4.0 is represented by these kinds of situations.

5.7 FUTURE TRENDS IN INTELLIGENT MANUFACTURING

The development of intelligent manufacturing is expected to witness the merging of deep learning with other innovative technologies. Here are some emerging trends to observe:

5.7.1 Edge Computing and Real-Time Data Processing

Edge computing is processing the information closer to anywhere it comes from like on a manufacturing floor and not as centralized data centers. This method is especially appropriate for critical manufacturing tasks since it lowers potential and enables real-time decision-making. The trend toward edge AI, which combines AI algorithms directly into edge devices, is anticipated to continue growing in the future. A new degree of automation and intelligence will be possible as a result of improving manufacturing systems' decision-making abilities. Manufacturing equipment sensors are capable of gathering enormous volumes of operational data. By processing this data, locally edge computing makes it possible to spot trends that point to approaching failures before they interrupt production. The downtime of systems and malfunctions can be prevented by using proactive maintenance. The edge computing with AI models can adjust the production parameter of the manufacturers. The usage of adaptive optimization keeps the manufacturing process effective and reduces the resource consumption. Unlike relying upon a centralized server in a cloud, in edge computing in intelligent systems of manufacturing, processing occurs at, or rather relatively close to, the point of origin, such as sensors, machines, or systems. The advantage of this form of processing, which involves analyzing key information at the edge, is that bandwidth consumption is reduced along with processing delay, thus encouraging applications in intelligent systems as well as robotics in manufacturing. Edge computing, when paired with AI and IoT, produces robust and effective industrial systems that can adjust to changing production demands, guarantee quicker reactions to irregularities, and increase overall operational efficiency.

5.7.2 Digital Twins and Virtual Simulation

Digital twins are virtual visualizations of real manufacturing systems. Deep learning can be integrated with digital twins for modeling scenarios, predicting output, and optimizing production constraints. Proper improvement and fast iterations do not interfere with the general physical operation going on. Real-time analysis of high-dimensional, multi-sensor data by DL-supported digital twins can show microscopic patterns or anomalies.

With predictive models like Transformers or LSTMs capable of predicting machine failures or quality issues days or weeks ahead, maintenance and exclusive down times can be avoided. "Intelligent manufacturing" utilizes digital twins, which are digital replicas of "actual things" or measures based on information that is often derived from the IoT and other supplementary sources, and use this information to replicate the behaviors of an "actual thing" in real time. With the help of "cutting-edge" analytical and machine learning tools, this provides the intelligent manufacturer an unparalleled opportunity to "increase understanding" based on how the digital twin is capable of learning from its surroundings through the aid of deep learning tools. By emulating actual circumstances, it facilitates enhancing the designs of products, predictive maintenance activities, and even conducting dynamic simulations. A significant element of Industry 4.0, digital twins, foster innovation and develop more versatile and data-based industrial processes.

5.7.3 AI-Driven Automation and Decision-Making

The artificial systems function just like humans. Various deep learning models, which work in collaboration with AI, are engaged in the process of offering support in human decision-making. It also includes a wide array of intelligent systems to assist operators in performing complex tasks and advice, enhancing safety. Deep learning thus enables the robots to comprehend human intention, voice commands, and gestures in real time to facilitate safe and seamless collaboration. This collaborative integration of AI systems and devices that work along with machines, robots, and humans to improve processes is called collaborative AI for intelligent manufacturing systems. With the assistance of collaborative AI systems, which utilize deep learning tools, there is better assessment of data in a real-time environment and better information sharing between machines. This also enables the interactions of robots with humans, which is also a major advantage. With collaborative AI systems, there is better learning from interactions between people, resulting in the flexibility of production. This is also a very important component of intelligent systems where there is better cooperative work of many agents, such as AI systems, to effectively implement challenging processes such as adaptive production.

5.7.4 Sustainability and Green Manufacturing

By improving resource usage, cutting wastage, and lowering energy consumption, deep learning is important in sustainable industry. AI-driven sustainability developments in the future will focus on creating circular economies and eco-friendly production techniques. Deep learning algorithms reduce waste and help guarantee product quality by predicting the optimal requirement of raw materials. These models analyze past production data to determine the exact quantity of materials needed for product optimization. This approach minimizes overuse of raw materials and significantly reduces wastage. Deep learning-based visual inspection systems that identify defects in real time reduce the production of defective goods and enable timely adjustments. By eliminating the need for redundant or rework, this lowers the quantity of material waste. AI models maximize energy use by analyzing usage patterns and making recommendations for improvements. By using precise process controls, intelligent systems reduce material waste. Designing sustainable materials and recycling procedures are made easier by deep learning. AI facilitates comprehensive evaluations of environmental impacts.

5.8 CONCLUSION

In conclusion, production systems become well-organized, adaptable, and data-driven because they are laid on a backbone of deep learning-based intelligent manufacturing systems. The use of AI, machine learning, and advanced analytics allowed manufacturers to optimize their product quality, detect possible failures, and optimize production processes with so far unimaginable precision. Thanks to this, complex techniques, like dynamic supply chain optimization and real-time quality checks, can be executed by deep learning automation within a knowledge base. This provides flexibility in industrial operations. There are, however, challenges like implementation cost, scalability, and model interpretability that still remain. Despite all this, deep learning promises much in the future in terms of reduction in downtime, better management of resources, and flexibility in customization. Thus, deep learning has become an essential component in Industry 4.0. Intelligent manufacturing will continue to unveil new possibilities in innovation, sustainability, and competition in the industry in accordance with technology.

REFERENCES

1. Mandloi, B., Dubey, G. P., & Tahiliani, K. (2023). A LSTM based Deep Learning Model for Smart Manufacturing. *2023 6th International Conference on Information Systems and Computer Networks (ISCON)*, Mathura, India, pp. 1–4, https://doi.org/10.1109/ISCON57294.2023.10111964.
2. Hou, M., Li, P., Cheng, S., & Yu, J. (2024). CNN-Based Defect Detection in Manufacturing. *Advanced Control for Applications, 6*(4), e196. https://doi.org/10.1002/adc2.196
3. Qin, Y., Xiang, S., Chai, Y., & Chen, H. (2020). Macroscopic–Microscopic Attention in LSTM Networks Based on Fusion Features for Gear Remaining Life Prediction. *IEEE Transactions on Industrial Electronics*, vol. 67, no. 12, pp. 10865–10875, Dec. 2020, doi: 10.1109/TIE.2019.2959492
4. Chen, M. Y., Lughofer, E. D., & Egrioglu, E. (2022). Deep Learning and Intelligent System Towards Smart Manufacturing. *Enterprise Information Systems*, 16(2), 189–192. https://doi.org/10.1080/17517575.2021.1898050.
5. Wang, J., Ma, Y., Zhang, L., Gao, R. X., & Wu, D. (2018). Deep Learning for Smart Manufacturing: Methods and Applications. *Journal of Manufacturing Systems*, 48, 144–156. https://doi.org/10.1016/j.jmsy.2018.01.003.
6. Barari, A., de Sales Guerra Tsuzuki, M., Cohen, Y. et al. (2021). Editorial: Intelligent Manufacturing Systems Towards Industry 4.0 Era. *The Journal of Intelligent Manufacturing,* 32, 1793–1796. https://doi.org/10.1007/s10845-021-01769-0.
7. Liang, S., Rajora, M., Liu, X., Yue, C., Zou, P., & Wang, L. (2018). Intelligent Manufacturing Systems: A Review. *International Journal of Mechanical Engineering and Robotics Research*, 7(3), 324–330. Doi: 10.18178/ijmerr.7.3.324-330
8. Essien, A. & Giannetti, C. (2020). A Deep Learning Model for Smart Manufacturing Using Convolutional LSTM Neural Network Autoencoders. *IEEE Transactions on Industrial Informatics*,16(9), 6069–6078. https://doi.org/10.1109/TII.2020.2967556.
9. Vahid, N., & Farrokh, S. (2021). A Review on Deep Learning in Machining and Tool Monitoring: Methods, Opportunities, and Challenges. *The International Journal of Advanced Manufacturing Technology*, 115(9), 2683–2709. https://doi.org/10.1007/S00170-021-07325-7.

10. Jiang, Y., Dai, P., Fang, P., Zhong, R. Y., Zhao, X., & Cao, X. (2022). A2-LSTM for Predictive Maintenance of Industrial Equipment Based on Machine Learning. *Computers & Industrial Engineering*, 172(Part A), 108560. https://doi.org/10.1016/j.cie.2022.108560.
11. Gan, W. (2024). Semiconductor Wafer Defect Detection Based on Machine Learning. *Transactions on Computer Science and Intelligent Systems Research*, 6, 128–133. https://doi.org/10.62051/wr098130.
12. Zhang, W., Yang, D., & Wang, H. (2019). Data-Driven Methods for Predictive Maintenance of Industrial Equipment: A survey. *IEEE Systems Journal*, 13(3), 2213–2227. https://doi.org/10.1109/jsyst.2019.2905565.
13. Liu, S., & Cheng, H. (2024). Manufacturing Process Optimization in the Process Industry. *International Journal of Information Technology and Web Engineering*, 19, 1–20. https://doi.org/10.4018/IJITWE.338998.
14. Rai, R., Tiwari, M. K., Ivanov, D., & Dolgui, A. (2021). Machine Learning in Manufacturing and Industry 4.0 Applications. *International Journal of Production Research*, 59(16), 4773–4778. https://doi.org/10.1080/00207543.2021.1956675.
15. Xie, T., Huang, X., & Choi, S. (2021). Intelligent Mechanical Fault Diagnosis Using Multisensor Fusion and Convolution Neural Network. *IEEE Transactions on Industrial Informatics*, 18(5), 3213–3223. https://doi.org/10.1109/tii.2021.3102017.
16. Li, X., Wang, B., Liu, C. et al. (2020). Intelligent Manufacturing Systems in COVID-19 Pandemic and Beyond: Framework and Impact Assessment. *Chinese Journal of Mechanical Engineering*, 33, 58.
17. Liu, C., Tang, D., Zhu, H., & Nie, Q. (2021). A Novel Predictive Maintenance Method Based on Deep Adversarial Learning in the Intelligent Manufacturing System. *IEEE Access*, 9, 49557–49575. https://doi.org/10.1109/access.2021.3069256.
18. Li, W., Liang, Y., & Wang, S. (2021). *Data Driven Smart Manufacturing Technologies and Applications*. Springer Nature. https://doi.org/10.1007/978-3-030-66849-5
19. Muduli, K., Kommula, V. P., Yadav, D. K., Selvan, M. C. P., & Kandasamy, J. (2023). *Intelligent Manufacturing Management Systems: Operational Applications of Evolutionary Digital Technologies in Mechanical and Industrial Engineering*. John Wiley & Sons.
20. Huang, R., Li, J., Li, W., & Cui, L. (2019). Deep Ensemble Capsule Network for Intelligent Compound Fault Diagnosis Using Multisensory Data. *IEEE Transactions on Instrumentation and Measurement*, 69(5), 2304–2314. https://doi.org/10.1109/tim.2019.2958010.
21. Ghadoui, M. E., Mouchtachi, A., & Majdoul, R. (2023). Intelligent Surface Roughness Measurement Using Deep Learning and Computer Vision: A Promising Approach for Manufacturing Quality Control. *The International Journal of Advanced Manufacturing Technology*, 129(7–8), 3261–3268. https://doi.org/10.1007/s00170-023-12457-z.
22. Chaudhary, A., Sharma, V., & Alkhayyat, A. (2024). *Intelligent Manufacturing and Industry 4.0: Impact, Trends, and Opportunities*. CRC Press.
23. Wang, J. (2024). *Intelligent Manufacturing System and Intelligent Workshop: Parameter Optimization, Process Planning, Workshop Scheduling, Typical Case*. Springer Nature.
24. Kumar, K., Kakandikar, G. M., & Davim, J. P. (2022). *Computational Intelligence in Manufacturing*. Woodhead Publishing.
25. Banjanović-Mehmedović, L., & Mehmedović, F. (2020). Intelligent Manufacturing Systems Driven by AI in Industry 4.0. In *Handbook of Research on Integrating Industry 4.0 in Business and Manufacturing*. IGI Global.
26. Kumar, K., Zindani, D., & Davim, J. P. (2019). Intelligent Manufacturing. In *Industry 4.0. SpringerBriefs in Applied Sciences and Technology*. Springer, Singapore, pp. 1–17. https://doi.org/10.1007/978-981-13-8165-2_1

27. Jiang, Y., Dai, P., Fang, P., Zhong, R. Y., Zhao, X., & Cao, X. (2022). A2-LSTM for Predictive Maintenance of Industrial Equipment Based on Machine Learning. *Computers & Industrial Engineering*, 172, 108560.
28. Tercan, H., & Meisen, T. (2022). Machine Learning and Deep Learning Based Predictive Quality in Manufacturing: A Systematic Review. *Journal of Intelligent Manufacturing*, 33, 1879–1905. https://doi.org/10.1007/s10845-022-01963-8
29. Fernández Martínez, A., Gonzalez Val, C., Martín, D., López, A., Muros, J., Llopis, A., Masood, J., Muiños-Landin, S. (2024). Reinforcement Learning in -Based Approaches in Manufacturing Environments. Doi: 10.1007/978-3-031-46452-2_11.
30. Sadiku, M. N. O., Ajayi-Majebi, A. J., & Adebo, P. O. (2023). Artificial Intelligence in Manufacturing. In: *Emerging Technologies in Manufacturing*, pp. 13–32. Springer. https://doi.org/10.1007/978-3-031-23156-8_2

6 AI and ML Techniques for Manufacturing Domain

Pankaj Kumar and Shashi Kant Singh

6.1 INTRODUCTION AND BACKGROUND

6.1.1 INTRODUCTION

A manufacturing system can thus be defined as an organized and well-coordinated system of resources, manufacturing tools, processes, and people who are organized with a view of efficiently transforming as many units of the manufacturing resources available into finished products. The goals of the system include organizing production in such a way that a range of targeted intermediate goods is produced based on the necessary materials, while maintaining a high quality and meeting the organizational needs for intermediate and final goods. The essence of a manufacturing system includes structures that contain tools and equipment used in cutting, molding, assembling, and finishing based on the type of manufactured product. These machines are used together with manpower; however, due to the increasing use of robots, most repetitive and dangerous operations are performed by these machines.

The material handling is one of the important components in the design of any manufacturing system because it provides guidance for the movement of the material within the production process both in the initial state and in the form of subassemblies and final products. Conveyors and automated guided vehicle, as well as robotic arms used for transporting there abouts, make certain that each workstation takes components in the right quantity at the right time available as opposed to spending considerable time sourcing for them. Further, human operators are needed in the operation of the system especially where flexibility, quality control, and changes to the routines in the production are desirable. They observe machine functionality, check products for compliance, and make on-the-spot judgments about problems.

Modern manufacturing systems incorporate information and control systems in their manufacturing operations. Real-time data like the state of manufacturing equipment, inventory, and other manufacturing processes are captured by technologies like Manufacturing Execution System and Enterprise Resource Planning, which help firms in enhancing their production efficiency and layout slow moving processes. The outcome of the enhanced chance for identifying probable breakdowns through analytics and machine learning (ML) reduces downtime and minimizes repairs expenses related to equipment.

Technology has enhanced the operational efficiency of manufacturing systems while at the same time improving flexibility. Automation and robotics contribute significantly to effecting high-speed repetitive functions with a lot of accuracy and

DOI: 10.1201/9781003582465-6

are used to prevent exposure of workers to dangerous conditions that may be fatal. ML and artificial intelligence (AI) are used to enhance processes, facilitate defects diagnosis, and optimize suggestions, thus raising efficiency and minimizing squander age. Further development of the Industrial Internet of Things (IIoT) improves manufacturing by integrating a network of sensors in objects so that data can be gathered in real time at every step of the process. It is crucial for manufacturers to be able to respond quickly to problems and maintain the quality due to real-time data from IIoT devices.

The major distinctions between a manufacturing system and an intelligent manufacturing system are therefore based on technology, flexibility, adaptability, and their ability to respond to changes within the production system. Where both of these systems work to transform materials into the final products, it is imperative that one considers the fact that both of these industrial models represent two distinct phases of the manufacturing process with significant peculiarities with regard to automation, decision-making, and performance.

6.1.1.1 Technology and Automation Level

Conventional manufacturing processes also depend on rigid automation and may include the use of apparatus that is programmed to produce the same output through uniformly defined operations. Generally, in these systems, automation is done in a sequential fashion, thus providing for very little flexibility. Scheduling and introducing change in product type calls for manual handling and reprogramming of the machines, which is expensive and time consuming. Moreover, data utilization in traditional systems is generally kept to fundamental process control and lacks real-time evaluation features.

Intelligent manufacturing systems apply solutions like AI, ML, and IIoT into the new manufacturing processes. They implant sensors and interconnected devices at various stages of the manufacturing conveyor line to acquire and analyze data in real time continually. This is effective because it provides the basis for predictive maintenance, process analysis, and subsequent changes, as well as for the creation of autonomous systems. Wise intelligent systems are based on the flexible automation, when different automated subsystems can modify parameters during the operation according to the changes of the production demand and the variability of the production processes.

6.1.1.2 Decision-Making and Adaptability

The majority of the decision processes in the traditional manufacturing system are usually carried out by operators or management. Automated procedures are performed by operators who have to monitor the overall process, the detection of abnormalities, and the correction of problems as and when they occur. The following decision-making process is highly dependent on humans, which translates to slow response to any issue since, and it is not very robust. There are systemic approaches that are more suited to consistency for those organizations with high-volume, low-variation production requirements, and modifying those elements for change can sometimes be done offline, but then the change disrupts production.

Smart manufacturing systems shift decision-making processes from conventional manual decision-making systems by utilizing data and technologies from artificial neural networks and ML. Analyzing the data by its patterns and shape, the system can identify problems, for example, wear of equipment or lack of efficiency in a process. The above systems are flexible in nature and can dynamically accommodate production fluctuations, market dynamics, and sometimes even some unfortunate events like delay of the supply chain. For instance, if one machine in an intelligent system detects some tweak in vibrations, it will inform the maintenance crews or even self-correct the parameters that may lead to breakdown, hence reducing down time.

6.1.1.3 Flexibility and Customization

While it is effective for environments that involve large volumes of work with little variation in the components needed, traditional systems are extremely rigid. They are most suitable for low-variability production environments, where many similar items are manufactured consecutively; reconfiguration costs and downtimes act as inhibiting factors to adjusting production lines. In conventional systems, generating or making special goods typically implies stopping a line to change tools, setup equipment, or align machines, thus cutting productivity.

The nature of intelligent systems is more flexible because they are easier to accommodate changes in the design of the product or the demand, and the production volume of the product. Malleable automation and modifiable tools enable the intelligent systems to switch between the variants without much interference. This flexibility is important for manufacturers facing consumer preferences that have called for personalized or custom designed goods. For instance, an intelligent manufacturing line of electronics might easily jump from one model variant to another or change features without requiring intervention and hence work less time on the changeover, which means faster time to market and more time to make the next product or enhance features.

6.1.1.4 Information Flow and Transparency

Traditional manufacturing often lacks real-time data integration and relies on isolated systems. Information flow is slower and segmented, leading to limited transparency in the production process. Data is typically collected after production stages for later analysis, which makes it difficult to address issues in real time and can result in delayed responses to problems, inefficiencies, or resource waste.

Intelligent systems provide a high level of transparency across all production stages through IIoT and integrated data systems. Each machine and sensor are interconnected, continuously feeding data to a centralized system that monitors performance, quality, and efficiency in real time. This real-time transparency enables immediate responses to fluctuations in supply, demand, or machine status. By creating a "digital twin" of the physical production environment, intelligent systems allow manufacturers to simulate changes and anticipate outcomes, thus minimizing risks and improving operational decisions.

6.1.1.5 Human Involvement and Skill Requirements

People are more involved in traditional systems, and operators are involved in the process of operating the machines and over seeing their corresponding problems, and the quality as well. A lot of technical know-how is required to some equipment for operating them and fine tuning them manually. Consequently, these systems demand additional operation labor but tends to sacrifice the flexibility of manufacturing production.

Intelligent systems delegate most of the tasks carried out by a human worker in an organization to mere oversight and choice-making. People observe the data interfaces and act upon it as and when it sends a signal to them instead of constantly having to interfere with the production process. Knowledge about data statistics, AI and ML concepts, and ability to operate and solve issues related with automations systems is valued. This shift not only minimizes the frequency of making repetitive manual operations, but then it also optimizes the position of workers to create and fine-tune activities.

AI and ML application in the manufacturing sector is taking the industrial automation to the next level with the design of the intelligent manufacturing systems, in line with the Industry 4.0 and 5.0 objectives. Of importance, it is evident that both AI and ML not only make work more productive by automating regular processes, but also allow for the development of a self-optimizing and evolving system in which data is at the center of decision-making.

6.1.1.6 Predictive Maintenance

The integration of AI and ML is incredibly important when it comes to predictive maintenance that is so vital for cutting costs related to machine breakdowns, as well as managing time spent on maintenance. ML is where historical data captured by such devices as sensors and equipment logs are analyzed to determine likely patterns of equipment failure. This material introduces the idea that given possible failures, a kind of AI will inform a maintenance schedule only when required, thus avoiding the possibility of unanticipated equipment breakdowns, diametrically lowering repair costs, and optimizing equipment life. This active approach increases equipment reliability to its highest level, meaning that the equipment will be very productive most of the time.

6.1.1.7 Quality Control and Defect Detection

Other application areas, which have been adopted by AI and ML, are quality control. Many traditional quality checks methods are very slow and inaccurate and require a large amount of manpower. Using AI technologies of computer vision, in manufacturing systems, products can be inspected for defects at a very high level of throughput. ML models working on the video from previous production runs can identify faults and alert about possible quality problems with suggestions for enhancing the procedures. This has implications in increased product quality, improved customer satisfaction, low material scrap, and fewer reprocessing or product returns costs.

6.1.1.8 Process Optimization and Automation

AI and ML are very useful in process optimization where there is a large data from the production lines that the algorithms interpret to give the best operation conditions. Further, by analyzing such data, the parameters relating to temperature, speed, and pressure can be learned and finely adjusted in order to ensure sustained manufacturing productivity. In addition, automation by AI eliminates the need for people to solve multiple manufacturing procedures that require little or no personal input, thereby improving productivity and efficiency and at the same time reducing human interference. Another type of ML is named as reinforcement learning (RL) that allows systems to find out the right course of actions to achieve goals from trial to trial and also promotes self-automation.

6.1.1.9 Demand Forecasting and Inventory Management

Demand forecasting is one of the important elements of the supply chain, and with the help of AI, demand forecasting accurately determines the kind of demand for the next period based on previous sales data, seasonality, and macroeconomic indicators. This helps manufacturers to have an optimal inventory management system, avoid cases of stock out or overstock, and correspondingly coordinate their production plan with that of the market. As for any inherent forecast error, it is rectified with time using the ML algorithms and results in better reduction of extra inventory and enhanced cash flow of the business.

6.1.1.10 Supply Chain Optimization

Disruptions in the manufacturing supply chain are costly, and the supply chain itself is becoming more intricate. This is where AI and ML come in handy in order to counter these complexities and disruptions by presenting real-time feedback on the supply chain of the manufacturers. The data collected from suppliers and logistics providers as well as the market conditions can be used by the AI systems to recommend the right suppliers, the best way to route the goods and materials, and how best to ensure they will get to where they are needed in good time. These two factors also act to improve the visibility and agility of the supply chain and enable the manufacturers to deal with change or disruption appropriately.

6.1.1.11 Human–Machine Collaboration

Substantial AI under Industry 5.0 means that it is not about replacing people, which is what human–AI mainly aims at improving. These tools can help your workers by giving them advice on what to do next, or even do simple tasks such as analysis for the workers. In manufacturing, this equates to tools that better inform workers so their routine decisions can be made quickly, providing them more time to zone in on the creative work like creating new manufacturing methods and the future planning of work. Cobots involve sharing human-interactive tasks that are either monotonous or require heavy tasks but must not harm the human partner at any one point.

6.1.1.12 Energy Management and Sustainability

AI and ML help achieve sustainable goals by improving energy and resource consumption in production plants. When studying patterns of energy utilization, the AI techniques can suggest how to decrease the consumption during specific high-demand periods or increase the effectiveness of the machines decreasing costs and negative impact on the environment. These systems are also used in waste minimization – an aspect relating to the efficient use of materials in determining opportunities for increasing resource efficiency and assisting companies in attaining sustainability objectives.

6.1.1.13 Product Design and Customization

Generative design, in particular, powered by AI, introduces manufacturers to a set of promising configurations of a certain product based on specified limitations (material, weight, cost, etc.). Besides increasing the speed of product design, it also allows design of lightweight and efficient products focusing on increasing differentiation opportunities for consumers. In addition, mass customization becomes manageable with the help of AI algorithms that can easily adapt production settings for large-scale production of customized products.

6.1.2 Background

The background research work presents brief overviews of works done by other authors, along with the focus of their work and the application of AI/ML in the manufacturing arena.

Maki and Loparo considered the application of neural networks to specify the fault in the manufacturing process and showed that AI has the capability to model the organizational correlation to specific values of the measured data to predict the equipment failures in the process. This was one of the first papers to show how neural networks could be used to supervise/manipulate manufacturing processes by analyzing signals detected by sensors [1].

The CNN-based approach for visual inspection in manufacturing context was studied by Villalba-Diez et al. [2]. The work explained how CNNs can be implemented to detect defects and irregularities on the surfaces of products during production. This work was among the first to directly apply deep learning to perform complex precise tasks such as detecting defects and replacing traditional image processing methods [2].

Supervised learning algorithms (regression and classification) were used for quality control in manufacturing by Schmitt et al. [3]. In the two case studies, the researchers also showed how to predict product defects and classify product quality using the models trained on historical data in real time. It presented one of the strong aspects of ML for improving the quality assurance activities in organizations that require high levels of product dependability [3].

Kaparthi and Bumblauskas used decision trees for the purpose of predictive maintenance, and where ML models were trained using sensor and maintenance data to predict potential failures of machines, it was a significant advancement toward data-driven prediction of required maintenance, which can be costly if the core causes are not addressed quickly and system reliability can benefit from overall [4].

RL has been introduced by Erharter et al. for the process improvement in manufacturing. Using RL algorithms, the researchers were able to align production parameters including the settings of the machines, movement of materials, and energy consumption in real time. RL was depicted as an effective means for the processes' optimization in the context of adaptation to new conditions, errors being corrected through a subsequent practice [5].

This research by Walas and Redchuk was primarily concerned with using IIoT and ML for real-time interpretation of massive data gathered from sensors. This also made the equipment condition tracking and the schedule possible in production in the manufacturing sector. In this paper, an emerging concept of IIoT was woven into the increasingly significant role toward delivering sophisticated data analytics and providing real-time process control in the advanced manufacturing systems [6].

Anandan et al. focused on smart IIoT platforms to develop a real-time health monitoring and failure prediction framework based on ML algorithms on analyzing sensor data from the industrial machines. This paper also explained that IIoT could offer the data platform needed for the real-time predictive maintenance using ML [7].

Saheb et al. suggested a holistically integrated AI and ML for realizing the paradigm of sustainable manufacturing, addressing energy reduction, waste minimization, and resource optimization across the manufacturing processes. This paper described an application of AI in promoting green manufacturing policies while putting environmental concerns as an important component in the manufacturing economy of the current world [8].

Soori et al. projected the concept of advanced digital twins embedded with AI and ML for modeling and improving the manufacturing process in real time. The authors showed how predictions about system behaviors, fault diagnostic capabilities, and optimization of production could be made using digital twins in manufacturing. In addition, it introduced the adoption of the digital twin technology with AI to improve the reliability, effectiveness, and predictive nature of manufacturing [9].

Darwish examined the possibility of using AI and human–robot interaction with advanced industrial technologies within the Industry 5.0 framework. But it highlighted how this weak form of AI recruitment was enabling the creation of more humanistic and cooperative manufacturing settings in preparation for Industry 5.0 [10].

6.2 FUNDAMENTALS OF AI AND ML TECHNIQUES IN THE MANUFACTURING DOMAIN

AI and ML in the manufacturing context are supported by an original set of basic techniques that enable us to extract information from raw data to be used for the development of models and improvement of processes. Such fundamentals facilitate the automation of manufacturing systems and promote efficiency as well as quality and outcome prediction formulating the basis for the intelligent environments seen in Figure 6.1.

6.2.1 Data Collection and Preprocessing

The data plays a critical role in AI and ML across the manufacturing context. Own equipment, devices, and sensors are the source of large data sets, including machine condition data, as well as data about environmental conditions within a factory. However, current data can be understood only if it is first preprocessed or prepared for consumption by these AI algorithms which includes cleaning the data, normalizing it, and structuring it in a manner that is interpretable by these ML algorithms. Data preprocessing is always an issue of handling missing values, noise, and feature transformation, or in other words, the conversion of raw data into engineering variables which can characterize the manufacturing environment, such as temperature trends, production speed, or vibration frequencies.

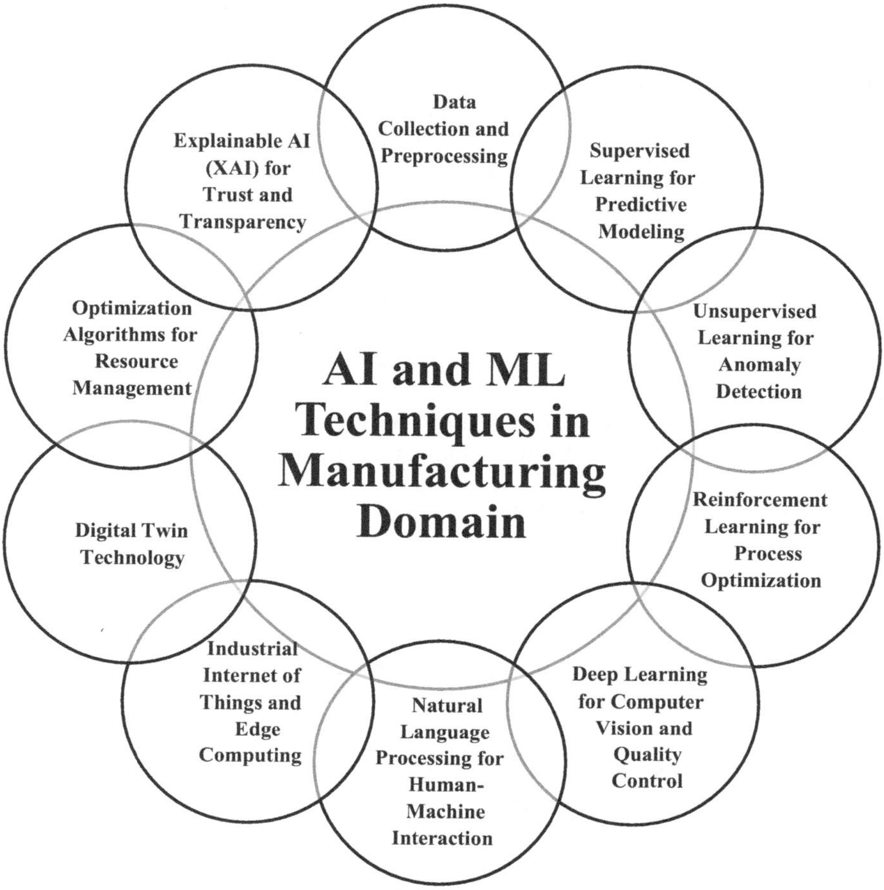

FIGURE 6.1 AI and ML techniques in the manufacturing domain.

6.2.2 Supervised Learning for Predictive Modeling

Supervised Learning is one of the most popular for learning in manufacturing when there is an access to the historical data containing labels [11]. In supervised learning, algorithms are trained on input–output pairs like production parameters and output quality and machine performance and maintenance. When applied, this training enables the model to identify the relationship in the data and make inference on new unseen data. One of the major use cases includes the one under the category of supervised learning, whereby models are trained to identify signs of possible equipment failure to plan the maintenance ahead of time to reduce the time that equipment will be out of service.

6.2.3 Unsupervised Learning for Anomaly Detection

This is particularly important in cases whereby input data may not be possible to categorize into labeled sets. In manufacturing, the unsupervised learning involved in clustering and anomaly discovering determines structure and outliers in the datasets devoid of prior class information. For instance, by categorizing sensor data of equipment, an unsupervised model can define a normal or standard regime of the equipment [12]. The baseline that is maintained is such that any new data which logically would not be expected to differ greatly from the previous data would be flagged as an outlier and identified by the system as indicative of perhaps equipment failure or low quality. It enables the management to avoid gaps in quality to be produced due to lack of necessary resources and also sustain quality in products to be developed.

6.2.4 RL for Process Optimization

RL is a kind of ML algorithm in which an agent decides, at every time step, the action it must take to completely pass a certain environment through making choices based on the reward level of the activity [13]. RL can be used in the manufacturing environment especially applied for process control where the parameters including temperature and pressure are managed depending on feedback about quality and/or speeds in the production line. The system in practice discovers which results in the best actions or behavior with regard to a certain goal, for instance, less energy use or increased traffic flow. RL is especially useful to enhance production in situations that would need constant tweak for efficiency in manufacturing industries.

6.2.5 Deep Learning for Computer Vision and Quality Control

One of the types of ML is known as deep learning, which applies artificial neural networks to analyze intricate data such as images, sound, and text that have not been structured. In manufacturing, CNNs comprise deep learning techniques related to the use of computer vision in features such as automated quality control by the use of images to inspect defective products. Skilled human workers do not have the capacity to check for minute details such as scratch, and development of deformities, but deep learning models can accomplish all that in real time as products pass through production lines. This technique is used in industries where appearance is high standard and cannot be compromised, such as the electronics industry, automotive industries, and the space industry.

6.2.6 Natural Language Processing (NLP) for Human–Machine Interaction

Advanced forms of NLP enable AI to understand the human language and therefore interact with the operators. In manufacturing, application of NLP may include voice control manufacturing; the operators speak to the machines, informing them what to do, where to find something or what ails them. Furthermore, using NLP chatbots or virtual assistants, technicians can receive answers to corresponding questions, solutions to certain machine issues, or step-by-step instructions for the maintenance process. This enhances a refined and natural engagement of the human operators with the manufacturing system.

6.2.7 IIoT and Edge Computing

IIoT is a key part of AI and ML in manufacturing since it supports the collection of real-time data from connected devices in the factory floor. In IIoT, devices like smart sensors or smart actuators collect data like temperature, vibration, energy, or runtime. However, to handle this data, especially with applications where real-time response is expected and needed, edge computing can be utilized to perform data processing locally. When IIoT is integrated with the AI algorithms in manufacturing systems, systems' productivity gains increased levels of automation because machines can minimize performance failures due to data gathered within the system.

6.2.8 Digital Twin Technology

The systematic digitalization of the concrete assets, processes, or systems is a process of expanding the manufacturers' capability to mimic, control, and enhance physical operations through the application of a virtual scenario. Data from the physical asset is run through current AI and ML algorithms to update the digital twin and allows the manufacturer to simulate changes, detect problems, and forecast breakdowns in digital before they occur in the physical asset. Digital twins create insights into the operations of the systems and enable better resource management, schedules for maintenance, and optimization of all processes.

6.2.9 Optimization Algorithms for Resource Management

Optimization algorithm is an important resource for dynamic management of resources in manufacturing: scheduling, inventory, and supply chain management. AI-based optimization models rely on the analyzed data in order to distribute resources that would generate the highest value with the lowest possible risk [14]. For instance, scheduling processes of machining practices incorporating availability of the machine, maintenance schedule, and flow of materials optimizes the production line, and inventory management takes care of proper stocking in-vogue with the forecasted demand, thus reducing the count of idle stocks.

6.2.10 Explainable AI for Trust and Transparency

Human staking holds that as AI and ML will be increasingly incorporated into the manufacturing operation; explainable AI is growing in relevance to guarantee that operators can comprehend and trust AI-designed decisions. Explainable AI techniques help in making the AI models more understandable for the manufacturers and help in understanding why an ML model predicted or recommend a certain value. In domains like quality control, explainable AI helps to understand why some product anomalies were highlighted in order to enhance both the system and the production line.

6.3 THE IMPACT OF AI AND ML ON THE MANUFACTURING DOMAIN

AI and ML are shifting the Industry 4.0 to Industry 5.0 in manufacturing through improved flexibility, operations efficiency, and decision-making. Following are the key impacts of AL and ML on the manufacturing domain, shown in Figure 6.2.

6.3.1 Enhanced Automation and Efficiency

- **Smart Robotics**: Sophisticated AI and ML robotic systems are being used in complex operations and also for monitoring and controlling operations such as assembly line, packing, and round the clock production systems by enhancing speed and quality [15]. From RL, a robot is able to modify its behavior to meet new assignments and conditions without human influence.
- **Process Optimization**: Looking at the production data, the ML algorithms are able to recognize the flaws within the processes. For instance, ML can alter some settings throughout its operation to keep running under the best conditions, hence minimizing loss and maximizing returns.

6.3.2 Predictive Maintenance and Downtime Reduction

- **Condition Monitoring and Failure Prediction**: ML algorithms also work based on data from sensors connected to the equipment to give early signals of failure to enable maintenance. This model leads to better cost control and reduction of unexpected outages of the airplane.

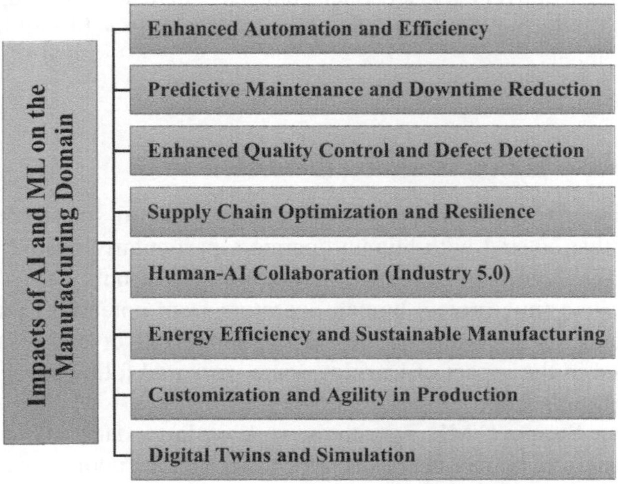

FIGURE 6.2 Impact of AI and ML on the manufacturing domain.

- **Maintenance Optimization**: Another is that predictive maintenance is the process of planning maintenance activities on when they are required rather than on when they were earlier programmed to be conducted, thereby prolonging equipment life spans and minimizing expenditure on maintenance.

6.3.3 Enhanced Quality Control and Defect Detection

- **Computer Vision for Inspection**: Computer vision systems powered by AI identify defects in products or their color, texture, surface, or assembly issues with great effectiveness and efficiency. This not only minimizes errors by human inspectors, but also ensures uniformity and saves time when inspecting the structures.
- **Automated Quality Analytics**: To this end, ML can keep learning from quality data, giving manufacturers a better insight into the requirements of higher standards in their products, identifying where defects originate from, and the subsequent enhancement of general product quality and reduction of workstation rework.

6.3.4 Supply Chain Optimization and Resilience

- **Demand Forecasting**: The sales and other factors using artificial neural networks analyze historical data and the market requirements to determine future sales patterns accurately to minimize the production of excess stock.
- **Logistics and Route Planning**: AI and ML can help improve logistics by getting routine tasks like determining the shortest distance between the supplier and the buyer and hence minimize fuel consumption when providing a delivery service. Such changes help to adapt the supply chain, especially during disruption, because of flexibility achieved by the new arrangements.

6.3.5 Human–AI Collaboration (Industry 5.0)

- **Collaborative Robotics (Cobots)**: Cobot refers to smart collaboration robots that coexist with human operators particularly in line operations where they can help to reduce fatigue prone and bulky exercises while at the same time protect human operators from potential hazards while enhancing their production efficiency. This kind of robot can be also designed in the aspect of learning some work and following the speed of the operator's work.
- **Decision Support**: ML algorithms work on large data sets to churn out information to human managers which they can act upon. For example, in production, it can predict the next step to take in the manufacturing process or even recommend the source of materials for the production and at the sometimes leave the decision-making to human beings.

6.3.6 Energy Efficiency and Sustainable Manufacturing

- **Energy Management**: AI can enhance efficiency in using energy by monitoring the use and identify peak times for operation and then manage use to decrease energy demands. It also helps save energy and efficiency comes close to achieving sustainable development objectives.
- **Waste Reduction**: Through the use of Regression, time to market and resource is decreased, hence reducing wastage such as over usage of material or repeating a particular process. For example, it is possible to reduce waste when using additive manufacturing that is assisted by AI while also meeting the industry's goal of deploying sustainable manufacturing processes.

6.3.7 Customization and Agility in Production

- **Mass Customization**: AI and ML help production lines to switch between different product models as per the client requirements for individual products. The inference of ML is used to predict consumer preferences of given products, while the adjustment of parameters to control specific manufacturing settings means that customization can be managed easily.
- **Flexible Manufacturing**: In a production setting, AI-based systems can easily deploy new solutions to respond to production needs, thereby allowing ramp-up or ramp-down. This flexibility is important for manufacturers interested in a production process that will allow them to meet the market needs without major reconfiguration of the production line.

6.3.8 Digital Twins and Simulation

- **Virtual Modeling**: Digital twins establish a digital copy of the physical manufacturing process or the tools being used in production. Real-time data is fed into these models using ML algorithms, which constantly update these models for them to be used by manufacturers for emulation, for evaluation of consequences, and for discovering opportunities for enhancement.
- **Optimized Process Testing**: AI and ML techniques can help organizations simulate various changes in production processes before an actual implementation is made, which means that such adjustments are tested in a virtual environment only and the corresponding trial-and-error costs are eliminated.

6.4 AI AND ML APPLICATIONS IN THE MANUFACTURING DOMAIN

The applications of AI and ML in manufacturing are redefining production, quality, and supply chain mechanisms. The following section elaborates the descriptions of the applications, along with examples to understand how value is created for manufacturing industries, shown in Figure 6.3.

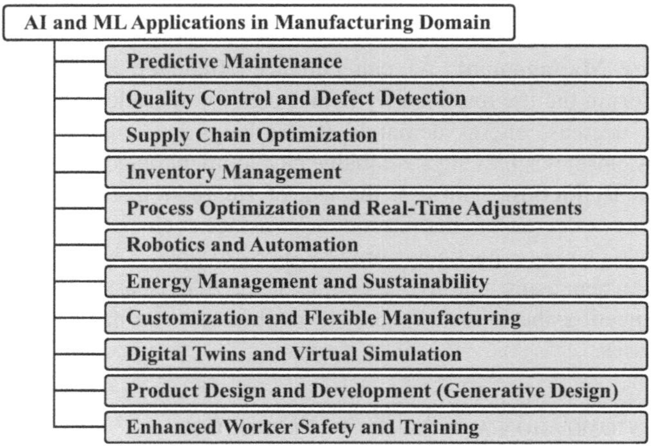

FIGURE 6.3 AI and ML applications in the manufacturing domain.

- **Predictive Maintenance**

  Practical application of predictive maintenance is based on using AI and ML when real data from the equipment sensors like temperatures, pressure, and vibrations are entered in the system to forecast equipment failure. This way, the manufacturers are only required to do maintenance, when necessary, hence little or no loss through frequent maintenance.

  One example of smart application is that General Motors (GM) applies it in its factories to detect impending failures of robotic arms on production lines. AI will help GM to analyze patterns of sensor data for anticipating when the part requires servicing and not after the machinery has already developed a fault, thus greatly cutting on the number of times a machine is stuck.
- **Quality Control and Defect Detection**

  Computer vision technology is applied in product monitoring during the process of its production to identify possible issues and abnormalities. This means that they are able to have quality checks in real time that are far better and more efficient than when using the traditional method of inspections.

  AI is also utilized by BMW in the assessment of vehicle parts through visual examination. Up-running cameras photograph the parts and AI algorithms check for defects in paint, assembly, and structural integrity on the production line. This makes high quality standards to be met and minimize situations whereby many substandard goods are produced and released to the market.
- **Supply Chain Optimization**

  AI and ML help improve the aspect of supply chain management through stock holding, demand prediction, and transportation virtually. With help of real-time statistics, AI algorithms consider historical sales, manager predictions, seasonal fluctuations, and other factors, such as markets, to predict demand in detail, manage storage, and identify optimal delivery routes.

In its supply chain, Siemens has employed AI. Siemens' AI system identifies inventory control because it uses production data and sales forecast to control inventory to remove over stock and stock shortage. Also, at the logistics level, to enhance transportation cost and time, the company has adopted AI, eradicating long routes.

- **Inventory Management**

  The intelligent inventory systems that incorporate AI keep track of stock and estimate when the ingredients shall be depleted, and place an order automatically when the stocks are low. It further assists in maintaining the right quantity of stocks by estimating the demand from trends of sale and the production calendar.

  Coca-Cola has applied this technology to control its inventory systems in several distribution centers. The AI system anticipates the users' requirements for the incoming raw materials and end products and manages the restocking process for overstocking or undersupply automatically [16].

- **Process Optimization and Real-Time Adjustments**

  AI and ML stabilize production parameters so as to maintain a production process in the best possible conditions. These variables are frequently checked through ML algorithms with a view of optimizing output and minimizing wastage by adjusting factors such as temperature, speed, and pressure.

  Procter&Gamble in its factories, for example, P&G, is now using AI to adjust the speed, volume, and frequency with which a detergent's ingredients are blended into a product, or the consistency of the output of shampoos. When it comes to manufacturing food products, the improper blend of ingredients leads to wastage of resources due to incorrect formulation; with the help of ML algorithms, the speed of mixing and the temperature are constantly checked to ensure quality and output [17].

- **Robotics and Automation**

  Robots and collaborative robots or cobots engage the human workforce in operations that are repetitive, exacting, or strenuous. These robots can also shape and improve their functionality by using RL and many other components of the ML family.

  At Amazon warehouses, robots controlled by AI are responsible for selecting goods, sorting and packing products, and effectively improving the rate of order fulfillment. Cobots share the workplace with their human counterparts taking over repetitive and time-consuming tasks like picking products on the shelves or sorting the packages [18].

- **Energy Management and Sustainability**

  The fourth one is smart energy management where AI is used to analyze the energy patterns and control energy through advising on the best times to use energy. This reduces cost and also acts in line with the company's environmental sustainability policy.

  In Schneider Electric-owned production sites, AI is deployed to analyze consumption in real time and to act on energy usage on its own. For example, it controls lighting, heating, and cooling depending on occupancy and production line, cutting on energy consumption [19].

- **Customization and Flexible Manufacturing**

  AI makes it possible to produce products and even services in large quantities but at the same time being customized to meet unique needs at a given instance due to flexible manufacturing lines. Manufacturers are able to use customer preference data to quickly and effectively customize products, thanks to the analysis offered by ML algorithms.

  Nike also uses AI to address customer needs and demands by addressing the fact that the firm produces customized products for the customer. Through AI-integrated design tools, Nike makes consumers to determine the color, material type, and design of the shoes. The specific parameters of production are then rapidly modified by the AI system and it is thus possible to satisfy specialized customer demands while continuing with typical production methods [20].
- **Digital Twins and Virtual Simulation**

  A digital twin is a digital representation of physical processes or systems of a production factory. These digital twins process production data in real time, thus modeling production processes through simulations for testing and scenario planning while not affecting real production lines.

  To illustrate, Rolls-Royce deploys the digital twins of its aircraft engines to experiment with various real-life situations. Creating a digital copy of the process of manufacturing the engines provides Rolls-Royce with the ability to track performance indices without direct interference and determine potential failures and organism's need in adjustments through simulations [21].
- **Product Design and Development (Generative Design)**

  Generative design tools are AI-based that generate and present different options for a part based on certain extra parameters like weight or strength or cost. These help to save time in the design process and allows engineers to evaluate new concepts in designs.

  General Electric applies generative design to parts of its jet engines. With the help of an AI-driven system, the product studies hundreds of thousands of design variants that correspond to the requirement of lightweight and durability. This has helped General Electric to design parts that are at the same time lighter and stronger, leading to enhanced fuel efficiency and performance [22].
- **Enhanced Worker Safety and Training**

  AI promotes the safety and security of workers since it supervises the conditions under which they work to identify risks. AI-based smart wearables and gadgets predict aspects such as the quality of the air in the workplace, the temperature, and avoid moving around during sensitive hours.

  Employing AI wearables, Toyota not only follows the physical state of its employees but also buzzes when they lift something improperly or enters a dangerous area. The following contributory factor is aimed at improving the overall working conditions and minimize work related accidents [23].

6.5 HOW AI AND ML SOLUTIONS CONTRIBUTE TO ACHIEVING MANUFACTURING EXCELLENCE?

AI or, to be accurate, ML is a very important factor influencing manufacturing excellence through efficiency, quality, flexibility, and sustainability. It is these technologies that are changing how manufacturers do business, providing answers that are effective for improving operational efficiency as well as overall results.

Manufacturing is one of the areas where AI and ML have made very impressive value additions, and one of the most remarkable areas that AI and ML have impacted is the predictive maintenance area. Conventional maintenance behavior recommends the use of planned or preventive measures or repairing a machine only when it has broken down. However, AI and ML solutions use actual data from sensors installed in the machines to identify the likelihood of the machine to fail. When and how the vibration, temperature, pressure, and other parameters change, AI can predict failures several days, weeks, or even months before they occur and the maintenance can be scheduled just before the failure. Such a transition from a predominately break-fix or reactive approach to contemplating and scheduling maintenance activities increases reliability and minimizes the frequency of equipment and asset failures, increases equipment reliability, and decreases repair costs and mean repair times, thereby improving the organizational and economic efficiency of asset utilization.

There is another field where I noticed AI and ML have a great perception, and that is, quality control. In the classical approach to manufacturing, quality assurance strategies use visual check, which can be labor extensive and riddled with inconsistencies. Computerized vision is a subfield of AI that enables line inspection of products to identify flaws or unevenness that is usually undetectable by vision. These systems can easily detect the slightest margins of variation in product qualities and thereby guarantee quality products. In addition, inspection data are integrated with ML algorithms in real time, which enhances the efficiency of the process, together with progressively increasing the accuracy of the algorithms used in quality control.

AI is also key to enhancing production processes and so is ML. Through processing of large history that is in terms of production, these AI systems can detect bottlenecks, cuts, and suggest small movements of production parameters such as temperature, speed, and type of material needed. Real time helps AI to constantly monitor the production process so that machines can be optimized in terms of their performance. This level of optimization is associated with less energy use, low wastage, and high overall through output. Further, AI systems can enable product differentiation within manufacturing since the production line can be easily redesigned to suit a particular design or type desired by the customer. This flexibility makes it possible for the manufacturers to act rapidly in satisfying the market demands by customizing their production while at the same time increasing their efficiency.

Regarding procurement and supply chain management, AI and ML improve evaluating decision-making and processes. Traditional Point of Sale (POS) systems being manually operated cannot anticipate change in demand patterns as accurately compared to AI-operated systems, which consider past sales patterns, market trends, and factors affecting demand. This results in improved storage control, and thereby a decreased likelihood of stockout or overstock situations. Also, AI is useful in logistics; in other words, certain buildings can define optimal ways to deliver goods by choosing the right path that takes less fuel and time. All these advancements assist the manufacturers to develop supply chains that are agile and robust – very important in the present unpredictable market situation.

They also bring energy efficiency and sustainability into the manufacturing unit and methods involved. With the help of analysis of energy utilization, AI is in the position to ensure that energy resources are utilized in projection with outlay, and thus, the issue of environmental degradation is also effectively tackled. For instance, AI in factories can automatically control lights, heating, and cooling depending on the production needs which in turn will save costs. In addition, AI provides more efficient use of materials to avoid waste, enhance the rates of recycling, and identify the areas that require reduction of resource consumption while manufacturing processes correspond to sustainable development objectives.

A key message one can infer from many of the articles is that AI and ML solutions are central to attaining superior performance in manufacturing. They provide the manufacturers to make huge prospects for acquiring operational effectiveness and important growth in quality, flexibility, and supply chain integration besides lowering the expenses and wastage. In other words, AI and ML are not luxuries that modern manufacturers can choose to ignore – they are the tools for driving consistent excellence in a field that changes at the speed of light.

6.6 AI AND ML IN MANUFACTURING: OPPORTUNITIES AND CHALLENGES

AI and ML are integrated into manufacturing with the benefits of performance optimization, product quality, adaptability, and eco effectivity. But as is the case with all technological interventions, there is a downside to incorporating AI and ML into organizational workflows. The opportunities and challenges of AI and ML in the manufacturing field are analyzed because this study focused on the enhanced technology of the factory automation industry.

6.6.1 Opportunities of AI and ML in Manufacturing

- **Improved Efficiency and Productivity**: Another area where the gains of AI and ML in manufacturing is the increase in production efficiency as a main benefit. It is used in manufacturing to enable the automation of the activities, thus minimizing on the repetitiveness and the common mistakes that testers are likely to make. Industrial robots can carry out functions like assembly, packaging, and material transportation respectively more efficiently than human operators. They lead to greater capacity, faster time to produce the products, and low overall cost of production. Furthermore, AI systems can also track production in real time and also make corrections to existing processes, improving them without direct operator input to ensure that machines and systems are running efficiently.

- **Predictive Maintenance**: AI and ML are impact maintaining strategies since they can now adopt a predictive maintenance model. Instead of working based on set time tables or waiting for some equipment to develop issues, AI applications analyze telemetered data from sensors mounted on the machinery to forecast failures. Thus, AI, by critically analyzing the patterns and outliers of machine activities, can predict low chances of a machine functioning correctly and suggest appropriate action. This also means that manufacturers can plan the maintenance of their equipment accurately, while also making it possible to avoid breakages that may be costly when spotted at a later date and time to also increase the life of the equipment.
- **Enhanced Quality Control**: The inspection can therefore be done automatically by using AI computer vision systems that will search for defects or variations on the products much to a high degree of precision. Visual inspection is very unreliable, especially in high production rates, but with the help of AI, not even the slightest flaw will escape the scanners. Furthermore, using ML capabilities, AI systems become adjusted with time getting better in efficiency and accuracy of results they deliver. These control standards are consistent and do not deviate much from the set standards which minimize loss or scrap and redo rates; hence, products developed have the best quality.
- **Optimization of Supply Chains**: These two technologies help in supply chain management by offering better insights information and decision-making. These technologies are capable of forecasting variations in demand and directing organizations in making the correct and proper adjustment to the production calendar and inventory based on the actual demand for certain products. AI systems also help through automation of order points and stock level and avoiding having too much stock in the first place. In the supply chain field, with the help of AI, the most suitable route for delivery can be determined, hence reducing the cost of transportation as well as time for delivery. Thereby, demand forecasting and supply chain transparency help manufacturers design more efficient and flexible supply networks.
- **Customization and Flexibility**: AI and ML favor the ability of manufacturers to change their focus on production of different products and personalize solutions. The customer data preferences allow the application of AI in production practices to facilitate the delivery of mass customization and achieving efficiency in production. Also, Flexible Manufacturing System (FMS) facilitated by AI means that production lines of the factory can easily adapt to change of product forms and variations without extensive redesigning and retooling.
- **Energy Efficiency and Sustainability**: There is energy management done by AI to analyze the consumption data of energy in the manufacturing process and suggest areas for improvement. This is possible because, through integrating AI systems, it is possible to self-regulate energy consumption depending on the production calendar. This would reduce the overall costs and is environmentally friendly, which helps toward sustainability goals in operations. AI can also support resource creation, reducing the amount of material used and increasing the effectiveness of recycling, with sustainability as a result.

6.6.2 Challenges of AI and ML in Manufacturing

- **High Initial Investment**: Some of the challenges that have been realized to hinder the manufacturing sector from implementing AI and ML include the fact that it is expensive to implement. The AI and ML deployment usually goes hand in hand with considerable investments; IT organizations need to obtain new hardware and software tools, train staff, and adapt the existing infrastructure. These costs could be costly to small manufacturers in their endeavor to achieve the sustainability status. In addition, incorporating AI and ML into an existing system may be also time-consuming and costly to make sure that they will work with the original system properly.
- **Complexity and Expertise Requirements**: AI and ML in manufacturing need extensive effort to implement and establish within production systems. Due to the emergence of complex problems, the new generation of AI models requires significant data for training, and the readiness of the models themselves also requires constant adjustments. These demands can sufficiently result in the creation of a skills gap where within the workforce available professionals with the required expertise and specialization are scarce. Some manufacturers may have to go to their expense or seek for data scientists and AI specialists; sometimes, this may be tough, given that in some industries the talent database is limited.
- **Data Privacy and Security Concerns**: Manufacturers have to gather large amounts of data from sensors, machines, and production systems on which AI and ML solutions depend. This data can be such as the manufacturing procedures that are specific to a particular company and the operations' details and, for this reason, can be invaded. Consequently, the uptake of both centers has the potentiality of eliciting staggering data privacy and security issues. Managers overseeing manufacturing companies must make sure that their data is secure and restricted from third parties.
- **Job Displacement and Workforce Challenges**: Application of such systems may trigger the elimination of particular positions as machines may be programmed to perform the tasks previously executed by people. Even though automation brings about efficiency, there are drawbacks such as eliminating some manual labor-related jobs, which creates unemployment or the need to train the workers to do other jobs. Risk placed on the companies includes crops depending on the automation of workers, hence leading to job elimination; companies must up upskill their workers for other tasks that may be created by the introduction of AI or ML systems.
- **Reliability of AI Models**: Not to mention that AI and ML models are perfectly capable of making mistakes. Though they may be refined, they may contain errors in a form of false positives or false negatives where wrong decision or actions are made. For instance, an AI-based defect identification system will fail to identify a particular defect or identify a product that is not defective as such. There are always consequences of a mistake in manufacturing ranging from formation of poor-quality products, wastage

of materials, and time among others. To achieve this, dependency on AI models requires having them frequently checked and validated to guarantee their efficiency.

- **Integration Challenges**: One of the biggest issues with the implementation of AI and ML is when the technologies need to be incorporated into otherwise established manufacturing structures. Some of these solutions can be outdated and inadequately compatible with contemporary AI technologies, and thus manufacturers can either refit their machines or buy new ones. Moreover, integration of voice and gesture control as a means of AI system performance, as well as the interaction of the latter with other components of the production complex, may involve certain adjustments, which consume time and resources.

6.7 CONCLUSION

Manufacturing systems are open, dynamic multitier formations where machines, automation, manpower, and technology create final products. As AI, robotics, and IoT technologies progress further into the manufacturing, manufacturing systems can become smarter and more flexible, thus leading to highly reactive sustainable and affordable production systems.

AI and ML are offering a great impact on the modern manufacturing by imparting it with high levels of flexibility, productivity, and elasticity. These technologies not only cause the automation of processes and improve their quality but also create conditions for cooperation between humans and AI, which distinguishes Industry 5.0. Through constant reinforcement of data analysis, AI and ML are making manufacturing proactively efficient, environmentally friendly, customer oriented, and capable of adapting to the rapidly changing market.

There is no doubt that the application of AI and ML in the manufacturing environment brings many benefits including efficiency, quality, and supply chain; however, there are some issues that need to be dealt with. This is due to the highly fixed costs of entry, the implementation process being a technical one and job threatened. However, if structured correctly with emphasize on investment within the employees of a manufacturing company, and focusing intensely on the use of AI and ML for cybersecurity purposes, a manufacturing firm stands to gain significantly in terms of production, efficiency, and competitiveness. You can clearly see that there are some benefits and some drawbacks of introducing AI and ML into the manufacturing domain.

REFERENCES

1. Maki, Y., & Loparo, K. A. (1997). A neural-network approach to fault detection and diagnosis in industrial processes. *IEEE Transactions on Control Systems Technology*, 5(6), 529–541.
2. Villalba-Diez, J., Schmidt, D., Gevers, R., Ordieres-Meré, J., Buchwitz, M., & Wellbrock, W. (2019). Deep learning for industrial computer vision quality control in the printing industry 4.0. *Sensors*, 19(18), 3987.

3. Schmitt, J., Bönig, J., Borggräfe, T., Beitinger, G., & Deuse, J. (2020). Predictive model-based quality inspection using Machine Learning and Edge Cloud Computing. *Advanced Engineering Informatics*, 45, 101101.
4. Kaparthi, S., & Bumblauskas, D. (2020). Designing predictive maintenance systems using decision tree-based machine learning techniques. *International Journal of Quality & Reliability Management*, 37(4), 659–686.
5. Erharter, G. H., Hansen, T. F., Liu, Z., & Marcher, T. (2021). Reinforcement learning based process optimization and strategy development in conventional tunneling. *Automation in Construction*, 127, 103701.
6. Walas Mateo, F., & Redchuk, A. (2021). IIOT/IOT and Artificial Intelligence/machine learning as a process optimization driver under industry 4.0 model. *Journal of Computer Science & Technology*, 21, e15.
7. Anandan, R., Gopalakrishnan, S., Pal, S., & Zaman, N. (Eds.). (2022). *Industrial Internet of Things (IIoT): Intelligent Analytics for Predictive Maintenance*. John Wiley & Sons.
8. Saheb, T., Dehghani, M., & Saheb, T. (2022). Artificial intelligence for sustainable energy: a contextual topic modeling and content analysis. *Sustainable Computing: Informatics and Systems*, 35, 100699.
9. Soori, M., Arezoo, B., & Dastres, R. (2023). Digital twin for smart manufacturing, A review. *Sustainable Manufacturing and Service Economics*, 2, 100017.
10. Darwish, D. (2024). Human-AI Collaboration in Industry 5. In Kumar, N., Pal, S. K., Agarwal, P., Rosak-Szyrocka, J., & Jain, V. (eds.), *Human-Machine Collaboration and Emotional Intelligence in Industry 5.0* (pp. 44–70). IGI Global.
11. Kumar, P., Singh, S.K. (2020). An Emerging Approach to Intelligent Techniques—Soft Computing and Its Application. In Balas, V., Solanki, V., Kumar, R. (eds), *Internet of Things and Big Data Applications. Intelligent Systems Reference Library*, vol 180. Springer. https://doi.org/10.1007/978-3-030-39119-5_13
12. Khare, S., Singh, P., & Kumar, P. (2024, March). LSTM Based Approach to Detect Fake News. In *2024 2nd International Conference on Disruptive Technologies (ICDT)*, Greater Noida, India (pp. 1501–1505). IEEE.
13. Kumar, P., Singh, S. K., & Choudhary, S. D. (2021). Reliability prediction analysis of aspect-oriented application using soft computing techniques. *Materials Today: Proceedings*, 45, 2660–2665.
14. Kumar, P., & Singh, S. K. (2017, May). A Framework for Assessing the Evolvability Characteristics Along with Sub-characteristics in AOSQ Model Using Fuzzy Logic Tool. In *2017 International Conference on Computing, Communication and Automation (ICCCA)*, Greater Noida, India (pp. 339–344). IEEE.
15. Patel, S. A., Patel, S. P., Adhyaru, Y. B. K., Maheshwari, S., Kumar, P., & Soni, M. (2022). Developing smart devices with automated Machine learning Approach: A review. *Materials Today: Proceedings*, 51, 826–831.
16. Singh, N., & Adhikari, D. (2023). AI in inventory management: Applications, challenges, and opportunities. International Journal for Research in Applied Science and Engineering Technology, 11(11), 2049–2053.
17. Pepper, J. E. (1999). Competitive intelligence at procter & gamble. *Competitive Intelligence Review: Published in Cooperation with the Society of Competitive Intelligence Professionals*, 10(4), 4–9.
18. Pandharikar, A., & Bussler, F. (2022). *AI-powered Commerce: Building the Products and Services of the Future with Commerce*. AI. Packt Publishing Ltd.
19. Jin, D., Ocone, R., Jiao, K., & Xuan, J. (2020). Energy and AI. *Energy and AI*, 1, 100002.

20. Mathews, A. (2024). *How Nike Is Using AI to Transform Product Design, Customer Experience, and Operational Efficiency.* AIM Research| Artificial Intelligence Market Insights.
21. Gupta, S., Iyer, R. S., & Kumar, S. (2024). Digital twin: Implementation. In Gupta, S., Iyer, R. S., & Kumar, S. (eds.), *Digital Twins: Advancements in Theory, Implementation, and Applications* (pp. 159–179). Cham: Springer Nature Switzerland.
22. Hackl, C., & Cronin, I. (2024). *Spatial Computing: An AI-Driven Business Revolution.* John Wiley & Sons.
23. Ramachandran Thampy Bindhu, V., & Kurumbadan Saseendran, A. (2024). AI revolutionizing manufacturing: cutting-edge advances: redefining manufacturing with intelligent solutions.

7 Development of a Cloud-Based Intelligent Manufacturing

Aradhna Saini, Rifa Nizam Khan, Pragya, and Mohd. Amjad

7.1 INTRODUCTION OF MANUFACTURING

The beginnings of a manufacturing machine system may be summarized as follows: a designer develops a concept, sketches it out (creates a model), and attempts to create actual models to be evaluated before assembling the entire structure. An overview of the production design of systems of industry development across many stages, from the beginning of Industry 1.0 to the current phase of Industry 4.0, is represented in Table 7.1.

In Industry 1.0 and 2.0, drawings are the information source, whereas in the physical sample, the platform, the system as a whole, is the message carrier. Physical prototypes must be put together using the traditional manufacturing system design technique to assess and confirm that the virtual space model properly matches the structure, ergonomics, and performance metrics. However, it is exceedingly expensive to validate the design using real prototypes. Simulations evaluating a model's performance and manufacturing feasibility in a virtual environment are essential to preventing needless risks on real prototypes [1]. The concepts of virtual, active, and virtual prototypes, among others, were introduced by several Computer-Aided Design software suppliers in Industry 3.0, including Siemens, Dassault, ANSYS, and PTC. A virtual prototype may be thought of as a sort of rehearsal where the information model replaces physics. The Virtual Mock-Up [2] idea, which stresses intricate connectivity as well as context interactions between evaluations of 3D designs, is one of the most popular virtual prototype concepts. The failure rate of physical prototypes is significantly decreased by the availability of virtual prototypes, which occasionally replace actual prototypes. The smart manufacturing system (SMS) performance may be assessed early to help save reconfiguration costs and losses when creating physical SMS designs that are modeled after the real production procedure in a virtual environment (e.g., Plant Simulation). The efficiency and convenience of SMS design might be significantly increased by using virtual reality (e.g., FlexSim). Designing a production system becomes much easier since virtual prototypes transmit information consistently.

One of the main paths for the global manufacturing industry in Industry 4.0 is smart manufacturing. The need for new smart manufacturing processes has increased

DOI: 10.1201/9781003582465-7

TABLE 7.1
Ranging from Industry 1.0 to Industry 4.0

Stages	1.0 Initial Industry	2.0 Second Industry	3.0 Third Industry	4.0 Fourth Industry
Period	1760s~1850s	1860s~1960s	1970s~2010s	2010s~Now
Mfg. paradigm	Stack manufacturing	Stack manufacturing	Stack customization	Stack individualization
Mfg. goal	Scale	Speed	Knowledge	Intelligence
Mfg. type of system	Mechanical manufacturing line	Self-acting Mfg. system	Computer-aided Mfg. system	Smart Mfg. system
Components of design	Machinery	Self-acting	Virtualization	Complex algorithms
Design goal	Acceptance	Interchangeability	Flexibility/ reconfigurability	Sustainability/ Intelligence
Design methods	Drawings in 2D	2D drawings	3D models and simulations	Virtual twins-based
Typical blueprint			Virtual prototype/ mock-up	Lifecycle virtual twins
Major challenges	Huge commissioning cost	Exorbitant commissioning fees	Complicated groups	Couplings in several dimensions

globally as a result of new national technologically sophisticated manufacturing projects. Even when the real goods and production processes are situated in a different physical place, an SMS may be divided into virtual models of various granularities in the virtual design process. To bridge the gap between the procedure's development and execution domains, high-fidelity cyberspace simulations that represent SMSs' real-world settings are crucial [3].

One answer is virtual twin technology. Due to fast-developing modeling and simulation capabilities, improved interoperability and IoT sensors, and increased tool and computer infrastructure availability, the virtual twin's concept is currently gaining. The virtual twins-based technique was initially used in the industrial system design field as a virtual twins-based simulation technique for the SMS setup following an analysis of current SMS development models. Developing a virtual twin during the SMS design part will be extremely helpful throughout the SMS's lifespan due to the superiority of virtual continuity, realistic modeling, and interdisciplinarity over conventional simulation.

Manufacturing in the cloud, also known as cloud manufacturing, is one of the key enabling technologies of Industry 4.0 that has the potential to successfully assist the economical utilization of manufacturing resources. This technology extends cloud computing to give on-demand manufacturing services to a large number of industrial users [1,2]. It does this by adhering to a service-oriented paradigm. Cloud manufacturing makes it possible for smart manufacturing networks to achieve increased productivity, utilization rates, and resource efficiency at the industrial network level.

This is accomplished through the comprehensive sharing and on-demand use of software, distributed computational, virtual, and physical production resources [2,3]. Through cloud computing, users have the ability to gain access to production systems, intelligent devices, and huge volumes of data that have been created by a variety of sources, such as other users, smart computation, and sensor systems [3]. There are a few outstanding research gaps that need to be addressed in order to successfully apply the cloud manufacturing paradigm. These gaps include the creation of cloud-based platforms, real user/production system interaction, and service-oriented self-acting utility supply [4–6]. A technique that is based on the cloud is applied in [7] in order to allocate work to Computer Numerical Control (CNC) machines that are accessible. The implementation of this strategy is predicated on the utilization of sensor networks on the manufacturing floor, knowledge fusion strategies, and the transmission of data via the internet. A service-oriented cloud-based strategy for adaptive process planning is proposed in [8]. This method relies on obtaining and evaluating information on the availability of machine tools, as well as their specifications and condition. The purpose of this technology is to facilitate the planning of distributed machining processes within a decentralized and dynamic manufacturing environment. It is designed to accommodate unpredictability in shop floor arrangements and to ensure that manufacturing services are accessible across the whole network [9].

7.2 HISTORICAL BACKGROUND OF MANUFACTURING

Manufacturing and industrialization systems have now advanced to the fourth generation of the industrial revolt after undergoing several inventions and iterative testing throughout the years. There have already been several advancements and modifications throughout this time. Figure 7.1's chronology illustrates the many phases of the industrial revolt, emphasizing significant discoveries and accomplishments that are also part of the more recent Revolt.

7.2.1 Revolts for Industrial

7.2.1.1 Revolt for First Industrial

In the early part of the 18th century, the first nation to become industrialized was the United Kingdom in the world to become industrialized. It was the nation that initiated the shift of the cotton industry from a cottage industry that relied on workers to an economy that was based on machines [10]. It is believed that the first industrial

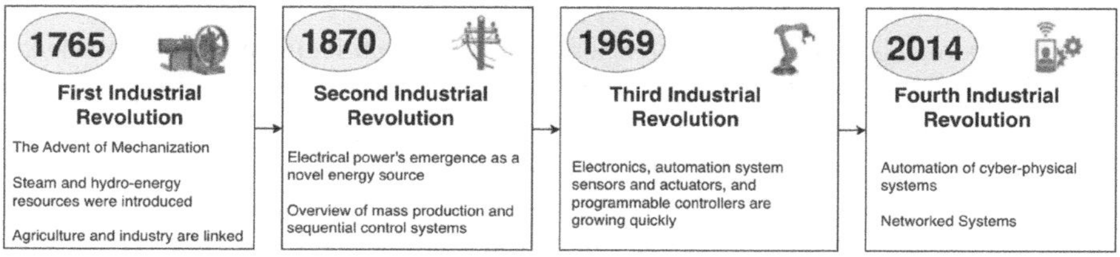

FIGURE 7.1 Chronology illustrates the many phases of the industrial revolt.

revolt in Europe and America took place between the years 1760 and 1820, shortly after the introduction of a new manufacturing process. Not only was the textile sector the first to use modern manufacturing procedures during this time period, but it was also the industry that produced the most goods, spent the most money on capital, and offered the most employment possibilities [11]. The invention of the spinning jenny by James Hargreaves in 1764, which was capable of producing many spools of thread at the same time, was a significant factor in the acceleration of the development of machining. The invention of coal, iron, railroads, and textiles marked the first industrial revolution in history. Because of the advent of machinery during this period, industry replaced agriculture as the main economic pillars of civilization. The invention of the steam engine and widespread coal mining created a new energy source that boosted all endeavors [12]. This was made possible by the expansion of railroads and the acceleration of material, human, and economic exchanges.

7.2.1.2 Revolt for Second Industrial

The second industrial Revolt, commonly referred to as the technical Revolt, took place between 1830 and 1914 [13]. New technological developments sparked the development of new energy sources, such as gas, oil, and electricity, which led to many creations. Therefore, the goal of the combustion engine's development was to make the most of these new resources. In addition, the steel industry started to expand in tandem with the rapidly rising demand for steel. The development of chemical synthesis also gave us synthetic fertilizers, colors, and textiles. The telegraph and telephone transformed communication systems, and the advent of the vehicle and airplane at the start of the 20th century altered transportation ways as well. Centralizing research and capital centered on an industrial and economic paradigm centered on new "large factories" allowed for all of these advancements. Chemistry also started along the path to the production of novel synthetic materials, such as salicylic acid, the function of bacteria in wound infection, and disinfectants and antiseptics, especially phenol and bromines. The electric systems created during this Revolt include transformers, electric generators, vacuum pumps, and gaslighting systems [14]. It was acknowledged that electricity was a universal energy transfer method. In the car industry, clipper ships, diesel engines, and railroads have all developed relative speed. Among the agricultural innovations were steel tools, irrigation and drainage pipelines, steam-powered threshers, mechanized reapers, and seed drills. It permanently altered the process of technological evolution by altering the connection between natural knowledge and how it influenced technology practices.

7.2.1.3 Revolt for Third Industrial

World Wars I and II also had an impact on the global economy and development. Following World War II, industrial advancements continued, and the years following 1969 are referred to as the third industrial Revolt [15]. The advent of nuclear energy, a new form of energy with potential greater than that of its predecessors, signaled the start of the third industrial Revolt. Transistors and microprocessors advanced throughout this Revolt, while computers and telecoms also gained popularity. Miniaturized materials were produced as a result of this new technique, which would lead to opportunities in biotechnology and space exploration. The third Revolt automated production via the use of information technology and electronics.

7.2.1.4 Revolt for Fourth Industrial

To increase German competitiveness in the manufacturing sector, a group of academic and corporate political specialists coined the phrase "Industry 4.0" in 2011 as the fourth industrial Revolt. It prioritizes analyzing real-time data and highly emphasizes connection through the Internet of Things and machine learning. Industry 4.0 connects the industrial internet and the Internet of Things to the production system so that it may share information, talk to the machines, and make choices based on the system algorithm. Essentially, Industry 4.0 includes autonomous robots, additive manufacturing, artificial intelligence, flexible industrial self-acting systems, and augmented reality [15].

7.3 CLOUD MANUFACTURING FRAMEWORK

Figure 7.2 shows the cloud manufacturing framework created in this study to allow distributed resources to be shared for efficient usage at the industrial network level. The cloud platform allows customers connected to the internet to dynamically share distributed manufacturing resources provided by various vendors within the manufacturing network. To determine the optimal manufacturing solution based on user requirements, the cloud platform gathers supplier bids and client requests for manufacturing services and then processes them using sophisticated decision-making algorithms. The platform has a database module that collects data from user input, an intelligent module that processes data, optimizes it, and generates workable solutions, and a decision support module that compares and evaluates solutions to accomplish these duties.

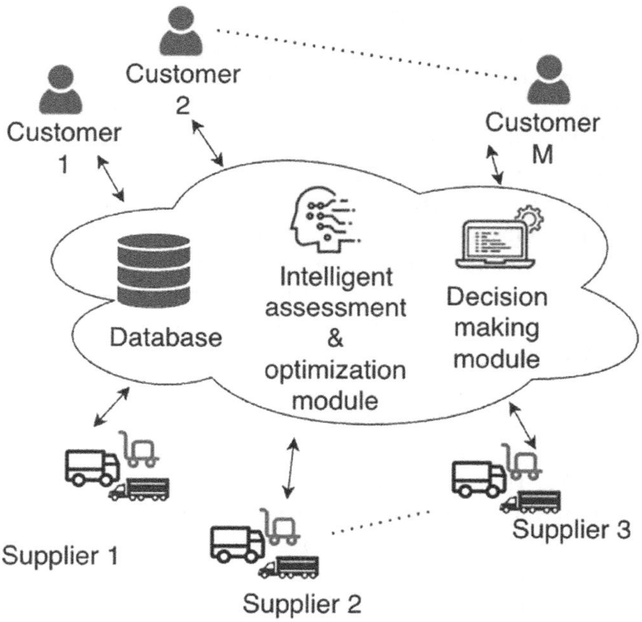

FIGURE 7.2 Level of the cloud user interface.

7.4 SMART MANUFACTURING SYSTEM DESIGN (SMSD) BASED ON VIRTUAL TWINS

From the suggested Function-Structure-Behavior-Control-Intelligence-Performance view, which includes 6 dimensions and 16 sub-dimensions, this part will analyze the research progress and challenges in the crucial processes of SMSD that might be improved by the virtual twin technologies.

7.4.1 Function Design of SMS Based on Virtual Twins

7.4.1.1 Process Planning Using Virtual Twins

Engineers use manufacturing process planning as a method to examine manufacturing in the early stages of Manufacturing System Design (MSD); engineers use process planning to examine cost, efficiency, and manufacturability based on the identification of manufacturing features from product design. It covers the selection and sequencing of production operations. Very little research has been done on how to handle complicated loadings and unpredictable disturbances in the process design process. Seventy-four percent of the planning time is required for acquiring sufficient process information and looking for the best options in the existing simulation-based process planning methodologies [16]. The first stage of SMSD that virtual twin technology might improve is process planning.

Planning accuracy and optimization speed are enhanced by the use of virtual twins for industrial operations. Using IoT technology and discrete event simulation, cyber-physical systems enable bidirectional mapping for re-manufacturing process optimization and planning. Based on the real-time mapping between the design model and the actual machining process, a virtual twins-based process evaluation methodology is proposed. It is anticipated that the resulting flexible production system would be able to handle a wide range of goods with little cost of reconfiguration. It is currently uncommon to use virtual twin technology for process planning [16]. The use of virtual twins in manufacturing process planning is expected to yield additional benefits and drawbacks, as well as the ability to quickly mine and learn from the data gathered.

7.4.1.2 Mechanical Design of Equipment Based on Virtual Twins

A thorough grasp of the equipment's machining process should be the foundation for any mechanical design work. For instance, a simulated twin model of the process of interaction between materials and the laser should be incorporated into the laser processing design machinery in order to improve understanding of the production process of laser materials through simulations [17]. The process of operating the actual equipment is also virtualized as part of the device's virtual twinning.

7.4.2 SMS Structure Design Based on Virtual Twins

7.4.2.1 Layout Planning and Topology Optimization Using Virtual Twins

The physical limitations of the designated site area significantly influence the SMS layout planning. However, a crucial metric for assessing the layout planning solution is the logistics intent. Virtual twin technologies can enable the automatic retrieval of layout information, making it easier to plan an optimal layout in the virtual twin of a physical SMS by quickly mirroring and validating the physical manufacturing process against its virtual model in cyberspace. The fundamental concept behind SMS topology design involves using optimization algorithms and numerical computing to identify the best topology structure while meeting various constraints within a specific design space. A well-known design approach for addressing the coupling and trade-off issues across multiple disciplines in designing large-scale complex engineering systems, such as SMSs, is multi-disciplinary design optimization. This approach considers how different disciplines interact, thoroughly examines and leverages the synergistic mechanisms of interaction in engineering systems, and maximizes the design of intricate engineering systems as a whole. Optimization should be straightforward in the virtual twin model used in the SMSD process [17]. A virtual twin-based graduated intelligent manufacturing system is capable of allocating and executing tasks for fixed-position assembly islands in real time. Overall, the coordination of industrial processes using virtual twins ensures that each piece of equipment is accurately positioned and utilized for the appropriate tasks, enhancing visibility.

7.4.2.2 Tooling and Buffer Design Based on Virtual Twins

The most important factor in enhancing production efficiency is auxiliary preparation time, which accounts for more than 20% of the manufacturing time of complex goods. The design of the tooling and buffer is an important stage in determining the production process's auxiliary time for preparation. Using takt time analyses and productivity balancing, it was feasible to determine the kind and quantity of machines as well as the buffer capacity in each process. However, because SMS involves stochastic logistics, significant interruptions, and various route patterns, tooling and buffer design are very challenging jobs. By bridging the gap between controlling and designing, the virtual twin technology provides a workable solution to the tooling/buffer designing problem. For instance, a technique based on virtual twins is used to dynamically clamp and position flexible tooling devices [18].

7.4.3 Behavior Design of SMS Based on Virtual Twins

7.4.3.1 Designing Equipment Behavior with Virtual Twins

Determining the actions of equipment and the sequence of actions for multi-process coordination by the process requirements and route is known as equipment behavior design. Deadlocks and needless collisions should be avoided. It is challenging to accurately replicate the real equipment, even if creating virtual equipment is helpful for safety and economically duplicating equipment's capabilities. Building a virtual twin of the equipment might help with behavior design, further diagnosis, and defect prediction for physical equipment operation. In a robotic production cell, integrated agent-based quick optimization algorithms with virtual twins offer a motion planning method. To improve accountability and production capacities, their virtual twins are developed by modeling the real state of the machine tools using sensory data. Additionally, a simulation method for robotic toolpath planning based on augmented reality communicates layout data between a virtual twin and a reconfigurable additive manufacturing system.

The MTConnect protocol and its components are used to transmit and store data. The optimization features about machine tool dynamics, energy consumption, cutting tool compensation, contour error estimate, machining trajectory, and machining status are all included in the virtual twin of Intelligent Manufacturing Technology (IMT). Additionally, being a crucial part of machine tools, the cutting tool's virtual twin is essential to machining solution optimization [18].

7.4.3.2 Work in Process (WIP)/Material Handling Based on Virtual Twins

Production that is not coordinated can quickly lead to issues like lengthy production cycles, unsmooth production, and the backlog of intermediate warehouses. Synchronized manufacturing lowers waste and increases overall efficiency. Due to the great degree of flexibility, robots are frequently used in SMSs for material delivery and handling. An efficient method for optimizing the design of work in progress and material handling in production systems is the use of simulation and emulation. Under the stack individualization paradigm, a flexible material handling solution should be able to handle the dynamic-change product production needs. Three factors must be taken into account when optimizing the design of work in progress and material handling: (1) how the manufacturing process affects logistics, (2) how manufacturing capacity requirements affect logistics facilities, and (3) how production time affects material flow. Virtual twin technologies might make it easier to assess these dynamic causes and implications. Through a design-for-manufacturing approach, virtual twin technology allows the system to achieve exceptional logistical traceability, controllability, and efficiency. For example, a proactive material handling technique based on virtual twins for a shop floor enabled by Cyber-Physical System (CPS) can represent the actual SMS production state [19]. Inspired by a colony of ants working toward a shared objective, they suggested an assembly grid plan to optimize space efficiency in place of the century-old assembly line mentality in the production layouts. It might increase adaptability to variations in the product. However, more accurate virtual models of work in progress must be created to map the real and virtual worlds and bridge the gap between design and production.

7.5.4 SMS Control Design Based on Virtual Twins

7.5.4.1 Process Optimization and Equipment Control Design Using Virtual Twins

Virtual equipment is often designed to mimic each machining process to direct the creation of controls by simulating the machining toolpath of different workpieces or parts. Establishing a virtual twin of physical equipment would allow designers to expedite the design cycle and make manufacturing process advancements in addition to verifying the equipment's performance. For example, virtual twins of the actual milling tools use a functional simulation system. The Standard for the Exchange of Product Model Data for Numerical Control (STEP-NC)-based virtual twin system is designed for a computer-aided manufacturing system. A virtual twin-powered cyber-physical system can independently operate a micropunching device. The virtual twin inspection system optimizes the inspection controls for workpieces with complex geometric surfaces. The huge amount of contextual data gathered from dispersed sensors in workpieces allowed the closed-loop virtual twins to circumvent the unpredictability of the inspection process [20]. The separation of sensory data makes it hard to gain useful information for calibrating equipment, even though some models have been developed to predict performance issues and avoid failures.

7.5.4.2 Commissioning Is Managed Via a System Based on Virtual Twins

Given the complexity and heterogeneity of SMSs in the context of Industry 4.0, the runtime validation of controls and the design are crucial for managing the quality of the product, but they are also difficult. Commissioning system control is a challenging process that requires modeling both low-level and high-level control functions in various environments of software and linking them via certain interfaces. This is a crucial stage in validating and confirming the basic design models.

Three primary methods are used in the commissioning of an SMS: semi-physical, physical, and virtual commissioning. To finish the physical debugging job, the physical commissioning must wait for the physical equipment assembly and control logic to be finished, which wastes waiting time. Errors in design, logic, coding, and other areas will unavoidably occur, with permanent effects like malfunctioning mechanical equipment. Numerous virtual simulation commissioning software packages are available, including Visual Components, Siemens Tecnomatix, Rockwell Emulate3D, and Simumatik3D [21]. A virtual twin may accurately depict how the physical equipment has changed over time, continually gather pertinent information, optimize and assess the existing state of affairs under certain controls, and ultimately support the design choice.

Several sets of equipment may be provided by several manufacturers during the SMS development process, necessitating the concurrent control design of numerous virtual machines. Typically, engineers who write control programs or code based on their own experiences do not make it easy for others to grasp the logical action flow or for the iterative optimization of the control debugging process to respond quickly [22].

7.5.5 SMS Intelligence Model Design Based on Virtual Twins

One significant example of the virtual twins paradigm in action is intelligence. In its manufacturing process, an SMS is thought to be able to achieve self-decision, self-perception, self-execution, self-improvement, self-learning, and autonomy, including the best possible control over the parameters. Its optimization incorporates big data and artificial intelligence technologies in addition to traditional and contemporary optimization control technologies. It is impossible to study and reason about the intelligence of an SMS without a virtual twin that accurately models the real system. SMS's industrial artificial intelligence may be divided into two categories: computational optimization models and data-driven machine learning models.

7.5.5.1 SMS Machine Learning Model Design Based on Virtual Twins

Complex, dynamic, and chaotic behaviors are characteristics of the SMS. Machine learning has advanced quickly in terms of both promising outcomes and usability to effectively meet the need for high-quality personalized products. Manufacturing equipment, production lines, workshops, factories, and cross-factory levels are among the various levels where machine learning-based intelligent control models are available [22]. One crucial difficulty in SMSD is the choice and design of a suitable machining learning system to manage dynamic events and facilitate intelligent process control. However, this technology will only produce deceptive results if industrial issues cannot be accurately represented.

7.5.5.2 SMS Computational Optimization Model Design Based on Virtual Twins

Numerous procedures from control and management optimization, including robustness/sensitivity analysis, network optimization, complexity theory, and large-scale optimization, are included in computational optimization in SMSs. To reduce the sensitivity to changes or disturbances as much as feasible, designers are looking for strong computational optimization techniques in SMSD practice. Therefore, finding a robust design that can withstand a wide range of system changes and disturbances is the primary objective of the computational optimization model design of SMS. To find reliable computational optimization models, the virtual twins technology offers a very secure runtime environment for simulating the complicated system. It is also standard practice to use hybrid autonomy models that combine computational optimization models with data-driven machine learning models. Virtual twin systems based on real-time data might help hybrid autonomy models, computational optimization, and alternative artificial intelligence to identify more effective production patterns and guidelines. A crucial design phase in production systems is often the abstraction of optimization issues and the coupling relationships between them.

7.5.6 SMS Performance Design with Virtual Twins

Numerous SMS plans have envisioned it as being extremely intelligent, versatile, autonomous, and adaptive. To handle increasingly erratic demands and changes, these SMS performance targets must be assessed and improved at the design stage [23]. Using virtual twin technology, researchers are working to enhance system performance (such as quality, flexibility, and reconfigurability).

7.5.6.1 Virtual Twin-Based SMSD that Prioritizes Quality

An important criterion for assessing a freshly designed SMS's success is its product quality. On the one hand, the virtual twins' technology might improve overall tolerance analysis, which is made possible by the mathematical modeling of tolerance standards from the product's point of view. A parametric space envelope-based tolerance modeling technique may support various computer-aided tools to meet specific tolerancing needs. However, from the standpoint of the manufacturing system, it is preferable in the ultra-precision manufacturing domain to perceive essential parts with full-field displacement [23].

7.5.6.2 Virtual Twin-Based SMSD with Flexibility

The stack customization, individualization, and personalization paradigm necessitate high SMS flexibility and rapid system design/reconfiguration technologies because of the frequent SMS changes. The SMS should be able to guarantee production's compatibility and scalability to satisfy consumers' demands for ongoing product development and services. Numerous research studies on MSD that represent production flexibility for various product orders have been carried out. Every component of SMS is intended to be documented using the Asset Administrative Shell approach in the Industry 4.0 blueprint. A comprehensive capacity management model helps manufacturing companies adjust or control their ability to respond to all possible demand situations. In general, an efficient SMSD solution that prioritizes flexibility should assess product upgrades as well as the integration of various product generations and architectures.

7.5.6.3 Virtual Twin-Based SMSD with a Focus on Reconfigurability

When a new kind, generation, family of goods, or model is released, traditional SMSD techniques usually limit themselves to manufacturing a family of products, single type, or generation incurring significant costs for redesigning or reconfiguring. This "new-product-then-new-system-design" reasoning becomes less effective as product upgrades and renewals happen more rapidly. Since the reconfigurability and adaptability of the design are uncertain due to unpredictable changes in the product, an optimized design for one product may not be feasible for the updated generation. This complicates the search for a design that can adapt to different types, generations, families of products, or models. Rethinking reconfigurability-oriented SMSD may involve utilizing virtual twin technology. For instance, leveraging the high reconfigurability of open-architecture machine tools can lead to a swift reconfiguration approach for SMSs powered by virtual twins. However, to enhance the efficacy and efficiency of the design and enable autonomous, intelligent reconfigurability optimization, it is essential to integrate computational optimization techniques with virtual twin technology.

7.5.6.4 Virtual Twin-Based SMSD with a Focus on Sustainability

Manufacturers are confronted with the problem of improving the SMS's sustainability in light of mounting pressure to minimize energy use. For SMS to save money, reduce emissions, and conserve energy, the design and choice of machining parameters must be optimal. To guarantee that it is always possible to preserve internal collaboration. Throughout the continuous development process, the SMS should be able to continually coordinate the relationships between various components based on the features of its internal structure. However, throughout the SMS design process, not much focus has been placed on explicitly defining and optimizing energy efficiency and carbon emission reduction.

The virtual twin's technology is a potent instrument in Industry 4.0 for comprehending and optimizing the interplay between all pertinent material, energy, and resource flows in an SMS [24]. For example, a paradigm for evaluating sustainability based on virtual twins might model feasible outcomes for various process strategies.

7.5.6.5 Virtual Twin-Based SMSD that Is Focused on Security and Safety

In SMS control, process safety is a major concern. During the design stage, the virtual twin's ability to forecast system problems can be utilized to optimize SMS information flow and enhance process safety. For instance, a Cyber-Factory blueprint based on virtual twins may incorporate the iterative design of cobots' safety functions to improve the avionics electronics' quality monitoring capability against manipulation attempts. A smart factory plan grounded in virtual twins was proposed [24] to facilitate safe data communication and product configuration. To bolster the safety of industrial systems, a virtual twin systems thinking technique is essential. A consistent language or ontology is necessary for logically linking SMS processes and modules. From a control safety perspective, the ability of controllers to adjust procedure behavior to manage failures without user intervention is known as fault tolerance. By employing active control mechanisms, the fault tolerance of SMS—also known as the system's robustness—can be enhanced. Adaptive control algorithms can further strengthen controller robustness through virtual twin technology.

In actuality, finding a genuine SMS that can accomplish all of the aforementioned objectives is challenging for many manufacturers. Additionally, the development of some performances will result in the decrease and degradation of other performance objectives in the actual SMS because of the diversity and contradiction of the numerous goals. For example, productivity and flexibility are typically incompatible. As a result, figuring out how to rationally set up and coordinate several objectives to collectively achieve the SMS's high overall performance is a challenging task. Solving this problem requires an understanding of the connections between various design aims. To improve design efficiency, it is advantageous to have a single environment that can be used to decouple and coordinate various planning goals [25].

7.6 SMSD MODELS BUILT ON VIRTUAL TWINS

Two models of virtual twin-based SMSD are being considered as a possible solution; however, few of the current models can completely satisfy the design criteria of SMSs.

7.6.1 Cloud Manufacturing and Collaborative Optimization (CMCO) Quad-Play Model

There is a process that transfers similarities between SMS's intelligence, structure, control, behavior, function, and performance models. Design efficiency might be greatly increased by utilizing this similarity mechanism. A quad-play CMCO is shown in Figure 7.3. (The architecture of the quad-play CMCO design model) architecture based on virtual twins [25] smoothens the fast customization of flow-type SMSD design. The flow-type SMS's control system structure and data collecting and processing model were referred to as the "Control Model." The linked optimization in the flow-type SMS's execution was identified as the optimization model.

The requirements of analysis, process plan, typology definition, layout design, and equipment and buffer configuration are all included in the CMCO Configuration Design dimension. Determining the motion of machine tool, buffering, and material handling are all included in the motion planning dimension. Designing the two-way sensing and controlling system is part of the Control Development dimension. Solving optimization issues in linked processes and exporting operation machinery to power the operation of SMS are two aspects of the optimization coupling dimension. The performance of an SMS is undoubtedly determined by its dynamics during operation. Typically, designers are only able to take the SMS into account during the design and development phase due to their inadequate

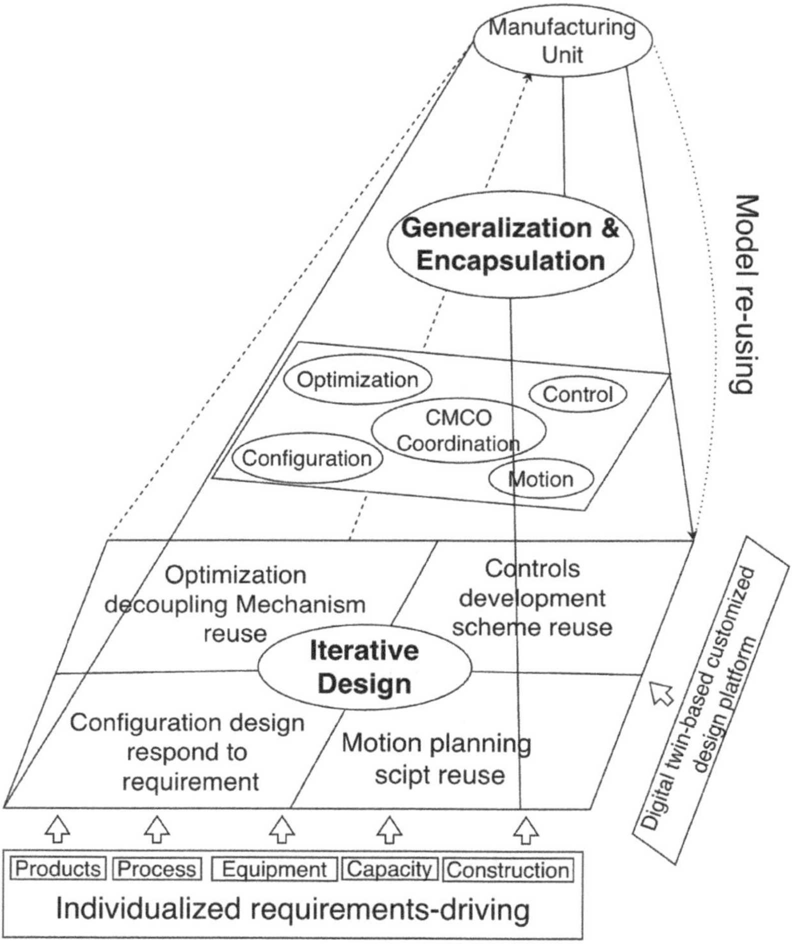

FIGURE 7.3 The architecture of the quad-play CMCO design model.

understanding of the dynamics; yet, they employ static intellectual entity thinking to study the SMS. It is difficult to carry out all the SMSD operations at the same time and create a single model that can perfectly copy all of the interactions and behaviors of the manufacturing process. The CMCO model offers four common paradigms for iterative design that realistic design objectives might use to address this difficulty. As a bi-level architecture, the CMCO model uses the symbols "FW" and "FB" to distinguish between the logic design level and the physical design level. The dynamic execution engine and the static configuration scheme are balanced by the iterative "execution-analysis-adjustment" optimization known as the CMCO model. Consequently, a possible method for successfully enhancing design efficiency in Digital Twin–based Smart Manufacturing System Design (DT-SMSD) is the CMCO architecture.

7.6.2 Shop Floor Virtual Twin Model

As a fundamental component of SMS, shop floor design and optimization are crucial. The tangible items on the shop floor, such as machine tools, are referred to as the actual shop floor. Virtual twins might facilitate virtual fault prediction, diagnosis, and maintenance, as well as the realization of the dynamic adjustment between industrial designing and execution [25]. This allowed for the simulation and prediction of the workshop's real-time operational performance, including manufacturing processes, process planning, and abnormal/errors. Following the establishment of the virtual model, a data-driven perspective might be used to construct an interoperability channel between physical space and cyberspace.

7.7 SMSD CASES BASED ON VIRTUAL TWINS

The production paradigm has changed from stack manufacturing and customization to stack personalization/individualization due to the growing variety of product needs and technological advancements. Dedicated manufacturing lines and reconfigurable/flexible production systems are being replaced by SMSs as the appropriate manufacturing systems. SMS's adaptability, independence, and sustainability are essential for making stack-customized, low-cost production possible. Open architecture, which is distinguished by a defined platform and interchangeable customized modules, is acknowledged as a possible remedy for SMS architecting [27]. By switching customized modules onto the platform, designers may dynamically redesign and reconfigure the SMS after process planning [26].

The size and diversity of module databases will increase dramatically due to the community's wild creativity of crowds. Rather than only creating uniform interfaces, SMSD's open architecture aims to eventually reach a deeper open-source level. Concurrently, the consensus on protection of intellectual property will be modified appropriately to better accommodate dispersed design and open inventions.

Unexpected circumstances involving various kinds of data would negatively impact the SMS. various levels of SMSD have various design elements, design goals, and key problems. Numerous studies have been conducted on SMSD at the manufacturing line level. For example, an optimization model based on virtual twins reduces the restriction or delay in a production line for water bottles. A virtual twin-driven method enables quick, individualized furniture manufacturing line design. The workshop types shown in Table 7.2 can be further divided into three categories: open shop, flow shop, and job shop [27]. The creation of useful standards and reference designs is a crucial first step toward the development of DT-SMSD [27].

7.8 INNOVATIVE PRODUCTION PLATFORM CAPABILITIES AND CHALLENGES

Intelligent production systems are capable of managing a lot of the complexity and challenges that today's industries face; there are still some challenges that come up during implementation. Several dependent variables suggest that when smart manufacturing technologies are being developed or when effective production equipment

TABLE 7.2
SMS Design at Different Levels

Level	Design Elements	Design Goal	Typical Blueprint	Major Challenges
Machine tool/center	Parts/components, controls, etc	Product quality	Machine tools, open architecture, etc.	Manufacturing Accuracy, etc
Mfg. units	+Robots, AGVs, etc	+Autonomy	Autonomous Mfg. units, etc	Deadlock Prevention, etc
Line of production	+Layout, typology, performance, etc	+Reconfigurability	Reconfigurable production line, etc	Bottleneck Prevention, etc
Workshop	+Material handling, etc	+Productivity	Smart workshop, etc	Adaptive Layout, etc
Factory	+Load balancing, intelligence, etc	+Flexibility	Smart Factory, etc	Compatibility with new products, etc
Distributed System	+Coordination mechanism, etc	+Sustainability	e.g., Decentralized Autonomous Mfg.	Consensus Efficiency, etc

is being upgraded in existing industries, they may face safety issues, absence of system cooperation and absence return on the expenditure of emerging technologies, and financial difficulties. Below are a description of the problems that SMSs confront and their potential fixes.

7.8.1 Smart Manufacturing Security Concerns

The phrase "intelligent production system" describes a manufacturing process that communicates with end users from machining or manufacturing units via an integrated network system. This requires access to the network, which is specially configured online. End-to-end encryption of data and a globally distinct identity for information and data security throughout the system are essential for connected internet exchange of data [28]. As a result, each network node must be protected against external risks and misuse of data. The most important consideration when developing networked systems, such intelligent production systems, is ensuring system and process security.

7.8.2 Integration of Systems

Integrating new technological equipment with old equipment is another hurdle in implementing an intelligent production system [28]. Implementing intelligent production technology presents various challenges due to the incompatibility of new and current equipment. Older equipment that uses certain communication protocols may not be up to date, while newer gadgets may use a different protocol. Additionally, a better transmission structure is required for interaction between machines and methodology interconnection. Modern production systems need an IPv6 connection to add more devices linked all together.

7.8.3 Interoperability

The power of different structures to understand and make use of each other's features separately is referred to as compatibility. Regardless of the origin of their software or hardware, this trait is capable of exchanging data and information among them. Interoperability is categorized into different four levels: semantic, systematic, technological, and operational. Operational interoperability connects CPS and Adaptive Control Framework (ACF) (addresses the conceptual framework). Systematic compatibility is related to principles, models, recommendations, and standards. Specifically, technical interoperability develops platforms and tools for technical and Information and Communication Technology (ICT) environments and related applications. Semantic interoperability [28] focuses on knowledge sharing across different institutional and individual levels. The interoperability feature may not be fully realized if the standards and communication protocols are not adequately aligned. The system's constraints regarding interoperability are influenced by variation in hardware capabilities, communication bandwidth, operating frequency, and modes of communication.

7.8.4 Safety in Cooperation between Humans and Robots

A robot, sometimes referred to as a compact machine, is a particular type of machine that can communicate with people in place of employment and work together by advancing the field of human–machine communication. The main priority ought to involve the safety and health at work of the workers; hazardous conditions should be avoided, and basic occupational health and security should be preserved. When establishing industrialized automation or CPS systems for an industry, the main goal should be to minimize any risks related to electrical, mechanical, thermal, vibrations, noise, radiation, material/substance, and the work atmosphere [29].

7.8.5 Being Multilingual

Innovative manufacturing processes need to be equipped to manage multinational processes and interpret every instruction given in the language of humans into the language of machines in order to direct the machinery to complete the required task [30]. For the term "smart manufacturing" to be effective and to incorporate artificial intelligence and state-of-the-art technology into production facility, it must be able to accept direction straight from the operator in the form of text or speech.

7.8.6 Return on Investment for New Technology

Integrating innovative technological advances in an existing industrial system requires careful consideration of the financial feasibility as well as investment return [30]. The adoption of newer technology is influenced by how long it takes to recover the value on investments using the revenue from the current system. The production losses during an upgrade would be compared to the higher cost required to adopt newer technology.

7.9 CONCLUSION

This chapter examines how virtual twin systems are incorporated into and support SMS design. A Function-Structure-Behavior-Control-Intelligence-Performance framework is proposed to analyze the main processes of DT-SMSD based on the definitions of SMSD and the benefits of DT-SMSD. The primary SMSD design processes that virtual twin technology could enhance are explored. While new blueprint models, such as the virtual twin shop floor and CMCO design architecture, are discussed, further development of DT-SMSD techniques is still urgently needed. The key enabling technologies that support DT-SMSD are analyzed, including blockchains, cloud computing, industrial artificial intelligence, data analytics, virtual reality, IIoT, and multi-domain physical–chemical modeling. Design examples are provided for various production paradigms and system levels. Following this, we suggest four potential avenues for further DT-SMSD research based on the insights gained from the evaluation and discussions. This study is expected to offer new perspectives on pressing business challenges related to advancing new SMSs in the context of Industry 4.0.

REFERENCES

1. Fowler JW, Rose O. Grand challenges in modeling and simulation of complex manufacturing systems. *Simulation* 2004;80(9):469–76.
2. Rooks B. A shorter product development time with virtual mock-up. *Assem Autom* 1998;18(1):34–8.
3. Wu D, Rosen DW, Wang L, Schaefer D. Cloud-based design and manufacturing: a new paradigm in virtual manufacturing and design innovation. *Comput Des* 2015;59:1–14.
4. Mahmoud MA, Grace J. A generic evaluation framework of smart manufacturing systems. *Proc Comput Sci* 2019;161:1292–9.
5. Zhang H, Liu Q, Chen X, Zhang D, Leng J. A virtual twin-based approach for designing and multi-objective optimization of hollow glass production line. *IEEE Access* 2017;5:26901–11.
6. Wang K, Lee T, Hsu Y. Revolt on virtual twin technology-a patent research approach. *Int J Adv Manuf Technol* 2020;107(11–12):4687–704.
7. Nujoom R, Mohammed A, Wang Q. A sustainable manufacturing system design: a fuzzy multi-objective optimization model. *Environ Sci Pollut Res Int* 2018;25 (25):24535–47.
8. Choi S, Kang G, Jun C, Lee JY, Han S. Cyber-physical systems: a case study of development for manufacturing industry. *Int J Comput Appl Technol* 2017;55(4):289–97.
9 Frontoni E, Loncarski J, Pierdicca R, Bernardini M, Sasso M. Cyber physical systems for industry 4.0: Towards real time virtual reality in smart manufacturing. In: DePaolis LT, Bourdot P, DePaolis LT, Bourdot P, editors. *International Conference on Augmented Reality, Virtual Reality and Computer Graphics* . Cham: Springer International Publishing Ag. 2018. p. 422–34.
10. Zakoldaev, D. A., Korobeynikov, A. G., Shukalov, A. V., & Zharinov, I. O. (2019, November). Digital forms of describing Industry 4.0 objects. In *IOP Conference Series: Materials Science and Engineering* (Vol. 656, No. 1, p. 012057). IOP Publishing.
11. Negri E, Fumagalli L, Macchi M. A review of the roles of virtual twin in CPS-based production systems. *Proc Manuf* 2017;11:939–48.
12. Shao GD, Kibira D. Digital manufacturing: Requirements and challenges for implementing digital surrogates. In *Winter Simulation Conference Proceedings*; 2018. p. 1226–37. IEEE.

13. Valckenaers P. Perspective on holonic manufacturing systems: PROSA becomes ARTI. *Comput Ind* 2020;120:103226.
14. Barricelli BR, Casiraghi E, Fogli D. A survey on virtual twin: definitions, characteristics, applications, and design implications. *IEEE Access* 2019;7:167653–71.
15. Zobel-Roos S, Schmidt A, Mestmäcker F, Mouellef M, Huter M, Uhlenbrock L, ... Strube J. Accelerating biologics manufacturing by modeling or: is approval under the qbd and pat approaches demanded by authorities acceptable without a virtual-twin? *Processes* 2019; 7(2):94.
16. Chen Y, Yang O, Sampat C, Bhalode P. Virtual twins in pharmaceutical and biopharmaceutical manufacturing: a literature review. *Processes* 2020;8(9):10889.
17. Tao F, Zhang H, Liu A, Nee AY. Virtual twin in industry: state-of-the-art. *IEEE Trans Ind Inform* 2019;15(4):2405–15.
18. Lu Y, Liu C, Kevin I, Wang K, Huang H, Xu X. Virtual twin-driven smart manufacturing: connotation, reference model, applications and research issues. *Robot Comput Integr Manuf* 2020;61:101837.
19. Yan J, Li B. Research hotspots and tendency of intelligent manufacturing. *Chin Sci Bull-Chin* 2020;65(8):684–94.
20. Cimino C, Negri E, Fumagalli L. Review of virtual twin applications in manufacturing. *Comput Ind* 2019;113(103130).
21. Qi Q, Tao F. Virtual twin and big data towards smart manufacturing and Industry 4.0: 360 degree comparison. *IEEE Access* 2018;6:3585–93.
22. Tao F, Qi Q, Wang L, Nee AYC. Virtual twins and cyber-physical systems toward smart manufacturing and Industry 4.0: correlation and comparison. *Engineering* 2019;5(4):653–61.
23. Konstantinov S, Ahmad M, Ananthanarayan K, Harrison R. The cyber-physical E-machine manufacturing system: virtual engineering for complete lifecycle support. *Proc CIRP* 2017;63:119–24.
24. Hasan, H. R., Salah, K., Jayaraman, R., Omar, M., Yaqoob, I., Pesic, S., ... & Boscovic, D. (2020). A blockchain-based approach for the creation of digital twins. *IEEE Access*, 8, 34113-34126.
25. Qian L, Gero JS, et al. Function-behavior-structure paths and their role in analogy-based design. *AI EDAM* 1996;10(4):289–312.
26 Zhang Y, et al. Intelligent feature recognition for STEP-NC-compliant manufacturing based on artificial bee colony algorithm and back propagation neural network. *J Manuf Syst* 2021. https://doi.org/10.1016/j.jmsy.2021.01.018.
27. Zhao P, et al. The modeling and using strategy for the virtual twin in process planning. *IEEE Access* 2020;8:41229–45.
28. Uhlemann T, Lehmann C, Steinhilper R. The virtual twin: realizing the cyber-physical production system for industry 4.0. *Proc CIRP* 2017;61:335–40.
29. Lu Y, et al. An IoT-enabled simulation approach for process planning and analysis: a case from engine re-manufacturing industry. *Int J Comput Integr Manuf* 2019; 32(4-5SI):413–29.
30. Liu J, et al. Dynamic evaluation method of machining process planning based on virtual twin. *IEEE Access* 2019;7:19312–23.

8 Digital Twin for Manufacturing

Kanya Devi Jayabalan, Gousia Thahniyath Mulla, Mouleeswaran Singanallur Kumaresan, and Sundaravadivazhagan Balasubaramanian

8.1 INTRODUCTION

8.1.1 INDUSTRIAL EVOLUTION

In the first industrial rebellion, production was mechanized using steam power and water. The second industrial revolution was defined by the development of the production line and the utilization of electricity for mass production. By automating manufacturing with computing technologies and embedded hardware, industries transformed the third industrial revolution. A digital manufacturing environment that combines cutting-edge manufacturing technology to build an interconnected production system that examines, transfers, and relies on data to execute wise decisions in the real domain is a general definition of the fourth industrial era. Industry 4.0 makes use of analytics, Artificial Intelligence, and the Internet of Things (IoT) to facilitate better operations and decision-making. The fifth industrial revolution, which combines multiple methods into a unified infrastructure, is finally predicted by experts to begin. Since it involves more than just a technology change, it is drastically different. It brings back the individual to the operating centre via a Human-Cyber Physical System aimed at profit generation. The observation or conviction that Industry 4.0, although significantly emphasizing computerization and the use of AI technologies to increase productivity and flexibility, partially ignores its fundamental concepts of social equality and sustainability is what gave rise to Industry 5.0. As a result, the perception of Industry 5.0 offers a different angle and point of view, emphasizing the value of innovation and research in assisting the sector in providing sustainable aids to individuals within the limits of the planet [1]. Figure 8.1 shows the time it took to move from one revolutionary era to the next was significantly reduced by rapid technological improvement.

Industrial Internet of Things (IIoT) and digital twin (DT) are the two key cutting-edge ideas of Industry 4.0. IIoT facilitates real-time gathering, analyzing, and processing of data from sensors positioned throughout an intelligent factory. On the other hand, Industry 4.0 can copy or portray real machines, processes, or people in cyberspace with remarkable accuracy because of DT technology. To fully realize the promise of DT, IIoT is therefore a crucial strategic component and a fundamental requirement. The physical experiences of people, processes, and products

DOI: 10.1201/9781003582465-8

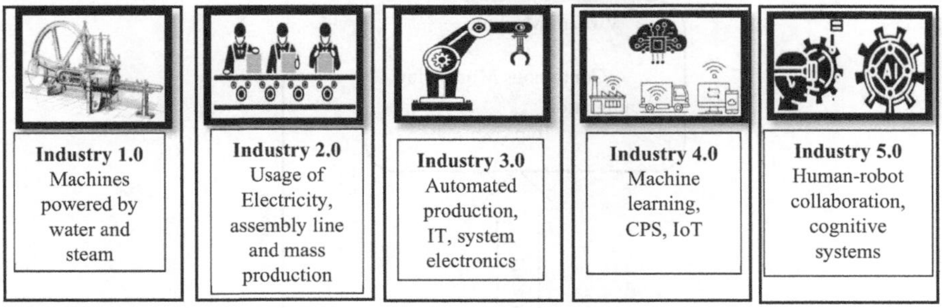

FIGURE 8.1 Industrial evolution.

are captured by IIoT as essential components of genuine DT to maximize field and manufacturing operations. Consequently, DT helps manufacturers construct superior goods, detect physical glitches prior, and make more accurate predictions.

8.1.2 DT Evolution

The idea of building similar spacecraft on Earth to mimic and forecast the behaviour of those in space was initially investigated during the NASA Apollo programme in the 1970s, which is where the term "digital twin" (DT) got its start. This programme recognized the value of physical twins, even if it was not a full DT system. As part of the University of Michigan's Product Lifecycle Management curriculum, Professor Grieves developed the idea of a "Virtual Digital Expression Equivalent to Physical Product" in 2003. This idea, which was first called the "Mirrored Space Model" and then the "Information Mirroring Model," established the framework for essential components for a DT, which includes the interaction between cyberspace and real-world space. Professor Grieves has finished the transition from entity to digital model in comparison to the "twin" proposed by the NASA Apollo programme.

The definition of DT, which has gained more prominence under Industry 4.0, is a digital model of a process or real-world system that permits continuous monitoring, examination, and improvement as depicted in Figure 8.2. Smart manufacturing can make use of a DT to boost part production efficiency and quality, forecast and prevent equipment breakdowns, and model and refine the production process [2]. By analyzing information from the real entity, the DT may track the physical object's performance, provide genuine feedback, and detect latent problems before they become issues. Additionally, before investing in real prototypes and assets, DT can be castoff by businesses to design, predict, and enhance goods and production processes throughout multiple industry sectors, including green energy, automotive, and aviation [3]. Therefore, DT can help in production processes such as the development of prudent judgements, overlays minimization, and growth improvement in various industries. Engineers and designers consider different situations and do refinements to save money and time using DT than prototyping and physical tests [4]. This ability is important in minimizing time-to-market and increase the production capacity to artefact manufacturers. The designing of DT is carried out by Computer-Aided Design illustrations with the aggregation of sensor data. So, the productivity is maximized by

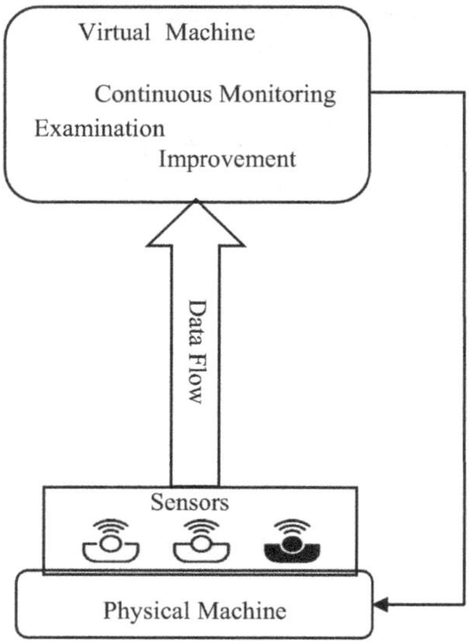

FIGURE 8.2 DT model.

making decisions based on data, detecting any problems before they arise, and tracking and assessing the functionality of tools and procedures in tangible intervals [5]. Engineers are able to observe a part's recital under various situations, including deviations in load, temperature, and pressure, by constructing a DT of the part. This facilitates them to antedate the part's performance in concrete settings, spot possible snags or malfunctions, and intensify its blueprints to boost performance [6]. Smart manufacturing can benefit from the DT in several ways. One benefit is that it enables continuous tracking of industrial processes, which facilitates the prompt detection and fixing of problems. It also makes it likely to examine and optimize processes and goods prior to manufacturing, which can save money and time.

With the use of performance virtual twins, manufacturing managers can enhance prototypes and performance of systems while generating new business prospects. At any stage of the production cycle, an all-encompassing DT for the engineering life-cycle enables the implementation and testing of ongoing improvements in a virtual environment that is significantly less costly to function than the actual one. Certain companies make use of DTs to mimic complete product lines and discover further operational ways to boost outcomes in partial manufacturing procedures [7]. An intelligent manufacturing technique digitizes all of its resources so that they may be examined and altered in virtual settings. Currently, DTs are used mostly for status monitoring, simulation, and visualization in smart manufacturing. Machines are constantly tracked via the IoT, and the virtual twin of a device can be utilized to ascertain its most recent state [8]. Live dashboards and warning systems can be cohesive with DT to monitor and diagnose an operating environment. These days, digital clones are only regarded as precise duplicates of real assets; they lack any additional services that would allow the real assets to act as sentient, autonomous entities. DTs can improve processes, increase output, recognize issues prior to, and continuously provide fresh insights in maintenance predictions [9]. A key advantage associated with this enhanced virtual twin architecture is the ability to offer more services beyond a flawless replica of DTs which aren't offered on real assets. Additionally, DT provides an exact duplicate of an actual setup, allowing for analysis and testing without affecting the original setup. For smart manufacturing processes, a DT can afford major aids in terms of output, lower expenses, and eminence of the product. DT will probably become a crucial tool for enterprises attempting to preserve their keenness in the international market as manufacturing grows more intricate and linked [10].

8.2 APPLICATIONS OF DT IN SMART MANUFACTURING

Applications of DTs in partial manufacturing enable the evaluation and adjustment of the efficacy of a product. With a DT, the total production procedure—from primary resources to completed merchandise—can be modelled. It can be applied to simulate diverse circumstances and envisage the behaviour of the system in specific circumstances. This makes it possible for manufacturers to spot possible problems and improve system performance [11]. In smart manufacturing processes, the DT can be allied to detection devices and other physical objects so that data collected throughout the production process can be used to update it in real time. Manufacturers are able to more accurately observe and regulate the equipment and render adjustments to optimize performance as a result [12]. A DT is capable of modelling how manufactured components would truly function in different operating conditions in virtual settings.

Testing is an integral part of the design process to evaluate the efficacy objectives of produced parts under operating circumstances as well as regulatory standards. By creating a virtual replica and using digital models for modelling and inquiry, the need to construct tangible prototypes can be removed. As a result, the approach or final item is of greater quality and is developed more quickly. At the production site, DTs are often used to track and enhance a whole line of production as well as every stage of manufacturing, including item investigation and development to making products [13]. Component analysis and modification using DTs are able to improve the component design optimization process. Companies can improve the precision and calibre of individual components produced by using this innovation to assess the designs of products in virtual settings.

8.2.1 Production Systems

Producers are able to minimize costs, improve quality, and increase productivity by employing DT as a dominant tool for ongoing industrialized system development to constantly improve industrial processes. To replicate and boost the efficacy of the real system, a virtual twin can be utilized in the framework of incessant progress of industrial systems. Manufacturers are able to now keep tabs on the efficiency of machines in an instant while matching it to expectations by leveraging the usage of DTs. The information can later be applied to upturn the machine's effectiveness and lifespan. This pulls down the idle time and boosts whole production by aiding producers to diagnose and resolve possible problems before they arise [14]. DTs are utilized for real-time manufacturing process review and inquiry in addition to optimization and simulation. Manufacturers can utilize DT to find drifts, patterns, and defects in their equipment by accumulating data from several sources and detectors.

Data-based decisions appropriate to optimizing the upshot and refining the overall result can subsequently be made using this information. DT can also be utilized to substantiate and inspect new manufacturing approaches or technologies before they are put into use in the real world. It reduces the time to launch the new products into the market and the probability of failures. The efficiency of product development is also escalated by providing additional details on predictable performance results. Industries use these statistics for making the necessary product modifications before the production begins [15].

The metadata of asset and production offered by DT technology is leveraged to optimize the process, discover the bottlenecks, and create new goods. If the condition and functionality of the equipment is well known by the production sector, the anomalies are detected in their operations more rapidly. This leads to planning the repair work and the substitution of auxiliary parts in advance to prevent expensive asset failures. Thus, DTs rise the artefact sturdiness and offer an innovative service-based profits for predictive maintenance. Virtual models of the used products offer complete data on workload capacity, defects, degradation spots, custom trends, etc. By better understanding the feature of product and catastrophe mechanisms, developers and designers may measure a product's usability and develop the future components' design. Based on unique usage patterns and product installation situations, this can offer customized products for different clientele. Based on empirical data, DT technology helps create virtual archetypes and run reliable imitations for feature testing [16–18].

Additionally, DT technology enhances product quality, traceability, batch changeover times, and waste reduction. By linking 3D models to equipment control code emulation and simulation, it facilitates effective design and development. Additionally, a DT eliminates the physical limitations of experienced engineers by enabling virtual troubleshooting and support. Dynamic supply chains with consumer interaction can potentially be built on top of this technology, establishing the information requirements and DT processes for the whole life cycle of the product, from asset creation to field use and real-world maintenance. In order to facilitate the flow of real-time sensor data as well as transactional and operational information from the company's core systems, enabling technology is developed by combining the physical asset and its DT, as described in conceptual architecture. The first step in building a DT is process design. Asset, time, or cost efficiency-enhancing attributes are added to the process design. Frequently, these are the fundamental presumptions that should serve as the basis for any upgrades to DTs [19–23].

8.2.2 Monitoring and Modifying the Part Production

The manufacturing processes, quality of goods, or even complete value chains can be boosted by exerting the DT concept. A DT of a specific device or process line might be created for part manufacturing, in order to incessantly track the manufacturing procedure in real time. This necessitates observance on variables like pressure, temperature, and rate of flow that may have a sway on the high standard of the finished product. Manufacturers might find places where manufacturing processes can be enhanced or reformed to increase yield and high-quality goods by probing data acquired through the DT. For example, the manufacturing process may be transformed to increase quality if the DT exposes that a precise machine is spawning goods with more flaws than others [24]. Furthermore, DTs are often employed to track energy consumption throughout the manufacturing of parts and ascertain locations where cost cutbacks are possible. DTs can also be used to implement continuous improvement at manufacturing localities.

The primary feature that sets DT apart from other major disruptors is its capacity to offer predictive assessments to organizations. The maintenance or operations team can assess an asset's long-term performance and contribution to the overall business performance with the help of the DT. Actually, it would be more correct to say that lifecycle analysis is aided by predictive analysis. From the moment an asset is designed until the end of its life, it generates data on it. This lowers the chance of industrial machine failures and many other business hazards. Businesses can test and certify a product using a DT before it is ever put into production. By creating a duplicate of the planned manufacturing process, a DT enables engineers to identify possible process flaws prior to the product entering production. In order to produce unexpected events, evaluate the system's behaviour, and suggest mitigation strategies, engineers might disrupt the system. It speeds up the development of new products, enhances risk assessment, and makes the production line more reliable. A virtual representation of a physical object can incorporate financial information, such as labour and material costs [25–29].

8.2.3 Method and Product Efficacy Enhancement

DTs are a cost-effective and time-efficient way to better control the industrial processes. Utilizing a DT could boost efficiency in the item's creation procedure and enhance processes in sectors like manufacturing. DTs help organizations increase the efficacy and productivity of their operations by providing a digital representation that is capable of being used for investigation and modelling. By using the potential advancements in statistical analysis and machine learning, enterprises can execute decisions based on data to increase productivity, reduce cost, and improve performance [30]. The technique can be very helpful for manufacturers in a variety of companies, spanning real-time quality predictions to doing away with costly testing procedures. DTs, which use intricate models powered by actual data collected via IoT devices such as detectors, are useful in improving current manufacturing procedures. A DT of a manufacturing line is a way to simulate how variations to the process of manufacturing will affect productivity and efficiency. By doing this, businesses can save time and money by determining which process modifications are most beneficial before putting them into practice [31]. Using the DT, manufacturing crews may analyze several data sources and reduce the number of damaged goods, which will increase efficiency and reduce prices throughout the component manufacturing procedures. Enterprises are able to increase output and reduce idle time. Additionally, the idea is applied to more rapidly anticipate maintenance issues. By using a DT, astute manufacturers can forecast the quality of the finished product, allowing them to make better judgements about material and process modifications. Assembly sectors have used DTs to guarantee stability during large-scale production [32].

DTs have several benefits since they improve products and processes and increase their efficiency. By using DTs, we can anticipate future challenges. Among other things, this reduces manufacturing time and gets rid of product defects. The DT is a great Industry 4.0 tool for evaluating new technologies electronically in order to mimic behaviours and reduce risks. They also maximize the incidence of events and states and allow for real-time monitoring operations. It is possible to simulate entire procedures in all their distinct phases due to DTs. Consequently, it is possible to optimize the entire process. It can be used directly in the design and manufacturing of products. It makes it possible to forecast how products will function and how manufacturing will proceed. Large amounts of data can be evaluated in order to build models based on reliable data that predict behaviours that maximize power generation activities. Because the DT reflects the condition and operation of power plants, it makes it possible to model the performance [33–35].

8.2.4 Predictive Maintenance

The purpose of predictive maintenance is to minimize downtime and save maintenance costs by monitoring equipment and forecasting when maintenance is necessary using data analysis tools and methodologies. Failures that could reduce production quality can be avoided with the help of early problem diagnosis. By using DT to study the core operations of their complex gear, manufacturers can predict when faults will occur and fix maintenance concerns before they halt production [36]. DTs can boost output, spot problems early, and continue to offer new insights into predictive maintenance. Finding the underlying reasons for the complications may be relieved with a spatial exemplary of machining methods via the use of the virtual twin during the making process.

One of the most important elements of predictive maintenance is condition monitoring [37]. Furthermore, predictive maintenance facilitates the early detection of defects that could subsequently worsen. Executives in the industrial sector should be able to make better decisions as a result of real-time equipment monitoring. The equipment will also last longer and function more efficiently overall. One of the elements influencing predictive maintenance's greater success is the achievements of manufacturing firms. Predictive maintenance is a component of predictive analytics in manufacturing [38]. Predictive maintenance solutions are essential for manufacturers because they can enhance the quality of their products, maximize precautionary or remedial actions done on resources, remove assembly deferments brought on using unplanned device idle time, and eventually save business outlays.

DTs are vital because they allow the system to run based on past demand data, weather forecasts, and other factors, ensuring nominal operating conditions in every situation. Network technology is connected to digital counterparts. Their ability to fix issues and provide better operational performance has made this digital screening component a crucial piece of technology for any business. DT technology gives businesses a full digital version of their products, which helps the industry identify any physical defects in hardware well in advance and take the appropriate action to resolve issues before they arise. In the corporate 4.0 concept, data is utilized to automate corporate processes. This makes the DT the perfect place to collect data from every part of the production process for analysis and modelling. When properly collected and designed, a DT can be used by vendors, data scientists, and other stakeholders to improve decision-making processes and influence corporate policy [39–41].

DTs enable engineers to test and model the item in a virtual environment, reducing current or potential production faults. Businesses who deploy a DT beat the competition and reduce time-to-market. An organization's risk can be greatly reduced by simulating the full product life in a digital setting, with all improvements done quickly and efficiently. Because the virtual replica confirms how an item will function in real life, the creation time is decreased. DTs have mostly been used in the sector. This is quickly changing, though, and many businesses, especially those integrating IoT into their daily operations, have an opportunity. The advantages of DTs will soon be felt in a number of industries. The DT approach made it easier to understand the different welding demands and concepts. Predictive maintenance can be included into business models as a benefit of building a virtual replica of a manufacturing plant or shop floor. The process of anticipating a machine or component breakdown and taking preventive action to stop it is known as predictive maintenance [42–45].

8.3 DT CASE STUDY IN MANUFACTURING

These days, DT is mostly used in engineering and manufacturing to create precise virtual objects and operational process simulations. Cyber physical systems can be modelled, simulated, and optimized with the help of the DT idea. It provides a comprehensive grasp of complicated physical procedures through diagnostic operations, modelling, tracking, enhancement, predictions, and physical wellness monitoring [46]. As a result, DTs enable businesses to produce more accurate projections, logical choices, and deliberate plans. In engineering, DTs are used to forecast how physical systems will behave and perform in the future. They aid in the collection of pertinent industrial big data, which supports decision-making processes and allows machines to behave in a self-adaptive manner. The utilization of DT in various fields is illustrated in Figure 8.3.

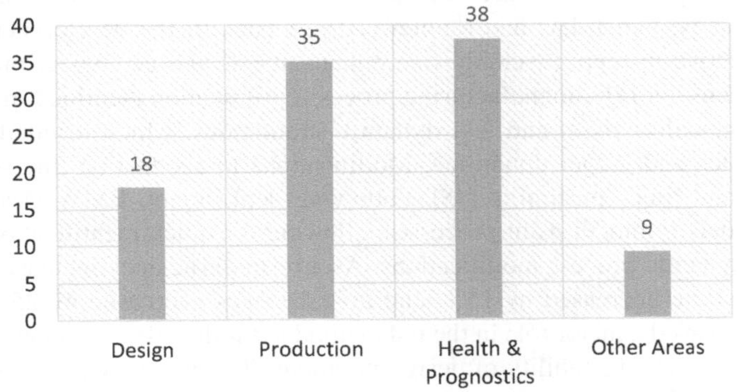

FIGURE 8.3 DT utilization in various fields.

Using virtual objects to monitor and control physical assets is another way that digital twinning is being used in production. Additionally, Industry 4.0 has facilitated high-tech innovations in tracking, detecting, and creating decisions. These encroachments, exclusively in IIoT, made it easier to accurately apply DT technology for continuous tracking and workflow optimization. In recent years, several technology companies have introduced DT services, including SAP, Oracle, and IBM. In a similar vein, IoT companies like Siemens and General Electric (GE) have developed or enhanced DT capabilities. Furthermore, producers may now take advantage of DT's advantages in a variety of fields due to developments in Industry 4.0 and the availability of technological assets. As a result, more complicated things including transportation networks, warehouses, and assembly line operations are now represented using DT. Lastly, DT is being used to transform production in asset-heavy industries like automotive, oil and gas, aerospace, and industrial products. The most common application for DT solutions is in production.

Through early problem detection, improved product design and construction, and more precise outcome prediction, DT may help manufacturing organizations address product concerns more quickly. DT can be applied in a variety of situations to achieve a range of goals. For instance, DT monitors and assesses wear and tear by simulating big mining trucks and airplane engines. Another example is a wind farm's DT, which can reveal operational inefficiencies. To extend product lifecycle management, Whirlpool Company implemented its digital renovation policy by investigating disruptive innovations like DT, IIoT, data-driven design, and augmented reality [47]. These represent only a handful of the numerous and quickly growing industries in which DTs could find use. In the context of reality, DTs are altering the approach we create, oversee, and care for chattels, from forecasting equipment breakdowns in complicated machinery to optimizing building energy usage. The vast bulk of current inquiries on DTs centres on hypothetical potentialities, dropping the entire scope of the benefits to mostly unrealized and deficient tangible instances. The sections that follow will highlight real-life instances of how several sectors are being transformed by DTs as well as diverse applications and practical deployments, to close this gap.

8.3.1 BMW

BMW's factory operations have been profoundly changed by the company's use of DT technology, which has had a noteworthy impact on the development of products, predictive upkeep, assembly line enhancement, and ecological programmes. Prior to the use of DTs, manufacturing process optimization identified inefficiencies through manual analysis and less dynamic simulations, which resulted in greater mistake rates and longer downtime. Modifications to production line setups were inflexible and time-consuming [48]. Following deployment, BMW used real-time digital models to model plant processes, allowing for quick identification of blockages and dynamic process modifications. As a result, efficiency increased by 20%–30%, downtime decreased by 15%, and mistake rates decreased by 25%. Physical prototypes played a major role in the old method to product development, which limited the pace and adaptability of design iterations. Testing procedures were limited to physical settings, which raised expenses and prolonged time-to-market. Virtual prototypes made possible by DTs enabled thorough testing in a variety of settings, leading to quicker design revisions and increased product dependability. BMW thereby cut R&D expenses by 20% and its time-to-market by 30%–40% [49].

The pre-DT process was primarily reactive or time-based in the maintenance domain, which resulted in production delays and frequent unplanned equipment breakdowns. Limited data insights resulted in less effective diagnostics. DTs made predictive maintenance possible after adoption by unceasingly tracking the state of machines and modelling possible problems. This proactive approach increased asset longevity by 15%–20%, reduced maintenance expenses by 25%, and reduced downtime by 50% [50]. BMW had difficulties monitoring and maximizing energy consumption and carbon emissions for sustainability. Inefficient use of resources and sluggish progress toward environmental goals were prevalent. BMW was able to lower its energy usage by 20% and emissions of carbon by 15% while also expediting adherence to green manufacturing standards due to the precise tracking and optimizing the energy use and emissions brought about by DTs. All things considered, DTs have transformed BMW's production processes, improving productivity, economy, and environmental performance while establishing a standard for creativeness in intelligent manufacturing systems. Figure 8.4 and Table 8.1 summarize the overall impact of BMW adoption of DT technology.

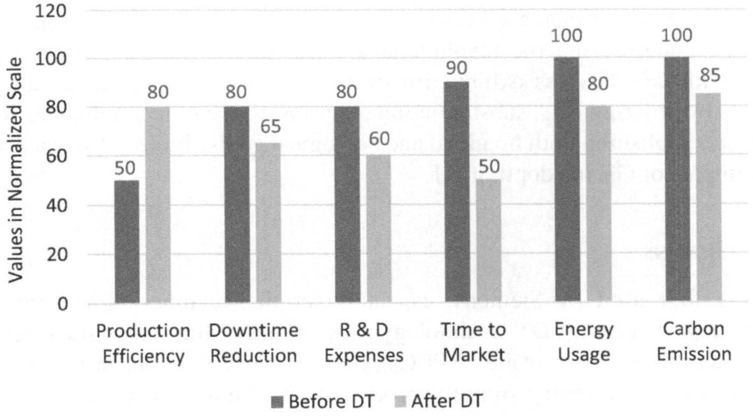

FIGURE 8.4 Impact of DT technology.

TABLE 8.1
Overall Impact of DT Utilization

Metric	Before DT	After DT	Improvement
Production efficiency	Moderate	High	+20%–30%
Downtime reduction	High	Significantly lower	−15%
R & D expenses	High	Reduced	−20%
Time-to-market	Long	Accelerated	−30%–40%
Energy usage	Higher	Optimized	−20%
Carbon emission	Higher	Lower	−15%

8.3.2 General Electric (GE)

For energy management and equipment maintenance, GE used conventional techniques prior to implementing DT technology. These techniques were primarily reactive and planned. Equipment failures were frequently addressed by maintenance plans after they happened, which resulted in unscheduled downtime and higher operating expenses. In a similar vein, energy management procedures lacked accuracy and had little real-time monitoring, forecasting, and optimization capabilities. These difficulties led to decreased asset lifespan, increased carbon emissions, and inefficiency. GE reformed how it loomed energy management and predictive maintenance by using DT technology. DTs made it possible to simulate and observe equipment operation in tangible time by provoking counterfeit copies of physical property. GE was able to foresee possible issues by using predictive analytics and take action before they caused any interruptions. The functional life of vibrant machinery was increased, and downtime was radically lessened by up to 25% due to this proactive maintenance strategy [51].

DTs provided GE erudite tools for energy management, allowing them to model energy use and maximize resource utilization. GE could adopt more energy-efficient practices, by modelling various operational situations, which would result in a 15% decrease in energy expenses and carbon emissions [52]. DTs' real-time perceptions helped make better decisions and match operations with sustainability objectives. The use of DT led to increased operational effectiveness, cost reductions, and sustainability, underscoring the revolutionary effect of this innovation on industrial processes for GE. GE has exhibited a standard in the manufacturing and energy industries by utilizing DTs, substantiating the prominence of technological advancement in accomplishing both financial and ecological goals. Table 8.2 summarizes the overall impact of GE in adopting DT.

8.3.3 Siemens

DTs were first used by Siemens, especially at their Amberg Electronics Plant in Germany. Utilizing DT technology, the plant, which manufactures PLCs Programmable Logic Controllers (PLCs), builds a virtual model of the whole production process. Everything from the production workflow to machine operations is included in this digital reproduction. Siemens has achieved notable strides by replicating and optimizing these processes, increasing its capacity to modify manufacturing volumes by 30%, increasing productivity by 20%, and improving space efficiency by 40% [53]. Additionally, the DT makes predictive maintenance possible,

TABLE 8.2
Overall Impact of Utilization of DT

Metric	Before DT	After DT	Improvement
Proactive maintenance	Leads to unexpected failures	Reduce downtime and increase lifespan of machine	25% reduction in downtime
Energy utilization	Physical optimization of energy usage	Real-time monitoring and problems prophecy	15% reduction in energy expenses

TABLE 8.3
Impact of Adoption of DT

Metric	Before DT	After DT	Improvement
Productivity	Limited capacity for real-time production process optimization.	Enhanced automation, predictive capabilities, and real-time process improvement.	+20%–30%
Space efficiency	Inadequate use of warehouse and manufacturing space.	Enhanced spatial organization and use due to digital simulations.	+40%

TABLE 8.4
Overall Impact of DT Utilization

Metric	Before DT	After DT	Improvement
Aircraft design	Greater use of physical prototypes and lengthier design and testing cycles.	Quicker design iterations using simulations and virtual models.	80% decrease in the assembly line and 50% decrease in development time.
Sustainability	Higher CO_2 emission	Lower	–25%
Material garbage	Higher	Significant reduction	–28.6% solid waste and –24.9% hazardous waste
Fuel efficiency	Suboptimal fuel efficiency	Optimization of fuel efficiency	12% reduced consumption

which lowers unplanned equipment failures and increases the machinery's lifespan. By modifying the DT model and making minor adjustments to the physical plant, Siemens can also promptly respond to shifts in demand [54]. The overall impact of Siemens adoption of DT is listed in Table 8.3.

8.3.4 Boeing

In several areas of its business, Boeing has used DT technology to improve productivity, creativity, and sustainability. Boeing has greatly shortened design and prototyping times by incorporating DT into the design of aircraft. This has allowed for quicker iterations and higher precision through virtual simulations. Assembly lines have become more efficient, downtime has decreased, and manufacturing efficiency has increased due to real-time monitoring and production optimization of the process [55]. DTs are also used in prophetic service, which reduces maintenance expenses and operational downtime by allowing continuous surveillance of aircraft systems to anticipate and prevent failures.

DTs in the management of supply chains offer predictive analytics and real-time insight, which improve inventory control, encourage proactive logistics, and cut down on delays. Continuous monitoring and fine-tuning of aircraft systems has also led to fuel efficiency and productivity optimization, which has resulted in saving money and environmental benefits. DTs have also helped Boeing achieve its sustainability goals by lowering emission of carbon and material garbage via more efficient operations [56]. Table 8.4 summarizes this.

TABLE 8.5
Impact of DT Utilization

Aspect	Impact (%)
Asset life	+15%
Operational hazards	–20%–25%
Decision-making efficiency	+10%–15%
Reliability	+20%–25%
Defect rate	–10%

With the usage of DT, Boeing was able to save assembly hours by 80%, software development time by 50%, and aerospace engineering first-time quality by 75% during the development of the T-7A aircraft [57]. This made it possible for the aircraft to be designed and fly for the first time in just 36 months. Boeing also improved the first-time systems quality and materials for both defence and commercial airlines by 40% through the introduction of DT assets. Boeing may also use DTs to conduct virtual tests on novel materials and designs, which speeds up innovation and enhances aircraft safety and dependability. DTs are also used in Boeing's in-service aircraft, where performance data is tracked to guarantee optimal operation and preventive maintenance.

8.3.5 IBM

To promote creativity and efficiency in operation in a variety of industries, IBM has incorporated DT within its portfolio. The business uses its knowledge of AI, the IoT, and cloud computing to offer cutting-edge DT solutions that facilitate process optimization, predictive maintenance, and real-time system tracking [58]. Manufacturing uses IBM's DT extensively to model production processes, identify inefficiencies, and streamline workflows. IBM uses DTs in the energy sector to improve resource allocation, forecast equipment failures, and monitor infrastructure. IBM also helps create smart cities by utilizing DTs for sustainability projects, traffic control, and urban planning.

IBM's solutions frequently integrate its Watson IoT platform with DT technology, offering actionable insights via machine learning and data analytics [35]. By using these technologies, businesses may increase overall system reliability, decrease downtime, and foresee possible problems. This method speeds up innovation, reduces operating costs, and improves strategic decision-making. Table 8.5 provides more information on the impact of DT adoption [59].

8.4 DT FRAMEWORK FOR INTELLIGENT MANUFACTURING SYSTEMS

A significant DT framework created especially for predictive analysis is suggested in this section. To guarantee precise forecasts and useful insights, it integrates deep learning algorithms, tangible prediction, and sophisticated data collection. This framework attempts to address issues like mechanical failures and complicated decision in diverse systems by fusing the advantages of DTs and predictive analytics.

8.4.1 Background

As the industries continue to establish and work on increasing the efficiency and reducing the breakdowns or malfunctions, DT steps in to solve it through predictive analysis. During production, predictive analysis plays a role as it focuses on accurate predictions to handle the unexpected disruptions in the normal operations while at the same moment upholds the maximum productivity. DT works on this cause as its feature is to observe the developing patterns from the already obtained data from a vast number of physical systems. This also helps in pin-pointing the oddities that may arise in the future. The strategy introduced by DT proves to be preventive as it consumes the resources effectively and curbs the expenses that might pop up due to unexpected failures. They further extend their helping hands in predictive analysis by their potential to predict the possible outcomes and simulate different ambiences. Testing can be done by the manufacturers on the aftermath of modifying procedures, resources, or system settings in a virtual space so that there is no hindrance in the actual business.

The digital model can undermine the behaviour of the actual system and replay the dynamic behaviour virtually in real time because these inputs of the system like pressure, temperature, torque, vibration, and even energy consumption are continuously fed into the model. This data design is supported with predictive analytics to predict equipment failures and sophisticated machine learning algorithms to anticipate the remaining useful life (and identify anomalies) very well. It is so because such models are self-optimizing over a certain time because of the sensitivity of fault detection, feedback, and growth of prognostic knowledge. However, DT infrastructure interacts repeatedly with the clouds platform and edge computing devices, providing the opportunity to process big data in large scale and make decisions in real time. This type of technological cooperation may allow manufacturers to bring the Mean Time Between Failures and Mean Time to Repair to minimum possible values and decrease production downtimes and optimize maintenance periods by changing the paradigm of condition-based and predictive maintenance to the paradigm of reactive and time-based maintenance.

This factor assists them in improving strategies and increasing production efficiency besides improving system reliability. DTs are also able to offer a controlled and safe environment where modelling the effects of system failures can help to create effective backup plans. The other notable advantage of DTs in predictive analysis is that, due to the optimization of the process and waste reduction, DTs can make the contribution to the environment and effectively utilize the resources. Predictive maintenance can assist in energy saving since the machines will work at their best performance and computer simulations of production conditions will allow one to make informed decisions that can be sustained by the sustainability objectives. In conclusion, the predictive analysis of intelligent manufacturing is based on the use of DTs and enables the assertive preparation of servicing, optimization of functions, and sustainable practices.

8.4.2 Objective

The proposed structure framework is established so that it will accomplish the following objectives:

- The overall architecture of anomaly detection of the DT systems is aimed at improving the decision-making, operational reliability, and effectiveness of intelligent manufacturing systems. The first objective is early detection, which is finding out the deviations or the irregularities in real time and preventing any possible application of systems breakdown or interruption. The system uses the real-time data and statistical analytics to identify the anomalies at the early stage to take actions in time. This improves the overall functionality of the system, reduces the maintenance cost, and minimizes the downtime.
- The second objective is to improve the decision-making process. It is achieved through quick and data-driven response to the identified anomalies. The framework compiles machine learning and predictive analytics to provide valuable information to managers and operators in order to understand the nature and severity of abnormalities. This is done by making sure that the judgements are made using the most current and accurate information and not on a hunch or delayed analysis of the data, which will lead to better outcomes and more optimal use of the resources.
- Constant observation of manufacturing procedures and equipment is also stressed in the framework. Through continuous smooth control, it ensures the functioning of all system parts within predefined limits to minimize the risk of failure without being identified to escalate into a critical failure. Second, long-term monitoring provides an in-depth knowledge of the health of the operations and helps in long-term planning and maintenance strategies.

8.4.3 Proposed DT Methodology

The general structure of the DT framework is presented in Figure 8.5, which contains Data Acquisition Layer, DT Layer, Anomaly Detection Engine, Decision-Making Support, and monitoring interface functional modules.

8.4.3.1 Acquisition Layer

One of the components of the DT system, the data gathering layer, is responsible to gather, analyze, and transmit data of the actual production environment to the digital one. The first stage of this layer involves installing IoT devices and physical sensors on production lines, robots, and equipment. These sensors present the real-life data that is needed to monitor and assess performance of the system by recording critical attributes such as temperature, vibration, and pressure. Sensors can also be integrated organically into the digital space effortlessly with the help of IoT devices, which ensures the uninterrupted flow of data. Edge computing nodes are necessary to process the unprocessed data collected by sensors. This pre-processing is to be

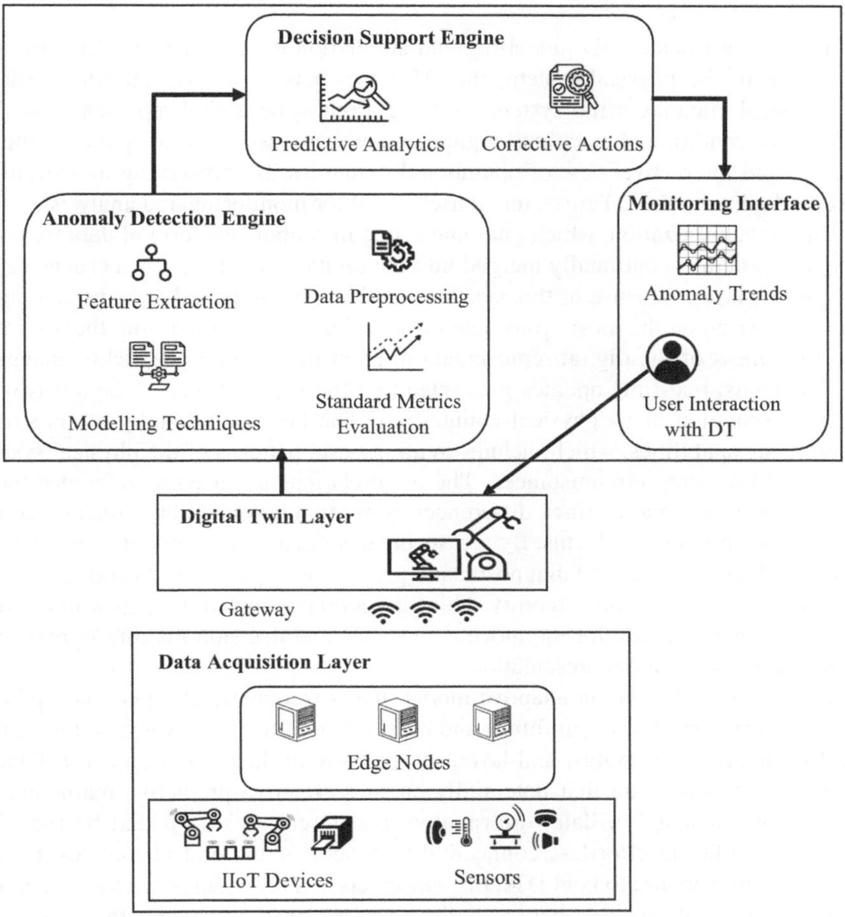

FIGURE 8.5 Proposed DT architecture.

done in order to increase the quality of the data by eliminating irrelevant information and noise-sifting.

Edge nodes also simplify real-time analysis by performing local calculations, reducing the dependence on centralized systems, and minimizing the latency. This strategy will result in the extraction of actionable insights in a short period of time, and this will be easy in making decisions. The data stream management is part of the layer as it provides effective and reliable data transfer. It makes use of protocols such as OPCUA Open Platform Communication Unified Architecture (OPCUA) that are highly reliable and secure regarding data exchange within an industrial environment and MQTT Message Queuing Telemetry Transport (MQTT) which is lightweight and suited in the requirements of connecting the IoT. These protocols allow the DT to reproduce the real world through ensuring the consistency and integrity of the streams.

8.4.3.2 DT Layer

By using sophisticated 3D modelling and simulation to replicate the structure and behaviour of the physical system, the DT Layer acts as the virtual equivalent of the physical manufacturing system, offering a real-time digital representation that reflects the condition of machines, equipment, and processes, allowing for a comprehensive and interactive view of operational dynamics. By preserving an extremely precise depiction, the DT turns into a useful tool for monitoring and analysis.

Data synchronization, which guarantees that instantaneous form of data from the physical system is continually merged into the digital counterpart, is a crucial function of this layer. Because of this synchronization, operators and systems can make decisions based on the most up-to-date information while maintaining the accuracy and timeliness of the digital representation. Even in dynamic or quickly changing environments, real-time updates guarantee that the DT continues to be a trustworthy representation of its physical counterpart. The layer additionally offers strong simulation capabilities, which include creating basal patterns of the physical system in typical operating circumstances. These simulations are used as reference models to identify anomalies since differences between a predicted baseline and actual data suggest possible problems. By measuring desired and true performance, the DT Layer enables sophisticated diagnostic and prognostic capabilities, boosting the system's ultimate efficacy and stability. This all-encompassing strategy guarantees that the DT is an active tool for monitoring, analysis, and decision-making in real time rather than just a static representation.

The DT is said to be an adaptive model that is frequently changed and updated with the variation of physical things and portrays conditions for working, the equipment status, resource status, and layout in the form of data management. DT technology is one invention that potentially enables effective predictive maintenance. A two-way exchange of data, information, and forecasts is provided by the twin system, by offering effortless connectivity between actual and virtual realms. As various sectors endure to hold DTs, the way assets and procedures are tracked down, analyzed, and optimized is being totally transformed. DT provides the users with intellectual application services, which include operation optimization, design optimization, fault diagnosis, and fault prediction. These are just enough to execute the data handling needed for predictive maintenance. DT has the potential to universally configure repairs choices, and the choice of repairs timing does not require physical evaluation. The DT demonstrates the virtual conception prototype of the equipment with the help of picturing interfaces. This model communicates with the real-time data of the physical objects and can evidently and instinctively present the fault statistics of the machinery and present circumstances to the operatives.

The necessities such as maintenance decision-making and fault caution will too turn out to be very direct and reliable. In summation, the DT is a contrary engineering feat in which the occurrences in the real domain is simulated in the virtual space. It can produce perceptions and forecasts regarding the performance and behaviour of the physical asset. DT enables manufacturers to optimize and test the tasks virtually prior to putting changes into practice in the real world, and DT can be unceasingly enhanced by gathering data, performance evaluation, and offering suggestions for improvement. Thus, DT technology can improve production scheduling and planning and lessen the effect of fabrication downtime on site by combining virtual and real-world interactions to automatically optimize algorithms.

8.4.3.3 Anomaly Detection Engine

An essential part of the DT architecture is the anomaly detection layer, which uses ML and sophisticated analytics to find departures from typical operating conditions. It is made up of a number of modules that cooperate to guarantee precise detection and trustworthy system performance insights. The Feature Extraction Module emphasizes on discovering and acquiring key performance indicators using the primary data collected by sensors. In order to highlight metrics that are most pertinent to identifying anomalies, these key performance indicators—such as thermal thresholds or vibration patterns—are developed using domain-specific knowledge. By ensuring that the analysis focuses on significant attributes, this module lowers complexity and improves the precision of later phases.

By normalizing the extracted data to ensure consistency across various variables, the Data Pre-processing Module gets it ready for analysis. By preventing scaling problems that might affect model performance, this normalization guarantees that the data is comparable. The module also handles common problems with data quality by smoothing noisy signals to remove random oscillations and handling missing values using imputation techniques. For robust anomaly detection, a clean and trustworthy dataset is produced by these pre-processing steps. Lastly, to identify irregularities in the pre-processed data, the Modelling Techniques component uses sophisticated algorithms. Depending on the type of data, this can include deep learning techniques like auto-encoders or Long Short-Term Memories as well as machine learning models like decision trees or support vector machines. By simulating conventional patterns of behaviour and recognizing aberrations, this layer delivers actionable information, enabling prompt interventions and preventive steps. These modules work together to create a unified and effective anomaly detection layer, which guarantees the dependability and operational excellence of the system.

In the anomaly detection layer, deep learning methods are essential, especially when examining intricate time-series data. Neural networks called auto-encoders are frequently employed for unsupervised anomaly identification. They are made to learn and then reconstruct a reduced version of the input data. Any notable differences between the actual data and the recreated output throughout this reconstruction phase suggest possible anomalies. This method works particularly well for identifying complex relationships and patterns in the data that conventional approaches might overlook. Another effective method for managing sequential data is the use of Recurrent Neural Networks, including their more sophisticated variations such as Long Short-Term Memory networks. These models are perfect to analyze time-series data in industrial systems since they are specifically made to handle data with temporal dependencies. Recurrent Neural Networks are able to identify abnormalities when sequence deviations occur because they have learned the typical patterns and sequences of operational data. The efficacy of the anomaly detection layer in intelligent manufacturing systems is increased when auto-encoders and Recurrent Neural Networks work together to offer strong capabilities for detecting anomalies in complicated datasets.

8.4.3.4 Decision-Making Support

The decision-making support is the key component of anomaly detection architecture. It contributes in operational efficiency by providing positive and planned guidance. This module will do the pre-emptive analytics using the past as well as the current data to test the possibility of arising anomalies. It works on analyzing the trends and patterns that help in recognizing the possible faults in the system by implementing well-developed technologies such as statistical forecasting and machine learning models. Any failure in the system can be minimized, and the allocation of the resources can be configured by confronting the problems before they become grave due to this prescience.

The module provides tailored recommendations on remedial actions other than forecasting. An example of this is where the system can recommend specific maintenance or adjustment of operating parameters in case an anomaly shows that an element of a machine is worn and tear. Such ideas are often prioritized by the level of seriousness and urgency of the identified issue, which ensures that urgent problems are addressed first and routine ones are managed masterfully. This module reduces risk of operation and system reliability and enhances productivity in the intelligent industrial setting, since it allows making informed decisions using data.

8.4.3.5 Monitoring Interface

The monitoring interface must participate in the anomaly detection structure to track the performance of the systems; therefore, it provides an interactive space as well as being user friendly. This interface is a short and straightforward description of the working order of machine, equipment, and processes, and thus, it predicts the actual-time anomaly progress. It supports the users to identify the trends and see the features of the system change over time, by giving trend analysis, and indicating the discovered anomalies. Since it offers real-time solutions to emerging problems, this proactive presence facilitates functional stability.

The interface makes operators interact with the visualization of the DT as well as real-time monitoring. The users are able to explore more about specific components or processes by exploring complex virtual images of real-life systems. This is practicable and enhances understanding and making of effective decisions. The monitoring interface is a powerful device to maintain the system performance and improve the efficiency of the work in intelligent industrial settings as the interactive DTs are merged with real-time data display.

8.5 DTS SETBACKS, THREATS, AND COMPLICATIONS

8.5.1 Recurring Setbacks and Restrictions

Numerous papers examined the dangers and threats that might affect the digital and physical components of the DT. The sections that follow provide descriptions of them. We have examined the multiple advantages of DT technology in the present paper. Not with standing these benefits, the technology nevertheless faces typical difficulties, such as those encountered by IoT and Artificial Intelligence technologies. The problems include challenges in installing and changing legacy systems Technovio as well as data standardization, administration, and security. Computer-aided design models, IoT sensors, libraries of historical data, and real-time data saved in numerous formats within a few other systems are just a few of the sources of data that DT solutions retrieve. It can be quite difficult and complex to combine this variety of data into a coherent, single model. Any errors in this data might lessen the efficacy of the DT's way of providing solutions, heightening the importance of making sure the data is accurate and comprehensive [60]. Additionally, scaling DT technology to handle massive quantities of data and complex prototypes can be problematic and is a major barrier. For example, the amount of processing power and storage space needed to handle and process data grows along with the size of the data and the complexity of the models. This necessitates infrastructure and effective algorithms that can meet the DT system's requirements. According to Technovio (2024) [61], all of these elements highlight the vitality of strong data governance structures and accessible technical infrastructure to fully utilize DT technology.

Furthermore, to make full use of the potential advantages of digital (software) technologies, the embodiment of DTs requires the administration, organization, and assimilation of data and models that arise across many technical domains. However, integrating several models, data sources, and associations to construct DTs can be a challenging undertaking. However, there are nevertheless numerous impediments to be addressed in the design, construction, and evolution of DTs, specifically:

i. Dealing with a variety of models from different fields,
ii. Guaranteeing a bidirectional synchronization between the physical systems and DTs they stand for, and
iii. Promoting collaborative enhancement in every stage of the cycle.

Further glitches consist of the need to modernize the obsolete IT setup, connectivity, the seclusion and safety of subtle data, and the deficit of a consistent modelling procedure. Predominantly in the manufacturing sector, the inadequate use of DTs is endorsed to the absence of conventional standards and approved compatibility. Furthermore, the restricted espousal of DTs might be expounded by the absence of conventional standards and endorsed interoperability, mostly in the manufacturing industry. The substantial cost of implementation and intricate architecture are other significant obstacles that could seriously slow down the usage of DT technology. The primary challenge to the wider application of DT expertise is the prohibitive costs of implementing them, which are caused by the surged requirement for detection devices and computational power. A substantial upfront venture in infrastructure building, upkeep, and safety measures is required for the deployment of DT systems. It is expensive and requires a significant operational investment to maintain DT infrastructure. It is anticipated that the emergence of DT technology will be slowed considerably by its significant fixed expenses and intricate infrastructure. The last significant obstacle preventing DT advancement is communication networks. 5G and other quicker and more unwavering communication interfaces are essential to tackling this. 5G is of paramount importance in smart cities, according to new research [62], which highlights its perspective to:

- Establish a much wider network of sensors and gadgets;
- Provide ubiquitous swift connectivity;
- Improve redundancy as well as dependability; and
- Facilitate extremely low electrical energy consumption.

Table 8.6 provides a summary of the aforementioned difficulties.

Furthermore, the usage of DT technology by organizations will be safeguarded by the need of robust IoT infrastructure bases and a profounder comprehension of data required for analytics. To assurance that the right points are taken while creating DT systems, it is necessary to consider the gains and minuses of the anticipation of DTs. It is apparent that the complications tackled by data analytics and the IoT are similar to those faced by the use of a DT. The modelling and construction of the DT provide unique obstacles in addition to the privacy and infrastructure issues that the DT bonds with data analytics and IoT from the user's point of view. Owing to the dearth of a standardized moulding practice, the subsequent hurdles in all forms of DT development relate to the modelling of such systems. Whether it is physics-based or design-based, a standard strategy should be adhered to from the creation of DT to its simulation. In addition to guaranteeing the flow of information between the creation step and deployment of a DT, standardized methodologies guarantee user and domain knowledge.

TABLE 8.6
Recurring Setbacks and Restrictions

Key Challenges	Summary
Data fusion challenges	Combining data from Computer-Aided Design models, IoT sensors, antique archives, and instantaneous systems is complex. Inaccuracies reduce solution efficacy.
Scalability issues	Increasing data size and model complexity demand higher computing power, storage, efficient algorithms, and scalable infrastructure.
Coordination of models and data	Difficulties in assimilating, coordinating, and administering diverse engineering models and data sources.
Standardization issues	Lack of standardized modelling and recognized interoperability, particularly in manufacturing, limits implementation.
Cost challenges	High deployment costs due to sensors and computational resources. Upfront expenditure for administration, safety, and logistics.
Groundwork complexity	Expensive maintenance and operational hassles slow down DT deployment.
Communication networks	Challenges in communication networks necessitate faster, robust technologies like 5G to facilitate operational reliability and accurate information transmission.

8.5.2 Deployment Setbacks

Since DT technology is still in its infancy, it must overcome certain hurdles and constraints to be implemented in the modern era. These include exorbitant expenses, intricate data management and upkeep, a dearth of clear guidelines and rules, and concerns with communication and cyber security. For the majority of applications, DTs' technological maturity and capacity are still in their development. Future studies must have to offer an efficient method to evaluate DTs from the standpoints of technical proficiency, societal readiness, and maturity. Furthermore, there nevertheless remains a great deal to be completed to absolutely incorporate sustainable, autonomous, and approved DTs into practical situations. Overcoming such and other barriers will become more achievable as technology develops further within the parameters of innovation and sustainability. Tools and technologies for processing and analyzing data will be essential facilitators for developing DTs [63].

There is a substantial knowledge vacuum regarding the practical implementation of DT concepts. Research ought to give priority to DT deployment strategies that are efficient and have a good cost-benefit ratio. Decision-makers must be educated on the practical and appropriate implementation of DTs, given their near-miraculous potential and recurring mentions [64]. Table 8.7 lists some of the DT deployment setbacks. This goes beyond merely fixing technological problems; it also involves realizing how vital human factors are. Gaining expertise and improving skills are two crucial elements for this technology's successful implementation. The focus going forward will be on utilizing the skills and talents of experts who are proficient at negotiating the complex world of DTs. These professionals will be crucial in helping the manufacturing industry, in particular, deal with the challenges of carrying out and supervising DTs [65].

TABLE 8.7
Deployment Setbacks

Key Aspects	Summary
Technological maturity	Demands improvements in maturity, societal readiness, and technical competence.
Integration in real-world scenarios	Emphasizes autonomous, sustainable DTs. Requires overcoming technical hurdles and leveraging sophisticated instruments for evaluating and dealing with data.
Human factors' function	Gaining competence and improving skills are essential. Specialized professionals are crucial for navigating complexities and training others.
Findings from industrial study	Non-technical barriers, such as scarcity of expertise, outweigh technical challenges. Persistent technical issues include a lack of data/model standardization.
Sector-specific needs	The manufacturing sector relies on experts to address deployment complexities and ongoing management.
Critical roles of specialists	Manage data integration, security, and large data volumes. Foster team training and a culture embracing advanced technology.

A recent survey also made it clear that it is paramount to focus on the technical challenges of DT implementation and, at the same time, to consider human factors that are required to ensure the success of this technology implementation, including skill development and competence. In a study aimed at gaining insights into the major challenges in implementing DTs, 61 experts working in the industry were engaged in an investigation. These accomplices were to rate the likelihood that some problems, classifications, and definite obstacles will lead to conflicts in the implementation of the DT. The conclusions that followed the findings were that, even though there were still technical problems like the harmonization of models and the absence of data, the main hurdles were non-technical. The information indicated that the absence of the expertise and specialized knowledge was more apt to become the reason of the implementation problems in DT [66]. It is impossible to overestimate the flagrancy of these non-technical elements. In order to overcome the difficulties of organization and running of DTs, it is essential to involve specialists who have specialized training and knowledge. They must deal with complexities of working with large volumes of data, combining different sources of data, and ensuring the security of data. They also play a vital role in inculcating a culture of valuing this innovative technology and training other personnel in the organization.

8.5.3 Confidentiality, Security Hazards, and Unanticipated Consequences

Security concerns about the integrity, confidentiality, and accessibility of information and resources must be taken into account when treating DTs as critical systems. Enhancing DT's security concerns requires taking into account both digital and physical attack types. All security risks related to endpoint, facility, IoT, and communication infrastructure access are included in the physical attack. Digital attacks target software-related security risks, including subpar coding and updates, preset security configurations, and elements like the setup and statistics systems. As mentioned before, the innovations required for DT implementation include cloud computing, virtualization, big data, IoT, and AI. The use of these innovations and the collaboration of DT with the physical thing in the real world creates some security risks. They are vulnerable to various attacks that have not been thoroughly investigated up to this point [67]. Analyzing the dangers and attacks that target the IoT, AI, and data transmission components of DT is essential, as is considering potential remedies to lessen the security threats.

Data trust and reliability confront DT with yet another key problem. To guarantee data quality, at each phase of development, DT systems must be integrated with a very safe framework and improved upon regularly. One technique for improving data reliability that can solve issues with data security, privacy, and trustworthiness is block chain technology. Other issues include distributed decision-making, seamless integration, verification, and reliability and viability within the production unit that must be addressed before DT can be used [68]. Numerous articles examined the dangers and threats that might affect the digital and physical components of the

DT [64,69]. The following is a list of these risks, possible restrictions, and unforeseen consequences:

- Security and data integrity.
- Weak software protection may result from improper coding that allows unlawful entry into the source code or DT software.
- There may be significant risks to data transmission and communications from or to the cloud and IoT. Denial of Service, distributed denial of service, spoofing, and wiretapping are among the most well-known dangers.
- Cloud data storage is sensitive and subject to numerous hazards, particularly those about privacy and trust, particularly in public clouds.
- The IoT and DT devices must be physically secured because an attacker could destroy, damage, or even steal them.

In order to achieve the transformative powers of the DTs to the fullest extent, we should promptly address the technological challenges that are revealed in Table 8.8, while at the same time building an environment of open collaboration between academicians, technology developers, and business professionals. This collaborative approach will play a key role in overcoming all the challenges. It is clear that the anonymity and security of the DTs gives a block in an enterprise setting: first, because of the high level of usage of data, and second, because of the risk such an activity poses to valuable system data. The two primary technologies facilitating the use of DTs, IoT, and data analytics should adhere to the new rules regarding privacy and security to overcome this barrier. Confidentiality and safety of data help to address trust hitches with DT. It has challenges with trust between the organization and the user. Further arguing and clarification of the technology is necessary in order to ensure that organizations and end users comprehend the advantage of a DT, which will aim to shatter the barrier of trust.

Another strategy for overwhelming the confidence issues is model authentication. Ensuring operator trust requires approving that DT functions as planned. More knowledge leads to more confidence in DTs. By providing extra understanding into the procedures that guarantee confidentiality and security standards adhered to

TABLE 8.8
Confidentiality, Security Hazards, and Unanticipated Consequences

Threats	Insight
Data integrity	Software protection may be weakened by illegal manipulation of the DT system or its code brought on by shoddy coding.
Data communication risks	Threats include Denial of Service, Distributed Denial of Service, spoofing, and eavesdropping.
Cloud storage risks	Risks associated with sensitive data on the cloud include privacy and trust challenges, particularly in public cloud systems.
Physical security	DT and IoT devices are vulnerable to damage, destruction, or theft by attackers.

throughout development, the technology that allows for it will help overcome obstacles with confidence. Making sure domain-use information is taken to all of the functional and development stages of a DT modelling leads to additional difficulty as an effect of the requirement for standardized use. This assures compatibility with areas like IoT and data analytics, aiding the DT to be successfully utilized in the upcoming time.

8.6 CONCLUSION AND FUTURE INVESTIGATION WORK GUIDELINES

A computer-generated representation of an actual scheme that is employed to observe, govern, and enhance the physical matching part is called a "DT." In the perspective of smart manufacturing, a virtual replica of an industrial plant or manufacturing process can be created by a virtual twin. This helps producers to detect potential problems as well as areas for improvement, assess and enhance their methods of production, and create sound decisions about supply distribution and assembly timing. A company's promotional value can be significantly increased by using DTs to improve costs and time efficacy, ensure seamless merchandise or procedure functioning, and foster performance excellence. DTs assist businesses in achieving better decision-making, operational optimization, and enhanced productivity through the efficient utilization of information and powerful analytics. They can help identify product issues before they result in damage and part production failure. Therefore, by employing DTs to forecast and analyze issues and mistakes in the production process and products, businesses could extend the lifespan of their tangible assets and machinery. DTs can also be rummage-sale to advance the part production productivity by streamlining production processes and reducing downtime. With the increasing allocation of cognitive assets towards the application of them, DTs' potential in smart production is essentially immeasurable. DT may continuously produce the insights needed to improve goods and expedite processes as they acquire novel abilities.

The next direction of the DTs approach to smart manufacturing should be to incorporate industry. AI, IoT, and machine learning to make decisions and improve efficiency 4.0 innovations. It is essential to focus on DTs with IoT real-time monitoring, the creation of multifaceted twins with multi-scale data combining to gain deeper insights into processes, and complex analytics to optimize the performance. Predictive capabilities based on AI/ML, environmental sustainability via scalability, and real-time response to supply chain changes should also be investigated in research. Also, there is the necessity to maximize supply chains by modelling them virtually, increase cooperation between stakeholders by using virtual platforms, enable human–machine interaction to make more effective decisions, and manage cyber security issues in order to safeguard the work of DTs against possible risks. The DT technology is being applied in many industries such as healthcare, automotive, and aerospace, among others. Future research can focus on designing scalable solutions of the DTs which are easy to modify and apply in different manufacturing environments. Finally, with the help of smart production, real-time monitoring, optimization, and cooperation, the production process may be changed radically due to the DT technology.

REFERENCES

1. S. Attaran, M. Attaran, B.G. Celik, Digital twins and industrial internet of things: uncovering operational intelligence in industry 4.0, *Decis. Anal. J.* 10 (2024) 1–14.
2. Z. Gao, A. Paul, X. Wang, Guest editorial: digital twinning: integrating AI-ML and big data analytics for virtual representation, *IEEE Trans. Ind. Inf.* 18 (2022) 1355–1358.
3. M. Singh, E. Fuenmayor, E.P. Hinchy, Y. Qiao, N. Murray, D. Devine, Digital twin: origin to future, *Appl. Syst. Innov.* 4 (2021) 36.
4. P.F. Borowski, Digitization, digital twins, blockchain, and industry 4.0 as elements of management process in enterprises in the energy sector, *Energies* 14 (2021) 1885.
5. A. Yasin, T.Y. Pang, C.T. Cheng, M. Miletic, A roadmap to integrate digital twins for small and medium-sized enterprises, *Appl. Sci.* 11 (2021) 9479.
6. J. Ulmer, S. Braun, C.-T. Cheng, S. Dowey, J. Wollert, Usage of digital twins for gamification applications in manufacturing, *Proc. CIRP* 107 (2022) 675–680.
7. P. Stavropoulos, D. Mourtzis (Eds.), in: *Digital Twins in Industry 4.0, Design and Operation of Production Networks for Mass Personalization in the Era of Cloud Technology*, Elsevier, 2022, pp. 277–316.
8. Q.-T. Nguyen, T.N. Tran, C. Heuchenne, K.P. Tran, in: *Decision Support Systems for Anomaly Detection with the Applications in Smart Manufacturing: a Survey and Perspective, Machine Learning and Probabilistic Graphical Models for Decision Support Systems*, Kim Phuc Tran (Ed.), CRC Press, 2021, pp. 34–61.
9. H.H. Hosamo, P.R. Svennevig, K. Svidt, D. Han, H.K. Nielsen, A Digital Twin predictive maintenance framework of air handling units based on automatic fault detection and diagnostics, *Energy Build.* 261 (2022) 111988.
10. J. Leng, D. Wang, W. Shen, X. Li, Q. Liu, X. Chen, Digital twins-based smart manufacturing system design in Industry 4.0: a review, *J. Manuf. Syst.* 60 (2021) 119–137.
11. G. Mylonas, A. Kalogeras, G. Kalogeras, C. Anagnostopoulos, C. Alexakos, L. Muñoz, Digital twins from smart manufacturing to smart cities: a survey, *IEEE Access* 9 (2021) 143222–143249.
12. M.I. Ali, P. Patel, J.G. Breslin, R. Harik, A. Sheth, Cognitive digital twins for smart manufacturing, *IEEE Intell. Syst.* 36 (2021) 96–100.
13. Q. Liu, J. Leng, D. Yan, D. Zhang, L. Wei, A. Yu, R. Zhao, H. Zhang, X. Chen, Digital twin-based designing of the configuration, motion, control, and optimization model of a flow-type smart manufacturing system, *J. Manuf. Syst.* 58 (2021) 52–64.
14. D. Ito, H. Ishida, Digital twin technology for continuous improvement at manufacturing sites, *Benefits* 2 (2020) 66–70.
15. D.A. Howard, Z. Ma, J.M. Aaslyng, B.N. Jørgensen, Data architecture for digital twin of commercial greenhouse production, in: *2020 RIVF International Conference on Computing and Communication Technologies (RIVF)*, IEEE, 2020, pp. 1–7.
16. S.M. Hasan, K. Lee, D. Moon, S. Kwon, S. Jinwoo, S. Lee, Augmented reality and digital twin system for interaction with construction machinery, *J. Asian Arch. Build. Eng.* 21 (2) (2022) 564–574.
17. K. Schützer, J. de Andrade Bertazzi, C. Sallati, R. Anderl, E. Zancul, Contribution to the development of a Digital Twin based on product lifecycle to support the manufacturing process, *Proc. CIRP* 84 (2019) 82–87.
18. Y. Zheng, S. Yang, H. Cheng, An application framework of digital twin and its case study, *J. Ambient Intell. Humaniz. Comput.* 10 (3) (2019) 1141–1153.
19. E. Bottani, G. Vignali, G.P.C. Tancredi, A digital twin model of a pasteurization system for food beverages: tools and architecture, in: *2020 IEEE International Conference on Engineering, Technology and Innovation (ICE/ITMC)*, IEEE, 2020, pp. 1–8.
20. W. Shengli, Is human digital twin possible? *Comput. Methods Programs Biomed. Update* 1 (2021) 100014.

21. Y. Liau, H. Lee, K. Ryu, Digital twin concept for smart injection molding, in: *IOP Conference Series: Materials Science and Engineering*, 324, IOP Publishing, 2018.
22. M.J. Kaur, V.P. Mishra, P. Maheshwari, The convergence of digital twin, IoT, and machine learning: transforming data into action, in: *Digital Twin Technologies and Smart Cities*, M. Farsi (Ed.), Springer, Cham, 2020, pp. 3–17.
23. L. Cattaneo, M. Macchi, A digital twin proof of concept to support machine prognostics with low availability of run-to-failure data, *IFAC-PapersOnLine* 52 (10) (2019) 37–42.
24. Q. Qi, F. Tao, T. Hu, N. Anwer, A. Liu, Y. Wei, L. Wang, A. Nee, Enabling technologies and tools for digital twin, *J. Manuf. Syst.* 58 (2021) 3–21.
25. V. Kharchenko, O. Illiashenko, O. Morozova, S. Sokolov, Combination of digital twin and artificial intelligence in manufacturing using industrial IoT, in: *2020 IEEE 11th International Conference on Dependable Systems, Services and Technologies (DESSERT)*, Kyiv (online), IEEE, 2020, pp. 196–201.
26. A. Khan, F. Shahid, C. Maple, A. Ahmad, G. Jeon, Toward smart manufacturing using spiral digital twin framework and twinchain, *IEEE Trans. Ind. Inform.* 18 (2) (2020) 1359–1366.
27. C. Semeraro, M. Lezoche, H. Panetto, M. Dassisti, Digital twin paradigm: a systematic literature review, *Comput. Ind.* 130 (2021) 103469.
28. E. Sujová, D. Vyslou ž ilová, H. Čierna, R. Bambura, Simulation models of production plants as a tool for implementation of the digital twin concept into production, *Manuf. Technol.* 20 (4) (2020) 527–533.
29. W. Sun, S. Lei, L. Wang, Z. Liu, Y. Zhang, Adaptive federated learning and digital twin for industrial internet of things, *IEEE Trans. Ind. Inform.* 17 (8) (2020) 5605–5614
30. C. Lo, C. Chen, R.Y. Zhong, A review of the digital twin in product design and development, *Adv. Eng. Inf.* 48 (2021) 101297.
31. M. Liu, S. Fang, H. Dong, C. Xu, Review of digital twin about concepts, technologies, and industrial applications, *J. Manuf. Syst.* 58 (2021) 346–361.
32. T.Y. Melesse, V. Di Pasquale, S. Riemma, Digital Twin models in industrial operations: state-of-the-art and future research directions, IET Collaborate. *Intell. Manuf.* 3 (2021) 37–47.
33. R.B. Roy, D. Mishra, S.K. Pal, T. Chakravarty, S. Panda, M.G. Chandra, S. Misra, Digital twin: current scenario and a case study on a manufacturing process, *Int. J. Adv. Manuf. Technol.* 107 (9) (2020) 3691–3714.
34. Y.K. Liu, S.K. Ong, A.Y.C. Nee, State-of-the-art survey on digital twin implementations, *Adv. Manuf.* 10 (1) (2022) 1–23.
35. S.K. Jo, D.H. Park, H. Park, Y. Kwak, S.H. Kim, Energy planning of pigsty using digital twin, in: *2019 International Conference on Information and Communication Technology Convergence (ICTC)*, Jeju Island, IEEE, 2019, pp. 723–725.
36. G. Falekas, A. Karlis, Digital twin in electrical machine control and predictive maintenance: state-of-the-art and future prospects, *Energies* 14 (2021) 5933.
37. J. Yang, Y. Sun, Y. Cao, X. Hu, Predictive maintenance for switch machine based on digital twins, *Information* 12 (2021) 485.
38. S. Mi, Y. Feng, H. Zheng, Y. Wang, Y. Gao, J. Tan, Prediction maintenance integrated decision-making approach supported by digital twin-driven cooperative awareness and interconnection framework, *J. Manuf. Syst.* 58 (2021) 329–345.
39. T. Bergs, S. Gierlings, T. Auerbach, A. Klink, D. Schraknepper, T. Augspurger, The concept of digital twin and digital shadow in manufacturing, *Proc. CIRP* 101 (2021) 81–84.
40. P. St ączek, J. Pizo ń, W. Danilczuk, A. Gola, A digital twin approach for the improvement of an autonomous mobile robots (AMR's) operating environment—a case study, *Sensors* 21 (23) (2021) 7830.

41. K. Mykoniatis, G.A. Harris, A digital twin emulator of a modular production system using a data-driven hybrid modeling and simulation approach, *J. Intell. Manuf.* 32 (7) (2021) 1899–1911.
42. P.K. Rajesh, N. Manikandan, C.S. Ramshankar, T. Vishwanathan, C. Sathishkumar, Digital twin of an automotive brake pad for predictive maintenance, *Proc. Comput. Sci.* 165 (2019) 18–24.
43. C. Zhou, F. Zhang, B. Wei, Y. Lin, K. He, R. Du, Digital twin–based stamping system for incremental bending, *Int. J. Adv. Manuf. Technol.* 116 (1) (2021) 389–401.
44. K. Alexopoulos, N. Nikolakis, G. Chryssolouris, Digital twin-driven supervised machine learning for the development of artificial intelligence applications in manufacturing, *Int. J. Comput. Integr. Manuf.* 33 (5) (2020) 429–439.
45. M. Caporuscio, F. Edrisi, M. Hallberg, A. Johannesson, C. Kopf, D. Perez-Palacin, Architectural concerns for digital twin of the organization, in: *European Conference on Software Architecture*, Springer, Cham, 2020, pp. 265–280.
46. M. Bertoni, A. Bertoni, Designing solutions with the product-service systems digital twin: what is now and what is next? *Comput. Ind.* 138 (2022) 103629.
47. Digital Transforms Physical, Innovator spotlight: Whirlpool corporation, 2024, Online: https://www.ptc.com/en/technologies/plm/digital-innovation/innovator-spotlight-whirlpool.
48. BMW Group, 2023. This is how DIGITAL the BMW iFACTORY is. https://www.bmwgroup.com/en/company/production.html#tabs-65c6b3da29-item-1bdb23dd33-tab
49. Place North West, 2023. CASE STUDY | BMW enjoys 'vast efficiency' of digital twin factories. https://www.placenorthwest.co.uk/case-study-bmw-enjoys-vast-efficiency-of-digital-twin-factories/?utm_source=chatgpt.com
50. HYSCALER, 2024. Introduction to Digital Twin Technology in Manufacturing with Unprecedented Efficiency and Innovation. https://hyscaler.com/insights/digital-twin-technology-manufacturing/
51. GE, 2022. Sustainability Report. https://www.ge.com/sites/default/files/ge2022_sustainability_report.pdf
52. SIEMENs. The journey to a sustainable Digital Enterprise has begun. https://www.siemens.com/global/en/products/automation/topic-areas/sustainable-industries.html
53. SIEMENS. Digital Twins with potential. https://www.siemens.com/global/en/company/stories/industry/the-digital-twin.html
54. LITSLINK. 2024. What is Digital Twin in Manufacturing? https://litslink.com/blog/what-is-digital-twin-in-manufacturing-inspiring-industry-examples
55. Boeing Scopes 1–3 Greenhouse Gas Emissions Supplement to the 2024 Sustainability and Social Impact Report. https://www.boeing.com/content/dam/boeing/boeingdotcom/principles/environment/pdf/GHG_Emissions_Supplement.pdf
56. Digital Twin Insider. 2024. The Performance of Digital Twins across Industry: https://digitaltwininsider.com/2024/06/20/the-performance-of-digital-twins-across-industry/
57. AI-powered process discovery helps drive procure-to-pay optimization. https://www.ibm.com/case-studies/global-manufacturing-company
58. IBM. 2023. IBM Watson to watsonx. https://www.ibm.com/watson/iot
59. IBM Building Information Modelling (BIM) and Digital Twin Services. 2022. https://assets.applytosupply.digitalmarketplace.service.gov.uk/g-cloud-13/documents/92284/948821848318740-service-definition-document-2022-05-12-1058.pdf
60. K.J. Kuehner, R. Scheer, S. Strassburger, Digital twin: finding common ground – a meta-review, *Proc. CIRP* 104 (2021) 1227–1232.
61. Digital Twin Market Analysis North America, Europe, APAC, Middle East and Africa, South America - US, Germany, UK, Japan, Canada, China, France, India, Italy, Brazil – Size and Forecast 2025–2029. https://www.technavio.com/report/digital-twin-market-size-industry-analysis

62. H. Russell, Sustainable urban governance networks: Data-driven planning technologies and smart city software systems, *Geopolitics. Hist. Int. Relat.* 12 (2020) 9–15.
63. D.M. Botín-Sanabria, A.S. Mihaita, R.E. Peimbert-García, M.A. Ramírez-Moreno, R.A. Ramírez-Mendoza, J.D.J. Lozoya-Santos, Digital twin technology challenges and applications: a comprehensive review, *Remote Sens.* 14 (6) (2022) 1335.
64. M. Hearn, S. Rix, Cybersecurity considerations for digital twin implementations, *IIC J. Innov.* 11 (4) (2019) I 07–1 I 3.
65. A. Sharma, E. Kosasih, J. Zhang, A. Brintrup, A. Calinescu, Digital twins: state of the art theory and practice, challenges, and open research questions, *J. Ind. Inf. Integr.* 30 (2022) 100383.
66. J. Trauer, M. Mutschler, M. Mörtl, M. Zimmermann, Challenges in implementing digital twins – a survey, in: *Proceedings of the ASME. International Design Engineering Technical Conferences and Computers and Information in Engineering Conference. Volume 2: 42nd Computers and Information in Engineering Conference, CIE.* St. Louis, Missouri, USA, August 14–17, 2022.
67. C. Alcaraz, H. Lopez, Digital twin: a comprehensive survey of security threats, *IEEE Commun. Surv. Tutor.* 24 (3) (2022) 1475–1503.
68. M. Li, Z. Li, X. Huang, T. Qu, Blockchain-based digital twin sharing platform for reconfigurable socialized manufacturing resource integration, *Int. J. Prod. Econ.* 240 (2021) 108223.
69. G. Thahniyath, P. Mishra, S.R. Moorthy, Two phase secure data collection technique for wireless sensor networks, *Indones. J. Electr. Eng. Comput. Sci.* 26 (1) (2022) 512–520. http://doi.org/10.11591/ijeecs.v26.i1.pp512-520.

9 Internet of Things for Intelligent Manufacturing Systems

Banu Priya R and Mouleeswaran Singanallur Kumaresan

9.1 INTRODUCTION

Today's rapid state of advancement imparted to digital technologies thus supervised the birth of Intelligent Manufacturing Systems (IMSs), within which the Internet of things (IoT) is able to metamorphose the classical methodology in manufacturing to a connected, automated, and databased environment. The IoT production processes by means of integration of smart sensors, connected devices, and cloud-based analytics. Such a smooth interconnectivity gives the manufacturers the ability to acquire, process, and analyze large quantities of data that makes the production processes more efficient, the product quality better, and the cost of operation smaller[1,2]. Additional areas of operation that the IoT is given are predictive maintenance, optimization of the supply chain, and energy-efficient operations that make the manufacturing systems more resilient and adaptive to the evolving demands [3].

However, it has several critical problems, some of which restrict the implementation of IoT in IMS at its large scale. The process of integrating IoT into legacy systems is even more complex due to the problem of interoperability, the high cost of implementation, and the problem of security. The other barrier to complete-fledged acceptance of an IoT in IMS is the fact that as manufacturing environments become more digitized, they can now be readily targeted by cyber-attacks; therefore, one approach to protecting data and network resilience becomes iconic towards the uptake of an IoT [4]. The missing part of the picture is the applications and the architectures of effective real-time data processing, and communication among the IoT devices is lacking in the current systems [5]. Despite the tremendous effort that has been done in terms of recognizing the potential of IoT towards improving manufacturing, the gap towards developing roadmaps that can help overcome these challenges as well as enhance the cost efficiency and scalability of the implementation of IoT remains very wide [6].

This chapter aims at outlining the narrowed divide that explores the various key features such as elements, uses, and issues that include the IoT of IMSs. In addition, it explores the key challenges including security threats, integration issues, and interoperability limitations and provides innovative answers to enhance the scalability, efficiency, and cybersecurity aspects of manufacturing using IoT [7]. In the same research, the authors examine the use of modern technologies, such as edge

DOI: 10.1201/9781003582465-9

computing, artificial intelligence (AI) analytics, and blockchain technology, which can play a crucial role in ensuring the safety of data, decentralized operation, and real-time decision-making in IMSs [8].

These are prominent areas that add a comprehensive standard of understanding to the application of IoT in the manufacturing sector to enhance productivity, optimism in resources management, and competitive ability in the dynamic world [9]. Such discoveries will form an adequate foundation to the future advancements in IoT-based manufacturing such that industries that believe in implementing smart, connected, and autonomous productions systems will find it easy to comprehend high-end practical solutions.

9.1.1 Key Contributions of the Research

- The core aspects of IoT are discussed in terms of their applications and benefits in optimization of production, quality control, and predictive maintenance. Some of the challenges being solved include cybersecurity threats, interoperability issues, and integration complexities among other challenges.
- The proposals are presented in support of blockchain, AI-powered analytics, and edge computing as the possible solutions to the challenges outlined above.
- Industry 4.0 emerging technologies are concerned with digital twins and 5G and cloud-edge integration to provide a flexible strategic approach to scaling and cost-efficient implementation of IoT by the manufacturing ecosystem.

Although a lot of efforts are undertaken in defining the role of IoT in IMSs, there are still gaps to be addressed by different research studies. The majority of the current studies have been focused on the advantages of the IoT applications without being aware of other crucial issues that need a comprehensive approach such as, but not limited to, interconnectivity and cybersecurity, excessive implementation costs, and compatibility with legacy systems. One of the aspects that have not been sufficiently addressed is the fact that most of the studies fail to address scalable and adaptive network structures in a seamless IoT implementation in large-scale manufacturing processes. To address these gaps, this framework suggests an all-encompassing one, which incorporates blockchain as a safe and decentralized paradigm of data handling using AI-driven analytics to real-time decision-making, whereas the edge computing is concerned with data processing in the vicinity. The possible gains of such advanced technologies include scalability, safety, and cost-effectiveness and allow making smooth transitions to the operations of the IoT in smart manufacturing.

9.2 LITERATURE REVIEW

Cioffi and others [10] came with a complete research study dedicated to the role of IoT in bringing out the feature of sustainable manufacturing in Industry 4.0. This review proceeds to assert the potential to improve the sustainability of IoT systems through the optimization of resources and minimizationof wastes using the real-time data to make improved decisions. The challenges of sustaining practices of consuming energy and complexity in the integration of IoT and legacy systems seem to be some issues that have been reported in the reviews.

The article by Chigilipalli et al. [11] is the review of how IoT can be used along with additive manufacturing (3D printing). It is claimed that such use of IoT in additive manufacturing will transform how the process is monitored, controlled, and customized in a product. It has been stated in the paper that real-time data processing, interoperability of 3D printers, and IoT platforms have issues and suggestions to make the integration of IoT in this manufacturing sector seamless.

As Yang et al. show in [12], Internet of Medical Things (IoMT) can aid in the development of smart manufacturing ecosystems. This review addresses the role of C-P-IoT integration to monitor production processes, predictive maintenance, and automation in realtime. In conjunction with this, security issues concerning data breach risks and cybersecurity measures in IoMT environments are discussed.

Mishra et al. [13] delivered a literature review on the merging of IoT with Product Lifecycle Management environments. This integration will improve tracking of product data and collaboration in the design in realtime and enhance overall manufacturing efficiency. The paper further mentions that IoT integration will help in the visibility of the supply chain, fewer delays in production, and improved quality of the product through insights obtained in every stage of the product lifecycle.

Hu et al. [14] presented a review of Industrial internet of things intelligence in smart manufacturing wherein AI-driven analytics and blockchain have improved decision-making and data security from IoT environments. The review focuses on using IoT for predictive maintenance, monitoring, and autonomous systems, analyzing the need for edge computing integration to further enhance the scalability and response time of IoT-based systems in smart manufacturing.

Kumar et al. [15] included IoT applications, including Industry 4.0, when it comes to decentralization of networking in place of centralized control systems. The authors would once again take notes regarding the impact of cloud platforms in the creation of smart choices concerning the applications of IoT, and predictive maintenance and adaptable manufacturing procedures. They have however also noted that the implementation of the IoT systems in the currently established setups in manufacturing is expensive and complex.

Gao et al. [16] undertook a bibliometric study to investigate the ever-growing research in IoT-assisted smart manufacturing; the review identified some of the prominent research topics concerning data-driven optimization, energy management, and robotics integration in manufacturing. The other emerging area of concern is the use of AI and Machine Learning as tools to enhance production efficiency and minimize wastage. The paper calls for additional research toward scalable IoT solutions for implementation in huge manufacturing systems.

Singh et al. [17] conducted a bibliometric analysis of the literature on IoT applications in smart manufacturing and highlighted key emerging trends, which include increasing use of AI-driven predictive models with relative importance on real-time monitoring, and automated manufacturing systems. The gaps include the research associated with integrating heterogeneous IoT devices, and standard protocols are needed to enhance interoperability in diversified manufacturing systems.

In manufacturing, Wang et al. [18] tracked inventory-related issues and logistics in realtime. IoT has more impacts than these because it enables manufacturers to maximize the allocation of resources to reduce lead time and maximize efficiency of the supply chain, as far as the visibility of the supply chain is concerned. Another problem is related to interoperability and involves combining blockchain and cloud in addition to IoT to have a more efficient and transparent supply chain operation.

Chen et al. [19] explained how IoT can introduce flexibility and customization of the processes of manufacturing to make them naturally adaptable to the evolving market needs. It also outlines the difficulties encountered in the course of MaaS-as scalability and costs implementation and integration of the IoT with cloud-based solutions to effectively manage data and make decisions.

The articles give a broad picture of the study addressing the use of the IoT in intelligent manufacturing, such as predictive maintenance, cybersecurity, real-time monitoring, and supply chain management, among others. The papers provide diverse focal points on the changing role of IoT technologies in a manufacturing environment and analyze some of the barriers to the increased adoption of IoT.

9.3 METHODOLOGY

9.3.1 System Architecture Design

The conceptual model of the proposed IMS-SIS based on the IoT. The architecture is a Multiples layer architecture that ensures seamless data acquisition, processing, storage, and real-time decision-making. The key layers that establish this architecture are:

Perception Layer (Data Collection)
Edge Layer (Real-Time Processing)
Network Layer (Secure Data Transmission)
Cloud and AI Layer (Advanced Analytics and Storage)
Application Layer (User Interaction and Decision-Making)

The bottom layer of the IoT-enabled IMS is the Perception Layer since it gathers real-time Radio Frequency Identification (RFID) tags and actuators.

The real-time processing and preliminary analysis is carried out in the edge layer with their respective low latency and lower system congestion. In the context of edge computing, the raw sensor data is localized at the machine level, and then, decision-making is performed at higher levels. The edge AI reviews data to identify anomalies, is made aware of machine failure forecasting, and makes use of optimization in manufacturing processes. These are instant decisions that maximize the efficiency and dependability of production procedures.

The network layer shall ensure a very secure and reliable transfer of the data throughout the IoT devices, edge nodes, and cloud infrastructure. It does all these through well-established 5G in the facilitation of speed and efficient connection. It is also this very layer that utilizes such encryption methods as to defend the information by using blockchain technologies. In this way, data integrity will be ensured, unauthorized access may be blocked, and other cybersecurity threats will be defended, therefore creating a highly robust and authoritative network of smart manufacturing settings.

Process optimization is complimented by the predictive analytics. The models of AI and machine learning are used to study production trends, predict possible failures, and enhance operational efficiency. In addition, there is a digital twin technology installed in this layer in realtime to simulate and optimize processes.

This is the layer where the user interface is the application where the user can observe, make decision, and control the processes. Operators/engineers will be linked to dash boards which will give real-time status updates of key performance indicators, predictive alerts, and system diagnostics. These AI decision-support systems will be beneficial in optimization of processes, improved utilization of resources, and constant process enhancement. This will make sure that there is an increase in productivity with limited downtimes, and all knowledge acquired in the manufacturing process can be applied.

9.3.2 Data Acquisition and Processing

The key processes in an IMS that has been facilitated by the IoT are data acquisition and processing. This process, which starts with use tags and smart actuators in the productive environment, fully captures, transmits, and analyses the real-time data. It enables incessant learning of applicable parameters application.

After these data points are taken, incoming data will be formatted in the edge layer where refineries and edge computing devices of real-time filtering, anomaly detection, and preliminary analysis to achieve the value of minimizing network congestion and responsiveness are installed. After the initial acquisition and processing, the appropriate data are sent to the cloud, where trained and developed AI and machine learning models process the trend variations, production optimization, and predictive maintenance. In addition, integration with blockchain allows security. It will be aided by the creation of a complete data collection and processing system that will facilitate smart decision-making that will enhance the manufacturing capacity of a process, reduce downtimes, and provide the adaptive optimization of the manufacturing process in realtime.

9.3.3 Security Enhancement Using Blockchain

The interface of Security Enhancement Using Blockchain is fantastic in offering integrity, transparency, and confidentiality of data in relation to the IoT-enabled IMSs. Blockchain is an inalterable decentralized file of all transactions that is why it is appropriate in safeguarding the vast amount of data that is being produced in the manufacturing setting. It can catalogue all the messages– sensor reading to production parameters – that are transmitted to it by making all the blocks in the chain stored in time-stamped logs-audit-worthy.

The high security mechanism is essentially the means of counteracting as many threats as possible with regards to cybercrime; data theft and unauthorized entry can somehow take place. There is a potential threat of attacks to conventional data storage systems, but a decentralized architecture like blockchain disseminates the information between multiple nodes, which makes it difficult for miscreants to replace data. In addition, the clarity of the blockchain also provides the ability to audit every transaction by the manufacturing ecosystem and traceability and accountability.

Therefore, peer-to-peer communication between IoT devices, edge nodes, and centralized systems can be secure, in addition to ensuring the integrity of the data, due to blockchains. This implies that confidential manufacturing information, including machine performance indicators and production plans, will be safely shared without the dangers of man-in-the-middle attacks. Furthermore, it can be used as well to facilitate safe and effective smart contract implementation whenever some preset conditions are automatically met.

9.3.4 Mathematical Model for Blockchain-Based Security in IoT Manufacturing

9.3.4.1 Data Integrity and Hashing Mechanism

Each transaction or data packet D in the IoT system is secured using a cryptographic hash function H, ensuring immutability:

$$H\left(D_i\right) = h_i \tag{9.1}$$

h is the unique hash value of D. Any modification to D results in a completely different hash $H\left(D_i'\right) \neq h_i$ ensuring data integrity.

9.3.4.2 Blockchain Transaction Verification

To validate transactions, a **Proof of Work (PoW)** or **Proof of Stake (PoS)** consensus mechanism is used. In PoW, miners solve a computational puzzle:

$$H\left(h_i + n\right) \leq T \tag{9.2}$$

n is the nonce (random number),

T is the target difficulty threshold.

If a valid nonce is found, in **PoS**, transaction validationbased on stake S of a participant is:

$$P(V) = \frac{S_v}{\Sigma S} \tag{9.3}$$

$P(V)$ is the probability of validator v being chosen, ensuring a fair and energy-efficient process.

9.3.4.3 Latency and Computational Overhead Analysis

The total delay in blockchain verification consists of transmission delay, computation delay T_c, and block propagation delay T_p:

$$T_{\text{total}} = T_t + T_c + T_p \tag{9.4}$$

9.3.4.4 Security Enhancement Factor

The effectiveness of blockchain in securing IoT data can be modelled as a security enhancement factor, SEF.

$$\text{SEF} = \frac{1}{P(A)} \tag{9.5}$$

$$P(A) = \left(\frac{Na}{N}\right)^{51\%} \tag{9.6}$$

where *P(A)* is the probability of a successful attack. Since blockchain is distributed, an attacker must control at least **51%** of nodes (*N*), making the attack probability:

Na is the number of compromised nodes.

Algorithm: Blockchain-Based Security in IoT

// Initialization

The blockchain_chain is initialized as an empty list. Define hash_function H(data). The consensus_type is set to either PoW or PoS. The difficulty threshold T for PoW is established here. Initialize N for total nodes, Na for compromised nodes, and initialize stake list S[v] for each validator v.

// Step 1: Data Acquisition and Hashing

FOR each incoming IoT data packet D_i DO

Generate hash for data packet h_i ← H(D_i)

// Generate hash for data packet

Store <D_i, h_i> in buffer

END FOR

//Step 2: Block Formation

Group n data records into block B_k ← {<D_1, h_1>, <D_2, h_2>,..., <D_n, h_n>}

```
//Step 3: Consensus Mechanism
        IF consensus_type = "PoW" THEN
        Initialize nonce ← 0
        WHILE TRUE
trial_hash ← H(h_k + nonce)
        IF trial_hash ≤ T THEN
        assign B_k.nonce ← nonce;
        append B_k to blockchain_chain;
        BREAK;
END IF
nonce ← nonce + 1;
END WHILE

ELSE IF consensus_type = "PoS" THEN
FOR each validator v DO
        P_v ← S[v] / SUM(S);
        // Calculate selection probability
END FOR
Randomly select validator_v based upon P_v;
IF validator_v verifies B_k
        append B_k to blockchain_chain
END IF
END IF

// Step 4: Block Propagation and Transmission Metrics
        Broadcast B_k to all peer nodes
        Measure T_t (transmission delay), T_c (computation delay), and T_p
        (propagation delay)
        T_total ← T_t + T_c + T_p

// Step 5: Security Enhancement Factor (SEF)
        P_attack ← (Na / N)^0.51
        SEF ← 1 / P_attack
```

```
// Step 6: Audit Log and Traceability
        Log B_k in the audit system
        Allow real-time integrity checks through previously stored hashes

// Optional Step 7: Smart Contract Execution
        IF any sensor value > threshold THEN
        Trigger maintenance alert by executing smart contract
        END IF

END
```

9.3.5 Overview of IoT Architecture

IoT architecture is hierarchical in nature for the definition of IoT devices, networks, data processing systems, and users making the entire IoT ecosystem. It defines the standards for collecting, transmitting, processing, and ultimately putting end-users to use in applications pertaining to IoT. IoT architecture generally constitutes several layers, each of which is responsible for one or more specific tasks to enhance the general efficiency, scalability, and performance of the system. Below is an account of the major layers of the IoT architecture:

9.3.5.1 Decision-Making

Making decisions with IoT has in its essence real-time data driving decisions towards improving operational efficiency. IoT systems gather huge data analyzed by means AI. These insights inform decisions regarding inventory management, production scheduling, and predictive maintenance. As an example, when a machine learning model has the capability of forecasting a breakdown of a particular component, it can also initiate maintenance to prevent occurrence of any downtimes. Indeed, therefore, decision-making is among the most important primary pillars of manufacturing to optimize the use of resources, save costs, and streamline the processes [20].

The knowledge in this case is gathered data and knowledge applied in the analysis of information to be used in decision-making in IoT. It is the process of processing sensor data using AI and other sophisticated analytics alongside past trends. This kind of knowledge will allow optimization of processes, prediction, and better management of resources. In a smart factory, an example is that the data concerning the machines is gathered and examined to enhance the functionality of the machines. Analyzed and processed via machine learning, resources can provide suggestions for optimizing the performance of the overall system [4].

One and only one physical system that exists in location will involve real machinery, sensors, and devices capable of acquiring and recording data from the outside. These include wearable technology linked to a range of other ambient environmental sensors and industrial machinery. Sensors and actuators are integrated into these systems, thereby building that bridge between the physical and digital realms. For example, conveyor systems or robotic installations are monitored for abnormalities and performance in a manufacturing facility. It uses all the data coming from these devices in the IoT application to analyze and act when that comes into play.

9.3.5.2 Machine Learning

Such machine learning algorithms and their processes find application in providing systems with the capability to actually improve performance over time. The pattern and trend-based prediction will increase uptime by predicting equipment failure in the course of the generation. For example, unattended Machine Learning algorithms can parse sensor data for trends indicating failure and schedule preventive maintenance. This is a very versatile tool for increasing self-direction and responsiveness in IoT systems.

9.3.5.3 Semantic Model Reasoning

Semantic model reasoning is, thus, applying semantics to IoT data in terms of inferring meaning from that data. In short, it concerns endowing data therefore collected from devices with context through the ontologies and knowledge representation paradigms. It further allows the interoperability of IoT devices since it helps machines comprehend the meaning of the data in a human-readable format. For example, semantic models may be applied in smart cities to understand data from streetlights, traffic signals, and cars, allowing better urban planning and more informed decision-making [7].

9.3.5.4 Sensing Components

Sensing components are tools that fit hardware devices for sensing applications in the IoT, which translates environmental changes into electrical signals that processing units can apply. These components include motion, gas, pressure, and temperature sensors. The applications are innumerable, considering monitoring irregularities in industrial machinery or air quality in smart cities. Sensing components also maintain tight, real-time feedback on conditions surrounding a system or environment and enhance decision-making speed and accuracy by Industrial internet of things systems.

9.3.5.5 Wi-Fi

Wi-Fi provides the common wireless communication medium for connecting IoT devices with local networks or the Internet. In homes, factories, and offices, Wi-Fi can be the most preferred for its higher data speeds and ease of use. Connecting IoT sensors, devices, and control systems through this technology would have remote access for any process, function, and result, making seamless communication between devices and cloud platforms. For example, appliances, lights, and security can interconnect in smart homes to be remotely controlled using mobile apps. Hence, manufacturing equipment could transmit real-time performance data to monitoring centres through Wi-Fi.

9.3.5.6 Ethernet

Typically, Ethernet connects devices through a wired networking mode for reliable and high-speed data transfer within IoT systems. It is commonly preferred in industrial circumstances, where consistent performance matters most and low-latency action is vital. Ethernet could provide interlinkage among the sensors, equipment, and control systems in an industrial set-up and guarantee rapid data transmission. Ethernet works exceptionally well for IoT devices in environments that may not be suitable for wireless communication or for relying upon it.

Like other types of applications for mobile IoT devices and applications, Long-Term Evolution is the protocol that gives rather high-speed wireless connection. Its quick data rates also make it adequate for IoT applications in remote or underdeveloped locations. IoT devices can send a large amount of data over great distances using Long-Term Evolution, so it can be an added advantage for applications like smart cities and agriculture. For example, sensors deployed in agricultural fields could send weather and soil moisture information using Long-Term Evolution to the cloud platform. Its broad coverage makes Long-Term Evolution a great candidate for remote or hard-to-reach deployments of IoT.

9.3.5.7 Sensors

Sensors are the key element of IoT in detecting and measuring physical properties. They convert data from the real world into signals that can be understood by IoT systems and then further used for analysis. For example, in production, sensors are used to keep track of product quality, health of the machine, and worker safety. For example, temperature sensors can monitor the machine temperature and prevent it from overheating. Intelligent systems are engineered these days, where the very basic and continuous data collection from different types of sensors is carried over IoT applications.

9.3.5.8 Radio Frequency Identification (RFID)

RFID is the new attribute in IoT systems that uses goods or assets from IoT systems. Through electromagnetic waves, it recognizes and tracks tags attached to an object automatically. RFID tags are widely used in production asset monitoring, supply chain tracking, and inventory management. For example, goods or raw materials could be tagged with RFID tags, and the readers can track their status during production. This enables manufacturers to increase traceability and facilitate processes.

9.3.5.9 Perception Layer (Sensing Layer)

The most basic layer in IoT is the perception layer, and it is responsible for collecting information from the real environment. Sensors, actuators, and any other equipment that are monitored in parameters such as motion, position, pressure, temperature, and humidity, are configured here. Real-time data is captured by these devices and conveyed to the next levels for processing. Manufacturing, for example, uses sensors to manage inventories, detects irregularities, and monitors equipment health.

9.3.5.10 Network Layer (Transmission Layer)

Gathering all information through sensors in the perception layer, it should be transmitted for processing. This transmission, which the network layer implements, can be realized with several different communication technologies. This layer also ensures that data and transmitted information from IoT devices are safely transferred to platforms for processing and stored. It should connect equipment, control systems, and remote monitoring tools to enable smooth data flow in manufacturing.

9.3.5.11 Application Layer

The interface where the end user interacts is the application layer. It contains the specific software and applications that provide the certain services with the processed data. Applications can be domain-specific, such as energy management applications, smart agriculture systems, or predictive maintenance in manufacturing. Commonly, it uses dashboards or mobile applications to make insight from the previous layer to be conveyed to decision-makers in a simple and practical form [8].

9.3.6 Components of an IMS

As IMSs aim for future manufacturing, as shown in Figure 9.1, operational and technology combinations for the maximization of output, quality enhancement, and operational efficiencies include data-driven platforms. Robotics, AI, machine learning, IoT, and real-time data analytics are integrated in a very responsive, flexible, and efficient manufacturing environment. Well-adapted IMS components cause higher levels of automation, intelligence, and predictability throughout the manufacturing life cycle of the organization.

Intelligent design systems themselves harness AI in designing products, intelligent processes in surveillance, and optimization of operational processes, and intelligent planning and scheduling systems are employed to reconfigure production pathways. High-end maintenance diagnostics and control techniques can be deployed to ensure continuous operation and to avert possible downtime of machinery. They are interconnected in minimizing the lead time to customer demands, minimizing the costs, and enhancing the quality of the products that prepares the manufacturers to stay successful throughout the Industry 4.0 and operate in an extremely competitive world market.

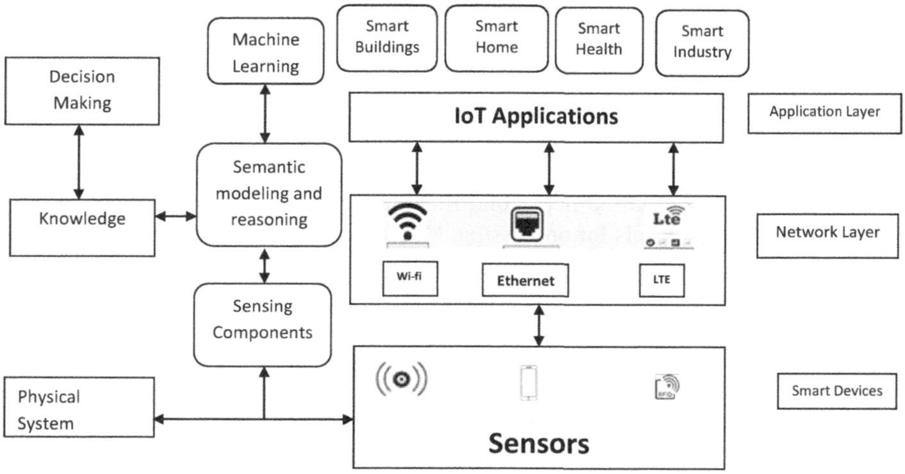

FIGURE 9.1 Components of an IMS.

9.3.6.1 "Intelligent Process" Characterizes an Interesting Term

Intelligent Processes oversee and optimize manufacturing processes based on AI algorithms and real-time process data of IoT devices. AI continuously tracks and changes the environmental conditions within which production is being conducted, to facilitate the greatest productivity, least wastage, and best quality.

9.3.6.2 Intelligent Design

This module supports fast design cycle and designs that fit production and performance specifications in terms of cost, manufacturability, and material characteristics.

9.3.6.3 Intelligent Management

Smart data management uses intelligent management systems, data analytics, and ERP systems in order to streamline production in various aspects, including resource allocation, the coordination of supply chain, and overall big picture corporate decision-making. This leads to strategic alignment of production with corporate goals as well as providing real-time visibility of operations.

9.3.6.4 Intelligent Planning

An intelligent planning tool is an AI predictive and optimization tool whereby future needs can be predicted and manufacturing operations optimized. This part will ensure that production time is better scheduled, and the resources are used in the best way possible by use of past data and making anticipation on future material requirements.

9.4 RESULTS AND DISCUSSION

9.4.1 IoT Sensor Deployment in Manufacturing

Although intelligent monitoring is indeed highly desired by modern industrial environments due to the sheer need of sensors, predictive analytics is made possible. The position of such sensors is as much tactical positioning through the different production lines, machinery, or even essential infrastructure to measure numerous parameters, such as temperature, pressure, vibration, humidity, tool wear, energy consumption, and machine usage. According to the IoT Institute Chairman Behnud Khosroshahi, condition-based monitoring and early fault detection in manufacturing processes are now made transparent with sensor data acquisition. Moreover, the RFID tags also make it possible to trace raw materials, components, and finished products in the supply chain. The sensor nodes therefore communicate via industrial-grade protocols like MQTT, OPC UA, and 5G to the industry-grading processes of data transmission of low latency and high reliability. Edge computing is usually performed near the sensor nodes in order to process and filter the local data and reduce the network load with enhanced response. These signals are connected to cloud or AI systems, and with the help of data analytics and machine learning models, optimized workflow, predictive maintenance, and overall equipment effectiveness are realized. The application smart IoT sensor installation converts the manufacturing base of the past into a smart, data-driven, and adaptive manufacturing process, thus opening the door to Industry 4.0.

TABLE 9.1
IoT Sensor Deployment in Manufacturing

Sensor Type	Measured Parameter	Typical Value Range	Unit	Application Area
Temperature Sensor	Machine/Tool Temperature	–40 to 150	°C	CNC machines, injection moulding machines
Pressure Sensor	Hydraulic/ Pneumatic Pressure	0–10,000	kPa	Pneumatic tools, hydraulic presses
Vibration Sensor (Micro-Electro-Mechanical Systems MEMS)	Vibration Speed (Root Mean Square)	0–25	mm/s	Motors, gearboxes, spindles
Proximity Sensor	Distance/Object Detection	0.1–30	mm–m	Robotics, material handling systems
Humidity Sensor	Relative Humidity	10–90	% RH	Cleanrooms, electronic component storage
Current Sensor	Electrical Current Flow	0–100	A	Motors, heaters, power lines
Gas Sensor (Carbon Monoxide , Volatile Organic Compounds VOCs)	Gas Concentration	0–1,000	ppm	Welding booths, chemical storage areas
RFID Tag/Reader	Item ID/ Tracking	0–5	m (range)	Inventory, raw material tracking
Load Cell/Force Sensor	Load/Force	0–5,000	N / kg	Press machines, weighing stations
Ultrasonic Sensor	Distance/Level Measurement	2–400	cm	Fluid tanks, Automated Guided Vehicles, package detection

The purpose of IoT sensor deployment in the manufacturing environment is to enable real-time monitoring, control, and optimization. Table 9.1 shows "IoT Sensor Deployment with Sample Values in Manufacturing", which presents a comprehensive representation of different types of sensors, their measured parameters, typical value ranges, and relevant fields of application. For example, temperature sensors are used widely in monitoring machine and tool temperatures, which typically operate from –40°C to 150°C to ensure that the machines do not overheat and radiate steady thermal performance. Pressure sensors monitor liquid pressure in hydraulic and pneumatic systems, thus sensing abnormalities that can lead the complete unit into failure. Vibration sensors mainly based on Micro-Electro-Mechanical Systems technology are vital for predictive maintenance by identifying mechanical defects in motors and rotating equipment through vibration intensity change detection. Proximity sensors can position objects and initiate automation control; humidity sensors are employed when very delicate atmospheric conditions are needed, for example, clean rooms and electronics production. Current sensors track the consumption of electric power and can therefore report faults, while gas sensors protect workers by detecting dangerous emissions. RFID systems further facilitate the tracking of materials and inventory along the production line. Load cells and force sensors carry great importance in quality inspection and weight-based operations, while ultrasonic sensors assist fluid level measurement and navigation for robots. In all of these ways, using various sensors, manufacturers collect data to enhance process reliability towards intelligent adaptive energy-efficient production within Industry 4.0.

9.4.2 Blockchain Implementation for Secure Data Management

Blockchain technology finds increasing acceptance in smart manufacturing for providing secure and tamper-proof data management. Since then, a huge amount of sensitive data has been generated by IoT devices, edge nodes, and cloud infrastructures generated in manufacturing environments, needing a decentralized and transparent security framework. Blockchain and its unsaturated registry keep the records of every transaction or data exchange in a correct time order with a cryptographic signature, thereby preserving the integrity and discovery of the information. Blockchain is useful in IoT-enabled IMS to reduce the possibility of data manipulation by unauthorized agents by distributing records over a peer-to-peer network, with each node validating the transactions with consensus mechanisms such as PoW or PoS. This eliminates points of failure, enhances fault tolerance, and offers a more powerful protection barrier against cyber-attacks such as data tampering, spoofing, and replay attacks. Moreover, blockchain systems with smart contracts will automate certain manufacturing systems based on a set of pre-defined events; predictive maintenance will be initiated, upon the violation of the vibration standards.

Table 9.2 displays the statistical findings of introducing blockchain to facilitate the safety of managing data in IoT-based manufacturing systems. The rate of data tampering has also been minimized by a margin of 14 to a mere 1 per year as evidence of the fact that the application would ensure the integrity of the data by its immutability

TABLE 9.2
Blockchain Implementation

Parameter	Before Blockchain	After Blockchain	Improvement (%)
Data tampering incidents (per year)	14	1	92.86
Average data retrieval time (ms)	250	190	24.00
Unauthorized access attempts detected	22	4	81.82
Traceability accuracy (%)	76	97	27.63
Smart contract automation rate (%)	0	89	—
Data storage redundancy (%)	10	60	500.00
Mean time to detect anomalies (minutes)	45	18	60.00
Compliance with data regulations (%)	68	95	39.71

ledger. Data retrieval time was cut down to 190 ms on average as compared to 250 ms which is a result of better accessibility to decentralized records. The most recent access attempts were more than 80% lower and indicated a heightened level of access control and enhanced authentication. Between 76% and 97% accuracy of traceability demonstrates the visibility of the supply chain, which is enabled in the end-to-end manner by blockchain. Nearly 89% of all critical processes of manufacturing will be automated under a smart contract, which will simplify the processes and minimize human error. Redundancy of data became 500% more, and this will enhance availability as well as fault tolerance of data storage at the distributed nodes. Furthermore, mean time to detect an anomaly decreased to 18 minutes as compared to 45 minutes to have a better real-time monitoring. The rate of data compliance has risen to 95% after being 68% previously, which is why blockchain is involved to make the process more transparent and auditable. Altogether, these statistics are indicative of the way that the power of blockchain can be used in the field of data security, operational stability, and compliance with regulations into their lands around Industry 4.0.

9.4.3 AI-Driven Predictive Analytics for Anomaly Detection

Predictive Analytics is an AI-based system that expands the ability of detecting anomalies in smarter manufacturing systems through IoT sensor and edge devices. These models that have been trained on the past readings and the present readings would have temperature, vibrations, and pressure data, among other crucial parameters, as an effective way of not being able to have a critical prediction by actors into serious failure. As the real-time equipment condition monitoring indicates behavioural patterns, predictive models can be used to execute proactive maintenance and reduce unplanned downtime. Moreover, techniques of unsupervised learning like clustering or autoencoders are highly potent in the discovery of either unknown or rare anomalies without having to be fed on labelled datasets. These AI models would thus be able to perform fast in-situ analysis so that relevant low-latency decision-making could occur with decreased reliance on cloud architecture in combination with edge computing. In general, AI-based predictive analytics can be used to provide evidence-based maintenance in state, to make operations more efficient, and to be more productive, becoming the basis of Industry 4.0.

9.4.4 Comparison Table for Model Performance

Predictive Anomaly Detection for IoT-enabled Manufacturing Systems: This section compares the predictive hidden anomaly detection performances of various AI models. The comparative performance of these AI models is presented in Table 9.3. The best model, so far in this comparison, for spatial pattern recognition in sensor data is Convolutional Neural Networks, with a 95.1% accuracy and 93.0% F1-score. Recurrent Neural Networks, especially the Long Short-Term Memory variants, excel further in temporal data analysis and provide the highest recall (94.3%) and the closest F1-score (93.5%). They demonstrate expectation evidence to pay attention to the location of the anomaly detected in sequential order over time. Support Vector Machines have significantly balanced performance of 90.3% accuracy coupled with

TABLE 9.3
Performance Comparison of AI Algorithms for Predictive Anomaly Detection

AI Model	Precision (%)	Recall (%)	F1-Score (%)	Accuracy (%)	Detection Latency (ms)
Convolutional Neural Network	94.2	91.8	93	95.1	210
Recurrent Neural Network (LSTM)	92.7	94.3	93.5	94	270
Support Vector Machine	89.5	87.6	88.5	90.3	150
Decision Tree Classifier	85.3	83.9	84.6	87	130
Autoencoder (Unsupervised)	78.1	81.5	79.8	82.6	180

fairly low detection latencies (150 ms), suitable for real-time classification tasks demanding quick decision-making. Decision Trees perform slightly faster than that (130 ms latency) but their accuracy is underwhelmingly moderate (87.0%) making them more suitable for rule-based interpretable systems, preferably less complicated. One area that unsupervised methods like autoencoders have shown can perform well is with regard to detecting anomalies that are unknown or happen to be new. They are however less precise than the supervised models at 78.1%. They, nevertheless, have a moderate recall of 81.5, which highlights their usage in detecting anomalies in exploration during complex manufacturing conditions. AI models must be selected based on the requirements of the system, be it speed or accuracy or ability to process unknown patterns of anomalies.

9.4.5 Performance Metrics and Comparative Evaluation

A performance measure and comparative analysis have significant functions to determine the performance of predictive anomaly detection algorithms in IoT-based manufacturing systems. Such parameters are accuracy, precision, recall, F1 score, and detection latency– all of them are fundamental benchmarking measures in comparison to the AI models. The overall correctness of the predictions of the model is the accuracy; the proportion of true anomalies to the predicted anomalies is precision and therefore must be minimized to false alarms. Recall denotes the fitness of the model in detecting actual anomalies, which is essential to avoid undetected failures. Detection latency reveals the quickness of detecting anomalies in realtime. A comparative evaluation among models such as Convolutional Neural Networks, Long Short-Term Memory, Support Vector Machine, Decision Trees, and autoencoders shows deep learning models (Convolutional Neural Networks and Long Short-Term Memory) winning the highest precision and recall, thus making them appropriate for recognition of complex patterns and temporal anomaly detection. Support Vector Machine and Decision Trees represent fair enough scores on domains that mostly require fast decision-making under the level of complexity. Autoencoders can be valuable in terms of unsupervised scenarios where anomalies are ill-defined. This evaluation empowers manufacturers to choose the suitest model according to application-specific needs, thereby gaining from being very reliable, efficient, and adaptive.

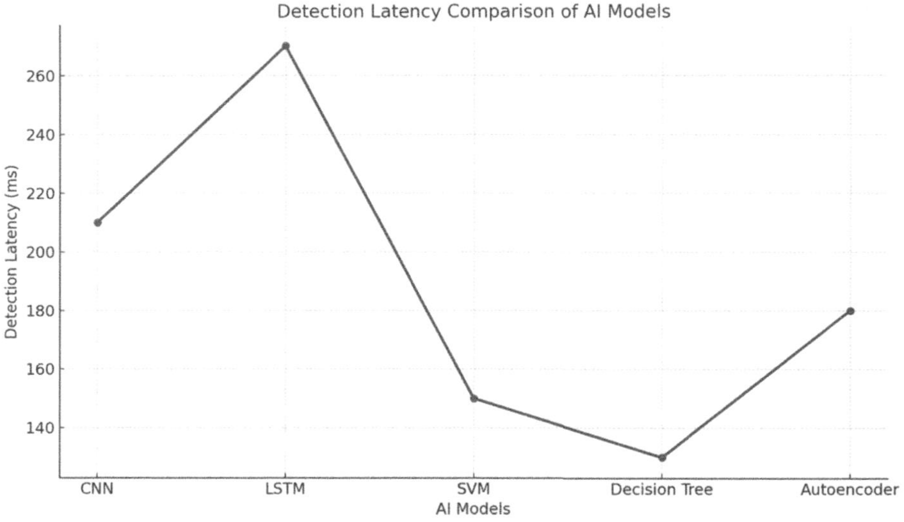

FIGURE 9.2 Comparative evaluation.

Figure 9.2 shows the detection latency associated with various AI models meant for predictive anomaly detection, which is compared in several IoT-enabled manufacturing systems. Among these models, the Decision Tree presents the least latency at 130 ms, rendering it potentially best for all applications requiring fast response times; the Support Vector Machine also presents relatively speedy detection at 150 ms. All of these, however, can be compared to Long Short-Term Memory networks, which take the highest time at 270 ms due to the complexity of computations involved in processing data sequentially. Between the two, Convolutional Neural Networks and autoencoders are latencies of 210 and 180 ms, respectively. It again compares the balancing act between speed and depth of analysis and ultimately indicates which type of model will be suitable to apply, depending on how real-time a requirement might be versus the complexity of the anomaly within intelligent manufacturing.

9.5 CASE STUDY – NETWORK MODELLING AND ANALYTICS

Advanced sensing technologies produce enormous volumes of data in the context of large-scale IoMT [15] in manufacturing, which offer important insights into production performance and machine conditions. IoMT creates massive data streams, such as power profiles gathered from individual machines during the creation of discrete parts, as it links multiple machines within a manufacturing system. Tens of thousands of power profiles are produced by the system; each variation contains important information about the operation of the machine and the process. By allowing to modify procedures and maintain machinery, these variations especially peer-to-peer disparities in power profilesimprove product quality and lower rework rates.

However, the sheer amount of data created makes it extremely difficult to manage and optimize a large-scale network of interconnected units. Making educated decisions requires gleaning pertinent insights from the data, both from a network of machines and from individual machines. Advanced information-processing skills are essential to achieving IoMT's full potential, but not much has been done to solve the core problems with big data analytics in extensive IoMT settings.

The case study suggests creating virtual machine network models as a solution to these issues. The first model, which focuses on long-term monitoring data from individual devices, is a tailored peer-to-peer network [16]. Each machine part's power profile data is represented as a node in this model, and changes in the signal waveform at various production phases offer important information about the performance and health of the machine. In the second model, which is a Population Machine-to-Machine network, each node stands for a separate machine, and the node attributes are aggregated properties or dominating profile patterns. In order to monitor and repair machines more effectively, engineers and managers can use this approach to find machine communities that have comparable operating circumstances.

Parallel graph analytics is the third model that has been suggested [17]. Conventional serial computing techniques are inadequate for effectively describing networks and delivering real-time analytics because of the enormous number of machines and the enormous volume of data. The capacity of IoMT to grow and add more machines, creating intricate network topologies, links, and communities, is what gives it its power. Thus, in order to optimize the vast IoMT network and enable real-time analytics and predictive decision-making in smart manufacturing settings, parallel algorithms are crucial. Manufacturers may improve machine performance, better manage their operations, and realize the full potential of IoMT in a smart manufacturing environment by combining these sophisticated network models with parallel processing and predictive analytics.

The main technological procedures for building and refining will be described in the next four subsections. These steps are not meant to be all-inclusive or comprehensive; rather, they are meant to offer fundamental concepts for the IoMT network.

9.6 CONCLUSION

This is because the IoT is a new era of intelligent, integrated, and streamlined production processes to organizations. According to the IoT technologies, it enhances productivity, reduces expenses, enhances quality of all products, and achieves the real-time data collection, predictive analytics, and the free-flowing communication between machines, systems, and operators. Old manufacturing processes are becoming data-driven and flexible to better network inventory management, worker safety, machine tracking, and predictive maintenance-related operations and better coping with an ever-changing global market that is dynamically evolving. The power of the smart manufacturing system will also be enhanced as the IoT will keep expanding in the future along with the use of AI, 5G connection, edge computing, and blockchain. One of the forces that will drive innovation and productivity will be integration at scale so that organizations can be relevant enough to satisfy the demands of sustainability, speed, and personalization that are constantly on the rise. In order to be driven in the sphere of industry innovations, the manufacturers should adopt the IoT; it is not an option anymore. IoT can shape the future of intelligent manufacturing, and implemented adequately, it can make the industrial systems much more efficient, profitable, and resilient.

REFERENCES

1. Khayyat, M.M., Munshi, R.M., Alabduallah, B., Lamoudan, T., Ghith, E., Kim, T-H., & Abdelhamid, A.A. (2024). "An improved biometric stress monitoring solution for working employees using heart rate variability data and Capsule Network model." *PLoS One*, 19(12), e0310776. https://doi.org/10.1371/journal.pone.0310776
2. Zhang, P., Li, F., Zhao, R., Zhou, R., Du, L., Zhao, Z., Chen, X., & Fang, Z. (2021). "Psychological stress detection according to ECG Using a deep learning model with attention mechanism." *Applied Sciences*, 11(6), 2848. https://doi.org/10.3390/app11062848
3. Liu, S., Liang, Y., Lin, Z., Qin, Y., Huang, Z., & Hooi, B. (2025). "Multi-task opinion enhanced hybrid BERT model for mental health analysis." *Scientific Reports*, 15(1), 3332. https://doi.org/10.1038/s41598-025-86124-6
4. Salih, A., Raisi-Estabragh, Z., BoscoloGalazzo, I., Radeva, P., Petersen, S. E., Menegaz, G., & Lekadir, K. (2023) "A perspective on explainable artificial intelligence methods: SHAP and LIME." arXiv preprint. https://doi.org/10.48550/arXiv.2305.02012
5. Bipro, S.S., Kabir, S., & Motin, M.A. (2023) "Monitoring stress using electrocardiogram signal." *Computing in Cardiology*. https://www.cinc.org/archives/2023/pdf/CinC2023-204.pdf
6. Khayyat, M., Munshi, R.M., Alabduallah, B., Lamoudan, T., Ghith, E., Kim, T.-H., et al. (2024). "An improved biometric stress monitoring solution for working employees using heart rate variability data and Capsule Network model." *PLOS One*, 19(12), e0310776. https://doi.org/10.1371/journal.pone.0310776
7. Anwar, Y., Liu, Y., & Wang, Y. (2021). "Psychological stress detection according to ECG using a deep learning model with attention mechanism." *Applied Sciences*, 11(6), 2848. https://doi.org/10.3390/app11062848
8. Liu, Y., Wang, Y., & Wang, Y. (2024). "Multi-task opinion enhanced hybrid BERT model for mental health analysis." *Scientific Reports*, 14, 86124. https://doi.org/10.1038/s41598-025-86124-6
9. Li, X., Wang, Y., & Wang, Y. (2024). "Integrated improved Harris hawks optimization for global optimization problems." *Scientific Reports*, 14, 58029. https://doi.org/10.1038/s41598-024-58029-3
10. Cioffi, R., Sorrentino, A., & Palumbo, M. (2020). "IoT in sustainable manufacturing: review and future research directions." *MDPI Sensors*, 10(8), 2897.
11. Chigilipalli, S., Kuo, J., & Yu, J. (2021). "Internet of Things in additive manufacturing: Applications and challenges." *MDPI Journal of Manufacturing*, 6(2), 50. https://doi.org/10.3390/asi6020050.
12. Yang, Z., Zhang, J., & Liu, L. (2019). "IoT-enabled smart manufacturing and cyber-physical systems: a survey." *Journal of Manufacturing Science and Engineering*, 141(9), 092502. https://doi.org/10.1115/1.4044766.
13. Mishra, S., Jain, V., & Singh, H. (2020). "Integrating IoT with product lifecycle management in manufacturing systems: a review." *Journal of Advanced Manufacturing Technology*, 56(4), 292–306.
14. Hu, B., Sun, Z., & Zhang, S. (2021). "Industrial IoT intelligence for smart manufacturing: a comprehensive review." *IEEE Transactions on Industrial Informatics*, 17(2), 1212–1222.
15. Kumar, M., Sharma, R., & Verma, S. (2020). "IoT applications in Industry 4.0: A comprehensive review." *Procedia CIRP*, 91, 1735–1740.
16. Gao, H., Wang, X., & Li, Y. (2021). "A bibliometric analysis of smart manufacturing and Internet of Things." *Computers in Industry*, 130, 103474.
17. Singh, A., Kaur, P., & Rana, S. (2021). "Smart manufacturing: A bibliometric review and future research directions." *MDPI Electronics*, 9(12), 1580.

18. Wang, H., Xu, M., & He, Q. (2020). "Applications of IoT in supply chain management and logistics in manufacturing." *Journal of Industrial Information Integration*, 17, 100116.
19. Chen, Y., Liu, Y., & Zhang, L. (2021). "Manufacturing-as-a-Service (MaaS) for smart manufacturing: challenges and future perspectives." *Journal of Intelligent Manufacturing*, 32(1), 33–48.
20. Li, J., Li, X., Zhang, Y., & Zhang, J. (2024). "Integrated improved Harris hawks optimization for global and engineering optimization." *Scientific Reports*, 14, 7445. https://doi.org/10.1038/s41598-024-58029-3

10 Industrial Internet of Things and Cyber Manufacturing Systems

Vanitha C. N. and Anusuya P.

10.1 INTRODUCTION

The Industrial Internet of Things (IIoT) and Cyber Manufacturing Systems (CMS) are two of the key drivers that have been recognized to be disruptive technology enablers of manufacturing as smart, connected, adaptable manufacturing processes. These are a part of the efficiencies that would be realized on the eventual implementation of the Industry 4.0 vision and its promise of more connected, intelligent, and adaptable production systems to cope with changing market requirements. Now think of computers chattering with machines as data stream passes data nonstop. Instead of depending solely on hands-on fixes, factories also monitor live-restarts to inform decisions in real time. One flows into another, from sensors to software, with actions formed by analytics. This fusion of hardware and smart systems enhances results throughout production lines. Order replaces chaos and precision is born. Problems are experienced with quicker responses, smarter adjustments. Outcomes tighten, and waste slips away. Each makes contact so that nothing runs blind.

Moving after Internet of Things (IoT), IIoT emerges as machinery exchanges information within factories [1,2]. This is a network of devices, sensors, and actuators that is used to collect, share, and process data from manufacturing processes in real time. These connected devices allow manufacturers to have an amount of control over the operations they supposedly have never experienced before, thereby helping to usher in new levels of efficiency, productivity, and cost-effectiveness. For instance, through IIoT, manufacturers are in a position to keep an eye on their machinery and equipment in real time, recognize problems before they appear or even prevent them, and decide with a level of preciseness how resources such as energy are being used, hence cutting down on so much time and money lost because of break down and misuse of resources. For instance, an IoT application in a factory might detect the vibration level of a particular machinery and alert that there is something wrong with the machinery before even it reaches a worse state where it needs to be replaced.

Alongside IIoT and CMS, this notion is one step further through building virtual replicas, known as digital twins, of actual manufacturing elements. It is an integration of digital and physical environments to give manufacturers the chance to replicate their processes, the ability to experiment, and changes made right away without affecting the real environment [3]. These Cyber-Physical Systems (CPS) coordinate

 DOI: 10.1201/9781003582465-10

physical and computational processes to the functioning of machinery and the manipulation of data, hence increasing the level of automation. For example, in the smart factory where CMS technology has been implemented, an actual production line can be created as a replica, where changes can be introduced within the production schedule, and the bottlenecks can be detected along with live updates from the IoT sensors and real-time adjustment of the production line can be developed. Such capability improves adaptability in operation and recovery, valuable factors for manufacturers amidst the growing environment dynamics and stiff competition.

Enablement of predictive and prescriptive analytics is one of the biggest advantages of IIoT and CMS. The old-style manufacturing systems have always engaged in firefighting manufacturing control systems, where they only act when there is a problem. But here's how it operates: IIoT-linked systems go on the defensive and move to prevent problems before they occur, that is things like broken machines, defective products, or shipment delays. As a result, because sensors are constantly aggregating data, patterns develop that indicate anything that might go wrong later. These signals are sent by interconnected devices that feed information into analysis tools. Imagine alerts that appear just as a motor starts acting funny, not after it dies completely. Machines are learning from previous behaviour so things are fixed earlier rather than too late. In other words, repairs are not made on schedule but whenever a need arises.

On the wild frontier of intelligent machines, IIoT is the natural partner of CMS, aligning closely with Industry 4.0 concepts. They enable connected systems to communicate freely and share their charge without any clunky hitches. This linkage means factories can adjust without delay, adapting to what buyers need now, not last year's plans. It enables faster development of new designs and gets old items some fresh updates to keep them relevant, all thanks to flows of responsive technologies. In each of the manufacturing stages, CIO combined with CMS brings intelligence to the operation.

One incredibly interesting shift that IIoT has brought to CMS is how much focus factories are now putting into sustainability. Now, thanks to the smarter systems monitoring every volt, machines sip power rather than guzzle it. Waste descends when sensors detect leaks or tiresome equipment spinning idle too long. Imagine live tracking inside plants like little devices screaming warnings before electricity drains into the void. Digital replicas of production lines allow teams to experiment with changes without laying a hand on a single bolt and they skip the safety risks associated with real-world tests. Cleaner output arises naturally when design takes place inside of software in the first place. Efficiency accelerates, while fumes diminish, not because regulations require it but rather the data illuminates the way forward. There's a smaller clean-up job when decisions are based on patterns, not guesses. Factories breathe easy when tech shapes rituals baked into old routines. Green steps are more palatable when they save money as well. Advancement buzzes softly in background updates, not grand pronouncements. What once would have been a pollutant now fuels improvement in the background. And operations reduce their footprints simply by taking note of what they never did before.

But the connection of IIoT to CMS transcends the shop floor. It reaches critical parts of the entire production network including suppliers, and buyers as well. With data on connected devices, factories can see every step of the supply chain.

This clarity gives them a sharper eye on how they watch stock, predict orders, and deal with shipping. The CMS reinforces this by translating numbers into intelligent information that can lead decisions rather than be driven by issues. Imagine that smart system discovers what is causing the late arrival of materials and reschedules early so customer deliveries are still on time. If there is one thing that ties CMS to intelligent manufacturing systems in an explicit fashion, it's goals. When flexibility shakes hands with greener methods at modern factories, productivity soars. Imagine infrastructure where CPS funnel information into cloud platforms, while sensors push data through industrial internet conduits. A mirror image of real-world actions shapes virtually, by the second. Decisions are born from all these inputs, never static, but taking shape moment by moment. But now focus intelligence kicks in through different ways as algorithms can learn patterns silently behind the scenes. Machines tune behaviour using predictive patterns cultivated through piles of operational data. Optimization is not the result of loud pronouncements; it is simply gradual silent additions, gradually accumulating. It works more efficiently when it makes its own decisions and speculates what is going to be next. Here live data begins to play a role in the location where CMS meets Intelligent Manufacturing System (IMS). There is one system that collects the loads of info about the way machines operate; there is the other system that implements smart algorithms to operate fast, snafus are being preempted far way in advance, and all they know is that they are incredibly intertwined. Factories can also work more rapidly with each other since they do not need someone to enter them at every single moment but can also switch their route in the middle of the steps when it is necessary because they can manage their resources more sharply. Because CMS is a combination of digital signals and the real objects, new production directions are tested by IMS.

What are the other places where IIoT systems shine and CMS? Quality checks. Machines find out defects before people see them. Consider fewer mistakes, higher standards. It is not magic, only sensors relaying real-time data. Results show up faster now. Decision-making becomes faster as well, with less waiting around. There are fewer delays down the line. The performance goes up without additional efforts. That kind of gain matters. The common methods used in quality assurance include frequent auditing which is both ineffective and consumes a lot of time. Conversely, quality problems can be evaluated on the fly and remedied by different IIoT sensors and analytics using artificial intelligence (AI) algorithms. Indicatively, methods such as AI with imaging can be used to detect defects on products on the surface to ensure that only perfect products are released into the market.

With the growth in the complexity of IIoT and CMS implementation, concepts of Industry 4.0 are increasing in their applicability of promoting integration from the supply chain right through to the Operational Technology layers. As such, 5G, blockchain, and augmented reality (AR) are conforming to the IIoT and CMS to provide further value. For instance, new generation networks such as 5G networks help in delivering real-time information for applications within a large, geographically dispersed manufacturing ecosystem [4]. The technology of blockchain decentralization improves and provides security and audibility for data in various fields, including supply chain and quality assurance [5,6]. AR, on the other hand, provides training and remote support and improves workforce and operation skills.

However, the implementation of IIoT and CMS comes with its own set of problems that have been described below. For example, cybersecurity risks or attacks translate into considerable risks to complicated manufacturing instituting systems [7,8]. Security implies the application of tools like encryption, detection of suspicious activity, or blockchain; all these factors serve to make systems credible and operate effectively. Due to the rapid increase in data particularly where little shops are big factories, managing size becomes difficult. Most scaling issues can be resolved without raising an alarm by use of smart panel designs and balanced workloads. The entry of big machines into IIoT and CMS usually conflicts rather than collaborates. Clear rules and middleware layers are used to direct old and new technologies to work together, with operations proceeding as the performance is improved on a board-wide basis.

Truth is, IIoT and CMS push factories away from old-school hands-on methods toward smarter, quicker systems. Because of these tools, setups adjust on the fly, upkeep runs smoother, and choices hit closer to the mark – outcomes get stronger without extra strain. It can be seen that as the integration gets finer, IIoT and CMS will have a much higher impact on the future of manufacturing in Industry 4.0 encompassing innovation, sustainability, and competitiveness.

10.2 LITERATURE REVIEW

IIoT and CMS have evolved the manufacturing industry, whereby smart factories and intelligent manufacturing have come into operation. Ryalat et al. [9] presented an architectural design of a smart factory that includes CPS and IIoT under the framework of Industry 4.0. They also underscored the importance of integration of the system in order to attain agility and modularization in production through CPS and digital technologies.

The synergistic combination of blockchain and AI has been considered to address the IIoT cybersecurity issue. Tyagi, in his work (2024) [10], outlined that blockchain offered trust and secure and indelible means of transferring information within the IoT and IIoT networks. With the integration of these technologies, the weaknesses in the management of devices and access are also solved. Souri et al. [11] also put forward a cloud-based cyber-attack detection architecture titled Ensemble Bagged Trees Detection along with feature selection approaches for the hyper-automation process in the IIoT environment. In large-scale settings, their approach was successful in managing security threats.

To solve the problem of intrusion detection in IIoT networks, Soliman et al. [12] proposed a deep learning (DL)-based system through the Telemetry of Things (ToN)-IoT dataset to demonstrate high accuracy in detecting cyber threats. It focused on biased samples and overfit problems by using superior classification methods. Also, Abikoye et al. [13] reflected briefly on how IoT and CPS can support Industry 4.0 through interconnectivity and smart interconnectedness for manufacturing, specifically examining interconnectivity issues.

In Banerjee and Choppella [14], the authors described a knowledge-driven approach towards dynamic reconfiguration of IoT and CPS control systems using ontological models to support control design and real-time flexibility. I thus confirm that this approach greatly improved the error rate and speed of development across the above domains. Furthermore, Fu et al. [15] studied decentralized failures in CMS and illustrated the risks of multiple coupled physical service networks for anyone who wants to design more robust system architectures. In Wu et al. [16], the authors discussed the utilization of the DT technology for CMS and performed edge–Cloud architecture on small defect detection tasks. This approach includes multi-modal inputs and comprehensively demonstrated DL models for real-time application in manufacturing industries with high accuracy rates. Also, machine-integrated intelligent detection systems have emerged in IIoT development. In the IIoT context, the scalability and efficiency of the proposed mechanism were investigated by Prince et al. [17] where IEEE standards and DL were used to enhance the protection of IoT devices from cyberattacks. This is due to hyper-automation, which you know has risen significantly due to Industry 5.0-intended IIoT and CPS frameworks. Earlier, scholars have shown superior approaches to the enhancement of security and functionality. Another detailed model that was presented by Nayem et al. aimed to examine malice and improve action setups in IIoT. All these strategies do not only assist in enhancing safety but also enable an easy transition in line with the requirements of the industrial practices. The influx in the use of IoT, IIoT, and CPS in factories and critical systems raises concerns on a growing basis – security vulnerabilities are discovered at the same rate as new designs are being created. Despite the high rate of its adoption, the vulnerabilities are ingrained in the constitution of how things are constructed. Issues are not slowing down with the increased connection between devices more frequently than ever. Such challenges and potential solutions have been described and analyzed by many of the authors, in some of the fields such as honeypots, CPS architecture, and the use of intelligent decision-making systems.

Franco et al. [18] provided a detailed overview of honeypots and honeynets in the case of IoT, IIoT, and CPS. The tools are used by attracting attackers like bait and can thus be used to attack paths and trends of real systems are not on real systems, but only on those that are captured by the researchers and practitioners. Yet there is a second layer that can be seen in the context of this effort in comparison to typical tools such as firewalls or Intrusion Detection Systems – one piece constructing individual yet linked shields in cybersecurity. Such a review obliterates existing honeypot and honeynet configurations, probes into what makes them take their form, and then lines directly on empty places that must be filled to make them stronger. Alternatively, Pivoto and colleagues [19] considered the issue of analytics in 2021 how CPS are designed to execute in spaces of Industrial IoT connected with Industry 4.0 demands. What is introduced is an image of fundamental CPS designs, including information on how they operate, what technology supports them, and what their purposes are. Instead of merely enumerating sections, it emphasizes the reason why integrating operations on different levels of factories is so important and in the process of quests into how these systems can be foundations to enhance the performance of IIoT. Some gaps stand clear. Corresponding new requirements arise when developing superior cyber-physical mechanisms to handle skin fungi issues related to smart factories. Rather, Krol Rymarczyk and Wyrwizi [20] research from 2023 provides a wider perspective on how this type of technology can monitor and control factory work. Inside their conception has a brainy heart – processes that make decisions quickly and execute live copies of models of physical setups. The arrangement saves on waste, identifies hiccups during their occurrences, and maintains operations smoothly. One result? A movement into much customized products, more cheerful consumers, not only shorter queues but smarter ones too.

Altogether, it is possible to emphasize that these works identify the developmental possibilities of the application of IIoT and CMS in smart production while also pointing to the problems of cybersecurity, system reliability, working productivity, and time-adequate adaptability.

10.3 FUNDAMENTALS OF CMS

This section presents multiple integrated approaches for the Design and Deployment of the IIoT and CMS. These methods adopt IoT, CPS, AI, and cybersecurity to create effective, responsive, and adaptable manufacturing systems.

CMS is defined here as the implementation of many technologies in manufacturing processes so as to improve the adaptability of manufacturing systems. This section explores three core principles that define CMS: CPS, digital twin technology, and Data Analytics and AI Integration. The basic architecture of this system is shown in Figure 10.1.

10.3.1 Cyber-Physical Systems

The second aspect of IoT is CPS, which combines computer control and networks with physical infrastructure. Manufacturing systems in CMS are supported by CPS, which connects physical systems with computational and control systems. This integration allows monitoring, feedback, or decision-making in real time. Integration of physical and virtual environments makes it possible to introduce higher levels of automation, giving the processes necessary flexibility.

CPS is the central platform of advanced manufacturing systems since it facilitates discrete interactions between the physical and computational layers. This is done through an interconnected system of instrumented sensors, actuators, and controllers that constantly watch over the physical infrastructure, accumulate data, and feed it to decision support systems. The collected data enables CPS to not only operate in real time but also anticipate problems in advance, keep big systems from failing, and maintain production. For example, in car production, CPS can analyze the speed of an assembly line, and lack of the interference of human input can alter speeds or

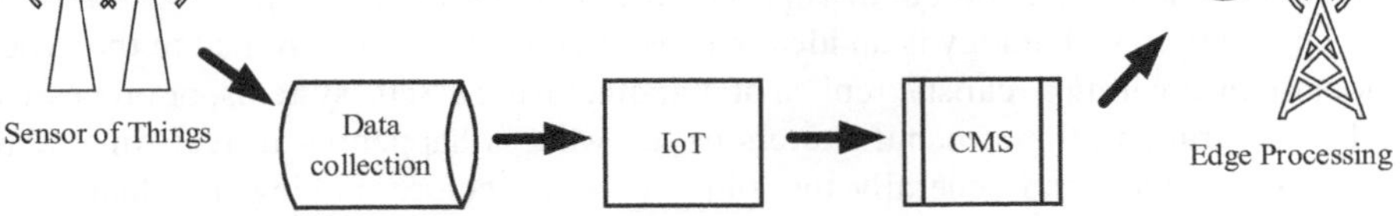

FIGURE 10.1 Basic interaction architecture of IIoT and CMS.

sequences for productivity and to avoid logjams. Such dynamic adaptability raises efficiency and enhances operational performance by cutting costs at this level [21].

Another great strength of CPS is its capacity to enhance the interactivity between human agents and machines as well as to create an improved production environment. Built with compatibility with AR, the operations with CPS can easily present real-time data and come up with a decided course of action without much delay. Regarding the application of the concept of CPS in production, in cases like for instance, product customization, manufacturers gain the ability to change production lines proactively according to customer needs as they get ready for this, without having to spend such a long time closing and opening the production line. In addition, CPS supports predictive maintenance on the machines as they help to detect the occurrences of wear and tear in them before organizing their maintenance. This avoids some random breakdowns and also gives long service to the industrial machinery. The more industries integrate CPS in manufacturing processes the closer they get to Industry 4.0 objectives of highly flexible, efficient, smart manufacturing environments.

10.3.1.1 Key Features of CPS in CMS

- These include the temperature, pressure, or vibrations of machinery and other equipment that are installed with permanently installed sensors sending data on the equipment parameters in real time.
- CPS is in a position to use algorithms to make an instant adjustment as it processes data. For example, if a machine displays some level of wear, then CPS can lessen its use or notify the maintenance crews.
- CPS integrates numerous machines and systems in the production line to ensure a proper flow of communication.

10.3.1.2 Applications of CPS in Manufacturing

- In a smart factory, through sensing, CPS alters the flow of processing depending on the variation of demand for products or the material status.
- Through energy consumption programmes, CPS guarantees that all machinery is properly utilized, thereby minimizing wastage.
- CPS identifies and prevents failures or defects that may occur in a production line out of its ordinary working.

10.3.2 Digital Twin Technology

Digital twin technology refers to an interface that builds a virtual model of a physical object, a structure, or a process, and corresponds to the actual version as it evolves. Digital twins offer manufacturers the ability to observe key operations, run trials, and assess the impact without disrupting those processes physically.

Digital twin technology is an ideal means of connecting the physical to the cyber domain by creating a realistic replica of manufacturing assets, systems, or processes. This integration allows manufacturers to see what is happening in real time, play "what-if" games, and generally fine-tune processes before making the changes in the physical domain. For instance, digital twins of aerospace manufacturing jet engines let engineers apply various stress conditions, detect possible failure, and determine performance characteristics, all of which can take place without interrupting the actual process. It improves decision-making and helps to eliminate costly mistake-prone paradigms such as trial and error, and also helps to reduce time wastage and resource consumption.

One of the defining aspects of digital twin technology is that it can pull in data from multiple data sources that are native to the IoT, machines, logs, and records of the production and marketing processes of a product. It is for this reason that multiple data sources can be integrated in support of the predictors to spearhead maintenance and process optimization based on pattern and trend discovery. Furthermore, digital twins promote efficiency by giving all the stakeholders complete visibility of the processes. For instance, in a smart factory solution, the exact representation of a production line can be accessed remotely, thus providing engineers and managers the ability to make decisions together. Thus, the implementation of digital twin technology allows industries not only to succeed operationally but also to be ready for market needs without losing time on making changes to the production process, which is critical during the modern manufacturing market constantly evolving.

10.3.2.1 Key Characteristics of Digital Twins

- The fleets can be created with accuracy based on the geometries of the physical asset, the operational parameters, and the environment.
- Information is exchanged between the virtual and the real models to retain the synchrony of the distributed model with the actual system.
- It should also be said that Digital Twins elaborate different options and calculate performance under different circumstances.

10.3.2.2 Applications of Digital Twins in CMS

- Another example of the digital twin use is in manufacturing to diagnose the cause of machine failure or to predict when certain machines may need maintenance.
- As a result of workflow emulation, further enhancements of production sequences are achieved by reducing the downtime of the digital twin.
- They help the trainers to understand the real processes of the industries and offer the operators the digital twin as a risk-free environment to learn complicated operations.

10.3.3 Data Analytics and AI Integration

Big data and AI are critical components of converting numerical, unprocessed information into valuable insights as applied to CMS with potential for growth and improvement. Starting with fresh eyes, makers now spot weak spots faster because smart analysis reveals hidden trends – patterns emerge where none seemed visible before. When machines hum inside factories, their sensors feed live details into systems that learn from past behaviour, so warnings pop up just in time. These alerts let fixes happen early, stretching life out by acting ahead instead of waiting for breakdowns.

Machine learning digs through heaps of varied data to spot weak spots in workflows and then suggests fixes. Simulations, guided by smart algorithms, reshuffle page priorities depending on how users move around and return most often. Patterns caught early keep output steady, flagging odd traits before they slip past defined benchmarks. Tied to AI, these steps smooth operations while making sure what gets built stays up to par. Happy customers follow, quietly, from things simply working right each time.

Finding patterns in how people buy helps companies guess what will sell next. Because of these insights, stocking the right amount becomes easier over time. When shopping habits shift, factories adjust quicker than before. What customers choose today shapes tomorrow's supply plans. Predicting changes in demand turns out smoother when past choices are studied closely. For instance, in the car industry, AI analysis can forecast the potential of certain car models to create demand, thus optimizing the available resources. Data analytics when combined with AI provide a strong foundation for proactive, future-proof manufacturing systems that are well-equipped to handle change and constantly evolving at the rate that is characteristic of the Industry 4.0 paradigm.

10.3.3.1 Key Components of Data Analytics in CMS

- Smart devices, IoT, and communication interfaces monitor and gather a huge amount of data from machines, systems, and processes.
- Methods such as filtering and normalization are employed on the data in order to pre-process the data for correct analysis.
- The analysis process brings professional quantitative and qualitative methods, which use ML algorithms for patterns and insights generation.

10.3.3.2 Role of AI in CMS

AI enhances CMS by offering predictive and prescriptive capabilities. Prescriptive AI models predict likely failures or production delays using historical and live data, and predictive models give suggestions to enhance performance like changing the production plan or distributing again of resources.

10.3.3.3 Applications of Data Analytics and AI in CMS

- Predictive analytics by ML provides insight into production by analyzing data and recommending areas of concern.
- Defect recognition in products is being done by computer image recognition, thus maintaining the quality of what is in the market.
- AI is capable of foreseeing market trends and customers' demands before the manufacturers counter them.

10.4 SYSTEM MODEL

10.4.1 System Architecture Design

The architecture for IIoT and CMS is created to provide a closed-loop integration between actual manufacturing processes in industrial facilities and the virtual world representing the same processes. There are multiple layers with specific roles and technologies within the architecture, all to create a high-performing and very dependable system. The physical and virtual platforms of IIoT and CMS are built following a system architecture that supports structures that are physical in form and virtual in operations. In Table 10.1 below, the proposed architecture including multiple components is listed with its description and example technologies.

10.4.1.1 IoT Sensors and Actuators

IoT sensors and actuators found in this layer refer to devices that are designed to work beneath and inside the physical layers of structures to monitor, detect, and control specific conditions and phenomena. The foundation of the IIoT system comprises IoT sensors and actuators that are the source of data as well as the means for controlling production processes on the shop floor. This layer includes:

Smart Sensors: Examples of such parameters include temperature, vibration, and production rates, acquired in real-time employing Micro-Electro-Mechanical Systems sensors and other innovative IIoT-enabled tools.

Actuators: Finally, the actuators work on mechanical systems utilizing the processed data for operation at their best. This layer is a layer of digitizing access points to physical processes, or ways to automate thickness.

10.4.1.2 Communication Networks Layer

This layer is for transferring data between devices so this layer plays a significant role in its process. Several key technologies under communication include:

5G Networks: The asymmetric digital subscriber line is a fast-speed and low-delay network that is best suited for real-time applications.

LPWANs: There are certain wireless technologies such as Long Range and Narrowband IoT for transmitting messages over large power and distance. For very low-power and long-distance communication, specific wireless technologies like Long Range modules and Narrowband IoT are also suitable for sending messages.

Industrial Ethernet: Ensures reliable and high-quality data transmission, enabling properly function essential systems.

Together, these networks can be integrated to create a scalable communication network suitable for high device density and bursty data rates.

TABLE 10.1
List of Components

Component	Description	Example Technologies
IoT sensors & actuators	Monitor and control physical processes in real time	Micro-Electro-Mechanical Systems sensors, industrial actuators
Communication networks	High-speed, low-latency networks for data exchange	5G, LPWAN, industrial Ethernet
Edge–cloud infrastructure	Combines local (edge) processing with centralized (cloud) storage	AWS IoT, Microsoft Azure IoT Hub
CPS	Integrate physical operations with computational models	CPS platforms, Siemens MindSphere

10.4.1.3 The Architecture of the Edge–Cloud Hybrid Infrastructure Layer

To balance real-time responsiveness with the need for extensive data analytics, this layer combines two computing systems.

Edge Computing: It is a real-time data processing so that the time taken from the source to analysis is reduced. Edge devices reduce data points and perform calculations which minimizes the time for making decisions while minimizing communication costs.

Cloud Computing: This includes AWS IoT Core or Microsoft Azure, for instance, which can handle vast amounts of data and use scalability for maintenance, optimization, and insights.

This approach provides optimum throughput for both domestic and international processing requests.

10.4.1.4 Integration between CPS

CPS facilitates live communication and coordination between physical events and computer simulations that use models from cyber and actual worlds. Key features included under CPS are

Digital Twins: It is a process-analogical models that embody, monitor, and run in real-time decision and real-time what-if simulation.

Feedback Loops: It is a sustained adaptive control mechanism and supervision procedure that may alter activities in response to modifications in the system or within the environment.

CPS makes sure that the system continues to remain malleable, resourceful, and elastic.

10.4.2 Data Management Processes

The CMS environment creates a lot of data; hence, the efficient management of data remains an important factor.

Various data management processes are involved and shown in Figure 10.2. For collecting data use protocols such as the MQTT or CoAP to collect highly structured data feed from IoT devices. Methods like moving averages and Kalman filtering exclude low-quality data and data fluctuations. By defining actual domain-related factors such as the wear rate of tools and the energy cost, the most significant pieces of information can be distinguished. With the help of normalization and standardization techniques, employing a similar analysis for different models is possible.

The emerging IIoT comes with sensor networks which use those elements for what we call the Comprehensive Machine System. This would mean real-time data acquisition by reserving distributed sensors, actuators, RFID tags, cameras, and industry controllers. These machines only keep track of machine health data with respect to energy consumption, production speed measuring, environment conditions, and real product quality monitoring with massive inflows of data across structured and

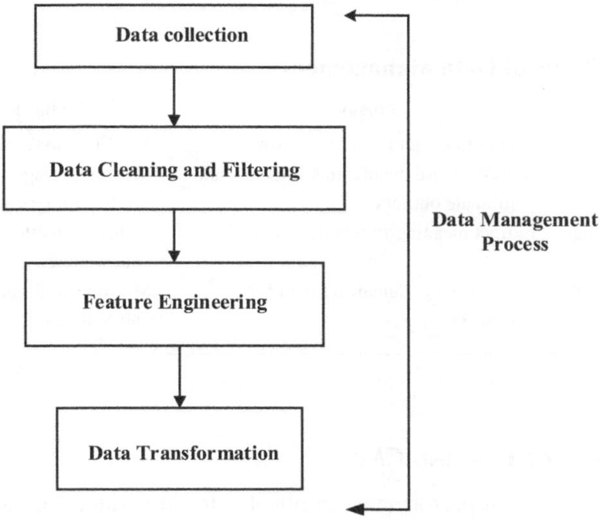

FIGURE 10.2 Data management process.

unstructured sources. The edge is where the most crucial pre-processing of this data takes place, hence prefetching latency and bandwidth consumption for centralization either on the cloud or on-premises storage solutions.

The data is stored and organized after its collection with some cloud platform, edge servers, or hybrid storage architecture. Next-generation CMS leverages big data frameworks, and distributed databases form the basis of its functionality in terms of the volume, velocity, and variety parameters of the industrial data the CMS is dealing with. Blockchain technology also gains ground as a solution to the issue of data security and immutability storage for IIoT-based CMS, which guarantees trust and traceability in manufacturing operations. In fact, data processing and analysis have much to do with actionable insights and informed decision-making. Predictive analytics include real-time fault detection, maintenance schedule identification, and resource optimization using advanced AI, ML, and digital twin model development. Using stream processing methods, IIoT-driven CMS constantly analyzes data to identify patterns and anomalies improving production efficiency while minimizing cost lost due to downtime. Table 10.2 below gives the steps and tools involved in the process of managing data.

All in all, however, data privacy and security will continue to be at the top of priorities in IIoT and CMS making manufacturing data often sensitive and quite critical to business operations. Data integrity and protection from cyber threats will also be guaranteed through incorporating encryption protocols, multifactor authentication, and access control mechanisms. This is in addition to adherence to regulatory compliance with various standards like the GDPR, ISO 27001, and frameworks such as NIST to ensure that manufacturers are regulated by the best practices in industry.

TABLE 10.2
Process and Tools of Data Management

Step	Purpose	Techniques/Tools
Data collection	Gather raw data from IoT sensors.	MQTT, CoAP, REST APIs
Data cleaning	Remove noise, handle missing data, and eliminate outliers.	Moving average, interpolation, Kalman filters
Feature engineering	Extract meaningful features for analysis.	Statistical methods, domain knowledge
Data transformation	Normalize or standardize data for consistency.	Min-max scaling, z-score normalization

10.4.3 Layers of IIoT and CMS

There are eight layers of performance applicable for integrated IIoT and CMS applications from connection establishment to providing applications and maintaining reliable performance. Security is also very essential in IIoT and CMS, and the Security and Privacy Layer safeguards its data throughout the network. Measures include data encryption, use of blockchain for secure transactions, and identity and access management. This layer involves implemented anomaly detection systems for flow analysis of the network traffic to prevent attacks on the system [22].

The multiple layers of this system are shown in Figure 10.3 along with the layer components. The Application and Service Layer points to the contact between the system and its users. Propose is the implementation of a supervisory human–machine interface that includes the visualization of real-time data relevant to operators for monitoring the system and reaction to alarms. Closeness to integration with the infrastructure of ERP systems allows for the positive correlation between conclusions made using the CMS and the overall goals of business, for improving aspects such as inventory control and production planning. Applications can be designed for the manufacturer and target specific aspects such as energy efficiency, or quality control, making the system more versatile.

The architecture is also created to be flexible to accommodate the constant changes that are characteristic of contemporary production processes. The scalability and adaptability framework mean that the development of the system can be expanded in the future. Through modularity, one or more modules can be appended or substituted without affecting the other modules, and in this case, one can add sensors or other edge devices. Smart buildings are self-organized using AI algorithms to enable the architecture to adapt to increasing workloads or conditions to provide continuous efficiency.

10.5 APPLICATIONS IN MANUFACTURING

Different applications use the IIoT and CMS systems for the effective development of technology. Some of the applications are explained below and shown in Figure 10.4.

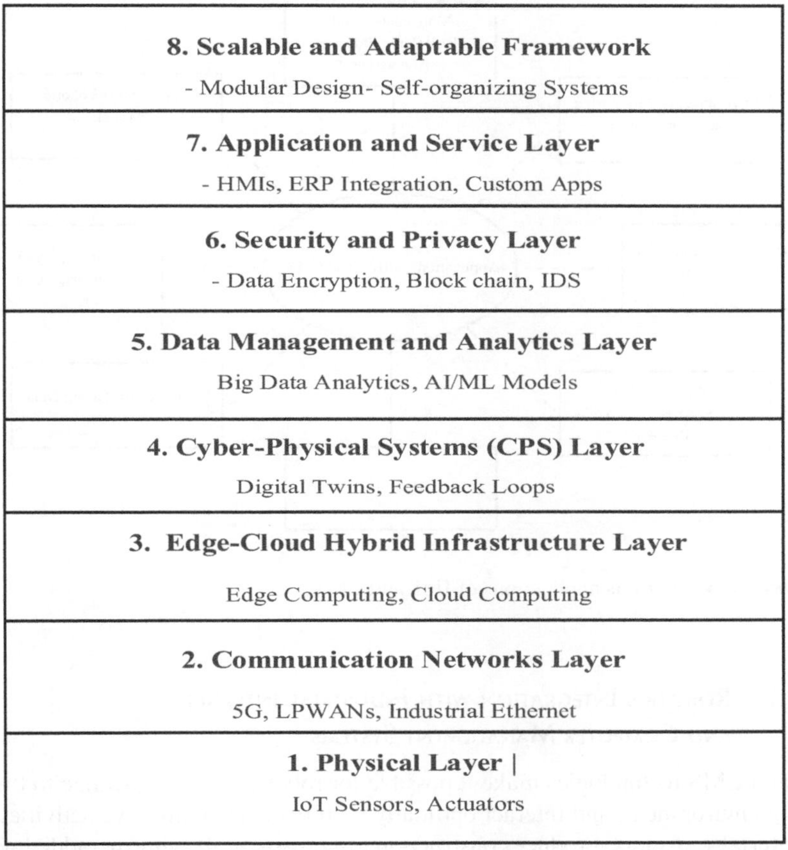

FIGURE 10.3 Layers of IIoT and CMS.

10.5.1 Advanced Usage of Distributed Sensing Processes for Maintenance

Distributed sensing harnesses the use of antecedent data acquisition of IoT devices to enhance the prognosis of maintenance plans. ML models therefore allow distributed sensors to continuously observe the conditions of the equipment and predict possible failure points other than at the time of a failure. The cycle pattern on the parameters including vibration, temperature, or pressure can be detected by these systems powered by AI and indicate wear and tear, rotor misalignment, or possible faults. This predictive approach decreases downtime, decreases the required amount of maintenance, and ultimately increases the user's lifespan, thus controlling profit margins. For instance, in a manufacturing hall, sensors placed on conveyor belts can monitor irregular vibrations and plan for repair only when they are due, not enslaving the machinery, and thus increasing its efficiency.

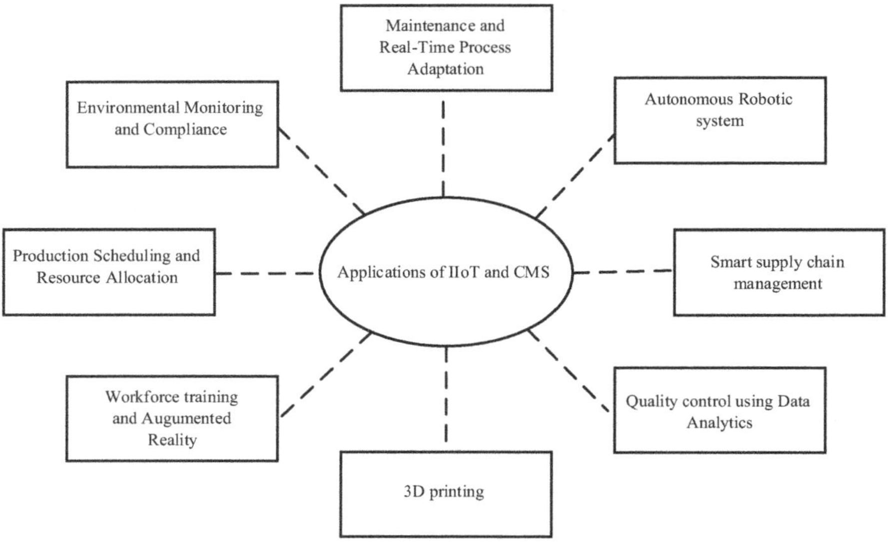

FIGURE 10.4 Various applications of IIoT and CMS.

10.5.2 Robotics Integration with Industrial Internet and Computer Management Systems

IIoT and CMS technologies make it possible for robotics to self-optimize to the prevailing environment, and interact optimally with man. They improve activities such as material transport, product construction, and testing, all with the added advantage of minimizing the risks associated with coming into contact with unfavourable conditions. For instance, cobots that are using sensors of the IIoT technology can work together with operators, flexibly changing positions. This leads to increased productivity through enhancing efficient working, and minimization of incidents and accidents. In line with this, such cobots can freely move from one type of work such as welding to packaging, hence absolutely enabling the assembly line to run uninterrupted due to changes in production demands.

10.5.3 Real-Time Inventory Management and Supply Chain Control

Thus, the use of IIoT real-time inventory control revolutionizes supply chain processes by evaluating stock, estimating future consumption, and managing shipment operations. Through the use of sensors and RFID tags on inventing items, their state of use and location can be constantly relayed, hence enabling timely restocking of the inventory. It reduces the stock levels of the products, maintains a low cost of holding stocks, and delivers the products. Moreover, self-automation demand forecasting technologies evaluate historical purchase records, the prevailing market conditions, and season to determine the future needs so as to make the corresponding decisions on supply chain management in advance. As an example, the e-commerce warehouse can make use of IIoT to monitor inventory and speed up the pick and pack operation and manage order prioritization and delivery satisfaction, providing better customer experience and lower operation expenses.

10.5.4 AI-Powered Quality Control

Automated imaging systems based on AI and data analytics are used in the quality assurance area whereby they are utilized in the proactive inspection of production and stopping when bad parts must be taken, and also in the detection of quality anomalies. These systems employ machine vision image pattern recognition to identify imperfections such as cracks, misalignment, or surface defects that might go unnoticed under manual inspection. Further, actual problems in quality can be predicted by using such variables as uniformity of the material, conditions within the environment, and performance of equipment. This minimizes wastage, improves the reliability of the end product, and hence increases customer confidence. For instance, to check the quality of weld in their cars, a car manufacturer can use AI technologies for inspection to enable efficient and accurate tests on weld quality.

10.5.5 Energy Management and Sustainability

IIoT sensors offer an accurate level of managing electrical power consumption in manufacturing plants and help avoid energy loss and costs. Such systems track the energy consumption of certain machines and determine how some of this consumption can be reduced. For example, during periods of low employment, during office nights or weekends, unnecessary apparatus may be switched off, which reduces energy consumption. Further, IIoT platforms help manufacturers monitor emissions and wastes they produce to reverse environmental policies. Facilities are now applying real-time data from sensors to help make sustainable manufacturing goals more effective in controlling carbon emissions, while also improving energy efficiency. For instance, smart grids using IIoT to coordinate energy usage can flexibly deploy energy consumption according to a more efficient method.

10.5.6 Complex Additive Manufacturing

The additive manufacturing benefits from related IIoT systems including real-time process monitoring, thus enabling quality manufacturing. Temperature, flow of material, and deposition of layers in 3D printers are monitored by sensors which eliminate the possibility of defects and guarantee accuracy. Another advantage of these systems is to support mass customization since they allow making specific complex designs in large quantities. For example, in aerospace, IIoT-integrated Additive Manufacturing (AM) can create lightweight and highly specific geometry components that can improve fuel efficiency, without compromising strength.

10.5.7 Training and Operations in the Light of AR

AR-based tools support workers by giving them real-time guidance and training and simultaneously improving efficiency and minimizing mistakes. Employees deal with complex assembly procedures or troubleshooting issues, using AR-enabled smart glasses to visualize guidance in steps. This reduces dead time and also increases the rate of acquiring new employees into the company. Furthermore, scenarios of operators during operation performance enable them to make real-world challenges in a virtual world without having to call for a repair or stop production. For example, maintenance technicians in a power plant can use AR tools for detecting damaged/faulty parts, and for guiding them on how to safely repair the damage without necessitating any special tools or expertise.

10.5.8 AI-Optimized Scheduling

It incorporates real-time schedules in determining the right process for making products to maintain efficiency and avoid hold-ups when responding to varying demands. Getting real-time availability of workforce, current status of machines, and stock of materials, the AI system generates optimal schedules that can be changed at the moment. For instance, in a food processing plant, AI can alter the timings in a manner that should provide the highest priority to the perishable stock without compromising on the turnaround times. This not only boosts organizational effectiveness in its operations but also customer satisfaction in delivery deadlines.

10.5.9 Environmental Sustainability

IIoT systems allow manufacturers to effectively assist in compliance with laid down environmental policies in discharge emissions, energy usage, and wastes generated. Real-time monitoring also checks that operation is still within legal constraints while large data analysis gives indications on how to reduce the consumption of resources and the effects of the organization on the environment. For instance, an IIoT-implemented system in a chemical plant can decide how best the raw materials can be used, where the effluent discharge can be minimized and waste products can be recycled, hence promoting a circular economy. Be it public awareness campaigns or sustainable business practices, such initiatives not only help implement sustainable practices but also build a positive brand image as the brand proclaims itself in a world that's gradually becoming more environment-friendly.

10.5.10 CPS and Digital Twins

When CPS and digital twins are combined, it is possible to link the actual physical space with the virtual digital space. It is defined as a virtual copy of an actual object or a business process, connected, and updated with real-time information. These may be system layouts, software estimates, or perhaps more broadly operational predictive planning. For example, to increase the efficacy of energy generation from a wind farm with turbines, there is the use of digital counterparts of turbines in that turbine wind farm which are able to predict how it will perform under different weather conditions. The system is expected to bridge the gap between the physical and virtual world, ensuring the scalability and efficiency of CPS.

10.6 IIOT-ENABLED ADAPTIVE SCHEDULING ALGORITHM (IIOT-ASA)

10.6.1 Methodology

The IIoT-ASA schedules production dynamically in response to up-todate machine-state information, workload status, and predictive failure analysis. This maintains peak machine utilization and minimizes cycle time, which results in less production downtime.

This study presents an IIoT-ASA that utilizes real-time data combined with IoT technology for improved task distribution. It takes the use of real-time IIoT sensor data, predictive maintenance, and smart scheduling to increase operational efficiency. At first, the IIoT sensors installed in manufacturing machines provide real-time data to the system. These are typically machine usage statistics, workload, and predictive failure probabilities. To ensure reliability, the algorithm first filters out machines that surpass a predetermined failure threshold. It subsequently ranks available machines in accordance with workload and utilization and orders manufacturing tasks in unified queue according to priority and estimated cycle time. The task allocation phase dynamically assigns the tasks with the least workload and utilization to the machines with the least workload and utilization to balance the resources. When the utilization of a machine reaches the predefined threshold, this machine considers different alternatives to not overloading itself. This kind of scheduling is dynamic, leveraging IIoT sensors to recalibrate its output iteratively, continually correlating failures from one machine with workloads in all the other machines, to update its solution in real time, as failures occur, or as workloads change. As a result, predictive maintenance alerts are now integrated into the system for additional efficiency. When a machine's failure probability is above the threshold (mean life lost per machine), then task reassignment is triggered to reduce the idle time. Moreover, as available real-time data ensures proper workload balancing throughout production lines, you do not face bottlenecks. Finally, the system analyzes the performance improvements made by IIoT-ASA. They are key metrics for machine utilization rate and cycle time reduction.

The proposed IIoT-ASA optimizes task allocation, machine utilization, and real-time decision-making within cyber-manufacturing environments shown in Figure 10.5. Cyber-manufacturing integrates advanced digital technologies, IIoT, cloud computing, AI, and big data analytics, enabling an intelligent, autonomous, and self-optimizing production system. The process starts with the acquisition of real-time records coming from IIoT sensors that are installed on production machines. These sensors constantly provide a flow of object operational parameters such as percentage hours used, power usage, workload and cycle time, temperature and vibration levels, and potential failure. The accumulated information is sent to a cloud-cyber manufacturing platform that harnesses AI analytics to transform the data into machine scheduling and downtime reduction.

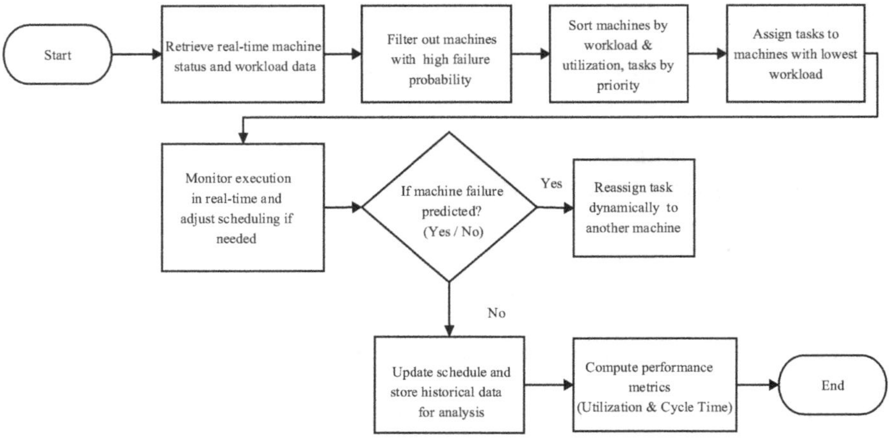

FIGURE 10.5 Process of IIoT-ASA.

Algorithm: IIoT-ASA

INITIALIZE

Collect real-time data from IIoT sensors on machine status (Ut_i, F_i, W_i)
Retrieve task queue with associated priority and estimated cycle time

PRE-PROCESSING

Filter out faulty machines: Exclude machines with F_i > Max Failure Threshold
Sort machines by ascending workload W_i and utilization $\mathrm{Ut_i}$
Sort tasks by descending priority Pr_j

TASK-MACHINE ASSIGNMENT:

For each task T_j in the sorted task list:
Identify machine M_i with the lowest utilization and workload
If Ut_i < Max Utilization Threshold:
Assign $T_j \rightarrow M_i$
Update Ut_i and W_i of machine M_i
Else, find next best available machine

ADAPTIVE SCHEDULING UPDATE:

Monitor execution in real time using IIoT feedback
If a machine failure is predicted (F_i increases above threshold),
Reassign tasks to alternate machines dynamically
If a machine becomes idle, assign the next highest priority task

OUTPUT OPTIMIZED SCHEDULE:

Generate schedule (*T*, *M*)
Store historical data for performance evaluation

EVALUATE PERFORMANCE:

Compute overall machine utilization improvement
Compute cycle time reduction
Generate visualization (graphs) for comparative analysis

Algorithm chooses some machines with high probability of failure through parameters and try to find an optimal task allocation for these unreliable machines. It then lists the machines that are available, and it ranks them according to load and utilization rate, and according to energy. Manufacturing orders are dynamically assigned to the best machines providing for balanced resources and platform down time reduction. This dynamic scheduling scheme requires to continuously look for new task schedules, which can result in a system that is very reactive when machines fail or unexpected load increases are experienced. Source: *Journal of Manufacturing Systems*. The merging of cyber-physical manufacturing with decision-making is supported in digital twin simulations. These digital models of the physical production system generate an analysis of several scheduling solutions and select the best one with AI-boosted optimization models, and at much higher production efficiency while minimizing disturbances.

10.6.2 Results and Discussion on IIoT-ASA

The application of IIoT-ASAIKI technology in a cyber-manufacture environment provided significant improvement on the machine's utilization efficiency and the cycle times. The algorithm used advanced techniques such as real-time data collection, dynamic task assignment, and proactive maintenance scheduling to deepen resource use and optimize productivity.

As compared to baseline operations, machine utilization increased by 20%–40%, as was observed by the outcomes. In the past, machines suffered from idle inefficiencies. For example, during the assignment of tasks, there was a significant delay, and workers were unproductively overloaded with work. Monitoring boosted via IIoT, however, makes it possible for machines to be assigned work tasks readily at the point of their availability, power intake, and health reading. Machines that were considered underperforming after the introduction of IIoT are now functioning at much greater efficiency, which ensures balanced production flow amongst all machines in the system simultaneously. Moreover, the implementation of predictive maintenance resulted in a reduced number of breakdowns and ultimately led to non-disrupted production.

The generated bar graphs explicitly show the comparison of improvements in machine utilization as in Figure 10.6a and cycle time before and after integrating IIoT as in Figure 10.6b. The first graph utilizes percentages of machine utilization before and after implementing the real-time task scheduling system, which

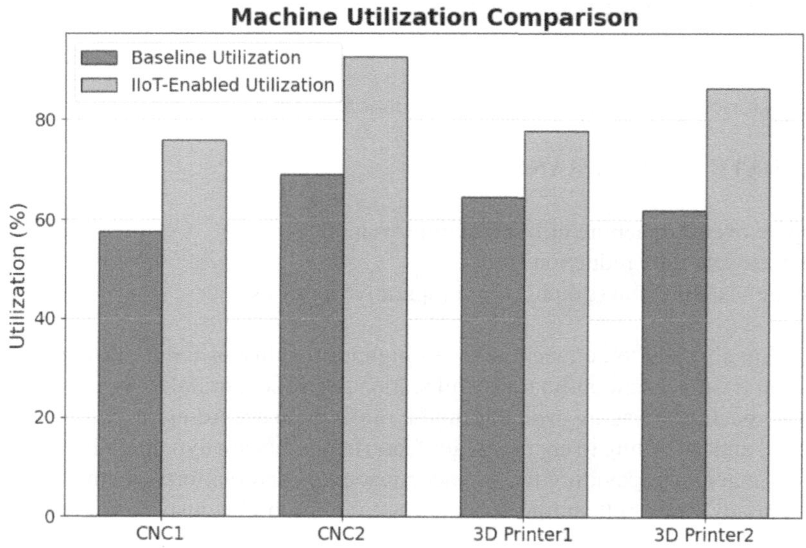

Machine Utilization Improvement (%): `[32.02 34.16 20.41 39.4]`

(a)

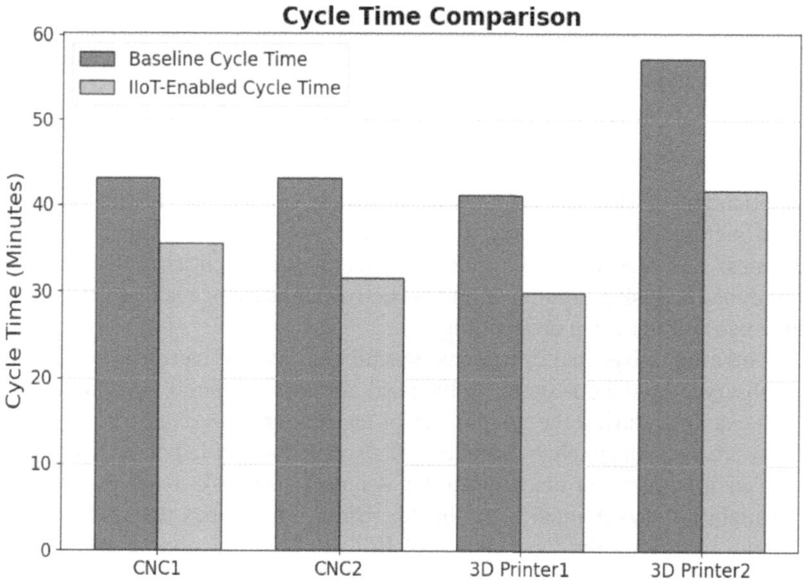

Cycle Time Reduction (%): `[17.51 26.81 27.27 27.25]`

(b)

FIGURE 10.6 (a) Performance of machine utilization. (b) Cyclic time performance.

significantly optimized the workload distribution. The second graph shows how cycle time reduced across various machines, showcasing the effectiveness of predictive analytics in scheduling and maintenance.

The comparison of scheduling methods Traditional Static Scheduling (TSS), Heuristic-Based Scheduling (HBS), and the new IIoT-ASA shows major gains in key factory metrics. The chart of cycle time reduction indicates that IIoT-ASA reduces the cycle by 30% outperforming HBS (18%) and TSS (10%). This boost comes from IIoT-ASA's ability to adapt schedules in real time and assign resources on the fly, which cuts down on idle time and streamlines work processes, and their performance comparison is given in Figure 10.7

In the same way, the machine utilization improvement graph shows that the suggested algorithm has an impact on utilization boosting it by 25%. This trumps HBS at 15% and TSS at 8%. The combination of IIoT-ASA's real time tracking and intelligent workload sharing optimizes how existing manufacturing tools are used.

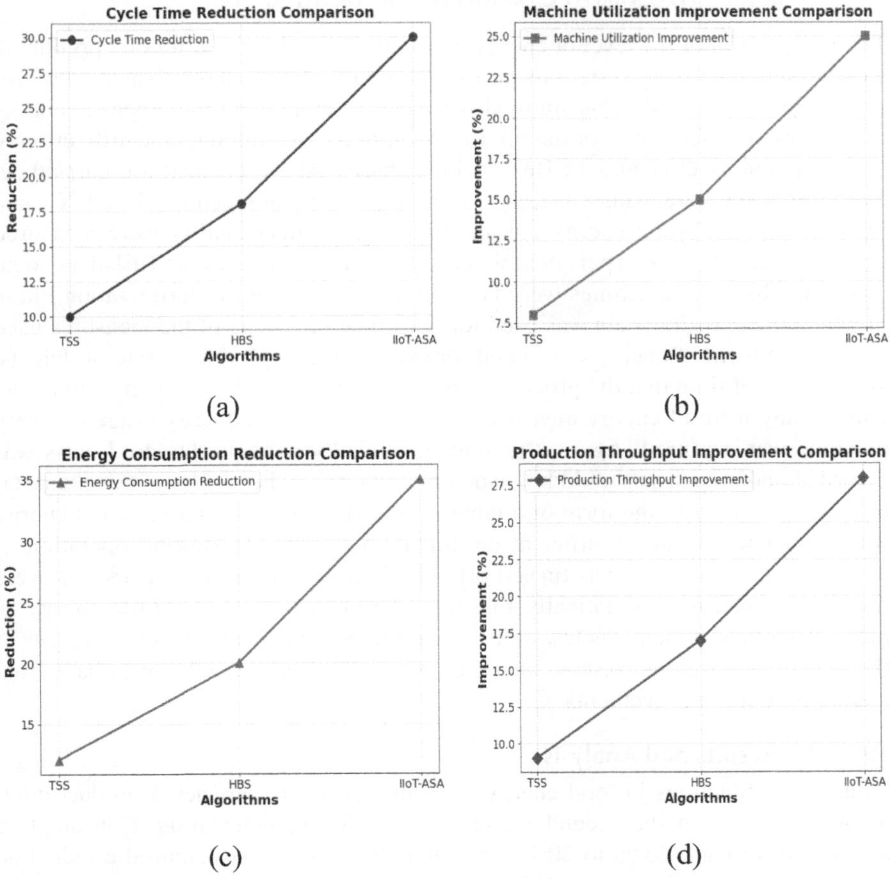

FIGURE 10.7 Performance comparison with existing methods.

This minimizes the likelihood of surprise downtimes and assures that operations are as efficient as they can be. The graph of power consumption drop [35%] indicates a significant fall in energy use with IIoT-ASA. Finally, completing the improvement in hot production graph demonstrates that IIoT-ASA raises process productivity by 28%. This is better than 17% for HBS and 9% for TSS. This bump in productivity comes when IIoT-ASA's predictive analytics help job sequencing better cut down on bottlenecks and enable machines to work more harmoniously together. Taken together, these test results demonstrate that IIoT-ASA significantly affects how well cyber-manufacturing systems function, rendering them more efficient, environmentally friendly, and productive. This makes it a promising way forward for the smart factories of tomorrow.

10.7 EXPERIMENTAL ANALYSIS ON A CASE STUDY

10.7.1 Evaluating Energy Efficiency and Production Quality in an IIoT-Enabled Cyber-Manufacturing System

The comparison of the level of energy consumption and the quality of a product in a cyber-manufacturing system using IIoT-based real-time energy display and process control is studied. This study also measures the percent increment in energy consumption, defect rates, or the improvement in the overall machine utilization of the compared baseline and the IIoT-enabled phases. An experiment was carried out assuming a simulated smart factory consisting of several machines like CNC and 3D printers. Real-time energy consumption and product quality were measured using IoT sensors. The experiment was divided into two phases: an IIoT-dependent phase in which the machines were not optimized, and a Post-Optimization Phase in which the real-time data was used for optimization. Some of the measures used were in the form of energy consumed for every product produced, rate of defects, and amount of time that the process takes. In the baseline phase, the machines ran without any form of energy measurement and control, and energy usage by every machine was captured. Again, the number of faulty ones per hundred parts was recorded and emphasis should be made on the fact that the results of the examination are presented in the form of a table. In the IIoT-enabled phase, actual energy was incorporated into an efficient optimization scheme. During no operation of a piece of machinery, it was turned off, and feedback from the sensors that were installed helped to automatically fine-tune the process to use as little energy as possible while producing as few defects as possible. The resulting performances of the machines were then assessed to give comparisons between the two phases that could point out improvements.

10.7.1.1 Results and Analysis

Significant reductions in total energy consumption while enhancing product quality were evident in the second phase of the IIoT implementation. Consumption levels were brought down to 20%–30%; in addition, machines showed a reduction in defective rates of between 25% and 50%. For instance, CNC 1 improved the consumption of energy by a quarter and 3D Printer1 reduced its defect rate by a third. Such enhancements were illustrated by bar charts contrasting between initial and IIoT-sourced values. Energy conservation was enhanced through efficiency in power control; machines that were not in use were switched off during times of inactivity.

At the same time, defect rates decreased since the performance of quality sensors caused feedback for the corrections in the process of product manufacturing resulting in enhanced accuracy. Figure 10.8a and b shows the energy enhancement and production performance of the above system. In light of these findings, energy efficiency and improvements in the quality achieved in IIoT cyber-manufacturing systems are highlighted. Based on the experimentations, the theoretical propositions concerning the advantages of IIoT in cyber-manufacturing systems can be supported. They posit that the integration of IIoT-based real-time energy monitoring and optimization yielded impressive energy slashing and quality enhancement. These empirical results highlight the fact that there is a great opportunity for IIoT to realize sustainable technology enablers for manufacturing systems that are aligned with the current global manufacturing trends of effective and efficient cost standards while not compromising on the environment. The review provides a description of how the industrial manufacturers can use IIoT for huge improvements of their processes, and improves the chances to turn to more sophisticated and sustainable environments for manufacturers.

The findings of applying IIoT for understanding cycle time, reduction of the cycle time, and increase of the machine utilization in an experimental context showed a significant increase in the manufacturing effectiveness. The findings indicated that, by using the features of IIoT such as real-time monitoring, and capability of intelligent scheduling, the production time cycle was minimized in the machines. Disregarding the bandwidth and latency constraints, the IIoT systems reduced the cycle times of tasks by 20%–35% to their baseline. This shows how because of IIoT and automation, not only production time is reduced but it also makes transitions from one operation to the other faster, therefore lowering total time needed and lead times.

Furthermore, the results of the studies revealed that improving the machine utilization was quite significant. Figure.10.9a and b gives the cycle time and machine utilization performance comparison. Machines that rose from low to moderate utilization due to time intervals such as idle time and unscheduled downtimes showed a range of 15%–25% improvement in the post-IIoT technology implementation scenario. Real-time information linked to amounts of work in machines and accurate forecasting reduced idle time and kept workload in proper ranges. Moreover, real-time alerts also minimize machine failures, which is essential for enhancing machine activity and productivity rates. The graphs that were developed from the analytical setup allowed us to compare the base state with the state after IIoT implementation and the effectiveness of IIoT integration plans. Lower cycle times are directly proportional to through put, and higher resource utilizations indicate better resource efficiency. In light of these results, the benefits of IIoT on state-of-the-art manufacturing can never be emphasized enough since it helps industries to work more efficiently, reduce operational expenses, and increase their level of competitiveness in the present-day global market.

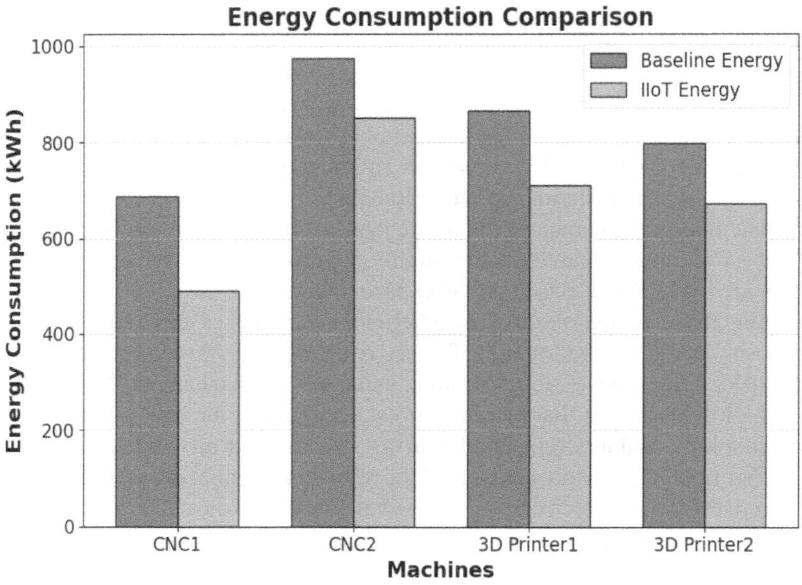

(a)

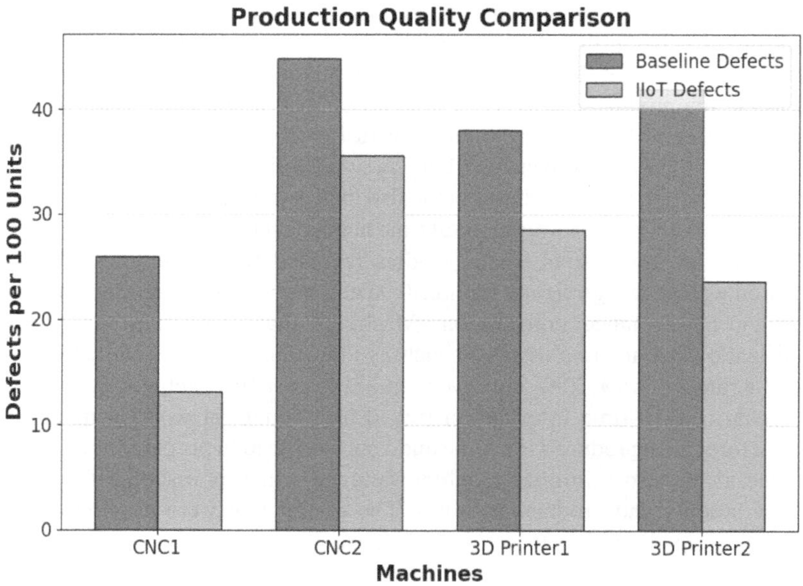

(b)

Energy Reduction (%): `[28.84 12.68 17.98 15.84]`
Defect Reduction (%): `[49.38 20.9  25.03 43.63]`

FIGURE 10.8 Performance analysis I of experimentation.

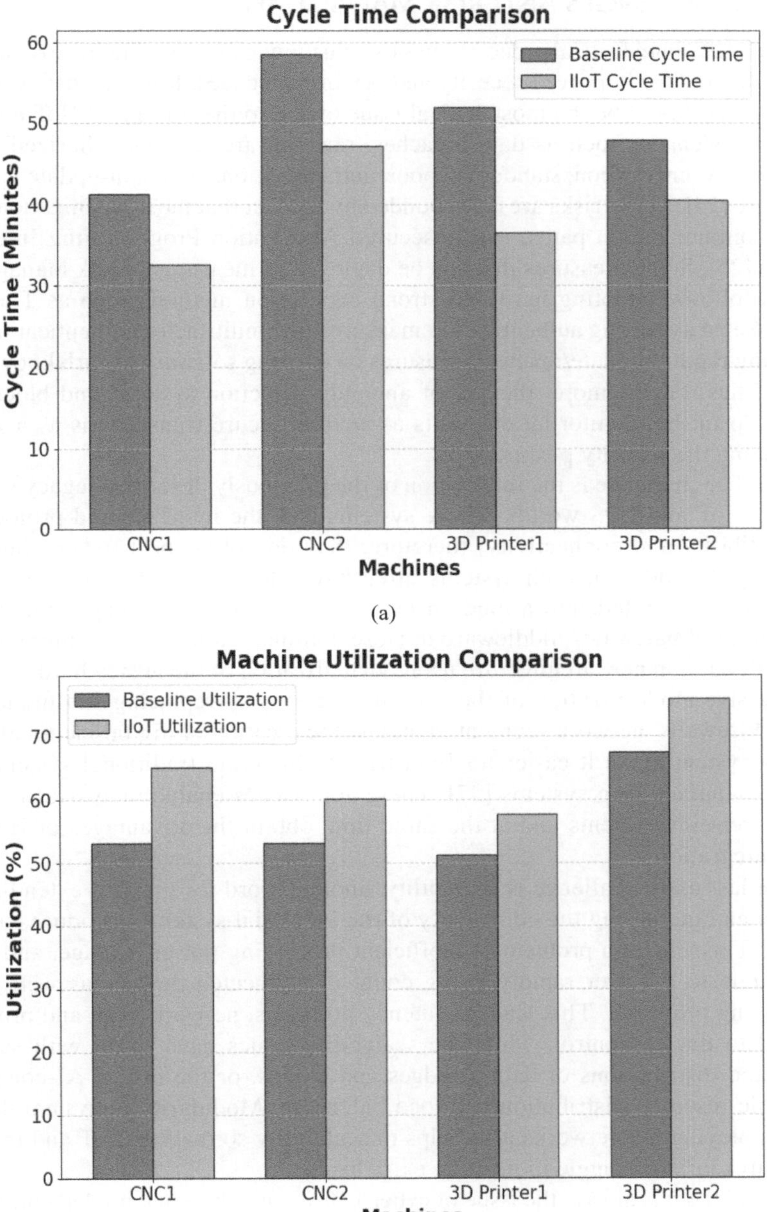

Cycle Time Reduction (%): [20.98 19.38 29.69 15.45]
Machine Utilization Improvement (%): [22.49 13.19 12.73 12.75]

FIGURE 10.9 Performance analysis II of experimentation.

10.8 CHALLENGES AND RISK MANAGEMENT

IIoT and CPS in industrial processes has its own unique factors, which are required to be considered for improved security and performance [23]. It seems that over security threats should be the most critical issue owing to the linking of IIoT and CPS systems. Menaces such as data breaches, ransomware, and unauthorized access bypass low encryption standards, poor authentication, and non-update patched software [24]. These risks are compounded by the fact that most organizations have open communication paths, and unsecured Application Programming Interfaces (APIs) [25]. Some measures that can be deployed as measures of risk management are as follows: adopting hard and strong encryption methods such as Transport Layer Security, strong authentication measures like multifactor authentication, and applying regular update/renewal measures on existing software to curb known vulnerabilities. Furthermore, the use of anomaly detection systems and blockchain will help in the monitoring of events as well as secure transactions as a way of enhancing the security posture [26].

Another challenge is the integration of the previously described legacy systems into the IoT and CPS worlds. These systems lack the interface and protocol for compatibility and connectivity; therefore, they do not support today's interconnectivity. In addition, such systems often have old security features that are at risk when integrated into a modern network. Additional challenges require the utilization of gateways/middleware to close communication gaps, running of current software on new architecture using virtualization of the legacy hardware, and progressive modernization of the central functions by replacing sub-modules in steps. Firewalls, network segmentation, and the creation of digital identical to the legacy system make it easier for industries to integrate traditional systems into smart manufacturing systems [27]. These approaches enable industries to retain the current investments and at the same time obtain the advantages of IIoT and CPS integration.

The last main challenge is scalability, another word for growth; extending the system and increasing the complexity of the industrial systems introduces a lot of issues. This causes a problem of inefficient processing power, storage, and bandwidth due to the ever rapidly rising count of connected devices as well as the data being produced. This leads to latency problems, network load, and problems related to device control, while the scalability issues have to do with subdivisions and distributions of data to edges and clouds, or the use of AI-conquered dynamic resource distribution and load balancing. Modularity in system designs and employing 5G networks also helps in scalability so that the IIoT and the CPS structures fail to struggle in meeting extra loads.

Hence, there is always the issue of cybersecurity attacks when implementing IIoT and CPS; the models cannot be implemented on a large scale; and the new models should be integrated with legacy systems. However, if industries adopt strong security measures and principles combined with loosely coupled, well-scaled systems integration, industries can develop safe, flexible, and efficient manufacturing systems that will sustain the cutting-edge environments of the contemporary world.

10.9 CASE STUDIES AND IMPLEMENTATIONS

10.9.1 Real-Life Applications of the IIoT and CMS

The applications of IIoT and CMS are scoped in numerous fields such as automobile, aviation, and medicinal industries. For instance, BMW employs IIoT robotics arms that are fitted with CMS for overseeing production lines and quality to improve production. Temperature, vibrations, and efficiency data are recorded by sensors within the machinery and fed to CMS to identify problems and avoid failure. Likewise, in the aerospace industry, Rolls-Royce uses IIoT and digital twins to track the performance of an engine during a flight, for prediction and effective maintenance [28]. These examples demonstrate the effectiveness and the possibilities of implementation of IIoT and CMS to obtain productivity, decrease the risks of failures, and stimulate development. Most specifically, performance and evaluation measures of IIoT and CMS initiatives are important.

There are numerous examples of industrial IIoT and CMS in the industry in the automotive and aerospace sectors, and in the pharmaceutical industry. Indicatively, BMW implements fog and edge IIoT empowered robotic arms tied to CMS to provide real-time monitoring and management of production lines to ensure continuous production and high-quality assurance. Machine sensors are inbuilt that capture the data of temperature, vibration, and performance on which data is implemented using a CMS to determine the deviations and eliminate the chances of failures. Similarly, Rolls-Royce aerospace applies the IIoT and digital twins to observe the performance of engines during flight to be able to schedule predictive maintenance and ensure that other processes continue to operate smoothly.

Performance assessment and comparison is essential to measure the effectiveness of IIoT and CMS deployments. Cognitive Equipment downtime, production efficiency, energy consumption, and defects produced are often measured. As an example, the Brilliant Factory as a part of General Electric IIoT service observes company Key Performance Indicator (KPI) across all manufacturing plants of that company. Using the above analysis tools, GE can analyze the entire production process, further optimize resources, and improve production efficiency. As we shall soon discover, the capacity to evaluate and measure their effectiveness not only confirms the effectiveness of these systems but also provides indication where improvements could be made.

Some of the successful implementations and their associated lessons and best practices highlight the need to consider more options and strategies than were previously considered. One of them is that bloated deployment strategies need to be avoided and replaced with a more incremental approach that practices smaller changes to avoid disrupting organizational processes and can step-by-step integrate new technologies into existing structures. For example, while taking the case of applying IIoT for smart factories, Siemens planned IIoT as the step-by-step process where attempts were made on a small scale before proceeding to the large ones, to develop the strategies. The final security best practice is cybersecurity, and Honeywell has a good example because it utilizes an anomaly detection system and has strict access control measures on the IIoT ecosystem. Moreover, the work of IT, operations, and engineering teams is coordinated to achieve organizational objectives and maximize the value of the systems.

Overall, the real-world applications of IIoT and CMS, along with critical evaluations and the best approaches' introduction, reveal the opportunities of the mentioned technologies. Through examples such as predictive maintenance in aerospace manufacturing, smart factories in automotive manufacturing, or trustful IIoT ecosystems, it is feasible to establish a basis for sound approaches towards sustainable and effective industrial processes. To assess the performance of IIoT and CMS, various aspects of functionality, productivity increase, and effect should be considered by key performance indicators [29].

10.10 FUTURE TRENDS AND RESEARCH DIRECTIONS

With advanced technologies, there has been a departure from the traditional manufacturing industries with excellent AI and ML innovation on the rise. For AI in manufacturing, it's no longer enough just to use analytics for equipment predictions – now it's all about predicting entire ecosystems. For instance, the application of DL is stated for the solution of multifaceted quality problems by analysis of many-factorized information received from different sensors, robotic, and control systems. Conversely, ML models also facilitate real-time adjustments of production schedules, given the availability of resources or demand for them. Subsequent research in this area of work covers reinforcement learning by enabling the AI system to become self-learning and thus handle new manufacturing problems without human assistance, greatly improving productivity and minimizing costs. 5G is expected to form the foundation of IIoT connectivity as it provides faster connectivity, lower latency rates, and real reliability for real-time communication between various devices for the exchange of data between CMS and IIoT. For instance, smart factories applying 5G to manage differentiated automation technologies such as autonomous guided vehicles and cooperative robots (cobots) require precision in controlling them within intricate and continuously changing environments. Furthermore, the communication of machines with machines gaining from 5G supports billions of devices, which creates the foundation of highly scalable industrial systems. Studies are ongoing to evaluate the applicability of new network slicing and edge computing techniques to enhance 5G manufacturing settings for safety and practical resource management.

The book coins "sustainable manufacturing" as a new business model that is infiltrating industrial strategies to thank IIoT and CMS. IIoT-based smart energy management solutions allow manufacturing companies to monitor and regulate their power usage on the fly, in compliance with sustainability goals. Applications and IIoT-enabled manufacturing facilities that use IIoT can benefit from waste heat recovery integration and addition of renewable power integration to remain cost-effective and sustainable manufacturing processes. CMS is a contributing factor, by being able to model the environmental impact of manufacturing before it happens for real. For the latter, new trends are emerging in extended producer responsibility (PLC: product life cycle), and IIoT extends the product life cycle and minimizes how a product is ultimately disposed of at its end of life. Another trend that is likely to continue expanding in the future is the integration of technologies such as quantum computing and IoT/CMS. This is expected to unlock new approaches for solving present complex computation challenges in manufacturing optimization. It is possible to achieve new solutions to several challenging problems like supply chain design or scheduling of production processes and real-time detection of defects. For example, a quantum-enhanced CMS could interpret large databases of data from complex interrelated IoT gadgets in a matter of a few seconds, allowing the manufacturers to make data-fuelled decisions instantly. Furthermore, quantum cryptography is projected to enhance the protection of IIoT systems from emerging cyber threats, or threats in general, through unprecedented security. Despite running as a topic of discussion in its early stage, studies and prototype quantum technologies that are in developmental phases are predicted to have higher growth rates, which will revolutionize manufacturing in ways that seemed nearly impossible before.

Therefore, it is necessary for IIoT and CMS to take advantage of advanced AI technology, and 5G networks, as well as focus on the development of sustainability in manufacturing industries for generating robust, effective, and environmentally sustainable manufacturing systems. As will be described below, advances made in these fields hold the potential to solve present-day problems to ensure smart and sustainable industrial environments in line with Industry 4.0 and beyond.

10.11 CONCLUSION

The IIoT and CMS technologies are, even as we speak, gaining momentum in changing the manufacturing industry and organizational world. The technologies of fabrication used in these systems have two important effects: They permit the uninterrupted incorporation of physical systems into computational infrastructure and control infrastructure that permits, as never previously, precise and efficient automation. This chapter evidently identified the main aspects and components of IIoT and CMS as well as their challenges, opportunities, and nature that will determine the form of future manufacturing. The IIoT-ASA that is introduced in this paper is an AI-powered scheduling and adaptive decision-making to implement the objective of AI-powered manufacturing to achieve the efficiency of resources, decrease wastes, and smart system functioning. The study findings highlighted the competitive edge of IIoT and CMS, providing manufacturers with competitive advantage as they get rolling down the road toward Industry 4.0 smart factories. The result of such system would be sustainable, competitive manufacturing systems with reconfigurable (in run-time) machine health monitoring and energy efficient functioning. In the future, the further innovation of IIoT and CMS will revolve around refining precision and intelligence surrounding production by incorporating more sophisticated AI models, blockchain for secure data transactions, and next-generation connectivity based on 6G, such that once the changes start being felt within the manufacturing sector, upgrading the smart factories to fully autonomous self-optimizing facilities would be a reality.

10.11.1 Summary of Key Insights

Near the close of this chapter there are even more basic perversions. One of the cornerstones for CMS is CPS, since they bridge efficiently physical and cyber worlds for control in real time. The use of digital twin technology makes it possible for system designers as well as managers to consider and take care of the various system aspects dynamically over its entire lifetime, and also provides a real-time window to simulate, optimize, and predict how the respective systems will function so that operational effectiveness can be enhanced while risks are reduced. Advanced data processing algorithms, analytics, and AI in general are turning up the intelligence of the ecosystem to enable predictive/prescriptive analysis, aiding manufacturers in managing processes better, raising product quality, and lowering any costs.

What's more, we outlined a number of real-world applications that IIoT and CMS are currently providing value to, such as predictive maintenance, adaptive production lines, and supply chains, and enhanced quality assurance. While all of these offer great opportunities, the main hurdles identified include cybersecurity issues, scalability concerns, and also whether it is possible to adapt systems that are already in place as well as best practices on how to address them.

10.11.2 Future of Manufacturing

The convergence of IIoT and CMS extends the concept of manufacturing intelligence to a more intelligent, flexible, and robust manufacturing ecosystem. With these technologies, it is possible to further adapt and customize the production environment systems as well as for the manufacturers to work more sustainably in response to changes in demand. Using new advancements in AI and ML, CMS should extend the capabilities of using resources effectively, eliminate any wastage, and improve the efficiency of manufacturing systems. Furthermore, the integration of 5G and the sophisticated connectivity solution will improve the capacity to deploy real-time applications at the distributed systems to support the context of fully autonomous operation. The emphasis on sustainability together with smart manufacturing based on IoT tools such as energy efficiency and cyclic production brings strategic goals of manufacturing businesses in line with global environmental ones. This integration of technological and ecological objectives makes explicit IIoT and CMS the foundational building blocks that underpin Industry 4.0 and beyond.

REFERENCES

1. Peter, O., A. Pradhan, and C. Mbohwa, Industrial internet of things (IIoT): opportunities, challenges, and requirements in manufacturing businesses in emerging economies, *Procedia Computer Science* 2023. 217: p. 856–865.
2. Munirathinam, S., Industry 4.0: Industrial internet of things (IIOT), Raj, P. and P. Evangeline (Eds.), in *Advances in computers*. 2020, Elsevier. p. 129–164.
3. Ahmed, U., J.C.-W. Lin, and G. Srivastava, Exploring the potential of cyber manufacturing system in the digital age, *ACM Transactions on Internet Technology* 2023. 23(4): p. 1–38.
4. Abdullahi, S.M. and S. Lazarova-Molnar, On the adoption and deployment of secure and privacy-preserving IIoT in smart manufacturing: a comprehensive guide with recent advances, *International Journal of Information Security* 2025. 24(1): p. 53.
5. Zhao, W., X. Yang, S. Qi, J. Wei, X. Dong, and Y. Qi, Secure blockchain-based reputation system for IIoT-enabled retail industry with resistance to sybil attack, *Future Generation Computer Systems* 2025. 166: p. 107705.
6. He, D., H. Wang, T. Deng, J. Liu, and J. Wang, Improving IIoT security: unveiling threats through advanced side-channel analysis, *Computers & Security* 2025. 148: p. 104135.

7. Alnajim, A.M., S. Habib, M. Islam, S.M. Thwin, and F. Alotaibi, A comprehensive survey of cybersecurity threats, attacks, and effective countermeasures in Industrial Internet of things, Technologies 2023. 11(6): p. 161.
8. Wu, M., Z. Song, and Y.B. Moon, Detecting cyber-physical attacks in CyberManufacturing systems with machine learning methods, *Journal of Intelligent Manufacturing* 2019. 30(3): p. 1111–1123.
9. Ryalat, M., H. ElMoaqet, and M. AlFaouri, Design of a smart factory based on cyber-physical systems and Internet of Things towards Industry 4.0, *Applied Science* 2023. 13(4): p. 2156.
10. Tyagi, A.K., Blockchain and artificial intelligence for cyber security in the era of internet of things and industrial internet of things applications, Biradar, R. C, Geetha, D. Nikhath, T. Nayana, H. and Mihai, L. (Eds.), in *AI and Blockchain Applications in Industrial Robotics*. 2024, IGI Global. p. 171–199.
11. Souri, A., M. Norouzi, and Y. Alsenani, A new cloud-based cyber-attack detection architecture for hyper-automation process in industrial internet of things, *Cluster Computing* 2024. 27(3): p. 3639–3655.
12. Soliman, S., W. Oudah, and A. Aljuhani, Deep learning-based intrusion detection approach for securing industrial Internet of Things, *Alexandria Engineering Journal* 2023. 81: p. 371–383.
13. Abikoye, O.C., A.O. Bajeh, J.B. Awotunde, A.O. Ameen, H.A. Mojeed, M. Abdulraheem, and S.A. Salihu, Application of internet of thing and cyber physical system in Industry 4.0 smart manufacturing, Singh, K.K., A. Nayyar, S. Tanwar, and M. Abouhawwash (Eds.), in *Emergence of Cyber Physical System and IoT in Smart Automation and Robotics: Computer Engineering in Automation*. 2021, Springer. p. 203–217.
14. Banerjee, A. and V. Choppella, A knowledge-driven approach for dynamic reconfiguration of control design in Internet of Things and cyber-physical systems, *IEEE Internet of Things Journal* 2024. 99: p. 1–1.
15. Fu, X., P. Pace, G. Aloi, A. Guerrieri, W. Li, and G. Fortino, Tolerance analysis of cyber-manufacturing systems to cascading failures, *ACM Transactions on Internet Technology* 2023. 23(4): p. 1–23.
16. Wu, Y., H. Cao, G. Yang, T. Lu, and S. Wan, Digital twin of intelligent small surface defect detection with cyber-manufacturing systems, *ACM Transactions on Internet Technology* 2023. 23(4): p. 1–20.
17. Prince, N.U., M.A. Al Mamun, A.O. Olajide, O.U. Khan, A.B. Akeem, and A.I. Sani, IEEE standards and deep learning techniques for securing Internet of Things (IoT) devices against cyber attacks, *Journal of Computational Analysis and Applications* 2024. 33(7): p. 1270–1289.
18. Franco, J., A. Aris, B. Canberk, and A.S. Uluagac, A survey of honeypots and honeynets for internet of things, industrial internet of things, and cyber-physical systems, IEEE Communications Surveys & Tutorials 2021. 23(4): p. 2351–2383.
19. Pivoto, D.G., D.G. Pivoto, L.F. De Almeida, R. da Rosa Righi, J.J. Rodrigues, A.B. Lugli, and A. M. Alberti, Cyber-physical systems architectures for industrial internet of things applications in Industry 4.0: a literature review, *Journal of Manufacturing Systems* 2021. 58: p. 176–192.
20 Król, K., T. Rymarczyk, and J. Wyrwisz, Cyber-physical platforms for monitoring and controlling industrial processes, in *Innovation in the Digital Economy*. 2023, Routledge. p. 73–84.
21. Yao, X., et al., Smart manufacturing based on cyber-physical systems and beyond, *Journal of Intelligent Manufacturing* 2019. 30: p. 2805–2817.
22. Espinoza-Zelaya, C. and Y.B. Moon, Resilience enhancing mechanisms for cyber-manufacturing systems against cyber-attacks, *IFAC-PapersOnLine* 2022. 55(10): p. 2252–2257.

23. Achamrah, F.E. and A. Attajer, Multi-objective reinforcement learning-based framework for solving selective maintenance problems in reconfigurable cyber-physical manufacturing systems, *International Journal of Production Research* 2024. 62(10): p. 3460–3482.
24. Balta, E.C., M. Pease, J. Moyne, K. Barton, and D.M. Tilbury, Digital twin-based cyber-attack detection framework for cyber-physical manufacturing systems, *IEEE Transactions on Automation Science and Engineering* 2023. 21(2): p. 1695–1712.
25. Shi, Z., B. Oskolkov, W. Tian, C. Kan, and C. Liu, Sensor data protection through integration of blockchain and camouflaged encryption in cyber-physical manufacturing systems, *Journal of Computing and Information Science in Engineering* 2024. 24(7): p. 1–25.
26. Li, Y., A.J.T.F. Mardani, and S. Change, Digital twins and blockchain technology in the industrial Internet of Things (IIoT) using an extended decision support system model: Industry 4.0 barriers perspective, *Technological Forecasting and Social Change* 2023. 195: p. 122794.
27. Fowler, D.S., G. Epiphaniou, M.D. Higgins, and C. Maple, Aspects of resilience for smart manufacturing systems, *Strategic Change* 2023. 32(6): p. 183–193.
28. Bleistein, T., M. Paulus, K. Gani, R. Becker, and D. Werth, IIoT and digital twin: a systematic literature review and looking beyond the state, *Applied Stochastic Models in Business and Industry* 2025. 41(1): p. e2923.
29. Ali, J., C. Iwendi, G. Shan, H.C. Wu, M.J. Alenazi, Z.B. Faheem, and C.N. Biamba, Performance optimization of software-defined industrial Internet-of-Things (SD-IIoT), *IEEE Access* 2024. 12: p. 169659–169670.

11 Intelligent Robotics in Manufacturing
The Role of AI-Driven Automation

Ashok Raj Rajendran, Rajiv Subramanian, Chanakyan Chandrasekaran, Vijayan Selvarangam, Mathiyalagan Ponnusamy, and Keerthivasan Navaneethakrishnan

11.1 INTRODUCTION

In hybrid manufacturing companies, artificial intelligence (AI) in robotics played a significant role due to the rapid advancement in transforming business processes and those techniques merge into conventional and non-conventional processes to transform the market demands. For companies to grow in a sustainable way they need to create effective financial plans, maximise product efficiency and optimise energy use. These factors are supporting developing resources and managing the financial performance in industries. Similarly, modern robots have activated advancement in manufacturing, enhancing accuracy and diminishing the defects of the products.

This will lead to scrap and rework savings, and spur better operational and financial outcomes. Prosperous production enhances production and market competitiveness. The energy monitoring and control sensor and AI technologies allow monitoring the energy consumption in real time and predicting its consumption. This contributes also toward the sustainability but most importantly also saves a lot of money.

These technologies allow the organizations to make proactive decisions based on data and immediately make decisions regarding development. Market research and customer behavior models can be exploited to enable the companies to develop the best pricing strategy when developing new products [1].

11.2 INDUSTRY 5.0

Two large concepts are now presently building the debate on Industry 5.0. In the initial vision of the future, there is collaboration of people and robots wherever feasible. Humans ought to be performing the jobs required which involve creativity, intuition, and emotional intelligence and the robots ought to be performing the jobs which they consider to be boring, dangerous, or highly precise. The second vision

DOI: 10.1201/9781003582465-11

is bioeconomy. It focuses on intelligent industrial utilization of bio-resources to enhance sustainability. According to European Commission, bioeconomy is production of renewable biological resources and transformation of these resources and waste streams into value-added products, food, feed, bio-based products, and bio-energy. It illustrates business divisions ranging from the chemical, energy, and biotechnology sectors to agriculture, forestry, and fisheries. The concept draws a large variety of scientific disciplines, including linguistics, information and communication technology, biology, ecology, and engineering. It also operates with local expertise and innovations [2].

Biologization is a macro-thesis of the bioeconomy, which requires the transformation of the functioning of industries with references to biological laws. This would transform many aspects. It is believed that bioeconomy could be a significant component of the next industrial revolution since it is valued by the environment as well as the economy.

The concept of Industry 5.0 relies on human–robot collaboration and bioeconomy, yet the new concepts of space exploration, space industries, and space mining are gaining popularity as well, which are provided in Figure 11.1. All these possibilities imply that industrial future will be larger, since the opportunities of using space resources become even bigger and the question of opportunities and moral issues emerges. Scientists are already telling us against consuming external earth resources in large quantities, lest we make the same mistakes that our ancestors made. It is likely that a recent addition would provide the world with a fresh dimension of industry development [3]. Space mining may soon be a contemporary day of the so-called gold rush.

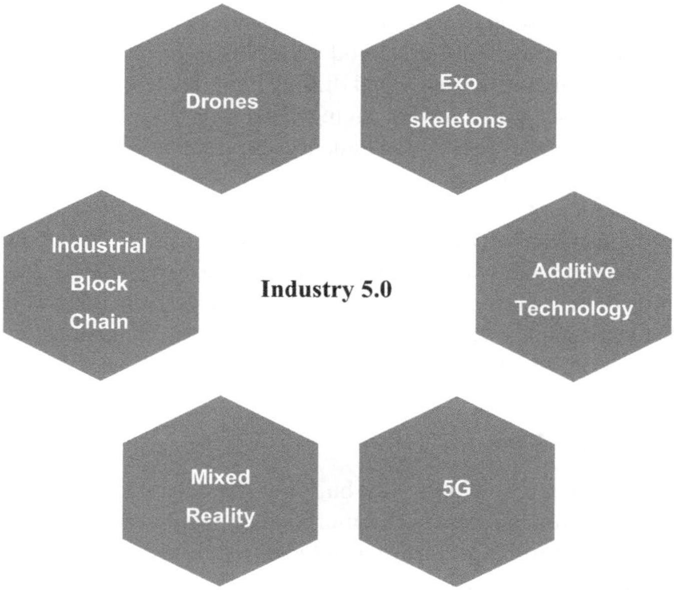

FIGURE 11.1 Technological pillars of Industry 5.0.

11.3 ROBOTS CAPABLE OF INDEPENDENT MOVEMENT

The expansion of e-commerce and direct-to-consumer delivery has placed an increased burden on the responsibility of warehouse managers in order to enhance operations like picking, packing, moving of inventory, and shipping. The use of mobile robots working alongside the human staff is becoming perceived as the necessity of improving the efficiency of operations and meeting these requirements. Other areas where such robotic systems are currently being used include hospitals, learning institutions, restaurants, and last-mile type delivery [4].

Two main types of mobile robots exist: Automated Guided Vehicles (AGVs) that travel using predefined paths and use sensors, lasers, barcodes, or magnetic tape, and Autonomous Mobile Robots (AMRs), which are more flexible and rely on sensors mounted on the robot, which are used to navigate, map, and avoid obstacles on their own. The NextAMR by Renesas illustrates the benefits of AMRs through the elimination of pre-coordinated routes, an autonomous route selection, and the navigation of humans and objects without posing a threat to them [5]. The NextAMR is adapted to low- and medium-capacity work. It implements RZ/V series-embedded AI MPUs to compute real-time data coordination and use less power. This is a depiction of how modern mobile robotic systems are superior in a dynamic environment.

11.4 PROBLEMS ASSOCIATED WITH PEOPLE–ROBOT COLLABORATION

The definition of robots is still a challenging one since current definitions either lack clarity, use terminology ambiguity, and include a forward-looking feature that is very similar to anthropomorphic features. A legal definition is essential and unquestionable, especially with the growing inclusion of robots in the human workplaces. The regulatory systems should be able to establish the distinction between robots and other types of automation such as unmanned aerial vehicles and cybernetic organisms. The law must provide guidance on the types of robots that can be allowed in the office environment and the limitations to the use of robots.

Remedial action should have clear guidelines in the case of malfunction and demarcation of responsibility. The determination of whether robotic systems execute as per set logic or adaptive learning is also important. It is necessary to set regulatory norms and certification standards. Rapidly implemented robotic technologies can also give rise to issues in the society and ethical concerns without proper legal provisions. The gaps that were revealed in the current regulations of drones indicate the need of corrective actions. As technologies of AI and robotics continue to develop, effective governance is set to turn into the ultimate goal of research and policy creation.

Scholars and practitioners in the industry still argue about the functions that robots will play in the work place. According to most scholars, the role of robots as helpers and additions to human work is a more acceptable and less controversial approach. In these cases, robots support human employees and do not replace them, which eliminates fears of job loss and perceived risks are reduced [6].

Reliability and effectiveness are the qualities that many stakeholders choose in robot assistants, assigning them repetitive or physically strenuous tasks. As a result, human workers are empowered to get engaged in activities that need higher-order cognition and creativity. The partnership approach to robots can help to adapt to them, unlike seeing them as competitors. On the other hand, others claim that by enabling the robots to directly compete with human beings in getting some jobs, it can prompt them to perform better. The integration of robots in the labor market will further complicate the dynamics of management and employees since there is an already established interpersonal competition in the firms. There are also empirical studies that examined the behavior of individuals where a robot is in control or oversees them.

11.5 THE EVOLUTION OF AI-DRIVEN ROBOTS IN MANUFACTURING

Table 11.1: memcpy Robotics and AI Modern manufacturing uses highly autonomous technologies which allow large-scale industrial transformation to be efficient, high quality, and cost-effective. The key point in the said transition is the integration of AI and machine learning with robotics to enable machines to learn, adapt, and respond to fluctuating production needs. AI-controlled AMRs are able to enhance flexibility, stability, safe interaction, and production, particularly in collaboration with humans through deep learning. These robots can understand their surroundings better with the help of machine learning, and detect objects, sort parts, and do quality inspections at an improved level. Lidar, cameras, and environmental sensors help them to collect real-time information and calculate the best course of action.

TABLE 11.1
The Future of Robots Powered by AI in Manufacturing

Future Trend	Description	Expected Impact
Hyper autonomous factories	Self-optimizing production lines, Fully automated	Reduced labor cost and increased Efficiency
Collaborative human–robot teams	Seamless teamwork between humans and intelligent robots	Flexibility and enhanced safety
Predictive analytics	AI identifies difficulties and provides remedies in real time	Less downtime and proactive maintenance
Mass customization	Robots flexibly change manufacturing to satisfy unique customization needs	Customer focus and greater product variety
Adaptive robots and self-learning	Robots learn new tasks autonomously from data and experience	Less programming and rapid deployment
Swarm robotics	Coordinate as a group for complex tasks	Resilience and scalability
Digital twin integration	Real-time virtual models for simulation and optimization	Reduced errors and better planning
Sustainable manufacturing	AI optimizes energy use, waste reduction, and resource allocation	Greener production, cost saving, and greener production

Consider the mobile manipulator types of robots, e.g., the AI-driven robots do not necessarily only affect the manufacturing sector, and other domains also include logistics, transportation, and healthcare. Smart robots also perform repetitive and correct job, like assembling and checking in a manufacturing field; in many cases, it performs better than humans [7]. Self-driving cars with AI analysis of the road situation and the rapid and safety-related decisions are also used. Surgery robots assisted by AI and performing sensitive tasks in the medical sphere can provide improved patient outcomes and are described by the high level of accuracy.

Reduction of waste production, resource optimization, and conservation of energy are also other sources of environmental sustainability through robotics. The collaborative robots or cobots are currently on the rise because of their capability to assist human hands in repetitive or precision-related tasks in a safe manner, which enhance productivity and work safety. This scenario of Lights-out manufacturing or the presence of machines that do not necessarily require being supervised by people can be put into more and more use, particularly by smaller enterprises that wish to save money on labor expenses. With a combination of industrial robots with a network of the Internet of Things, sensor data were possible to gather to monitor on-the-fly, predictive maintenance, and more informed decisions on operations. The empirical evidence is that robotics can be used to increase the efficiency of operations by the capability of reducing the expenses by as much as 30% and could decrease the error rate [8,9]. The transfer of the stationary, programmed machines into the mobile, intelligent AMRs is replacing the manufacture processes being conducted; the systems will be capable of moving the products, change according to the circumstances when there is a need to do so, and be able to interact with the human workers. Thus, it is approximated that AMRs will assume an increasing share of the routine or hazardous work in the supply chain, and it will liberate the human labor force to concentrate on other more strategically significant tasks.

11.6 ROBOTIC INNOVATIONS BASED ON MACHINE LEARNING

Machine learning as a branch of AI has extensive impacts on robotics in various areas as shown in Figure 11.2. Machine learning software on autonomous vehicles and remotely operated drones checks sensor information, such as LiDAR, radar, and cameras, to instruct on hazards on the road, the meaning of road signs, and speculate on behaviors of other road users and determine optimal routes. The technology improves the safety and responsiveness of systems within the operation environments. Furthermore, some of the websites have social-sensitivity applications, which are meant to support people in the case of an emergency. Machine learning in industrial automation allows production and logistics machines to learn through historical information, hence enhancing production, minimizing human-induced downtimes, and enabling operation with a lower degree of human intervention.

This phenomenon leads to a high level of productivity and low costs in the healthcare. Machine learning will provide surgical robots with the ability to interpret medical data and help them to perform accurate and minimally invasive surgeries. Also, there are other robotic platforms where the patients are monitored, assisted daily, and rehabilitated through personal progress-based rehabilitation. These examples

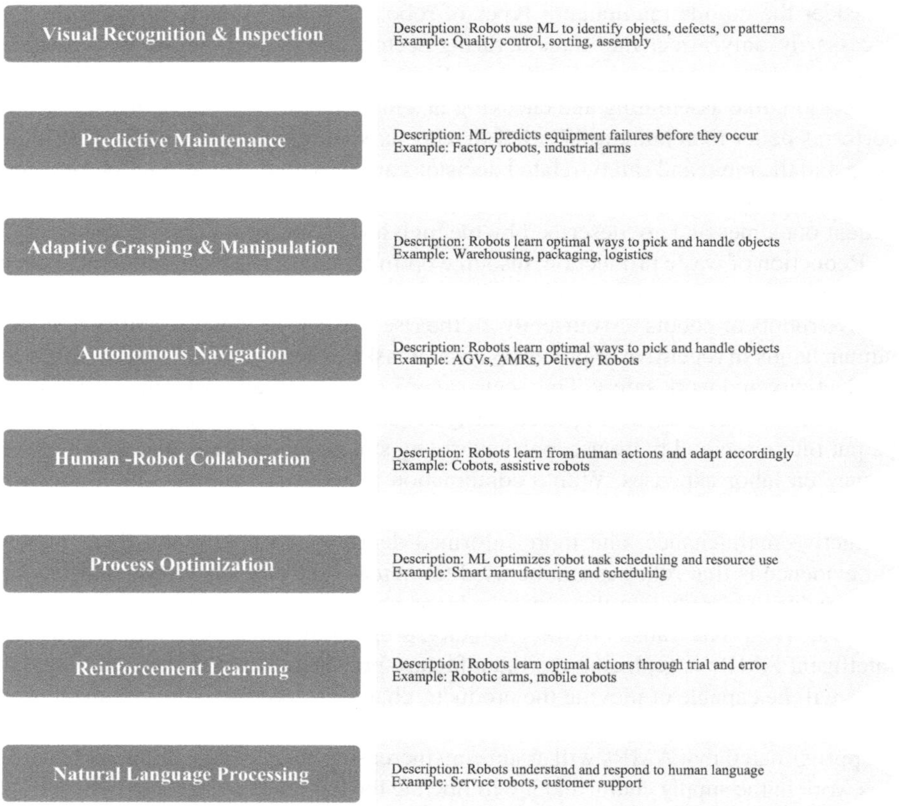

FIGURE 11.2 Applications of machine learning in intelligent robotics.

show that machine learning can enhance the intelligence, flexibility, and functionality of robots in the field of medical practice, and represent the practical value of AI-controlled robotics in decision-making and optimization in real time in the Industry 5.0 paradigm.

Recent developments as shown in Figure 11.3 indicate that the AI-based robots have transformed manufacturing and logistic industries. The AI and robot platforms synergies result in the formation of intelligent agents that can perform complex tasks at a high speed, accuracy, and flexibility. These robots automatically mechanize and learn by experience, hence improving efficiency over time. In manufacturing environments, AI-powered robotic systems can be used to simplify the working process, reduce the number of devices out of operation, and increase the quality of products [10].

In logistics, inventory, warehouse operations, sorting, and delivery are simplified, thus bringing labor and mistakes down, improving supply chains. Figure 11.4 shows that machine learning, computer vision, and natural language processing are technologies that enable robots to perceive the world around them and take real-time

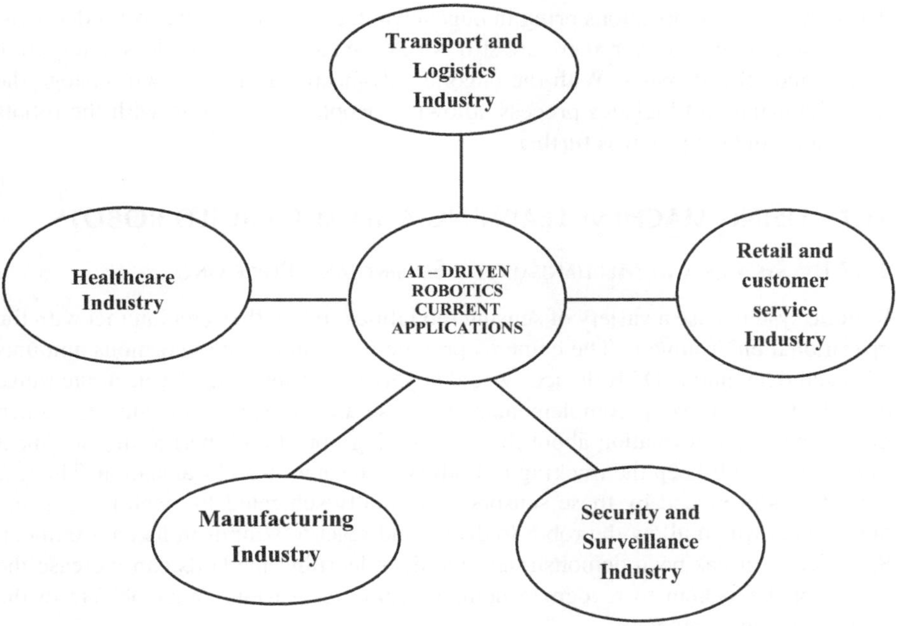

FIGURE 11.3 AI-driven robotics in various sectors.

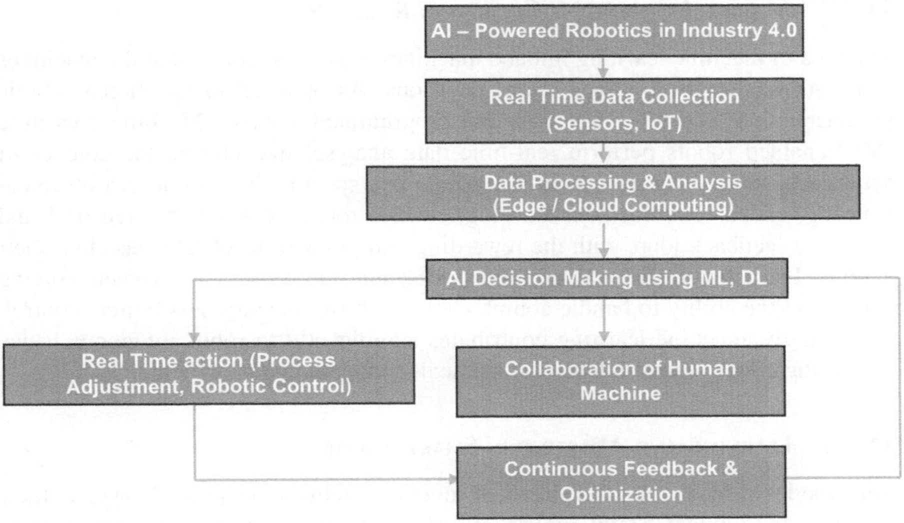

FIGURE 11.4 Integration of AI, Internet of Things, and robotics in industrial processes.

decisions. These innovations bring in huge advantages in efficiency, cost reductions, and productivity; however, there are still issues such as possible job loss, integration issues, and ethical issues. With the ongoing advancement of AI, it will change the manufacturing and logistics process, allowing people to cooperate with the robots and improving the progress further.

11.7 USING MACHINE LEARNING AND AI TO BUILD ROBOTS

11.7.1 Systems and Mechanisms for Sensing and Perceiving

Robotic systems use a variety of sensing modalities so that they can interact with the operational environment. The cameras provide the system with enormous amounts of visual data, and LiDAR devices would supply the system with the accurate range data. In the same vein, complementary to these are ultrasonic transducers, which give proximity information about the surrounding object and inertial measurement units, which will keep the tracking of both system rotation and translation. The raw data that is produced by these sensors is normally subjected to machine learning algorithms, which allow the robot to detect and react to stimuli in its environment. Specifically, it has been demonstrated that deep learning methods can increase the ability of the system to recognize humans, cars, and various other objects in the immediate environment.

Sensor fusion is an important process and based on multiple sensor data streams; sensor fusion is a process that gives a more detailed depiction of the environment. Integrative process: Through the combination of heterogeneous information provided by sensors, this integrative process enhances the perceptual expertise of the robotic platform prior to carrying out independent functions.

11.7.2 Making Independent Choices in Robotics

The idea of machine learning imbued machines makes us realize that the machines can also make out-of-the-box smart decisions. As opposed to traditional robotic platforms that faithfully follow a pre-programmed course, Machine Learning (ML)-enabled robots perform real-time data analyses and change the courses of action accordingly wisely. Machine learning one specific division of reinforcement learning, called reinforcement learning, enables robots to learn through trial and error in a feedback loop, with the rewarding and punitive feedbacks based on their actions. The approach helps to promote performance improvement, problem-solving skills, and the ability to handle complex jobs with significantly less human control. Accordingly, machine learning contributes significantly to robot autonomy, hence increasing effectiveness in logistics, medical, and manufacturing fields.

11.7.3 Learning and Adapting in Smart Robots

Machine learning enables the ability of robotic systems to adapt to changes in their working environment. Traditional robotic platforms are fixed on pre-written instructions. On the other hand, robots that possess machine learning are found to have the tendency to adjust their behavior as they continue to learn more data [11]. Considering the fact that the empirical environment is often subjected to sudden changes, it is now urgent to design robotic structures, which have adaptive resilience capabilities, and thus guarantee sustained effectiveness and operational adaptability.

11.7.4 Real-Life Uses of Robotics with AI

Robotics driven by AI is having a significant impact on a range of spheres of industry as shown in Figure 11.5, especially in the fields of manufacturing and logistics. Smart robots systems are transforming the operation of the enterprises by improving the efficiency of the operations as well as building organizational growth.

11.7.5 AI Is Used in Self-Driving Cars and Robots for Healthcare

Machine learning provides autonomous agents with the opportunity to react to the real-time situations of the roads and the clinical setting. These agents are improved by means of supervised and reinforcement learning at every interaction. They are able to observe patterns, decide the way things could go ahead, and manage their behaviors, which result in improved results. This lifelong learning enables them to deal with complex and real-world scenarios with little human intervention because they keep on adjusting to the changes in the environment. As a result, the machine learning-enabled robots can be more competent and also succeed in dynamic

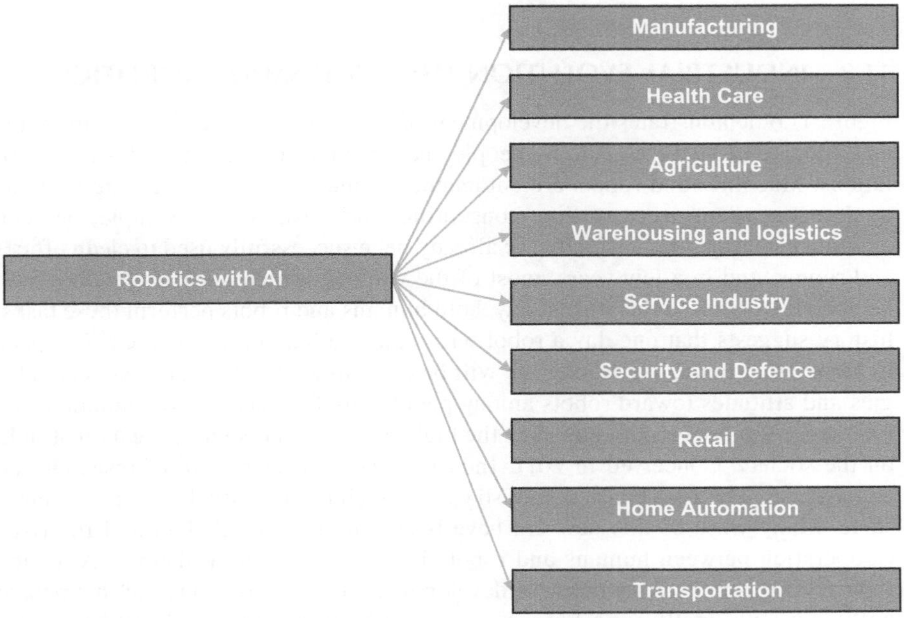

FIGURE 11.5 Robots real-life uses.

environments in various areas that include transportation, healthcare, agriculture, customer services, etc.

11.7.6 AI Does in Modern Robotics

The state-of-the-art robotic systems rely on AI technologies to obtain autonomy, adaptability, and real-time decision-making. Machine learning, computer vision, and natural language processing improve the performance and intelligence of a robot. Supervised learning enhances the accuracy of the task through the use of labeled data. Unsupervised learning finds patterns and identifies problems in the dynamically changing conditions. Reinforcement learning also enables the robots to refine their actions using the trial and error method particularly in navigation and manipulation of objects.

Computer vision enables robots to be aware of the data they see. This ability is essential in the sorting, packaging, and assembly tasks. The estimation of posture and tracking assists in accuracy in manufacturing of electronics as well as automobiles, where proper movements and positioning are essential. Natural language processing improves the interaction between human beings and robots. It enables robots to obey spoken or written instructions that comes in handy especially in collaborative robots, otherwise known as cobots. In the cases when natural language processing is combined with the Warehouse Management Systems and ERP software, robots are provided with real-time updates. They are able to perform tasks and handle inventory in order to streamline logistics and supply-chain operations.

11.8 INDUSTRIAL EVOLUTION THROUGH SMART ROBOTICS

Figure 11.6 demonstrates the development of smart robots. The attempts to divide and allocate tasks were made by people and machines during the industrial revolutions. Machines and robots are automated technologies that are taking over the monotonous, dangerous, or time-consuming work fast. As an example, one can mention cleaning robots which have already been successfully used to clean offices and rooms, and in a few years, most of the working which needs to be done will be done by robots. In the present day, both humans and robots perform these tasks; history suggests that one day a robot will replace a human in this area. The pace of automation in the day-to-day life will be determined by the emerging technologies and attitudes toward robots among people. Studies focusing on human–robot interaction cannot be ignored, since the high usage of robots will have a great light on the society. Conceived in 2011, Industry 4.0 has drawn a lot of research and conferences. The next phase is Industry 5.0, which has recently become the center stage. Many ways of this new era have been outlined by scholars and futurists. Cooperation between humans and robots is one of the central themes. Although Industry 5.0 is in its early phase of development, it is already apparent that people will work with intelligent robots in a way that is transformational and has a long

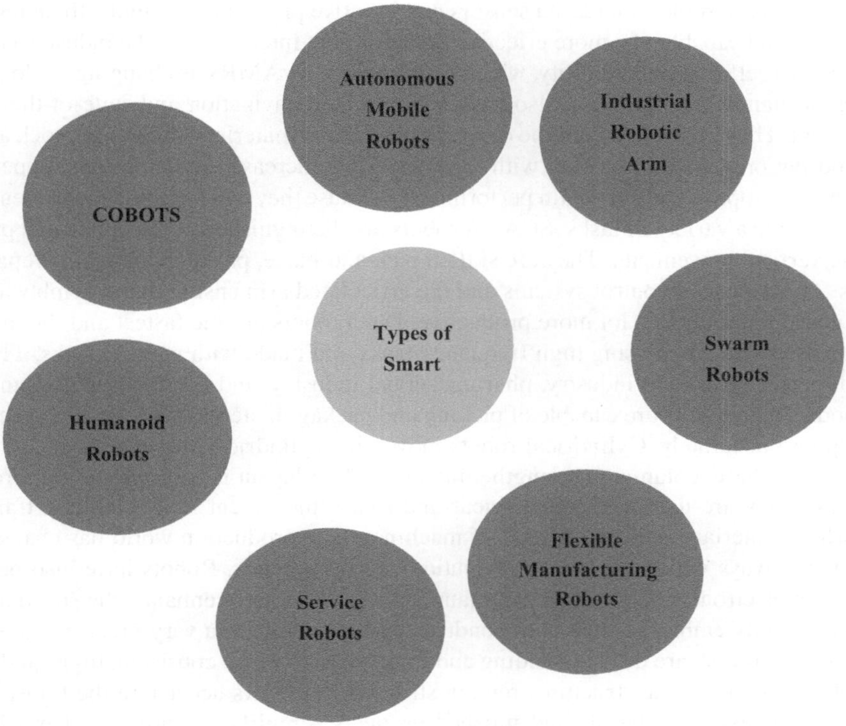

FIGURE 11.6 Types of smart robots.

reach. In the following section, Industry 5.0 is introduced in the comparison with Industry 4.0 and two prevailing concepts. It further talks about the major challenges and opportunities of robot collaboration. Lastly, the report also states areas of research that are open to further study.

11.8.1 Different Kinds of Smart Robots that Can Be Used in Manufacturing

The use of smart robots is growing on the production lines as they are employed to work alongside people in automotive and electronics industries to enhance productivity, quality, and sustainable growth. Due to advanced sensors and sophisticated programming, industrial robots are valued due to their strength, accuracy, and dependability, which perform tasks such as welding, painting, assembly, and material management. Their consistent performance has enabled them to become indispensable in the manufacturing processes all over the world, with the performance level boosting productivity as well as innovation. One of the significant developments is collaborative robots or cobots. They are programmed to communicate safely with individuals, and their increased sensors and intuitive programming make them more flexible and capable of a more effective human–robot interaction in the industry [12].

Smart self-directed mobility, which is introduced by AMRs, is changing the logistics of manufacturing. They also have sophisticated navigation and state-of-the-art sensors. They are tasked with the duty of transporting materials, managing stock and handling orders, and assisting with logistics. They increase the flexibility of operations and improve supply-chain performance because they can operate independently and handle a variety of tasks. SCARA robots are distinguished by the quick and precise vertical movements. They are skilled pick-and-place, pack, and machine repairers. The advanced control systems and the articulated arm ensure that assembly and material handling is a lot more productive. Delta robots are the fastest and the most maneuverable when using high frequency tasks and made with parallel links. They suit perfectly in food industry, pharmaceutical industry, and fast-moving consumer goods. Delta robots are capable of picking and packaging items that require a speedy response accurately. Cylindrical robots move on a cylindrical shape with the aid of a rotating base, column, and lengthening arm. Their layout is appropriate to narrow areas. They are used with rapid linear and rotary movement in assembling, transporting materials, and taking care of machines. The production world has changed in many ways which have been revolutionized by robotics. Robots have also been used in electronics and automotive manufacturing sectors to enhance the speed and quality of assembly, as well as to conduct repetitive tasks in a very precise manner. Industrial robots are used in welding and fabrication to make consistent high-quality welds that ensure the structures remain strong. The AMRs accelerate the transportation process of materials and finished products, simplify the process of moving materials, and minimize the use of human labor.

11.8.2 Application and Advantages

In Figure 11.7, there are figures that show the types of robots, their benefits, and the use. Robot coating provides a smooth finish, eliminating wastes and giving a high quality and uniform finish on each paint job. The combination of vision systems and AI will enable robots to identify defects and abnormalities to ensure the level of quality meets the standards. Speed and flexibility are the strengths of delta robots that are able to package and palletize, according to source [13]. Robots of inspection find defects and do a non-destructive test, enhancing product reliability and reducing the time of inspection.

11.9 SMART ROBOTICS AND THE FUTURE OF MANUFACTURING

In modern-day production facilities, robotic systems with AI can be used to automatize production lines and perform the work both repetitive and complex in a significantly faster and more accurate manner. Productivity is improved as well as better product quality is secured because it is possible, with the help of computer vision and machine learning tools, to detect defects in the product in real time. AI also facilitates proactive maintenance, in which the robot components observe the equipment and predict any failures and fix them, reducing unproductive downtime. In additive

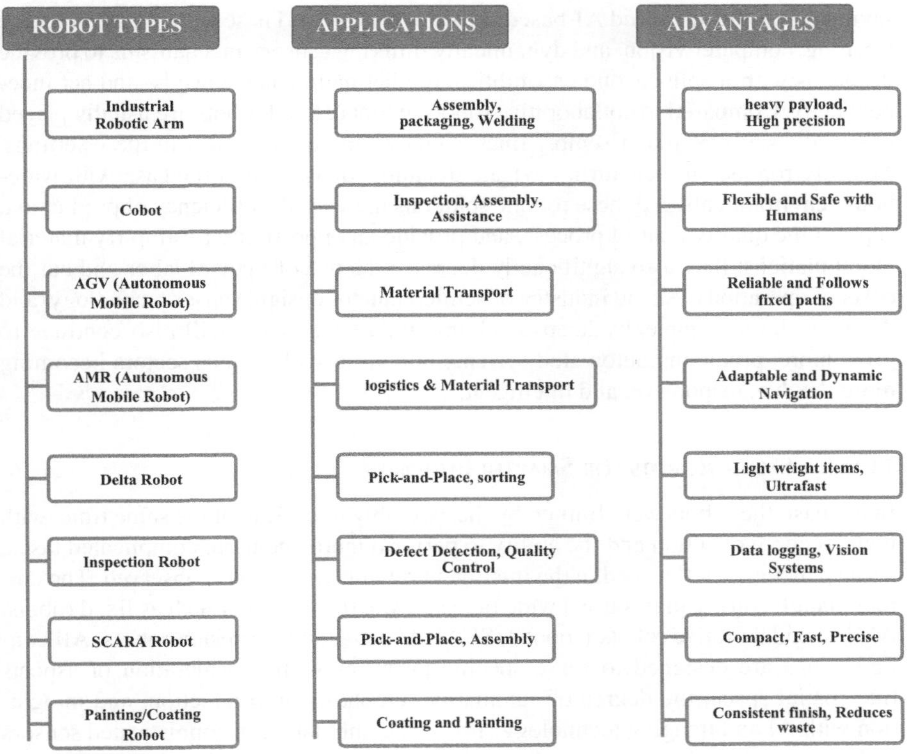

FIGURE 11.7 Robot types, advantages, and applications.

manufacturing, especially in 3D printing, AI helps to change the parameters of the design and streamline the production processes, leading to a decrease in the waste of materials. Robotic warehouse operations, including picking, packing, and sorting, reduce the use of manual labor and enhance the accuracy of the operations in the logistics operations. AMRs move across facility environments on their own, and as such, they speed up the delivery processes. The AI-controlled delivery robots are changing the last-mile logistics, being able to work with minimum human actions in both urban and industrial areas.

The unification of AI provides major improvements to the operations of the supply chain, especially in terms of enhanced control of the inventory, sophisticated demand prediction, and distribution mechanisms, thus enabling the quick business expansion. However, the deeper integration of AI also presents substantive issues related to job loss, the safety of the operating system, and system integration, and requires careful analysis and pre-emptive reducing measures. At the same time, the development of AI and hardware is driving the industrial robotics, which makes systems in the manufacturing sector and logistics smarter, more efficient, and more affordable. The modern-day industrial robots are capable of performing intricate tasks with a high sense of accuracy and flexibility, which is due to their powerful processors, energy saving parts, and advanced AI-based software platforms. These systems use machine learning, computer vision, and dynamically thinking sensory mechanisms to provide decisions within split-second capabilities, predict maintenance needs, and act independently. Compared to collaborative robots (cobots), fixed robots are usually placed in specific settings, like assembly lines, so they can operate safely in these settings. Mobility robots, on their turn, navigate dynamic areas, as it is the case with warehouse environments. All these robotic solutions increase the efficiency of production, support the quality control process, and provide an opportunity to simplify material manipulations; they also significantly decrease the use of manual labor and cut the costs of operations. As the industry of semiconductor design, sensor technology, and AI algorithmic complexity keeps evolving, industrial robots will also continue to grow more, producing automated systems in a variety of various sectors becoming more flexible, responsive, and intelligent.

11.9.1 Smart Robots for Smarter Factories

In the past, the robots were limited by the assembly lines. But, at the same time, with their freedom of action and the ability to perform more and more complicated tasks, a sharp increase of the need in the intelligent robotic systems was observed. The current manufacturing plants use a wide range of robotic platforms such as fixed robots, AMRs, collaborative robots (cobots), SCARA, delta, and Cartesian robots. All configurations are designed to serve specific purposes with consideration of aspects like spatial space, the degree of automation, emphasis on production, and integration with AI and imaging technology [14]. The combination of sophisticated sensors and machine learning programs has improved the decision-making ability of such systems, thus decreasing the dependency on people to carry out their operational activities. AGVs are also a major improvement in the automation of logistics. AGVs increase both the efficiency of handling materials because they are able to navigate plant floor scenarios without a pilot operator. Combined with manipulators, AGVs transform into the mobile robotic arm systems with a wide range of possible hitches, which boosts the flexibility of production.

These robots have sensors and neural networks that let them collect and send data to centralized systems. This lets them learn all the time and improve their performance, getting rid of obstacles and getting more small- and medium-sized businesses to use smart robotics The International Federation of Robotics says that in major robot markets outside of China, there are an average of six robots for every 100,000 workers. In the European Union, 99% of industrial companies are small- or medium-sized businesses. This means that there is a big chance to use smart robotics and move toward smart factory models. Smart robots help by making things cheaper, making less waste, and making better products. But there are still big problems that make it hard to adopt, like the need for a big initial investment, the need to change existing workflows, a lack of technical knowledge and space, and the fact that current programming methods don't support frequent changes that are common in customized, small-batch production.

11.9.2 Cognitive Intelligence in Industrial Robots for Smart Manufacturing

The general goal of cognitive robotics is to give intelligent robots the ability of human beings by modeling the human brain functional architecture. The human brain is one of the most complex and least comprehended biological systems, and an empirical knowledge is that its actions can be adjusted by external factors. In its modern evolution, the brain in its present form consists of around hundreds of billions of neurons and it controls a myriad of cognitive and physiological processes, including attention, decision-making, planning, multimodal sensory perception (visual, auditory, touching, taste, smell), speech production, memory formation, affective reactions, motor control, coordination, heart rate autonomic regulation, and respiration. The brain of a person performs millions of operations simultaneously, and thus, it is capable of performing multiple functions at once.

The neurons are organized into discrete groups known as netlets. In the response to the complicated stimuli, parallel neuronal groups in the different netlets are active in synchrony. Cutaneous, visual, auditory, olfactory, and gustatory sensory inputs are accessed by sensory afferents to determine the prevailing environmental parameters. The cerebral cortex encompasses the memories of the antecedent events by means of the fusion of the incoming data of the senses with the previously existing representations. Therefore, besides producing the most efficient response plans, it performs affective valuation of goals so that they can be navigated toward in a way that is as safe and efficient as possible.

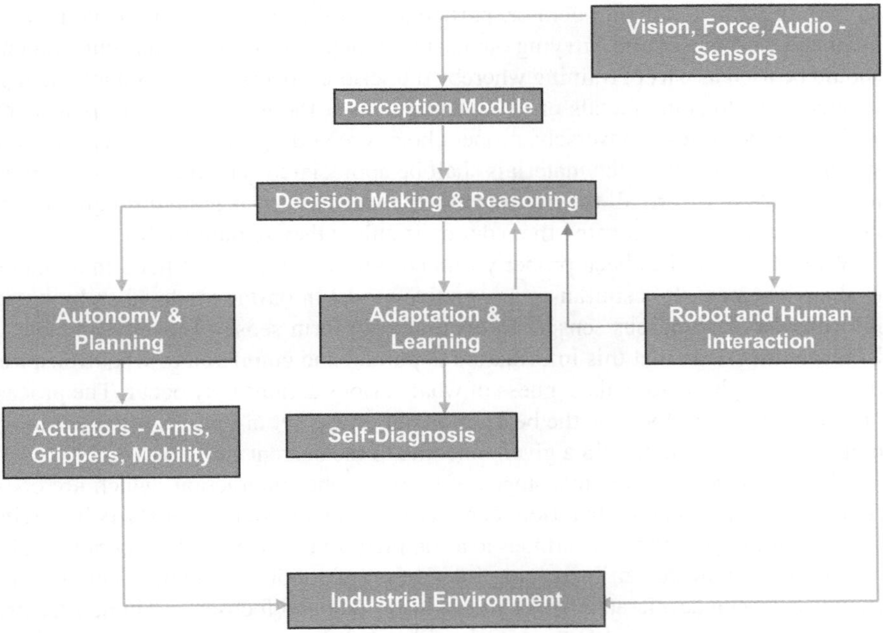

FIGURE 11.8 Integrated framework for adaptive robotics.

The whole system is shown in Figure 11.8. The accuracy of the computations produced by the brain in its everyday functioning is often accurate because its past experiences are used to make informed decisions. Not surprisingly, one of the main stimuli of the development of AI and robotics has always been this impressive potential. In this regard, therefore, researchers have indicated that the task of developing computational systems simulating the brain is quite challenging, and such projects demand that a systematic theoretical model defines how neurons interact with each other. The foundational AI research is based on the existing knowledge of the effectiveness of the functioning of the brain and its adaptability to environmental changes. What makes cognitive robots deviate off the typical robotic platforms is that their intelligence is based on the ability of the brain to grasp complex real-life happenings and take up highly challenging assignments with much precision. Scientists have emphasized that the development of cognitive intelligence in robots requires not only a strong knowledge base of cognition but also an advanced learning machine. All these are reinforced by mathematical models which explain human behavioral mechanisms.

Cognitive robotics is all about getting humans to learn by experience, but the ultimate aim of cognitive robotics is to enable machines to solve plenty of situations, make conclusions, and recollect what they have learned to use in the future. Cognitive robots are expected to scan the surrounding, make assumptions as to what may be wrong or altered, and act accordingly out of the correct course to complete a task. A good example of cognitive processes in manufacturing is the operation of automated heat treatment equipment in a high risk and precision critical manufacturing environment. A robot, in such cases, requires undergoing offline training to acquire similar skills as a human operator, particularly in the control of the related equipment and workpieces and carrying out heat treatment activities. Serious punishments should be used as part of training whereby the serious mistakes such as applying high temperatures to some metals or using equipment at the wrong time are punishable with harsh penalties. Conversely, proper choices regarding timing, temperature, and the process of handling the materials shall be appreciated. The memory of the robot must be able to record all the training experiences that it has gone through with the latest experiences overturning the older ones unless they remain useful.

When the robot has been properly trained offline, it may be utilized in an industrial environment. It is similar to a cognitive model in online mode whereby it uses information of numerous sensors to continuously form sense of its environment. It is during this stage that this information is purged and compared to what transpired in the offline phase, to make a guess of what various actions may occur. The process of selecting and performing the best action out of this set of options is done through motor actuation, resulting in a given outcome to the current situation.

The 5C model presents five stages of human–robot interaction, which are coexistence, cooperation, collaboration, compassion, and coevolution. It starts by having some common ground and continues to a complete and coordinated cooperation. This development indicates an increasing integration of robots and human beings. This change has been accelerated by AI and Industry 5.0, and focuses on Human-Centric Smart Manufacturing and Human-Cyber-Physical Systems. Human–robot collaboration has become the key to increased productivity by combining human flexibility with precision of robotic action. Intelligent agents, in this case, should be directed at the needs and values of people, which will allow them to learn autonomously and improve the health of the population.

Manufacturing environments in the real world are always changing and open, with multiple modes of input and interaction involving many people. In these kinds of situations, smart agents need to be able to understand and combine information from different sources, adjust to new situations, and get smarter over time by interacting with people and other agents. At first, multimodal fusion for human–robot interaction only looked at a small number of sensory channels, like visual, aural, tactile, and physiological inputs like Electroencephalography (EEG), Electromyography (EMG), and Electrocardiography (ECG). Smart robots involve putting AI into physical agents so that they can interact with their surroundings in real time [15]. This makes it possible for AI to reach into the physical world.

11.10 CONCLUSIONS

Industry 5.0 is a transformation of automation to human machine cooperation where production is improved by intelligent, adaptive, and human-focused technologies. Smart systems can now assist in real-time decision-making and autonomous navigation, and they can process tasks in various industries, thanks to the combination of AI, machine learning, and cognitive robotics. The robots will decrease the human labor force, enhance productivity, and facilitate efficient and sustainable operations. Even though there has been considerable improvement, issues of high prices, low awareness, skills shortage, and workflow interruptions have been a barrier to its wider adoption particularly among small- or medium-sized businesses. Nevertheless, with the development of AI technologies and their increased availability, intelligent robots will be at the center of the manufacturing, logistics, and healthcare industries. Cognitive robots are capable of adjusting to new circumstances and working in safety with humans due to the creation of a new type of robot, which is able to sense, learn, and act independently. This is able to improve decision-making, defect detection, and optimization of processes. Industry 5.0 does not only bring superior robotics but also facilitates in ethical, inclusive, and sustainable industrial practices. Through further studies and deliberate execution, the forthcoming phase of industrial revolution as spearheaded by smart robotics will see the creation of innovation and human value walking hand in hand.

REFERENCES

1. Plathottam, Siby Jose, Arin Rzonca, Rishi Lakhnori, and Chukwunwike O. Iloeje. "A review of artificial intelligence applications in manufacturing operations." *Journal of Advanced Manufacturing and Processing* 5, no. 3 (2023): e10159.
2. Doven, Gozde, Bulent Sezen, Kadir Alpaslan Demir, and Yavuz Selim Balcioglu."Industry 5.0: are we going to accept robots as co-workers in office environments? An empirical analysis." *Applied Sciences* 15, no. 3 (2025): 1591.
3. Alojaiman, Bader."Technological modernizations in the industry 5.0 era: A descriptive analysis and future research directions." *Processes* 11, no. 5 (2023): 1318.

4. Kumar, Suryakant, Jiuh-Biing Sheu, and Tanmoy Kundu. "Planning a parts-to-picker order picking system with consideration of the impact of perceived workload." *Transportation Research Part E: Logistics and Transportation Review* 173 (2023): 103088.
5. Moshayedi, Ata Jahangir, Li Jinsong, and Liefa Liao. "AGV (automated guided vehicle) robot: Mission and obstacles in design and performance." *Journal of Simulation and Analysis of Novel Technologies in Mechanical Engineering* 12, no. 4 (2019): 5–18.
6. Smids, Jilles, Sven Nyholm, and Hannah Berkers. "Robots in the workplace: A threat to—or opportunity for—meaningful work?" *Philosophy & Technology*, 33, no. 3 (2020): 503–522.
7. Rashid, Adib Bin, and MD Ashfakul Karim Kausik. "AI revolutionizing industries worldwide: A comprehensive overview of its diverse applications." *Hybrid Advances* 7 (2024): 100277.
8. Shah, Ronit, Arockia Selvakumar Arockia Doss, and Natrayan Lakshmaiya. "Advancements in AI-enhanced collaborative robotics: Towards safer, smarter, and human-centric industrial automation." *Results in Engineering* 27 (2025): 105704.
9. Zafar, Muhammad Hamza, Even Falkenberg Langås, and Filippo Sanfilippo. "Exploring the synergies between collaborative robotics, digital twins, augmentation, and industry 5.0 for smart manufacturing: A state-of-the-art review." *Robotics and Computer-Integrated Manufacturing* 89 (2024): 102769.
10. Soori, Mohsen, Behrooz Arezoo, and Roza Dastres. "Artificial intelligence, machine learning and deep learning in advanced robotics, a review." *Cognitive Robotics* 3 (2023): 54–70.
11. Arents, Janis, and Modris Greitans."Smart industrial robot control trends, challenges and opportunities within manufacturing" *Applied Sciences* 12, no. 2 (2022): 937. https://doi.org/10.3390/app12020937
12. Javaid, Mohd, Abid Haleem, Ravi Pratap Singh, and Rajiv Suman. "Substantial capabilities of robotics in enhancing industry 4.0 implementation." *Cognitive Robotics* 1 (2021): 58–75.
13. Huang, Ziqi, Yang Shen, Jiayi Li, Marcel Fey, and Christian Brecher. "A survey on AI-driven digital twins in industry 4.0: Smart manufacturing and advanced robotics." *Sensors* 21, no. 19 (2021): 6340.
14. Dzedzickis, Andrius, Jurga Subačiūtė-Žemaitienė, Ernestas Šutinys, Urtė Samukaitė-Bubnienė, and Vytautas Bučinskas. "Advanced applications of industrial robotics: New trends and possibilities." *Applied Sciences* 12, no. 1 (2021): 135.
15. Othman, Uqba, and Erfu Yang. "Human–robot collaborations in smart manufacturing environments: Review and outlook." *Sensors* 23, no. 12 (2023): 5663. https://doi.org/10.3390/s23125663

Index

U

V

For Product Safety Concerns and Information please contact our EU representative GPSR@taylorandfrancis.com Taylor & Francis Verlag GmbH, Kaufingerstraße 24, 80331 München, Germany